CONNECTING SPHERES

European Women in a Globalizing World, 1500 to the Present

SECOND EDITION

MARILYN J. BOXER
San Francisco State University
Stanford University

JEAN H. QUATAERT
Binghamton University,
State University of New York

with

Barbara Franzoi Bari
Antoinette Burton
Carolyn J. Dean
Donna Gabaccia
Sandra M. Gilbert
Sarah Hanley
Maryanne Cline Horowitz
Olwen Hufton

Sibylle Meyer
Gerda Ruth Neyer
Karen Offen
Mary Elizabeth Perry
Richard Stites
Frank Tallett
Luise White
Merry Wiesner-Hanks

Foreword by
JOAN W. SCOTT

New York • Oxford
OXFORD UNIVERSITY PRESS
2000

Oxford University Press

Oxford   New York
Athens   Auckland   Bangkok   Bogotá   Buenos Aires   Calcutta
Cape Town   Chennai   Dar es Salaam   Delhi   Florence   Hong Kong   Istanbul
Karachi   Kuala Lumpur   Madrid   Melbourne   Mexico City   Mumbai
Nairobi   Paris   Saõ Paulo   Singapore   Taipei   Tokyo   Toronto   Warsaw

and associated companies in
Berlin   Ibadan

Published by Oxford University Press, Inc.,
198 Madison Avenue, New York, New York 10016
http://www.oup-usa.org

Oxford is a registered trademark of Oxford University Press

Library of Congress Cataloging-in-Publication Data

Boxer, Marilyn J.
  Connecting spheres : European women in a globalizing world, 1500
to the present / Marilyn J. Boxer & Jean H. Quataert with Barbara
Franzoi Bari . . . [et al.] ; foreword by Joan W. Scott. — 2nd ed.
     p.   cm.
  Rev. ed. of: Connecting spheres: women in the Western world, 1500
to the present / edited by Marilyn J. Boxer, Jean H. Quataert. 1987.
  Includes bibliographical references and index.
  ISBN 0-19-510950-3 (cloth : alk. paper). — ISBN 0-19-510951-1
(pbk. : alk. paper)
  1. Women—History—Cross-cultural studies.   2. Women—Europe-
-History.   3. Feminism—History—Cross-cultural studies.
I. Quataert, Jean H. (Jean Helen), 1945– .   II. Title.
HQ1150.B63   1999
305.49094—dc21   99-19863
                                       CIP

Printing number:
10   9   8   7   6   5   4   3   2   1

Printed in the United States of America
on acid-free paper

In memory of our spiritual mother
SIMONE DE BEAUVOIR
1908–1986

ACKNOWLEDGMENTS

We want to thank the many persons who contributed to the first edition of *Connecting Spheres* and to the present volume. We include all those who with us have studied and written in women's history—our own students at Binghamton University, San Diego State University, San Francisco State University, and University of Houston—Clear Lake; our co-workers and colleagues throughout the United States and across international borders. We single out for special appreciation Karen Offen, Sandra Peacock, and Mary Elizabeth Perry for their helpful comments on the overview chapters, Albert Tong of the Center for the Enhancement of Teaching at San Francisco State University for his assistance in preparing the figures in Part III, and Rick Polk, graduate student in geography at Binghamton University, for our map of European colonial holdings. Janet Hamann of San Diego State University prepared our index.

One of the pleasures of authorship has been working with our contributors, whose excellent case studies have enhanced our work and deepened the analysis we present in this book. Joan Scott, once again, has provided a thoughtful foreword to our work. As co-authors we have also shared a rare and rewarding personal experience. The professional relationship that we created through our joint work in the 1970s on *Socialist Women* (1978) was sustained through the 1980s with our collaboration on the first edition of *Connecting Spheres* (1987) and, over three decades of intellectual and personal growth, has solidified into a deep and productive friendship. For us, the process of writing together—even crafting sentences that blend our individual thoughts into one coherent statement—is exhilarating and enlightening. We hope that the product of our joint efforts offers an equally compelling educational experience.

We wish not finally but again, with special emphasis, to acknowledge our appreciation for the love and support of our families: Claire, Larry and Samantha, Brian, Mary Jane, and Jenny; Don, Eliot, and Bethany.

M. J. B. and J. H. Q.
Berkeley, December 1998

Connecting Spheres

CONTENTS

PART II. WOMEN IN INDUSTRIALIZING, LIBERALIZING, AND IMPERIALIZING EUROPE

PART III. WOMEN IN THE ERA OF THE INTERVENTIONIST STATE

LIST OF FIGURES AND TABLES

FOREWORD TO THE SECOND EDITION

When asked to write a new foreword for the second edition of *Connecting Spheres,* I readily agreed. I soon realized, however, that what I had written about the first edition was still valid and that there was no point in trying to restate those points. So, I have asked that that foreword be reprinted.

Connecting Spheres is an impressive demonstration of the accomplishments of women's history and of the way the field has proceeded, as a dialogue between large overviews and small case studies. This new edition also shows how approaches to women's history have evolved over the past decade. The expansion of global capitalism, the emergence of attention to postcoloniality, and the debates about cultural and political differences among feminists in academia and at the UN world conferences on women, have all raised new questions about the historical past. These questions not only call for new kinds of knowledge, they also change the ways we have understood established areas, such as the field of European history. What have been the connections between European expansion and women's experience? How did feminist campaigns for rights in the nations of Europe refer to or depend upon differences with non-European women? How does attention to the differences between colonial powers and their subjects change our perspective about "women"? Is it possible any longer to speak about "women's" history as a single, separate entity?

These, and other questions, are addressed in the new overview chapters and in some of the individual essays. The result is that the term *connecting* in the title acquires new geopolitical resonance and our perspective on both women's history and European history is dramatically and importantly enlarged.

Joan W. Scott
Institute for Advanced Study,
Princeton

FOREWORD TO THE FIRST EDITION

In the fall of 1984, I arrived in Paris on my way to a conference at UNESCO on the history of women. At the airport an officious customs officer asked the usual question about the nature of my business in France, and then queried me on the topic of the conference I was attending. When I replied "the history of women," he responded mockingly, "Do women have a history, Professor? And what might it be?" I was taken aback not only by his hostility, but by the difficulty of answering such questions. Of course women had a history, but one so rich and unmined that no single phrase or story-line could capture it. The women's history movement of the last fifteen years has revealed the complexity and diversity of women's experience as well as the historically relative meaning of the term "woman" itself. Thus, the only way to know women's history, I thought, was to study it in all its variety. But to the customs man I only said something placating about how much I hoped to learn at the conference. I suspect that he did not believe there was anything new to learn because his view of women was fundamentally ahistorical. For him, women were probably defined by their bodies; they were objects of male desire or agents of reproduction, performing timeless, "natural" functions that do not figure in textbook histories. From this perspective the term "women's history" was an oxymoron, ridiculous, easy to ridicule.

The encounter with the official presented me with the very outlook women's history sets out to refute. In opposition to the idea of timelessness, women's history insists that women's experience is shaped in time. Even the most "natural"of functions, sexuality and childbirth, have been practiced differently in different epochs. Against the idea that the essential qualities of femininity never change, women's history offers a vast array of female types and extensive evidence about how ideals of femininity have changed. If the results of all this research have not yet reached French bureaucrats, they have been acknowledged in the academy and they are being incorporated into the history curriculum. *Connecting Spheres*, in fact, represents just such an acknowledgement and incorporation of themes long neglected.

Connecting Spheres illustrates the accomplishments of women's history in many ways. In its interesting format—a series of overviews and a group of individual articles—the book preserves the mode of inquiry from which this field has been fashioned. New information and insights have been steadily accumulated through careful study of specific subjects, making larger, more general syntheses possible. The title asserts that women are historical beings: they are affected by monumental developments such as demographic transitions and political revolutions and they are active participants in the movements and events of their times. *Connecting Spheres* shows that women consistently mattered in social, economic, and political terms; that women's history is not limited to the narrow course of feminist political movements in the modern period. The book offers a complex history, a patchwork quilt of colorful themes rather than a neat linear narrative. There are many characters here—queens and serving maids, factory workers and housewives, nuns and prostitutes, suffragists and antisuffragists, socialists and fascists—whose stories differ. Indeed, these stories must be told separately for their contexts, causes, and effects are different. There is no Woman in Western history; there are only women who cannot be reduced to singular character traits, behaviors, or outlooks.

Neither can women's lives be explained by one cause. *Connecting Spheres* requires us to look at many factors in order to explain the experiences of women. Thus, Sarah Hanley argues that statebuilding led to the promulgation of laws that gave parents greater control over their children's marriage choices in early modern France. In the process, errant daughters were more severely treated than sons. In the modern period, Donna Gabaccia points to the influence of Italian unification on economic developments that deprived peasant women of productive roles. In some periods, religious teachings were incorporated not only into church policy, but into education as well; scientific discoveries created new possibilities for women and reproduced prevailing beliefs about them. Technological breakthroughs have sometimes improved, sometimes worsened the conditions of wage-earning women. And ideas about separate male and female spheres—of work and domesticity, public and private—which now seem the source of women's subordination, were once used to justify demands for improvements in women's status.

If causality is complex, so is the notion of women's experience. In all ages there have been normative definitions of masculinity and femininity, but such received wisdom has had differing impacts on the different lives of women. Differences of social class often made it impossible for women in the same era to identify with one another: the world of hardworking peasant mothers, who nursed their own babies as well as the babies of the rich, was not the same world as that inhabited by noble women, who bore the children others cared for. The necessity to earn wages differed fundamentally from the desire to find fulfillment in work: hence, a nineteenth-century middle-class doctor had little in common with a lower-class factory girl. Religious differences have sometimes separated women of the same class; thus in late nineteenth-century France, Catholic middle-class women tended to conservative politics within the orbit of the Church, while their Protestant counterparts became leaders of major reform movements. There has been no eternal essence to "womanhood" that provided a common denominator for women's experience past or present. Women have always had to interpret their womanhood within the contexts and parameters of their lives.

Those parameters could be terribly confining, as disobedient daughters imprisoned in convents could testify; they could be confusing, as the doctors' debates on the role of women's organs in the reproductive process reveals; they could be flexible, as evidenced by the initial events of the Russian Revolution. But parameters alone—the pressures of economic conditions, the teachings of religious authorities, the legal strictures about marriage and citizenship—have never set the limits on human imagination and behavior. As always, the possibility for change—the very core of historical interest—resides in the variety of individual and collective behavior.

Connecting Spheres puts women into history where they belong—at each turning point and major development; in processes of change large and small; as objects of debate and active participants in events—in short, everywhere. After reading this book one can no longer ask if women had a history. For the answer is clearly yes. As a unified group we cannot say women had a singular, identifiable history. We can say, however, that they have always been part of history, experiencing its impacts and contributing to its movement. That statement seems so self-evident after reading this book that one wonders how scholars could have thought the contrary. Inevitably, we are left to ponder questions about the writing of history itself: How did it happen that women became invisible as historical subjects? How was it possible to overlook their participation for so long?

Joan W. Scott
Institute for Advanced Study,
Princeton

INTRODUCTION
TO THE SECOND EDITION

New Connections

In the decade since the first publication of *Connecting Spheres,* women's historians have been engaged in the lively methodological and theoretical debates over the fundamental nature of historical practice. The recent challenges have put under new scrutiny many long-held assumptions about doing history. In dispute are the basic categories of analysis, the validity of the historical "subject," the transparency of language, indeed—even the once sacrosanct distinction between fact and fiction. The net result is a powerful critique of many of the claims of the discipline. It is reminiscent of the one launched by women's historians in the 1970s against traditional methods of historical research and writing that all but silenced and obscured "women's" multiple roles, participation, and contributions in the past. *Connecting Spheres* was part of that earlier feminist project of revision. Purposefully, we have left intact our original introduction to preserve clearly the governing assumptions that were at the basis of this work in European women's history. These original formulations should provide, then, a useful backdrop against which to assess women's history as a continuously evolving and dynamic inquiry by historians of the present into the past.

As practicing women's historians over the past decade, however, we, too, have been grappling with the new theories of knowledge, many of which seem now to challenge profoundly the fundamental bases of women's history. The present revised edition reflects both our ongoing commitment to connecting women and history as well as the simultaneous ways that our thinking has broadened, deepened, and changed in light of the discussions over theory, method, evidence, and narrative structure.

The basic organizational framework of *Connecting Spheres* remains the same. It is divided into three overview sections, preserving for the five hundred years under investigation the same chronological divides that we heuristically offer as one perspective on women, time, and change. And we include innovative case studies to demonstrate methodological and interpretative aspects of "doing" women's history; some are new and reflect expanding research interests (e.g., on sexuality, Europe and Empire as well as the "fraternal" welfare state since the Second World War). Furthermore, we remain convinced of the validity of connecting spheres; the approach has proven a useful interpretive grid for women's history. Indeed, at a time when much of the wider literature was coining the notion of "separate spheres" (for the gendered character of middle-class life in Europe and North America), we

1

proposed important linkages, between public (which at the time essentially elided the political) and private; class and gender; urban and rural; sexuality and the evolving world economy. But our original matrix of connections now appears too limited. One purpose of the second edition is to reflect new relationships that challenge the narrative of European history unconnected to the wider context of imperialism and colonial rule and the historicized voice of European "woman" without the specificity of her class, race, geographic, or sexual position.

Significantly, reconnecting the history of Europe and its colonies (in the Americas and the East Indies) in the early modern period and, by extension, reexamining the expansion of European imperial rule into Africa and elsewhere during the nineteenth century shed new light on many of the standard accounts of European economic, political, and social developments. So, too, in the emerging world of global interdependency since the 1960s, the presence in the heartland of Europe of former colonial subjects, permanent "guest" workers, and generations of immigrant children raises new questions about the gendered, racialized processes that work continuously to reconstruct European identity. For example, the touted policy of assimilation in France of the 1990s founders on the symbolics of Muslim women's scarves.

Acknowledging the centrality of Europe's colonial ventures (and the struggles of decolonization) in history, however, requires a multidimensional model of influence that moves in many directions. It no longer is possible to speak solely of the European impact on the colonies, as if the meaning of colonialism was restricted to only "out there," overseas, in the colonies proper. From the very first encounters with indigenous peoples in the Western Hemisphere in 1492, the interaction between Europeans and colonial subjects had profound impact on Europe itself. In many significant ways, these connections were mediated by gender and race, providing a new lens on women's multiple stories as well. Often, there were parallel processes at work. For example, conquest of subjects abroad in the consolidation of imperial rule in the sixteenth century was matched in Spain by efforts to enclose religious women in convents and curtail their public works and ministerings. Similarly, the domestic model of middle-class respectability in late nineteenth-century England was exported to the colonies and served to reinvent racial boundaries and hierarchies in the colonial states of Africa, for example. Furthermore, if the sovereign individual identified by seventeenth-century philosophers and scientists as endowed with reason and autonomy was male, he was constructed against the archetypical "other," the female; indeed, the linkage of man and citizen seemed natural when set against the notion of woman as household dependent. Recent research, however, also demonstrates the extent to which indigenous and later slave populations in the Americas and Africa constituted rich sources of analogies and metaphors for the mounting contrast with "civilized" Europeans. These insights have led to important rereadings of many of the standard works of European literature, philosophy, and Enlightenment thought, including Western feminism, which owes a profound debt to eighteenth-century assumptions. In the process, then, Christine de Pizan and Mary Wollstonecraft, two of the most well-known prowoman authors contributing to the birth of feminism, become more complex figures. They are proponents of sexual equality to be sure, women whose visions contain key insights and understandings that still have the power to persuade and mobilize. At the same time, however, they universalized their particular Western, white feminist experience and drew explicit contrasts with religious or racial others.

Thus, sensitivities to the evolving context of global interactions force challenging new approaches to European history itself and call for new interpretations and analyses. Consequently, despite preserving the overall structure of *Connecting Spheres,* we have redesigned thoroughly the analytic contents of our overview sections. And we remain advocates of reintegrating the perspective of diverse women's lives and wider gender relations into the political and economic interpretations of European developments—with an eye, of course, to their reinterpretation through the analytic lens of gender. Therefore, *Connecting Spheres* remains a text in European women's history. It draws together the multiple stories of diverse women's lives and struggles in a world profoundly shaped by material and cultural interactions with peoples, territories, and empires outside of Europe. In this way, however, *Connecting Spheres* simultaneously is designed for a global historical perspective, demonstrating the complex ways European women were both complicit in and critical of a hierarchical ordering of the world that has apportioned resources, opportunities, and power on the basis of constructed notions of gender and race.

These new perspectives reflect a serious reexamination of the categories of "woman" and "gender," which still lie at the basis of women's history. In the first edition, we assumed as foundational the perspective of "woman as a social group"; our historical narrative in some ways contributed to the construction of a shared women's experience, which masked a much more diverse and conflictual reality. We do not have to adopt the postmodern cry of the "death of the subject" to recognize the challenges to the understandings of the categories of "woman," "gender," and "class" in the discipline. Indeed, it is partially the work of Western feminists of color, anthropologists crossing borders, and trenchant scholarship outside of Europe that has encouraged us to reexamine our own assumptions about the "voices" of European women. It is also, however, the impact of historical change that demonstrates forcefully our need to maintain fluid definitions and multiple perspectives. The changes in eastern Europe after 1989 brought a new set of women's voices into dialogue with women's studies scholars, making us rethink such fundamental concepts of Western feminism as the "public sphere" and giving new meaning to such foundational principles as "the personal is political." In some instances, the personal is altogether too political, too open, that is, to intrusion by forces of the state. Feminism transcends national boundaries but must be interpreted in specific political and cultural contexts and historical settings. We must understand all knowledge as "situated knowledges."

Although we are not full converts, we also have read, debated, and digested the writings of feminist critical theory by women's historians, literary critics, and political theorists. Like the new cultural historians, we ask of concepts and events not only what they mean but how they work.[1] Therefore, throughout the text we reconnect gender and race (which includes the construction of whiteness in the European case), rethink the relationship between the body, sex, and gender and, at times, show how notions of class and national identity come into being and their tense relationship with gender identity. The social categories of "woman" as well as "female" identity in the expanding Western world, then, are more complex and fluid notions, which are rearranged continuously at precise moments in time.

As the primary authors of *Connecting Spheres,* we remain committed to women's history as a distinct, enriching, and critical perspective on the past. It is one, we believe, that remains indispensable for the efforts in the present to work for more egalitarian bases to social relations, whether in local, national, or global arenas. The debates over the decade have not shaken our feminist politics; however, we acknowledge more clearly the multiple perspectives that comprise the basis of feminism and the continuous need for debate, dialogue, and alliances across class and culture. Indeed, we share with Jean Howard the call for a "committed historical practice."[2] In her persuasive formulation, it is the consistent commitment to greater equality in the ever-changing present that guides the historian's engagement with the past. In this light, perhaps we can even anticipate a third edition, which will reflect the many changes in contemporary strategies for achieving equality based on new inquiry into the social dynamics of the past.

NOTES

1. See, for example, Judith Butler and Joan W. Scott, eds., *Feminists Theorize the Political* (New York: Routledge, 1992); Ruth Behar, *Translated Woman: Crossing the Border with Esperanza's Story* (Boston: Beacon Press, 1993); Margo Hendricks and Patricia Parker, eds., *Women, "Race," and Writing in the Early Modern Period* (London and New York: Routledge, 1995); and Lynn Hunt, "Introduction: History, Culture, and Text," in id., ed., *The New Cultural History* (Berkeley: University of California Press, 1989), pp. 1–22.
2. Jean E. Howard, "Towards a Postmodern, Politically-committed, Historical Practice," in Francis Barker, Peter Hulme and Margaret Iversen, eds., *Uses of History: Marxism, Postmodernism, and the Renaissance* (Manchester and New York: Manchester University Press, 1991), pp. 101–122.

INTRODUCTION TO THE FIRST EDITION

Restoring Women to History

This is a book about women's history. But women, like men and children, live inextricably linked with other human beings. They are influenced not only by the unique experiences that befall every person but also by the inherited ideas and institutions they share with others of their generation. Whatever their differences of race, class, religion, sexual preference, language, and culture, they participate from birth until death in an ongoing tale of human action, reaction, perception, and interpretation. They inevitably belong to a social culture that we define as "civilization." To understand themselves and their world, they often seek knowledge about the past—of their family and of their collective ancestry. For most Americans of the late twentieth century, this means tracing human culture back across the ages of Western civilization to times past that, but for the work of historians, would have been lost. In some cases it is too late; we cannot all find our family tree, for the records of our forebears—especially if they were poor or persecuted—may have disappeared. So we study history and identify with the collective experience of our nation, of our people, however defined. But if we are looking for the history of women we have a special problem, for few female individuals appear in most accounts of the past. Yet common sense tells us women have always been part of the social fabric. Women's work, after all, was never done, and behind all great men, we have been told, stood women who nurtured and inspired them.

To help us find the story of these women we must begin by considering how history itself has been composed. The story of Western civilization stretches back beyond recorded time to the myths and legends told by ancient seers. Passed from generation to generation by storytellers, such tales form the basis of the earliest written narratives, the epic poems, the liturgies and dramas as well as songs which collectively constitute an important part of what we today call ancient history. Although in later times we have narrowed our definition of history from its original meaning of "a relation of incidents" to include only those "professedly true," to the "facts," the Greek word *historia* is the source as well for our word "story," a narrative of fictitious events. And, if asked to distinguish "history" from "story," most of us today would fall back on the common contrast between fact and fiction. History is a chronicle of facts.

Which facts? Obviously no history book, even one drawing on the largest computerized information banks, could contain all the facts, every experience of every person who ever existed anywhere. This would not be possible in Western civilization, or, say, American history even if—another impossibility—all such things were known. What we know as history is thus limited to those experiences and events that were deemed important enough to be remembered—and recorded for later and wider recollection. History is essentially what has been included in history books, the collective work of generations of writers who were chosen for that purpose by virtue of special knowledge, training, or position. Out of the vast, almost infinite, universe of human experience, they, the educated men who wrote the history books (and most historians have been men), created by their selection of events not just a story, but history. History, therefore, comprises selected experience, elevated into significant events by virtue of inclusion in historical narratives. And these choices were made according to the values and purposes of the historians.

History traditionally has been written to recount and to record important *public* events. Most of its conventional themes deal with wars and revolutions, outbreaks of violence, and contests of might for prizes of territory, political power and public place. In the many dramatic struggles for hegemony recorded by historians, from the city-states of ancient Greece to the nation-states of modern Europe, Africa, and Asia, most of the contenders have been men. Except for a few women born to the throne like Queen Elizabeth I, or called to martyrdom like Joan of Arc, most women took no part in military and political contests, or in other public events that were deemed worthy of incorporation in the annals of history. Nor, except for soldiers and servants, did most ordinary men. Traditional history was the platform of political elites; civilization the creation of civic leaders.

The story of common men enters the tale from time to time, if only implicitly: the invaders who terrorized early medieval Europe, the sailors whose muscle-power propelled the great explorers' ships, were, one assumes, men; but we know nothing of their lives except that they were there, on hand to obey and to work. The labor of ordinary men entered history only after a major philosophical reevaluation took place concerning the worth of work. And so, in the twentieth century, economic and labor history were born. But this was one hundred years after the "Declaration of the Rights of Man" had established the claim of ordinary men to political participation and the English political economists had exposed the labor theory of value. The definition of work, moreover, remained confined by limited notions about the sphere of production; much of women's work (unpaid and for family use) continued to be invisible to economic theorists and labor historians. Furthermore, it was the struggle of workingmen to live, organize, and fight for *political* power that became part of the broadened public record. The inclusion of these themes did not challenge the dominant understanding of historical significance: the focus remained on men (privileged and now the nonprivileged) struggling for power in the *public* arena.

The women who lived in the past continued to be absent from history. Despite an occasional allusion to an exceptional woman, a woman "worthy" because she nurtured, inspired, or, in rare cases, substituted for man, "her story" was not written. The history of women as a social group must of necessity focus on private and personal, not public and political, events. It therefore challenges the inherited assumption that historically significant events are publicly recognized events only. Most women through most of history have been excluded from arenas of public power, relegated to women's quarters and women's work, denied the apprenticeships and education requisite to autonomous existence. Defined primarily by relationships with men— fathers, husbands, sons, and lovers—women passed their lives subsumed within families. There were exceptions. When the family order constituted the public order and their families belonged to the leading circles, then some women gained power, privilege, and responsibility generally deemed incongruent with their "nature" as weak, dependent beings.[1] But even in these cases, their exploits were rarely preserved. Quite simply, women did not appear in the official accounts of male-dominated institutions or the formal records of political and economic associations that served as sources for the writing of history. Few men wrote biographies of women; few women had the leisure and education to produce autobiographies.

The omission of women from history books, then, can be explained without recourse to a conspiracy theory of history. Men never sat in council and decided to keep women down by eliminating their lives from the chronicles of history. Besides, Helen of Troy, Joan of Arc, Lucrezia Borgia, Charlotte Corday, and a few others who played important roles in men's stories won recognition. When women did something men considered important—inspired or defeated a powerful army, poisoned or fatally stabbed an eminent leader—their deeds were duly noted. Otherwise, they were relegated to the realm of daily routine, to the domestic functions prescribed for them by priests and philosophers, physicians and politicians, patriarchs of all callings who followed Aristotle, Aquinas, and, more recently, Freud, in defining women as imperfect men. Many of the great leaders of Western thought did trouble themselves to explain the nature of women's inferiority, locating the limits of women's possibilities for achievement in some weakness of spirit, mind, or body. When the ancient philosopher Protagoras and the Sophists declared that "man is the measure of all things," and Aristotle stated that "the female state [is] a deformity [which, however,] occurs in the ordinary course of nature," for purposes of reproduction of the species; and when Aquinas, over a millenium later, echoed the Greeks with his assertion that "woman is defective and misbegotten," they took the biological male as the model for human being. Scholars of all eras have followed suit and used terms, categories of analysis, and definitions that denigrate women, when they do not altogether ignore them. Even recently, in turning attention from heroes and headline events to obscure and ordinary occurrences, the habit remains strong, as witnessed by this statement in a review of Fernand Braudel's widely acclaimed work, *The Structures of Everyday Life:*

> While *Homo medievalis* was the prey of wolves, unidentified bacilli and viruses, he had, nevertheless, the permanent task of providing food and shelter for his family.

This example shows the use of sex-biased, though supposedly "objective" or "neutral," terms. Women as well as men fell victim to disease, and women perhaps even more than men shouldered the responsibility for feeding their families. No question, however, that "the family" belonged to "him"; the traditional family in Western cultures was a patriarchal, male-dominated and -defined institution and should be labeled as such. While women labored alongside men in fields and shops they won little recognition for their crucial work in production, or even in reproduction. They might "manufacture societ[ies]"; but "women's work," however essential to survival, was hardly the stuff of history.[2]

Partly because women's status has been subsumed under that of the men who were their masters and guardians, traditional interpretations of historical events were easily cast in universal terms and the long sweep of history was structured about turning points of limited significance for the female sex. Athenian "democracy" seems a less worthy ancestor of our own when we learn that its "rule by the people" excluded most men and all women (who lived secluded in women's quarters, if not as slaves or concubines). The twelfth-century "reform" of Catholicism in the Cluny movement appears less progressive from the viewpoint of nuns and managers of female monasteries who thereby lost their autonomy and gained male overseers. The Renaissance brought not "rebirth," but regress for some feudal noblewomen, those few of their sex who enjoyed power and influence in church and state as long as their families constituted the public order.[3] The "Great" Revolution of 1789 in France granted neither liberty nor equality to women; and in the interests of fraternity, Napoleon's lauded Code of Laws subjected women henceforth to discriminatory standards in marriage, sexual behavior, and education. Another major "democratic" upheaval of the late eighteenth century, the American Revolution, ushered in a long-sustained era of "common men," whose gains seem less progressive from the perspective of those women who lost legal rights and professional opportunities. Where colonial women could enjoy property rights and engage in business ventures or medical practices, their nineteenth-century descendants faced exclusion through new laws and professional organizations. Milestones of advancement for men may mark gravestones of opportunity for women.

Viewed from the perspective of women, history requires other signposts. A historian of the thirtieth century, dividing a total human history into chapters, books, and courses, might well deemphasize the "Renaissance" of the fifteenth century and the "Revolutions" of the eighteenth. Searching the record for "world-historical" events to serve as markers and turning points, this scholar might pause at the dawn of (what we call) the modern age, to acknowledge the import of the Enlightenment thinkers who saw that human intervention could liberate humanity from arbitrary rule and human invention could increase mastery over nature. But she or he might stop to erect a monument only in 1844 or 1877 or 1936 or 1967—choices based, as always, on values, and here selected for their significance in the struggle for freedom from the biological necessity of recurring childbirth that was imposed throughout earlier ages on half of humanity.

What have these dates to do with Western civilization? The dates are hallmarks in the conquest of reproductive freedom for women. The vulcanization of rubber in 1844 made possible the mass production decades later of safe, effective artificial contraception; the widely publicized trial of Annie Besant and Charles Bradlaugh in London in 1877 for distribution of a birth control pamphlet brought knowledge of new possibilities to the minds of millions; the legalization of traffic in contraceptive devices and literature, in the United States in 1936 and in France in 1967, after decades of criminal prosecution, offered release from unwanted pregnancy and hope for self-determination to vast numbers of human beings.[4] Isolated because of their sex, segregated into schools with curricula designed for "ladies," hired for jobs paying less than subsistence wages, deprived of rights to compete for many others by "protective" laws, biology was in fact destiny for women, all because of the "special needs" of the female organism, and the superior interest of the "race" (species) in their reproductive capacity. Freed from biological constraints, however, women can "leave off spending their lives in universal house-service," and more easily become "world-servants" rather than "house-servants," more "human," less "female," and more free to participate in the work which the pioneer American feminist Charlotte Perkins Gilman (1860–1935) believed defines the *human* species.[5]

With the political, ideological, and technological changes of the late eighteenth and the nineteenth centuries came a new sense of human agency that slowly allowed some women to achieve what we today call reproductive freedom. A new era in human history thus dawned, but the forces of the past had long-lived consequences for the future. For without a history of women, which provides the basis for understanding the temporal and cross-cultural variations in women's lives, historians, philosophers, poets, and scientists still too often spoke abstractly of women's so-called "nature," and, on the basis of inherited ideas or personal preferences, prescribed what women "ought" to be. Because of misleading notions of the "eternal feminine" or "natural woman," many discussions of women were (and are) *ahistorical*, ignoring differences in the female experience by era, as well as by class, race, culture, religion, marital status, and other attributes, both ascribed and achieved, that profoundly affect human beings. As the German existentialist philosopher Dilthey pointed out in the nineteenth century, "What [wo]man is, only [her] history tells." In our own time Simone de Beauvoir has written, "One is not born, but becomes, a woman."

There is a second source of distortion related to the absence of women's history. This is the tendency to view women only relative to men. To be sure, women have served men as nurturers, as mothers, wives, nurses, and teachers. Having seen women primarily in these roles, men tend to think of women in these terms—or, again abstractly, as the inspiration for their own actions and achievements, as the muses and "fair ladies" of writers and warriors. Modern men are defined by occupations "what does he do?" ask most typical parents about the prospective boyfriends of their daughters. "Who is she?" ask the parents of sons. Women today continue to be identified first and foremost by relationship to men—whose wife, daughter, mother, lover is she?

But this perspective leads us to ignore or to diminish women's own experiences and the real importance of their multiple contributions to social life. It obscures the other roles women play and the work that they do. More importantly, it suggests that change is impossible. Feminism, for example, seems less radical and more "natural" when the long tradition of female protest is known. Simone de Beauvoir, Betty Friedan, and Gloria Steinem are daughters of Mary Wollstonecraft, Flora Tristan, and Lucy Stone. Women's work in paid employment strikes many people even today as a new departure, because of misinformation about the economic contributions of women in the past. The importance of women's work to the premodern family economy is reflected in the eighteenth-century observation that "none but a fool will take a wife whose bread must be earned solely by his labour and who will contribute nothing towards it herself." False ideas about women necessarily lead to incorrect views of history and sometimes to fallacious assumptions about the "nature" of womanhood. Would the founder of psychoanalysis, Sigmund Freud (1856–1939), whose essays on femininity have exercised extraordinary influence on twentieth-century concepts of womanhood, have asked his infamous question, "What do women want?" if he had studied women's history?

While ideas, attitudes, and customs about women's nature and roles are passed on from generation to generation and serve to narrow options, all such notions are reinforced by, and, in turn, influence social structures. Institutions of law, government, business, and education reflect both age-old biases against women and the economic, educational, legal, and political liabilities long attached to female status. For example, laws that have denied women equal rights in voting, jury service, control of property, credit, choice of domicile, and so forth stem from the English common law, transplanted to the United States, according to which women upon marriage entered an institution where "the husband and wife are one and that one is the husband."

The present-day near-monopoly of power by men in government, business, and education also reflects old attitudes about women's weaknesses. In the nineteenth century, when traditional religious doctrine began to lose its force, "scientific" explanations were invented to justify the inherited interpretations of public life that excluded women's contributions. Doctors replaced priests in enforcing sanctions that restricted women's roles. Where the church had for centuries prescribed limited roles for women in religion, politics, and other social activities on grounds of women's moral weakness—the hereditary "curse of Eve"—now the medical profession utilized biological evidence of women's smaller brains, more sensitive nerves, and periodic procreative "illnesses," to the same purpose. As women's confidants, physicians gained access to intimate knowledge that they used to support a double standard in family and society. For example, they advised women that marriage was "the best of all purgatives to chase away their bad moods," and counseled men that "a modest woman seldom desires any sexual gratification for herself. She submits to her husband but principally to please him. . . . Love of home, children, and domestic duties are the only passions [women] feel."[6]

To break through chains of custom and law requires more than the lonely voice of reason. History is filled with men and women who pointed out biases that impinged on women's lives. Speaking in the fourteenth century, Chaucer's Wife of Bath opined that "there is no libel on women that the clergy will not paint." Aware of the power of holding the pen, she confronted androcentricity (male-centeredness):

> By God, if women had but written stories
> Like those the clergy keep in oratories,
> More had been written of man's wickedness
> Than all the sons of Adam could redress.

With Christine de Pizan's book, *The City of Women* (1404), the voices of real women began a rebuttal of the early misogynist (expressing hatred toward women) literature. Discovering through self-analysis and observation of other women that the evils attributed to her sex existed in male minds rather than in female nature, she also declared that "the books that so sayeth, women made them not." If contempt for women remained "public and unashamed" for several centuries more, henceforth at least it was countered by an equally long and vehement defense. Mary

Astell, an Englishwoman of the late seventeenth century, "despaired of learning anything about women from books, 'because the writers, being men, envious of the good works of women haven't recounted their great deeds.' "[7]

Almost two hundred years of "modern" feminism—often dated from Mary Wollstonecraft's *A Vindication of the Rights of Woman* (1792)—parallels demographic, economic, political, and ideological changes that have fundamentally altered the condition of women of various classes, races, and nations. Yet the old ideas persist; they appear, disappear, and reappear in new guises. Whatever the "true" nature of sex differences, they will never, as John Stuart Mill (and Harriet Taylor) pointed out in the 1860s, be known as long as old ideas preclude consideration of other possibilities.[8] Prerequisite to change is new knowledge and awakened consciousness. What the Wife of Bath and Christine de Pizan knew must become common wisdom. The potential exists today, thanks to the women's liberation movement of the mid-twentieth century and its academic wing, women's studies.

Founded in the late 1960s, women's studies began in response to demands by students, faculty, and community women to learn the "truth" about women. Foremost in the minds of these modern daughters of Christine de Pizan and Mary Astell was the need to find their heritage, to rediscover the past, to find women in history. The first women's studies courses, often taught by volunteer instructors to students seeking to learn regardless of university "credit," were typically history courses. Through the development of women's studies, this new feminism became "a major structure for thinking about our world." Women's studies, that is, provided a new perspective from which to view, to organize, to evaluate, and to reinterpret knowledge. Stoutly resisted by some disciplines, woman-oriented scholarship was more readily accepted by others, including some branches of history. Perhaps because it developed contemporaneously with the "new social" history, women's history at last won wide support for the opinions of the Wife of Bath and Pizan—that women's experiences differed distinctly from men's perception of them.

Women's history is not, however, altogether new. While the "history of women's history" is of recent origin, there have always been some historians who wrote about notorious women, often stressing their character and moral influence. Joan of Arc, Elizabeth I, and Marie de Medici did not lack biographers. Studies of witchcraft demonstrated that not all women have been content to sweep the family hearth with their brooms. However, as an inquiry into the lives of women of less than aristocratic origin or dramatically atypical behavior, women's history is closely related to movements for reform in female status and it parallels the quest for personal freedom in Western civilization. The "scientific," or systematic, study of women's history began in the early nineteenth-century debate on the evolution of women's rights of inheritance and the relationship of the family to the state. Social critics of both liberal and conservative bent recognized that the status of women, as of men, depended on the juridical and political status of the family in the social order. The immediate concern of conservatives was not "the rights of women," but revision of the laws governing inheritance, so as to strengthen the power of patriarchal families. For liberals, it was often the "rehabilitation of the flesh" from Christian connotations of sin. But in examining the role of women and the "social relationship of the sexes," these "social scientists" adopted a method with important implications for understanding women's history. Their studies of the status of women revealed the social and relational, as distinct from the biological or "natural" attributes of sex.

This was history *about* women. Women's history written also *for* women appeared in the early twentieth century when several economic historians—English and American women—produced pioneer works on the extent and contributions of female labor force participation and its implications. In this era also a lone female voice, Mary R. Beard, reviewed the political history of women's condition and protested as false and mischievous assertions of universal female subjugation. Until rediscovered in the 1970s, however, these works could do little for good or ill, for they were out of print and included on few lists of required or essential readings in academic history courses.[9] But 1970 brought to the forefront of Western consciousness a formidable challenge to the idealized separation of spheres along gender lines that most historians had accepted and reinforced in their work. Thousands of women—especially university students and faculty, journalists and government employees, all well-placed to gain public attention—began to recognize the false ground of the dichotomy and to insist that "the personal is political." That summer, *Time* magazine even published a cover story on "sexual politics." No longer would "political" and "public" be synonymous terms, both separate from and opposed to "personal" and "private." No longer could historians and other scholars ignore women's lives. In the same way that great interest in economic history followed closely periods of economic depression and labor unrest, that new programs in minority and ethnic group history emerged in the wake of racial conflict and civil rights movements, so a veritable avalanche of new studies on women filled the pages of journals and blanketed the shelves of bookstores in the decade after the "rebirth" of feminism. For the first time, courses on women in history—designed largely *for* as well as *about* women—appeared in college curricula.

While women in society continue, as they always have, to *make* history, they are determined today that their contributions will be recognized and *recorded*. Increasingly, feminists can ground their actions in theories drawn from the new scholarship in women's studies, often supported by knowledge learned in works on women's history. Scholars have compensated for the absence of women in conventional courses by rediscovery of the long tradition of feminism, reading works showing *Women, Resistance and Revolution* (1974), though *Hidden from History* (1973), and told to *Suffer and Be Still* (1972); now *Becoming Visible* (1977) and seeking *A Widening Sphere* (1977)—all titles of books on women in European history. After numerous works demonstrated women's contributions to male-defined history, historians of women moved on to a less "compensatory" approach, publishing *Women, Work and Family* (1978), *Fit Work for Women* (1979), and *A Heritage of Her Own* (1979), books that emphasize the value of women's experience apart from the politics and purposes of men. Historians of the nineteenth century, especially, have proposed the idea of "women's culture," meaning "the separate values, experiences, institutions, relationships, rituals, and consciousness that nineteenth-century women developed out of their separation from the male domain of public life and their restriction to the private sphere." *Ladies of the Leisure Class,* a recent example, draws on materials and insights from anthropology, psychology, and literature to show French bourgeois women as agents in maintenance of a pre-modern world view that validated their domestic and religious roles.[10]

Influenced by the new social historians, many of whom (men and women) chose women as subjects for investigation, historians of women spent a decade in retrieving the data necessary for new woman-centered works that are sensitive to the realities of women's lives. An innovative emphasis by social historians on systematic analysis of quantifiable data happily coincided with the recognition by feminist scholars of the role of earlier generations of social scientists in the "social construction of the second sex." Early in the development of women's studies, psychologist Naomi Weisstein exposed descriptions of women's "nature" by male psychologists as prescriptions reflecting men's desires, while psychologists Sandra Bem and Daryl Bem and political scientist Jo Freeman demonstrated the power of social processes to shape definitions of femininity, which serve to control female behavior.[11] This conjuncture led, not without some problems, to a fruitful union of the methodologies, sources, and theories in the new social history with the questions raised by the new women's history. The net result has been a lively debate over such issues as the impact of industrialization on women's work, family roles, and social power; the links between modes of production, the design of social space, and concepts of womanhood; and the nature of relationships among women within the subculture of women's purported separate sphere, including their collective action for economic as well as political and social goals. In short, considerable information about women has been uncovered, recorded, and analyzed. To borrow the construct of Joan Scott, "her-story" has been fashioned as has the social history of women—but as yet, only in part, for women's history needs to be integrated back into, and in turn, to restructure, political history.[12] The writing of a complete human "history," to replace the truncated "story," waits upon this task.

The progress of writing women's history can be divided into three overlapping phases. First came the task of *dismantling*: exposing assumptions, interpretations, and practices that led to the omission or distortion of women's presence in the past. Next followed the work of *discovery*: searching sources old and new for the data needed to add women's experiences to the corpus of materials that comprise the written record of history. This research "discovered," for example, a wide variety of women's movements that were part and parcel of the European political scene in the late nineteenth century and women's charitable activities that were used to launch a critique of male dominance and power. It also "uncovered" neglected feminist writers, established the centrality of the "argument about women" in Western thought, and traced the importance and influence of women's networks for family survival during periods of revolutionary upheaval and economic transformation. Furthermore, the popularity enjoyed and prestige won by the new social history and its practitioners motivated inquiry on such related topics as demographic patterns, family structures and functions, sexual attitudes and behaviors—all of which influenced and, in turn, were affected by women's lives. Through recognizing sex and gender as central categories of analysis, scholars in the new field created a history that paralleled and often intersected more traditional work. They challenged all historians to rethink old truths and to raise new questions in ways that included women's experiences and perceptions.

At this stage, the growing and sustained acceptance of the importance of women as both subjects of and agents in the historical process has produced a torrent of publications. Without slackening, it has moved women's history into a third phase: *reconstruction*, or integration of the new knowledge about women and female perspectives into the more traditional political and economic narrative. The "re-vision" of history from the perspective of women has produced a "double vision"—the seeing of two images—that now calls for integration.[13] As a step in this complex process of writing human history, this book connects women's lives to the major economic, social, intellectual, and political developments in the Western world during the last five centuries. It "re-views" the major events and ideas of half a millenium of Western history from the perspective of women's contributions and experiences. Beginning in the finite, earth-centered, male-defined world of Ptolemy, our narrative ends in a universe of ever-expanding horizons where both women and men move into space and face the discovery of new worlds, new life-forms, other galaxies—or, alternatively, of collapse through war and nuclear devastation.

The focus on women adds richness to the content of this chronicle. It also alters the perspective and, by emphasizing women in their own right, exposes the misconceptions through which their personal lives and collective values were denigrated or ignored by power elites and by historians. Less arithmetic than geometric, the effect of the change is to reshape our understanding of the relationship between individual and society in both the past and the present. It shows us that our social system rests on assumptions that contradict important values in society and it calls for a new perspective.

We begin each section with an overview chapter that presents a broad-ranging analysis of the main forces shaping and being shaped by women's experiences. The first deals with the early modern era, 1500–1750; the second concerns the "age of revolution"; and the third covers much of the twentieth century, 1890 to the present. We follow each overview with case studies that develop important themes of the period. They are designed to demonstrate the workings of women's history: to show the kinds of questions raised, the types of evidence used, the methods of analysis employed, the variety of concepts derived. As you will see, these case studies offer a dramatic illustration of what is missing in traditional histories. You will find that old interpretations take on new meaning when a new category of analysis—gender—is added to the historical perspective.

We open this new history by exploring important themes in the early modern period. Part I deals with religious reformation and political centralization. It reveals that both processes invoked ideas and created structures pregnant with meaning for women. For example, the consolidation of political power in centralized states both drew on the patriarchal family as a model and strengthened its authority. Absolute monarchies promulgated laws that enhanced the patriarch's power. However, the breakup of religious hierarchy fostered the spread of education and favored the growth of an individualism that began to undermine familial influence. These changes also reinforced an increasing differentiation of men's and women's roles that was based in a growing market economy. So problematic was the role of women in a changing but still male-defined society that even the scientists of the early modern period found difficulty reconciling their discoveries and their prejudices. Especially for women, the changes created contradictions between social ideals and social reality that gave birth to female protest.

The human story continues in an era of political upheaval and economic transformation. Part II focuses on change and continuity as a result of the "dual revolution"—the political revolution that restructured the state and redefined the political roles of subjects, and the industrial revolution that changed traditional methods and locations for the production of goods and the provision of services. When seen from the perspective of women, the change is less dramatic and perhaps less progressive than commonly portrayed. Excluded from citizenship and defined by their family and household roles, women struggled throughout the nineteenth century to appropriate for themselves freedoms promised by the loosening of inherited values and traditions. Counterposed against economic and demographic shifts that prepared the ground for new roles for women (as indeed for men) was a newly developing ideology of domesticity that sought to channel narrowly the female option. As men followed the dictates of production and increasingly found work separate from home and family, women discovered new means to reconcile gainful employment and domestic duties. Industrial homework, originally used by all members of the family to supplement agricultural income, became finally the preserve of women. The middle-class ideal of the wife without profession, the leisured lady free to embellish herself and her home, lay beyond the grasp of most rural and urban families. And even the lady of apparent leisure often worked hard to maintain her carefully controlled, and hardly carefree, domesticity. Our studies of a cross section of female experiences show that most women were concerned primarily with women's multiple responsibilities, and not with women's rights.

Finally the flow of women's history brings us into the present century. Part III treats the more familiar era of welfare states and developing countries, and of peoples connected by markets and media to others they may never know in all parts of the world. It brings us head on into conflict over women's roles founded in traditional views of women's nature, on the one hand, and the imperatives of both a new social organization and a new egalitarian ethos, on the other. When, after decades of struggle, for example, victorious revolutionaries in Russia sought to transform personal as well as political, spiritual as well as economic life, they begot massive resistance rather than promised revision in social relations. The circumstances of change, amid deprivation, destruction, and death, perhaps doomed all efforts at radical reconstruction. While war and revolution released women from traditional constraints and encouraged them to enter nontraditional roles, their new-found opportunities were contingent and short-lived. Changes came only as makeshift responses to the imperatives of economic, political, and diplomatic decisions. Yet, sometimes changes have unplanned effects and transform the consciousness of those forced into new roles. For some women today, altered self-awareness both reflects new roles and portends deep-seated readjustments in the social fabric. The history of the last five hundred years, however, suggests that this process will require a major reorientation in social values.

For more than half a millenium one idea has loomed large in the West—that people themselves, as well as their historians, came to regard as a central ingredient of liberal democratic society: the notion of the individual. Individualism has been identified by historians and philosophers of the modern Western world as one of its most important principles and as a universal goal. It was once popular to organize the history of Western civilization itself around the growing acceptance of the idea of individualism. Individual liberty and freedom for self-fulfillment were deemed essential to the progress of humanity. Personal happiness and social welfare demanded that individual sovereignty be limited only by social necessity. In art as in politics, unfettered individual liberty became the touchstone of an ideal, virtuous society. From Michelangelo's *David* to Beethoven's *Eroica Symphony* and Shelley's *Prometheus Unbound,* the Western world has celebrated the image of the rebellious individual who defied both natural and social constraints to test the limits of human potential. At its romantic extreme, human genius was released from all moral and social obligation. This glorification of individualism belonged to the story of (mostly male) elites.

Many people in Western societies today continue to take pride in individualism, considering personal dignity and self-determination as distinctive and supreme virtues of the free world. They may even pose individual self-expression as a universal ideal. This stands in stark contrast to societies, past or contemporary, that subordinate the rights of the individual to the needs of the state. But what happens to this ideal when history is revised to include women? To be a realistic goal for all, individual liberty requires changing the very fabric of society, a position that many are not willing to accept. One fearful response to the emergence of autonomous, self-defining women has been, "Who takes care of the children?" Another has been the feminist demand for shared parental responsibility. Still another is a nostalgic urge to turn the clock back.

While most people gradually have accustomed themselves to material changes, to automobiles and airplanes, to radios and television sets, to canned foods, frozen foods, and "fast foods," they have been less ready to accept concurrent changes in personal roles and social relationships, especially the "liberation of women." Thus the "subtle revolution" of women's increasing labor force participation and distance from family authority, which resulted from reorganization in structures and methods of work, and was accelerated by war, revolution, and rising material expectations, is at times misunderstood. It may even fuel attacks on nontraditional women. Seen by some as willful rejection of responsibility toward family, women's changing work patterns more often reflect their need to continue making the traditional female contributions to the family under changed circumstances. It may, however, also express women's responsiveness to the ethos of a society that treasures individual liberty as a precious value, and defines it as a kind of self-fulfillment free of social ties. This perspective ignores not only the role of women in the family and the benefits of family to men, but also the very real interdependence of all people. And it neglects the underlying social supports without which individuals could not achieve their goals. Moreover, it obscures the social basis for the survival of the individual and for the formation of individual psychological identity. This integral relationship between the individual and the social is highlighted by our reassessment of the historical experience of women.

We see our task today as that of creating a new social environment that facilitates the development of *individual* identity along with *group* responsibility—for both women and men of all diverse cultures and lifestyles. As historians, we participate intimately in this endeavor by relating a story of human experience that reveals the limits of unrestrained individualism and stresses the significance of social ties. The new history and the future world that include women alongside and equal to men must reconnect the many aspects of human existence heretofore divided into separate spheres and labeled as "men's world" (of individual achievement) and "women's place" (of social support).

The influence of history on our lives extends far beyond the knowledge we accumulate of the experiences of our forebears. For history, like all moral tales, has a power beyond cognition; it has a "mythic power to link our lives with larger forces."[14] Every generation constructs its own understanding of the past in order to connect the individual lives of its members with a collective identity. Through serendipity, sexual politics, or "the cunning of history," the body of knowledge created by feminist scholars of the last fifteen years is at hand today to aid in the task of revival. This new history, like the old, will reflect the values and purposes of the historians who write it. It is the hope of the authors that this book, by restoring women to history, will also restore history not only to women, but to all who seek to improve human understanding by transcending the separation of the personal from the political, of man from woman, of individual from group, of past from present.

NOTES

1. Joan Kelly-Gadol, "The Social Relations of the Sexes: Methodological Implications of Women's History," *Signs* 1, no. 4 (Summer 1976): 809–823.
2. *The Ladies Wreath* (1852) cited by Mary P. Ryan, "Femininity and Capitalism in Antebellum America," in Zillah P. Eisenstein, ed., *Capitalist Patriarchy and the Case for Socialist Feminism* (New York: Monthly Review Press, 1979), p. 166.
3. Joan Kelly-Gadol, "Did Women Have a Renaissance?" in Renate Bridenthal and Claudia Koonz, eds., *Becoming Visible: Women in European History* (Boston: Houghton Mifflin Company, 1977), pp. 137–164.
4. On 1844 and 1877 see Norman E. Himes, *Medical History of Contraception* (New York: Schocken Books, 1970), pp. 187, 243–245; on 1877, also J. A. and Olive Banks, *Feminism and Family Planning in Victorian England* (New York: Schocken Books, 1964), pp. 90–91. On 1936, see discussion of United States v. One Package of Japanese Pessaries in David M. Kennedy, *Birth Control in America: The Career of Margaret Sanger* (New Haven: Yale University Press, 1970), pp. 248–257. On 1967, when the Neuwrith Law authorized the sale of contraceptives in France, see Shari Steiner, *The Female Factor: A Report on Women in Western Europe* (New York: Putnam Publishing Group, 1977), p. 137.
5. Charlotte Perkins Gilman, *The Home: Its Work and Influence* (1903; reprint Urbana, Ill.: University of Illinois Press, 1972), p. 317; *Women and Economics: The Economic Factor between Men and Women as a Factor in Social Evolution* (1898; reprint New York: Harper and Row, 1966), p. 269; and "Our Androcentric Culture," in Gilman, *The Forerunner* I, no. 1 (1909): 24.
6. Angus McLaren, "Doctor in the House: Medicine and Private Morality in France, 1800–1850," *Feminist Studies* 2, no. 2/3 (1975): 45; William Acton, *The Functions and Disorders of the Reproductive Organs*, 8th American ed. (Philadelphia, 1894, orig. 1857) in Erna Olafson Hellerstein, Leslie Parker Hume, and Karen M. Offen, eds., *Victorian Women: A Documentary Account of Women's Lives in Nineteenth-Century England, France, and the United States* (Stanford: Stanford University Press, 1981), p. 178.

7. In Joan Kelly, "Early Feminist Theory and the *Querelle des Femmes,* 1400–1789," *Signs* 8, no. 1 (Autumn 1982): 14, 20.

8. John Stuart Mill, *The Subjection of Women,* in Alice S. Rossi, ed., *John Stuart Mill and Harriet Taylor Mill, Essays on Sex Equality* (Chicago: University of Chicago Press, 1970), p. 148.

9. Alice Clark, *Working Life of Women in the Seventeenth Century* (New York: G. Routledge and Sons, 1919); Ivy Pinchbeck, *Women Workers and the Industrial Revolution: 1750–1850* (1930; reprint New York: A.M. Kelley, 1969); Edith Abbott, *Women in Industry* (New York: D. Appleton, 1910); Mary R. Beard, *Woman As Force in History* (New York: Collier Books, 1946).

10. Sheila Rowbotham, *Women, Resistance and Revolution* (New York: Pantheon Books, 1974) and *Hidden from History* (New York: Pantheon Books, 1974); Martha Vicinus, ed., *Suffer and Be Still: Women in the Victorian Age* (Bloomington, Ind.: Indiana University Press, 1973); Bridenthal and Koonz, *Becoming Visible;* Martha Vicinus, ed., *A Widening Sphere: Changing Roles of Victorian Women* (Bloomington, Ind.: Indiana University Press, 1978); Nancy Cott and Elizabeth H. Pleck, eds., *A Heritage of Her Own: Toward a New Social History of American Women* (New York: Simon & Schuster, 1979); Louise A. Tilly and Joan W. Scott, *Women, Work, and Family* (New York: Holt, Rinehart, Winston, 1978); Sandra Burman, ed., *Fit Work, for Women* (New York: St. Martin's Press, 1979); Cynthia M. Patterson, "New Directions in the Political History of Women: A Case Study of the National Woman's Party's Campaign for the Equal Rights Amendment, 1920–1927," *Women's Studies International Forum* 5, no. 6 (Fall 1982): 586. Patterson and others now use the social history of that "women's culture" in new approaches to women's political history; Bonnie G. Smith, *Ladies of the Leisure Class: The Bourgeoises of Northern France in the Nineteenth Century* (Princeton: Princeton University Press, 1981).

11. Naomi Weisstein, "Psychology Constructs the Female, or the Fantasy Life of the Male Psychologist," in Michele Hoffnung Garskof, ed., *Roles Women Play: Readings toward Women's Liberation* (Belmont, Calif.: Brooks/Cole, 1971), pp. 68–83; Sandra L. Bem and Daryl J. Bem, "Training the Woman to Know Her Place: The Power of a Nonconscious Ideology," ibid., pp. 84–96; Jo Freeman, "The Social Construction of the Second Sex," ibid., pp. 123–141.

12. Joan Wallach Scott, "Survey Articles: Women in History II: The Modern Period," *Past and Present* 101 (November 1983): 154.

13. Kelly, "Social Relations," p. 811; Joan Kelly, "The Doubled Vision of Feminist Theory: A Postscript to the 'Women and Power' Conference," *Feminist Studies* 5, no. 1 (Spring 1979): 216–227.

14. Kathryn Kish Sklar, "The Uses of History," lecture at American Writers Congress (New York, October 1981).

I

WOMEN IN THE EARLY MODERN ERA: RELIGIOUS UPHEAVAL, POLITICAL CENTRALIZATION, AND COLONIAL CONQUEST

Overview, 1500–1750

There is nothing magical about the year 1500, the date we choose to start our story. It begins the century of the religious Reformation, which forged new links between state, church, individual, and society and transported as well the religious beliefs and attitudes to encounters with indigenous peoples in the establishment of empires in the Americas. It set a pattern of interaction between events and their consequences in Europe, Africa, and the Americas, intertwining the lives of women and men in far-off lands, and in effect bringing gender and race issues inextricably together. The unsettling processes of empire-building and economic restructuring fed a parallel move to domesticate European women and control colonial subjects. At the same time, some educated urban European women, testing their own voices based on personal experiences, duplicated many of the attitudes that reinforced patterns of imperial thinking. In the history of European women, indeed, gender and race intersect in complex and often tense relationships.

The events of the sixteenth century, however, had been long in the making. The *Respublica Christiana*—the medieval Latin Christian world of one God, one Church, one Empire—was already being transformed by changes internal to Europe. In the prior century, the church had not been able to assert a unifying influence and was fragmenting along geographic lines. The Gallican (French) church claimed administrative independence from the Holy See in Rome and, in disputes over authority, Catholic bishops often allied with their territorial princes or kings against the centralizing efforts of the papal court.

Furthermore, European consciousness of other peoples had been reactivated by Christian revival and reconquest. The conquest of the Americas followed on the heels of the establishment of dominion over the Canary Islands (1402) and the Catholic

19

kings' battles against the Moors, leading ultimately to the defeat of the Moorish kingdom at Granada (1492). This was accompanied by the compulsory conversion or
expulsion of the Jews (1492) and Moors (1502) from Castile. Consciousness of difference—to the English, the Irish were a "wild race" of men and Germans were
"drunks"—readily became framed in religious idiom in the figure of the Jew, Moor,
or Turk. Although "sincere" conversion promised reintegration into Christian society (most Spanish Jews opted instead for emigration), difference also was interpreted
as a matter of blood. Listen to the words of Lope de Vega (1562–1635):

> I am a man,
> And although of low birth,
> I am of pure blood,
> Never stained by Jewish or Moorish woman.[1]

Dominion over the peoples of the Canaries and later the Amerindians, for whom
the Christian principle of "just war" through reconquest did not apply (since their
ancestors never had been Christian converts), reworked the metaphor of "wild
beasts" who needed to be brought into the Christian fold. Not surprisingly, the Latin
church gave its blessings to imperialism in the Papal Treaty of Tordesillas (1494),
which divided up the "new" world to its west into Spanish and Portuguese empires.
In tales that glorified the exploits of the new explorers and conquerors, the painful
effects on the conquered were generally suppressed.

Simultaneously, new cultural values, which drew their inspiration from Classical Greece and Rome, had emerged in the urban, more secular environment of the
Italian city-states. A new norm of civic activism and political commitment was put
forth over and above the Christian ideal of contemplative monastic living. Concerned
with immediate circumstances and this world, its proponents were known as "humanists." Conscious of a deep gulf separating them from the medievalists, they spoke of
the need for a "renaissance," or rebirth. This rebirth would be guided by a study of
the rhetoric, poetry, grammar, history, as well as the moral philosophy, of classical
antiquity. In the formulation of the Italian philosopher Pico della Mirandola
(1463–94), it proclaimed the "dignity of man," a notion that still carries normative
weight. But the ideal of European "manhood" was complicated in practice because
it rested on construction of "others"—barbarians, cannibals, and the "wild" men, as
well as, of course, women, who were excluded from the political life of the city-states.
Furthermore, reconnection to the world of classical philosophy and politics reinforced the case for slavery, which had been endemic to antiquity. Of course, classical texts did not replace Christian scripture; humanism could be reconciled with religious beliefs and in fact exerted a powerful influence on the theology and philosophy
of medieval scholars (scholasticism). In turn, Renaissance works continued to reference both classical and Christian traditions and ideas. Particularly in northern Europe,
humanists in the sixteenth century were known as Christian humanists, and turned
their critical faculties to examining the scriptures. Indeed, what is meant by the Western tradition as opposed to the Eastern or "Middle" Eastern tradition, is the ongoing
reintegration of ancient classical ideas and notions with Judeo-Christian values and
beliefs in the geographic area of Europe and later of North America as well.

The sixteenth-century religious Reformation, which coincided with the transition to empire, was part of a profound crisis of authority that affected the evolution of the more secular realms of political community and family life in ways that also had far-reaching consequences for the lives of women. As reform ideas spread through towns, communities, and countries, religion and politics became more deeply intertwined. Many historians now label the period an age of "confessionalism," implying a significant recasting of the relationship between state, church, individual, and society. There has been a move away from seeing the "reformation" as theological struggles within a limited time frame (1517–55) to describing a much longer process of state and empire-building that drew on energies unleashed and justified by religious fervor and conviction. The nearly one and one-half centuries following Luther's call for debate at the church of Wittenberg Castle in 1517 involved a series of civil wars (in France and later in England) and international wars (in central Europe as well as in North and South America). In the course of these conflicts, both Protestantism (especially Lutheranism and Calvinism) and Catholicism were vitalized and structured in similar ways through doctrinal clarification, institutional growth, and new ritual forms. Church and state were more effectively able to impact the daily lives of subjects in urban and rural communities. These changes reinforced the move to centralize political authority based on a shared confessional identity, the origins of which can also be traced back to earlier efforts of European kings and princes, the so-called new monarchs, to establish their power against counterclaims of nobles and towns to their own inviolable "privileges and liberties." For many European subjects, the political instability of religious change and conflict reinforced the case for centralized authority; in other instances, patterns of control that were tested in the colonies doubled back into Europe.

This revision of boundaries among major institutions in the life of the polity—church, government, and household—necessarily affected female roles in diverse and complicated ways. As society became increasingly complex and the private realm more clearly delineated and described, which women gained or lost status? What new roles opened to religiously inspired women? How did definitions of female deviancy affect political authority in Europe and in Europe's colonies? Why did the patriarchal family become a symbol of dynastic authority? What are the linkages between state-building, patriarchal control, and colonialism?

So far, we have discussed the changing relationships between state and society in the context of religious reform. But the whole process of state-building and the imposition and maintenance of colonial rule was reinforced by economic changes that were shifting production and exchange from the Mediterranean to the wider Atlantic world. Between the sixteenth and the eighteenth centuries, a new Atlantic community was being formed through a developing triangular trading nexus between Europe, Africa, and the Americas. It marked an important milestone toward the increasingly global economy of the late twentieth century. In turn, these economic rivalries and colonial successes (or failures) reinforced state power and prestige in Europe itself.

Growing markets for new goods produced a "commercial revolution" in Europe, linking people across borders and oceans through their daily purchases of sugar, tobacco, coffee, or textiles. Consumption spread from a near monopoly of the rich in Europe to become a growing sign of the middling sorts in society. For many commentators, indeed, consumption was a proper female sphere of activity, helping to constitute feminine attributes of gender. Furthermore, there was a growing intersection of economic and political power among Europe's elites. For example, in England between 1604 and 1614, the families of one-third of the members of the House of Commons (in Parliament) were involved in colonial projects that produced new wealth. As significantly, new values were communicated in the very act of buying and consuming. In the late eighteenth century, the great English pottery firm Wedgwood, ever attuned to new market opportunities, designed a black teapot "to show off to better advantage the current feminine vogue for bleached white hands."[2] And a growing preoccupation with cleanliness and the body, which was expressed in a fashionable display of white linen garments, increasingly worked to differentiate elites from the "low" born by color and manners.

These commercial exchanges affected production throughout the regions of Europe, stimulating economic activities beyond that controlled by guilds, those urban corporations that had been responsible for most marketable goods manufactured in the medieval world. The availability of goods also changed the nature of production in the household and its gender role divisions. In the medieval period, most people lived and subsisted only because of a family household, whose members worked together to produce the food, clothing, and other goods essential to life. The economic changes of the early modern period brought new opportunities for commercial gain to those fortunate enough to produce beyond subsistence needs. Among the many factors in family life altered by economic development were the age at marriage, the number of children, the relative status of single and married women, and the place of residence selected by people as they sought strategies to survive and prosper. How did female labor in both urban and rural settings contribute to the economic development of early modern Europe? Did the nature and status of women's work change or remain stable in the period? How were women's lives impacted in urban settings when men left for administrative or artisanal posts in the colonies? In what ways did the extension of commercial capitalism reinforce the tendency of the new states to consolidate decision making under men's auspices?

Along with political and economic changes came intense intellectual ferment that has been termed a revolution: a scientific revolution. Indeed, "science" increasingly became a powerful authority in its own right, with its claims to truth and objectivity based on observation and critical methodologies as well as its stress on reason. Although science grew out of a male monastic and university culture, a number of women took part in the intellectual exchanges, inspired by new scientific methods and philosophical propositions that were beginning to undermine the old intellectual order. Conscious of themselves as a social group, they drew on science to propose extending education to women and restructuring domestic authority in order to improve the position of the female sex. These women writers were the descendants of a line of thinkers stretching back to the fifteenth century that today we would term "feminist." What accounts for the presence of debate on "the woman question" in one period of history and its relative neglect in another era? How did science itself reestablish hierarchies on the basis of gender and race? What particular voices were reflected in the writings of Europe's early feminists?

In the previous pages we have summarized briefly several lines of European development in the centuries we are investigating in Part I. We take a similar approach in the overviews to Parts II and III. Without doing injustice to the complexity of events, we want to familiarize readers with the broad themes of modern history before we turn to the changing roles of women. Since our purpose is to integrate women's experiences into the overall pattern of historical development in the West, we have raised general questions concerning the forces that have influenced most directly women's lives. These questions are designed to help you read more critically the ensuing narrative and case studies. Remember to bear in mind the multiple roles and situations of women in Europe as well as in the areas of political encounters outside of Europe. How does this unmistakable diversity of women's experiences and perspectives affect notions of a common female identity? What realities did women share?

Confronting Traditions: The Origins of the "Argument About Women"

The waning of the old feudal order in Europe was signaled by the growing importance of a new class of educated people. The group was urban and a product of the social mobility that commerce as well as new bureaucratic and university careers had introduced into the more static world of feudal Europe. Beginning in the mid-fifteenth century, its members served the new monarchs in their efforts to transform themselves from chief feudal lords (the first among equals) into sovereign rulers. It is the women of this group that primarily interest us here. As daughters of humanists, of businessmen, of clergymen, they benefited as individuals from the spread of learning, which still was limited to a tiny proportion of the population. In reading the venerable authors of the past, however, these educated women could not escape the prejudicial and hostile views about the inferiority of the female sex that were a part of secular as well as religious texts. Their response was to challenge the homosocial humanist culture by proposing alternative ways to assess women's condition. They initiated what became a tradition of "feminist" theorizing in Western thought.

Their earliest spokeswoman was Christine de Pizan (1364–1429), whom we have already met in the introduction. Their ranks included the Venetian poet Lucrezia Marinella (1571–1653), the British playwright Aphra Behn (1640–89), and women from whom we shall have occasion to hear more fully later on, such as Jane Sharp (fl. 1671), Elizabeth Cellier (fl. 1680), and Mary Astell (1668–1731)—all predecessors to Laura Bassi (1711–78), who in 1732 earned a doctorate at the University of Bologna (the Western world's oldest university, founded in 1088). What lay at the heart of their protest was the conviction that women were full human beings, not creatures restricted by nature or female biology. And their remedy was to open to women the fruits of their culture, the education in "arms and letters" as it was conceived at the time; women's true capabilities then would become manifest. Marinella wrote, "I wish that these [detractors of women] would make this experiment: that they raise a boy and a girl of the same age, and both of sound mind and body, in letters and arms. They would see in a short time how the girl would be more perfectly instructed than the boy and would soon surpass him."[3]

This conclusion contradicted the assertions of women's inferiority that had been passed down from ancient classical author to Christian writer in Western history to that date. Christine de Pizan has left a remarkable testimony of her own struggle when confronting the authority of these learned men. It was, she wrote, "too much [to hold], that so many famous men . . . should have lied, and in so many places, for I could scarcely find a volume [of moral philosophy], whoever its author, without . . . some chapters or sections blaming [women]."[4] Traditions represent accumulated wisdom based on shared perceptions and beliefs that become part of each generation's intellectual convictions. As Pizan recognized, there was a long tradition of misogynist thinking in the Western world, but it was man-made, not indicative of any natural state of affairs. And she and the other early feminists began to turn the historical record around in order to acquire a heritage to be proud of. An understanding of "history" was essential to their project. They set out to capture the exploits of great ladies—the "women worthies"—and to "discourse on the excellence of women."[5] Pizan's women assume the attributes associated with men; they are capable and intelligent and speak with authority and compassion. Indeed, she obliterates differences between women and men, since polarized thinking was one main source of misogynistic views. This position is an important contribution to feminist thinking. But at the same time, Pizan bases her arguments on concepts of religious and territorial "difference"—defending the universal claims of Christianity against Jews and Muslims, and eliding the true Christian community with France (against the English).

Writers such as Christine de Pizan initiated an intellectual defense of women that continued and gained credence during the famous four-hundred-year-long "Querelle des femmes" (argument over the nature of women). The time of Pizan, the Renaissance, was a period of intellectual ferment, empirical inquiry, and experimentation, but all that creative energy did not alter the general negative assessment of women's capabilities or the normative belief that women's proper place was ensconced in domestic life, subject to the authority of fathers, husbands, or other men. Two reasons account for the perpetuation of these ancient beliefs at a time of otherwise significant transformation of values. First, these beliefs offered a persuasive and comprehensive justification for common biblical assertions about women. Second, they supported the philosophically conservative bias of most scholars.

The inherited notions about women were an integral part of the structure of the dominant Christian philosophy of the Renaissance. To replace its method and argument by an alternative system of thought implied severing all ties to contemporary philosophical usage. Renaissance scholars, too, relied on previous authority in developing their arguments. The great Renaissance astronomer Galileo in the *Dialogue Concerning the Two Chief World Systems—Ptolemaic and Copernican* (1632) expresses the force of tradition when he has Simplicio, a confused peripatetic (a devotee of Aristotle), protest, "Who would there be to settle our controversies if Aristotle were to be deposed? What other author should we follow in the schools, the academies, the universities? What philosopher has written the whole of natural philosophy, so well arranged. . . . Ought we to desert that structure under which so many travelers have recuperated?"[6] Especially in a time of religious, political, and economic upheaval, continuity in the gender hierarchy would be reassuring.

Aristotle's system of thought rested on the principle of duality, in which one element was superior to another, and this position was incorporated by the scholastics into their own Christian edifice. The male principle in nature was associated with activity and perfection, while the female was conceived of as passive and deprived. The duality male/female was paralleled by the dualities active/passive, form/matter, and perfection/imperfection. In using this notion of male/female, we can observe how through time the classical and Christian views were merged to produce the characteristic gender belief system of the West so forcefully challenged by Christine de Pizan. Aristotle had argued that nature always sought to create the most perfect thing, which was the most completely formed. Such a creature, he claimed, was the male. Neither Aristotle nor his influential thirteenth-century scholastic follower, Thomas Aquinas, meant that females contradicted the intentions of nature. Both sexes were necessary to procreate the species. In explaining the purpose of female being, Aquinas synthesized his understanding of Aristotle with the account of the creation of woman in Genesis (1:26–7, 2:22–3):

> With reference to nature in the species as a whole, the female is not something manqué, but is according to the plan of nature, and is directed to the work of procreation.[7]

By the time of the Renaissance some doctors (as learned men were called) had turned against Aristotelian thought and argued that women were equally perfect (though lesser) beings. This progressive-sounding position did not translate into advocacy of greater equality for women, but it helped solve one potentially bothersome problem—to understand the successes of queens or the influence of strong wives. Renaissance doctors posited two intermediary types between the perfect woman (born from the dominant female semen in the left-hand side of the uterus) and the perfect man (resulting from the dominant male semen in the right side of the uterus): effeminate males and viragoes (strong, manlike women). Thus, the dramatic exploits and achievements of queens, abbesses, and heroines (Elizabeth I, for example) were credited to physiological "abnormalities," an explanation that obviated examination of the circumstances under which women could develop their potentials more fully. Later, a new literary category, too, was adopted to make sense of the writings of colonial women such as Anne Bradstreet in New England or Sor Juana in New Spain (Mexico), whose poetry was published in London and Madrid. In library catalogues and literary compendia, such work was grouped with neither the writings of women nor poets, but classified under a new label as the "Tenth Muse."

From an idiosyncratic understanding of female physiology, scholars were quick to generalize about woman's psychology, and here the learned medical voices blended in well with venerable theological beliefs. Prey to a hysterical animal within her (the uterus), woman could not control her emotions, nor discipline her sexual impulses, nor act in any consistent fashion according to reason. This justified her relegation to home and hearth and exclusion from participation in public affairs. Clergymen reached the same conclusion, though partly for different reasons. In the accounts of man's superiority over woman in the theological tracts of the medieval world, her passivity and imperfections were attributed to the malediction laid on woman at the Fall and to her uncleanliness during menstruation, a concept adapted by Christians from Judaic law. Eve's betrayal and the monthly "curse" were used to justify many of the restrictions placed on women's earthly participation in the life of the church. This was notwithstanding the basic Christian tenet that while woman was the inferior of man by nature, she was his equal by grace. There would be no difference in status of the sexes in heaven; they shared the same spiritual destiny. In the present world, however, women were enjoined to cover their heads in church and to wear their hair long as signs of submission. Not formed in the image of God, they were excluded from the priesthood, and because Eve's words had bewitched Adam, they were barred from preaching or speaking in church. Above all, they were subject to their husbands in marriage. Although marriage itself was considered an imperfect state, it was a necessary evil for weaker mortals unable to achieve the celibate ideal embodied in the priesthood. Church, custom, and law placed wives squarely under husbands' authority. Both classical and Judeo-Christian teachings and common proverbs praised Patient Griselda, the chaste, submissive wife of medieval literature.

These widespread beliefs represented a formidable obstacle to women's assuming authoritative public roles in social and political life. But such norms, or ideological notions, are insufficient to explain fully women's status and historic experiences. As we will see in the course of this chapter, these misogynist views played a decisive role in shaping women's experiences in certain contexts, while in others they were less influential. The reality of women's lives defies the reach of rigid gender norms. History demonstrates numerous contexts within which women exercised considerable authority, responsibility, and decision-making power that belied the image of them as weaker vessels. In these cases, the material conditions of women's lives overrode the values and norms that sought to channel life along certain ideal paths.

In the early medieval world, women of rank played an active part in public life as suited their central role in the management of family property. Many of the economic documents of the day—the sales contracts, letters of exchange, leases, and donations—identified men by their mother's name. Because of her extensive managerial functions of overseeing the serfs, paying and collecting rents, producing and exchanging goods, an upper-class woman was a well-known personage in the local community and her name alone was sufficient to identify her male offspring. Family lineage counted more than gender. Often, women's behavior was governed by practical and informal arrangements not codified in judicial statute. Women did whatever was needed to ensure the continuity of the family estate, particularly when warrior-husbands departed for military ventures, crusades, or pilgrimages. With the demise of the Roman Empire, central rule had broken down and public authority was being exercised by powerful families. There was an overlapping of jurisdictions and the early medieval world made no clear distinction between the public realm and the private sphere. To the extent, then, that women were part of the governing nobility, they exhibited considerable authority over a range of public activities. For a long time, well into the early modern period in fact, politics remained dynastic and family ties were essential to the exercise of political power. This meant that some women who were members of powerful aristocratic and dynastic families continued to play significant roles in conflicts among states as well as in political struggles over the centralizing efforts of the new monarchs within the states of Europe. On the same model, some women in religious orders, usually women of aristocratic heritage, exercised important administrative powers as abbesses and prioresses.

The Reformation and the Confessional States

Defying stereotypes, women in good measure also were instrumental in spreading the ideas of the religious Reformation to the communities, towns, and provinces of Europe after 1517. In their roles as spouses and mothers they were often the ones to bring the early reform ideas to the families of Europe's aristocracy and to those of the common people in urban centers as well. The important role played by women in the early Reformation should not surprise us, for they had been equally significant in supporting previous heresies that challenged the established order and at times the gender hierarchy, too. Many medieval anticlerical movements that extolled the virtues of lay men praised lay women as well. For example, the fourteenth-century followers of John Wycliffe in England, known as Lollards, encouraged women to read the Bible and recite the Scriptures at their meetings; evidence suggests that women might even have preached on occasion. Wealthy women of aristocratic families who were allied together in the southern French province of Carcassonne were the vanguard of the Albigensian heresy in the twelfth and thirteenth centuries. Albigensians professed a radical dualism of good and evil and held that Satan, the principle of evil, was an independent deity, not a fallen angel of God. The adherents were ascetics, who withdrew from the evil world around them to free their spirits. When St. Dominic, who later founded the Dominican Order, converted the area back to orthodox Latin Christendom, he took great pains to win over these influential noblewomen.[8] Since the message of the Reformation, like that of the earlier religious movements, meant a loosening of hierarchies, it had a particular appeal to women. By stressing the individual's personal relationship with God and his or her own responsibility for behavior, it affirmed the ability of each to find truth by reading the original Scriptures. Thus, it offered a greater role for lay participation by women, as well as men, than was possible in Roman Catholicism.

The way was paved by the movement of Christian humanism in France, England, and the Low Countries at the end of the fifteenth century. Religious reformers utilized the new learning to deepen and strengthen individual piety; they hoped gradually and peacefully to reform the church from within. Two of the outstanding humanists, the Dutchman Desiderius Erasmus (1466–1536) and the Englishman Sir Thomas More (1478–1535), both acknowledged the importance of bringing religious education to women. Erasmus summed up their belief in his treatise on Christian marriage:

> The distaff and spindle are in truth the tools of all women and suitable for avoiding idleness. . . . It would be better if [people] taught [their daughters] to study, for study busies the whole soul. . . . It is not only a weapon against idleness, but also a means of impressing the best precepts upon a girl's mind and of leading her to virtue.[9]

More ironically grounded his advocacy of improved education for women in the old prejudices.

> If the female soil be in its nature stubborn, and more productive of weeds than fruit, it ought, in my opinion, to be more diligently cultivated with learning and good instruction. I do not see why learning . . . , may not equally agree with both sexes.[10]

And, in the context of Christian schism, the Spanish humanist Jean-Louis Vives (1492–1540) published *On the Institution of the Christian Woman* (1523). He, too, felt that education for women, although separate and distinct in content and purpose from that of men, nonetheless was essential for good marriage and good society, which rested on harmonious relations among the sexes.

Influenced by these Renaissance and Christian humanists, educators opened new opportunities for women of the aristocracy, many of whom later patronized the new learning in their own courts and lands. The humanist movement helps account for the group of remarkably talented and renowned female rulers and educators of the sixteenth century, which includes Queen Elizabeth I (1558–1603), Lady Jane Grey (1537–54), and Catherine Parr (1512–48) in England; Marguerite of Angoulême, queen of Navarre (1492–1549) and Jeanne d'Albret (1528–72) in France; as well as Mary of Austria, queen of Hungary and regent in the Netherlands (1509–58). Encouraged and often educated by the humanists, women began to participate in the discussions over church reforms, to debate the Scriptures, and to speculate on theological problems.

Translation of Luther's ideas reached France by 1519 and struck a receptive chord among the educated French noblewomen. Many, like Marguerite of Navarre, never officially converted to Protestantism but nevertheless turned their provinces into asylums for religious fugitives in the decades of turmoil to come. Marguerite even sheltered the Protestant reformer John Calvin (1509–64). The elder sister of Francis I, the king of France at the time of Luther's revolt, she was excluded from succession to the throne by the Salic law. Marguerite was a devotee of the new learning, a true lady of the Renaissance who, it is said, read Dante in Italian, quite probably Plato in Greek, and Luther in broken German. She was a writer and poet of considerable merit in her own right; her most important work is the *Heptameron,* modeled on Boccaccio's *Decameron,* which presents the tales of travelers whose lives express virtue and honor and contrast with the debauched and depraved ways of clerics and monks. One charming (and protofeminist) story relates the adventure of a boat woman who cleverly avoids rape by two Franciscan friars and delivers them quaking into the hands of villagers, who are delighted to catch the hypocritical clergy. Many of her verses, such as "The Primacy of Scripture" or "Justification by Faith," expressed in poetic form basic tenets of Protestantism. Through the printing press, her writings, as those of Christine de Pizan, were made available to well-born urban women in France who were encouraged to read and study according to the ideal of the humanists. The future Queen Elizabeth I translated one of her poems, "A Godly Meditation of the Soul."

At the French court, under the auspices of Anne de Beaujeu (1441–1522), a whole generation of ladies-in-waiting, the daughters of many of the leading noble families, had been educated according to humanist principles. These noblewomen, tied together by bonds of blood and marriage and by their earlier association as young girls at court, were active in the French Reform movement. In the 1520s they sponsored the educational and religious reforms associated with the evangelical movement led by Lefevre d'Etaples; it stressed meditation, prayer, and a life guided by reading the Gospel. For their own daughters' educations, they often chose tutors of reformed leanings and even specified the curriculum.

The first generation of French Protestant women were the daughters, granddaughters, and close associates of these educated aristocrats. This group of Protestant (Huguenot) activists emerged around midcentury and openly advocated Calvinism and the French Reformed church that John Calvin was guiding from Geneva. All of these Huguenot women were strong-minded, independent persons and a disproportionate number of them were widows. They found in Calvinism a way to enhance their participation in the religious and political events of the day. Thus, they carved out more meaningful roles in society than was otherwise possible. They converted friends and kin, protected pastors and educators, and gave money and advice to their male associates. In the lands that had gone Huguenot, they helped reform the system of law, levy new taxes, reorganize economic life, and they debated the question of the proper structure of the Reformed church. Even after the decline of the Huguenot cause, its women continued to be active in founding schools and establishing poor relief.

But what about the common women who lived in cities? What accounted for their conversion? At the heart of urban lay religious life in western Europe, supporting both religious and secular causes, stood confraternities, associations that also fostered new urban solidarities. Organized around craft guilds, they sponsored banquets and celebrations, held plays and festivities, and arranged for processions on their saints' days and masses to honor the souls of their dead members, friends, and relatives. In Lyons and other important cities, these were men's experiences; women were less likely than men to be members of the confraternity. However, even before the Reformation, as a result of the emphasis on the new learning, urban women who had access to vernacular devotional literature joined reading groups and began to discuss and debate theological issues. The churchmen were not at all sympathetic to such activity. "Why they are half theologians," complained a Franciscan priest vigorously. "They own Bibles the way they own love stories and romances. They get carried away by questions on transubstantiation [the doctrine that in the Sacrament bread and wine become the actual body and blood of Christ] and they go 'running around from . . . one [female] religious house to another, seeking advice. . . .'"[11]

The Protestant movement affirmed the right of women to read the Scriptures in the vernacular. It offered women who previously had not found much room for expressing their religious beliefs a new and clearly welcomed option: that of joining with the men of their families to talk seriously about religious matters. Even at church, men and women could raise their voices together in song and share religious expression. The women who became Protestants in Lyons were not the most learned women of the city but precisely those who found in religion a rewarding outlet for their new educational interests. They belonged mostly to middle-class families of artisans, merchants, and members of the professions; their ranks included a disproportionate number of widows with employment of their own in dressmaking, midwifery, and innkeeping. The new opportunities for intellectual and spiritual growth that conversion to Protestantism implied complemented an independence that some middle-class urban women, like the aristocratic Huguenot women, already had obtained.

After a half century of civil wars, France remained a Catholic nation; in other parts of northern and central Europe, the Reformation was institutionalized by official decree and maintained by resort to armed leagues. Claiming the right of *ius reformandi* (the power to reform), many dynastic states and imperial cities opted for Lutheranism, introducing Lutheran bishops, doctrines, and forms of worship, encouraging clerical marriages, secularizing (nationalizing) church property within their borders, and closing the convents. Luther himself had called upon the princes and urban magistrates to oversee religious reform, and the strong arm of authority seemed all the more crucial in light of massive peasant rebellions and the Anabaptist challenge that rejected authorities of both church and state and threatened to turn the Reformation into social revolution. Indeed, the Reformation cemented a working alliance between secular and religious powers—between princes and urban and rural elites as well as clergy—over religious reform and social discipline. This was true in lands that went Lutheran (e.g., Saxony, the Scandinavian countries, the imperial city of Frankfurt), in Calvinist Geneva, Holland, and the Rhineland as well as reformed (post-Tridentine) Catholicism in Spain, Austria, Bohemia, Poland, and Bavaria. Through a shared commitment to reform the clergy and impose confessional conformity, Christianity was assuming the character of political ideology, providing legitimacy for state authority.

Reforming Female Behavior

These changes had an immediate impact on the lives of women of all classes. One important and positive result was the stimulus it provided to educate girls so that they could read the Bible and other devotional literature. In the Saxon city of Zwickau, as in other urban areas that became Lutheran, the city council set up a girls' school as early as 1525. Since it was designed primarily to instill correct moral virtues rather than to stimulate intellectual development, the new educational program did not appreciably improve women's position in society. Furthermore, by introducing a new moral sensibility, the reform movement affected ambivalently, if not negatively, two vocations that had been important for women in the pre-Reformation era: that of nun and that of prostitute.

The nunneries were closed down wherever the Protestant reform triumphed. The nuns "did not go willingly," however; they were among those who resisted reform most tenaciously. In a society that elevated spirituality to the highest level, a religious vocation for women offered opportunities unequaled in the profane world. Indeed, by dedicating a daughter to the church, a family could hope not only for reward from God but also for special respect from neighbors and local officials. For example, in the early 1600s, Benedetta Carlini, a young woman from a mountain village in Italy, was pledged to the church by her father in gratitude for God's having spared her and her mother through a difficult birth. From early childhood Benedetta won privileges beyond her gender. When she began to have visions and fall into trances during which God and Jesus visited her, she achieved a kind of power and fame that could bring profit to her entire village. According to historian Judith Brown, Benedetta's claims were later rejected by church authorities, who imprisoned her for the rest of her life (some thirty-five years), because they feared the power of "holy women" to influence the rest of society. In Benedetta's case, after one investigation by local religious leaders confirmed her claims to be a true visionary, emissaries of the pope undertook a second investigation and judged her guilty of fraud—a very serious offense in a society torn by religious conflict. The church, believing "all novelty is dangerous and all unusual events are suspect," punished impostors severely. The case against Benedetta rested on testimony by her cellmate that during some of the nun's trances she had initiated lesbian sexual acts. Henceforth, this talented woman who, as abbess, had supervised the convent and its staff, administered extensive agricultural properties, and overseen the production and marketing of silk, was deprived of all activity, forbidden to speak, and perhaps even made to eat on the floor.[12]

Convents had provided women uncommon opportunities and a place of refuge away from male supervision. Therefore, in Catholic areas female monasteries continued to be important and to perform essential social functions. Sarah Hanley demonstrates (chapter 1) that when conflict over family authority broke out, the convents often were used by families as "official detention centers" for errant female members. In some cases they also solved financial problems for families unable or unwilling to provide dowries sufficient to assure their daughters appropriate marriages. Admission to a convent cost only a fraction of the price of a dowry. In the early modern period, because of new religious sensibilities unleashed by the Catholic reform, new activist orders and religious sisters also provided much-needed public service, as the study by Olwen Hufton and Frank Tallett (chapter 4) reveals. They offered educational and vocational training to youths, oversaw children while mothers worked, and ministered to the sick in hospitals. Similarly, in sixteenth-century Seville (chapter 2), one of the major departure points for migrants to New Spain, religious women outside the convents became increasingly prominent in "healing work" in the city. Some beatas were employed by the city, working, for example, in prisons where they brought food and medicine along with religious exhortation to the ill and destitute.[13] Others joined private households to pursue philanthropy. The work offered a needed alternative to marriage, as more men were leaving for colonial pursuits. However, it fell under the watchful eyes of the Spanish Inquisition, which, in the climate of economic uncertainty brought on by colonial conquest, was determined to stamp out heresy and reinscribe proper gender behavior.

Because Protestant reformers celebrated marriage over the Catholic ideal of celibacy, family living became one of the bases of respectability in post-Reformation society. But Christian family living became equally important to Catholic authority. Church courts joined with secular institutions to oversee marital relations, especially in cases concerning disputed property rights, physical mistreatment, or sexual misbehavior of contending spouses. Historian Joanne Ferraro, examining the records of the patriarchal courts of Venice after the Council of Trent, has found that litigating couples commonly filed for (or against) separation simultaneously in ecclesiastical and secular courts. While divorce was proscribed by canon law, appeals for legal separation provided an opportunity for aggrieved spouses to obtain a public hearing and redress against abuse. Both institutions sought to regulate and stabilize marriage, the church often providing sanctuary and succor to women and sanctioning men who violated community and religious norms.[14]

The increasing "sacralization" of society in this era was accompanied by the criminalization of sin. The reformers, for example, made new efforts to curtail prostitution. They attacked the widespread and public presence of prostitutes, just as they railed against clerical concubinages and other forms of behavior that contemporary norms considered to be sexually immoral. Brothels had been a regular part of late medieval society, usually regulated by city officials. In England, licensed brothels survived until the reign of Henry VIII (1509–47); there, they had come under the jurisdiction of the bishop of Winchester and the women were known as "Winchester geese." Brothels signified a moral attitude that was willing to make concessions to human nature. Since in many occupations, marriage was only possible after completion of extended study or apprenticeship training, the population in urban centers typically consisted of large numbers of young, single men. In some places servants and other economically dependent men were even legally prohibited from marrying. Prostitution was considered economically preferable to indigent marriages.

Under the imprint of a new moral sensibility, however, the reformers now sought to banish prostitutes and to confine sex solely to marriage. City fathers, first under Protestantism and later under reformed Catholicism, developed novel institutional mechanisms to oversee and control the moral behavior of the populace, to "enforce order in society and in the household." For example, in Calvin's Geneva, the infamous consistory, composed of twelve male elders and the city's eight or ten pastors, met weekly to punish moral transgressions. In Zwickau, city councillors appointed a panel of clergy and magistrates to sit as a marital court; in Emden, East Friesia, the presbytery discussed "proper codes of dress and entertainment, familial conflicts and sexual deviancy."[15] The Zwickau panel often sought advice from the Lutheran consistory in Wittenberg. At the outset, in treating sexual offenders, the Genevan consistory made minimal distinctions according to gender. Calvin envisioned ideal relations between the sexes as "differentiated equality," allowing for neither "male tyranny" nor "female autonomy," but requiring instead reciprocal cooperation under male leadership. In practice, this meant that males were held as responsible for their sexual behavior as were females. Of 320 city inhabitants banished for marital troubles between 1564 and 1569, 56 percent were men. But by the early seventeenth century, the double standard had returned to Geneva; men, who were merely "sowing wild oats," received reduced punishment, whereas unchaste and adulterous women were "whipped through the streets and banished." Heightened moral concerns also brought a growing preoccupation with girls' virginity and wives' chastity.[16]

The reformers and moralists seeking to confine sexuality to marriage, treated premarital and extramarital intercourse as sex crimes—fornication and adultery. They also refused to dissociate sex from procreation. On the ground that it violated God's intentions and denied women the saving grace of bearing children for

Christ, they opposed contemporary folk notions about contraception. By the mid-seventeenth century, as we will see shortly, birth control practices spread among the men and women of some well-off European families that were ignoring these norms. But the power of prescription can be seen in the low rates of illegitimacy characteristic of the early modern period, in the face of relatively late marriages and considerable celibacy. The fate of women who bore bastards—and they were usually servants or wage laborers vulnerable to coercion by masters or seduction by lovers who promised but failed to wed—varied considerably. In parts of Germany, they were sometimes fully integrated into family life with undiminished inheritance rights for their children. More commonly, however, they faced social ostracism, including the denial of employment and shelter, as well as public humiliation. In France, unwed mothers, called *fille-mères* (girl-mothers), were required to file a "declaration of pregnancy" stating, often in great detail, the circumstances under which they had become pregnant. Often they gave birth in hospitals run by religious or other charitable institutions; these were unhealthy places dreaded by most people as symbols of poverty and of death. In some places, public officials subjected unwed mothers to considerable pressure to reveal the names of the fathers of their "illegitimate" children; in colonial America, unwed women who had refused to cooperate earlier might be prevailed upon to speak the truth while suffering labor pains. Such responses also must be seen in light of the importance of the moral economy to political authority vested in a patriarchal family. Besides, support of single mothers was felt to place undue burdens on public resources.

Religious reformers did not markedly transform women's place in society, and the reformers had never intended to do so. To be sure, they called on men and women to read the Bible and participate in religious ceremonies together. But Bible reading reinforced the Pauline view of woman as weak-minded and sinful. When such practice took a more radical turn in the direction of lay prophesy, as occurred in some Reform churches southwest of Paris, or in the coming together of women to discuss "unchristian pieces" as was recorded in Zwickau, reformers, Lutheran and Calvinist alike, pulled back in horror. The radical or Anabaptist brand of reform generally offered women a more active role in religious life than did Lutheranism, even allowing them to preach. "Admonished to Christian righteousness" by more conservative Protestants, Anabaptists were charged with holding that "marriage and whoredom are one and the same thing." The women were even accused of having "dared to deny their husbands' marital rights." During an interrogation one woman explained that "she was wed to Christ and must therefore be chaste, for which she cited the saying, that no one can serve two masters."[17]

The alliance of church, state, and elites was unequivocal. Equality in the Gospel was not to overturn the inequalities of social rank or the hierarchies of the sexual order. As the Frenchman Pierre Viret explained it in 1560, appealing to the old polarities again, the Protestant elect were equal as Christians and believers—as man and woman, master and servant, free and slave. While the Protestant reform thus failed to elevate women's status, it deprived them of the emotionally sustaining presence of female imagery, of saints and protectors who long had played a significant role at crucial points in their life cycles. The Reformers rejected the special powers of the saints and downplayed, for example, Saints Margaret and Ann, who had been faithful and succoring companions for women in childbirth and in widowhood. With the rejection of Mary as well as the saints, nuns, and abbesses, God the Father was more firmly in place. In Catholic Spain, where Mary continued to be an important figure of veneration, in the sixteenth and seventeenth centuries she became passive, a symbolic expression of female purity, piety, and obedience. Once a more active figure who had intervened in the daily lives of men and women, now the image of Mary reflected more perfectly Catholic and lay reformers' fears of disorder, and buttressed their efforts to deploy prescribed gender imagery to help restore and maintain order.

Political Centralization and Witchcraft

Partly because of the unanticipated enthusiasm that the challenge to authority had unleashed, the forces of confessionalism sought to enhance the powers of secular officials. Challenged by Anabaptists, with their greater emphasis on women's religious roles, and by peasant rebellions, Luther became more conservative, qualifying his notion of the priesthood of all believers and upgrading the responsibilities of the established male clergy. Calvinism represented a form of theocracy in which the clergy governed the public realm. Similarly, Reformed Catholicism strengthened Hapsburg rule as well as Wittelbach (Bavarian) kingship. The dominant conflicts of the age concerned delimiting contested lines of political authority, although often the struggle was couched in religious terms. In France, the Huguenots, typically southern French aristocrats, saw in Calvinism a way to counteract the centralizing tendencies of the Catholic Valois dynasty. Similarly, in central Europe, princes used Lutheranism to challenge the authority of the Catholic Austrian emperor.

The novel uses of religion to strengthen the political legitimacy of Europe's regimes help to explain the timing of the great witch hunts and the thousands of organized trials and executions of suspected witches that took place in the sixteenth and seventeenth centuries in Europe. During these two centuries witchcraft was a capital crime throughout most of Europe. Witchcraft trials are of central importance in European history, not only for what they say specifically about women's social position and vulnerability (since more often than not it was women who were executed as witches), but also for the light they shed on the socioeconomic and political changes transforming early modern life in Europe. As we will see shortly, the notion of the witch—absent in pre-Columbian America—was transported to the New World by the Spanish colonizers and became a source of indigenous women's resistance to colonial rule.

Historians once believed that there were two major outbreaks of witchcraft trials in Europe, the mass executions in fourteenth-century France and Italy and those in the early modern era. But research has shown conclusively that this picture was based on forgeries; in fact, there were comparatively few trials in the fourteenth century. It was in the half century before 1500 that the number of trials increased in France, southwest Germany, and Switzerland, foreshadowing the great outbreaks of the sixteenth and seventeenth centuries. This discovery has altered the interpretation of Europe's witch hunts.[18] The persecution and trial of witches were widespread phenomena in urban and rural areas of both Catholic and Protestant lands.

They concentrated, however, in border areas in which the lines of legitimate authority were in question. After nearly a half century of neglect, witch trials began to
multiply in the 1560s and sentiment rose to panic proportions by the end of the
century. There were mass trials in central Europe, as well as in France, England,
Switzerland, and elsewhere. The end of the century saw further geographical extension into the Rhineland between France and the Germanies and the Basque lands
between France and Spain. Events reached fever pitch during the decade of the
1620s; the trials continued throughout the century. Sweden experienced them for
the first time in 1669 and 1676 and the last major outbreaks occurred in Salem,
Massachusetts, in 1692 and in Paisley, Scotland, in 1697. The final legal execution
of a witch apparently occurred in Switzerland as late as 1782.

Who were Europe's witches? Those accused were predominantly women. In
Scotland, southwest Germany, and Switzerland, around four-fifths of the accused
witches were women. Similarly, in New England, 78 percent of the accused were
women. England recorded even higher proportions. In France, the appeal cases that
reached the Parlement of Paris, the highest court of law, indicate that significant numbers of "cunning men" or male magical healers were accused of malice. Overall, however, men were a distinct minority, for the most part located in areas where witchcraft was confused with heresy. The association of "witch" with "woman" predated
these mass-organized witch hunts, however. It harked back to Aristotle's notions of
female imperfection and the Judeo-Christian association of woman with evil and sin.
"The reason is easie" said James I of England (r. 1603–25) in discussing why women
were more inclined to witchcraft than men. "(F)or as that sexe is frailer then men is,
so is it easier to be intrapped in these grosse snares of the Devill, as was well proved
to be true, by the Serpent's deceiving of Eve at the beginning, which makes him the
homelier with that sex ever since."[19] Notions about witches, devils, sorcery, orgy,
and the evil-eye had long been part of popular beliefs in European and in other societies as well. When coupled with women's supposed weaknesses and sinful nature,
they reinforced disparaging cultural views of women. Yet, such ideas must be distinguished from witch hunting, which was prevalent in Europe and New England.
While continuing research makes generalization difficult, witch trials were efforts by
government and clerical elites to reinforce political authority; motives of the accus-
ers as well as accused, however, were exceedingly complex, and bring into question
the validity of any single historical category of "the witch."

Witches were typically female, however diverse their attributes, and all females
were potential witches; but they were not randomly selected. In England, they were
often old and poor, certainly less well off than those who accused them; and they
were nearly always in a fairly close relationship to the accuser, usually a neighbor
or relative, who could be either male or female. In Scotland, they were women with
a "ready, sharp, and angry tongue"; quarrelsome women who were married and in
their midlife and came from the bottom rungs of the peasantry. In Germany, large
numbers of widows were burned as witches. By contrast, in the British North American colonies, many of the accused were potentially wealthy women about to inherit
money or property, thereby posing a threat to male inheritance patterns. Furthermore, the accused frequently had a local reputation as a potential evil-doer; typically she was charged with having made a covenant with the devil. Some women

quite readily accepted the label for the power and enhanced status it might give them in the local community. As the Scot Agnes Finnie declared menacingly at her trial, "If I be a witch, you or yours shall have better cause to call me so." In other cases confessions were won by torture. In Puritan New England, witchcraft was in good measure about sin. Many women who confessed believed deeply in their sinful nature and vulnerability to the devil's temptations.[20]

Despite regional variations, the typical witch was not a young, immature woman but rather an adult, quite often a single or widowed and eccentric female who defied the boundaries of acceptable behavior for her sex. The new ideas of Protestantism as well as Reformed Catholicism required that women assume personal responsibility for their own salvation. In this new context witchcraft was an activity defined by law as criminal, for which the woman herself, not her husband or guardian, was responsible. On one level, pursuit of witches in the local community represented a particularly violent reaction by men and other women against this view of woman as an independent adult. But witch hunting served additional functions, particularly in areas recently converted to Protestantism. Calvinists believed that God was just and punished those who sinned with hardships; misfortunes, which were ever-present under subsistence conditions of poor nutrition, high mortality, pests, and plagues, were not God's tests of fidelity and strength but were clear indications of sin and of God's just punishment for transgression. Under these conditions, belief in witchcraft provided an alternative answer to the ever presence of death and disease. Psychologically, it shifted the blame from the afflicted people onto others like "evil" old women who were socially more vulnerable.

The multiple and useful functions served by witch hunts and trials testify to the variety of intellectual and social changes that were slowly transforming early modern Europe. A widespread motive throughout Europe as a whole was political—the trials were used to strengthen the authority of post-Reformation rulers and to confirm the legitimacy of the new regimes. The trials were not spontaneous but organized from above. They aided secular authorities in taking over jurisdictions that previously had been the preserve of the ecclesiastical courts. These magistrates passed statutes against witchcraft that included new, legal definitions of sexual and religious offenses, among them bestiality, adultery, and blasphemy. They instituted new mechanisms of social control, including sessions and courts created to handle the charges, countercharges, and appeals, and also to supervise the social and moral behavior of the territory's subjects. In other cases, as in seventeenth-century Rome, witch trials were part of the more general efforts by the clergy to discipline its population. In a revealing study, Sally Scully follows the trials of several "witches" by the Roman Inquisition. Surprisingly, in the case of the sisters Marietta and Laura Battaglia, which was brought before the Inquisition in midcentury, "witchcraft" was only one of many strategies they used to survive: "love magic" joined prostitution, medical healing, renting rooms, or selling books (and several were on the Catholic Index of prohibited works, no less!). From Laura's point of view, "witchcraft" was part of her economic life course, which allowed her to escape marriage. From the perspective of the authorities, her behavior expressed female deviancy and the need to discipline sexuality in order to reinforce social hierarchy.[21] But witch hunting remained important only as long as Christianity served as a legitimizing political ideology. In time, as European society became increasingly secular, witchcraft trials lost their cohesive force and function, and large-scale organized witch hunts disappeared from the scene of history. In terms of pressures toward conformity, they were replaced by a sense of personal guilt and, later, by new definitions of "insanity," lack of neighborliness, and various forms of perceived antisocial behavior.

Political Centralization and the Early Modern Family

The presence of witch trials in the various states of Europe and the North American colonies, which increased the level of misogyny in society, also served to strengthen weak lines of central authority. Everywhere in post-Reformation Europe, the task of princes, kings, and councillors, was to amass more effective powers in the new state bureaucracies by levying taxes, stimulating trade, and expanding political offices and public jurisdictions, including regulation of individual behavior. For example, in the first half of the seventeenth century Cardinal Richelieu, advisor to King Louis XIII and chief architect of the emerging system of French absolutism, opposed the nobility's recourse to dueling, thus striking a serious blow to aristocratic privilege. By upholding only the king's justice in the realm, he undercut the earlier rights of nobles to take the law into their hands. Similarly, in the next century, central government began to limit ecclesiastical power by curtailing the autonomy of religious orders. State-building in this instance impinged on one of the few areas of autonomy open to women outside the family.

In this critical process of state-building and consolidating power in the colonies abroad, rulers began to rely on a new analogy that entwined the authority of the state with that of the family. Kings ruled their realm as fathers ruled their roost, an early formulation of the popular idea that "a man's house is his castle." The legal subjection of wives to husbands and of children to parents reinforced, so the early modern political theorists assumed, the obedience of each subject to the growing claims of the centralizing state. Neither the authority of kings nor that of fathers was contractual; it was part of the natural order, akin to the power of God to command obedience from His flock. The analogy was persuasive because it mirrored actual changes in family structure and power, which the Reformation crisis had reinforced.

The changes unleashed by the process of reformation reorganized the moral basis of the family and strengthened the father's position over wife, children, and servants. To be sure, in permitting priests to marry and extolling the married life above the celibate ideal, the Protestant Reformation challenged the traditional medieval hostility to sexuality and particularly the deep-seated prejudices associated with the female body. Indeed, Protestants were forced to confront the nature of sexual differences in marriage. Furthermore, since marriage was no longer a sacrament but a civil transaction, reformers countenanced divorce; by the Ordinances of Wittenberg (1553) and those of Geneva (1561) adultery and desertion were recognized as legitimate grounds for divorce although, in practice, divorce was almost as difficult to obtain under Protestantism as it was under Catholicism. In eighteenth-century Geneva, for example, the city averaged only one divorce per year. Between 1670 and 1799, in all of England only 131 divorces were granted, usually to peers who wanted second wives to give them sons.

In important ways, the family had become a pivotal institution in reformed conceptions for Protestants and Catholics alike; it was given many important religious functions to fulfill. Its members were expected to spend evenings together reading and discussing the Bible and other devotional literature. Protestants were also enjoined to say prayers at meals. These family centered rituals offered new roles to women and some, now as pastors' wives, enjoyed new public duties, supporting their husbands' efforts but also engaging separately in charitable and educational endeavors in local communities. But it was the master of the house who was given ultimate authority. Paul had proclaimed, "Wives, submit yourself unto your own husbands, as unto the Lord. Children, obey your parents in the Lord." A Bible published in England in 1537 went further. It added to the patristic admonition the counsel that, if faced with a rebellious wife, a husband "endeavoureth to beat the fear of God into her head, . . . that thereby she may be compelled to learn her duty and do it."[22] Protestant interpretation of the Bible made such strictures a part of daily life.

Legal changes were reinforcing these patterns of family authority. Roman law had been introduced into Italy and southern Europe in the thirteenth century, and by the sixteenth, was spreading to Germany and northern France. Adoption of Roman legal principles paralleled the move toward political centralization, for the law was based on uniformity and consistency. In England, similar trends toward territorial standardization accelerated in the seventeenth century, elevating common law and parliamentary statutes over ecclesiastical and manorial laws. For our purposes, it was in matters of property that these changes had the most radical potential to affect economic, social, and family relations. Laws, however, must be seen as statements of principle and not as fully reflective of social practice. But the same principle, supporting property rights, could be used to justify what were clearly highly immoral practices by the standards of some contemporaries. Such is the case of slavery, which was the foundation of the plantation system of Europe's colonies in the Americas, from Virginia to Hispaniola (today's Haiti and Dominican Republic) to Brazil. The old Roman Law of Nations, the system of laws codified and commented on by the Roman emperor Justinian in the sixth century, had sanctioned slavery. Indeed, Spanish jurists justified the imposition of slavery in the case of the Canary Islands through the absolute right of private property in persons. In time, legal and religious arguments became intertwined. Listen to the French theorist of absolutism, Bishop Bossuet (1627–1704) defend the institution:

> To condemn this state [slavery] . . . would be not only to condemn human law (i.e., the Roman *jus gentium*) where servitude is admitted, as it appears in all laws, but also it would be to condemn the Holy Spirit which, speaking through St. Paul, ordered slaves to remain in their condition and which did not in any way oblige masters to free them.[23]

The importance of scripture to post-Reformation Europe served to reintroduce many of the biblical stories of slavery, such as Noah's "curse" and the prescriptions of Leviticus, into public debates and legal formulations.

Property remained essential to both state authority and early capitalist accumulation. Significantly, the legal changes which accompanied these political and economic transformations reinforced patriarchal controls over property as the basis of social stability and hierarchy. Therefore, with the move toward centralization of legal uniformity came a clear deterioration in women's legal status in early modern Europe. If the legal map remained exceedingly complex, the introduction of Roman law, and the elevation of common law in England, restricted women's legal options. For example, English ecclesiastical law had followed Roman civil law, which advocated community property in marriage and the equal division of parental wealth among all children. Continental medieval codes generally had afforded unmarried women and widows considerable rights to make wills, and to serve as witnesses in civil and criminal cases, or as executors of other testaments.

The turn to common law in England and the encroachment of Roman law throughout the states and city-states of the continent negatively affected women's rights of inheritance, primarily in two ways. (And historically, it was inheritance—of land among the wealthy and work tools, cows, or goats for the less well off—that comprised the major components of wealth, not wages.) First, the changing legal context reinforced the principle of primogeniture, a practice whereby powerful aristocratic families passed their lands to one son only, to preserve intact the foundation of their wealth. In England, in terms of real property, the principle of descent remained operative from the thirteenth century until 1925. In the absence of sons, however, daughters would inherit equally. Secondly, the changes increased the control of male heads of households. Expressed through common law, a woman's legal identity during marriage was erased—literally "covered"—by her husband's. As a *feme covert*, she could not contract, sue, or be sued independently of her husband. In France, in the sixteenth century, new laws and judgments severely curtailed the ability of married women to act in their own or their children's interests, to control their wealth, or choose their domicile. In England, a law of 1540 empowered husbands, who were already vested with control of their wives' estates, to extend their rights by long leases well beyond their own lifetime, and to retain the rents from the land.

These changes comprised a powerful set of legal constraints within which, of course, there was a wide continuum of possible behavior and practice. Nonetheless, their impact on family relationships made them a primary target of the feminist struggle in the nineteenth century that we discuss in Part II. Women's legal equality was one of the first demands of feminists pressuring for reform in both Europe and North America. Significantly, too, property rights that sanctioned slavery and oppressed women created a clear intersection of abolitionist and women's rights movements.

The family of the early modern period was not the institution that we think of today. The very term *family* was vague; the German language, for example, had no word for the grouping of parents and children that we think of as a family. In France, family meant lineage, a line, a dynasty—that is, a set of kinfolk who did not necessarily live together in one residence. It also referred, however, to persons living under one roof, which included parents and children as well as apprentices, servants, and lodgers. Furthermore, there was no notion of privacy; people often lived together in one room, worked, ate, and slept there.

Equally important, economic and political calculations were foremost in decisions to marry. Even among the landed peasantry or urban artisanal groups, marriage represented an economic alliance, a pooling of male and female resources

needed for the creation and survival of a household. For members of the aristocracy, a marriage reflected specific social and economic purposes—it solidified an
important alliance, enhanced the economic position of the group, or served political ends. Individual choice played a minimal role and family strategy overrode personal desire. Sarah Hanley (chapter 1) pursues this theme further by analyzing the
conflict in France between church and state over the conditions of marriage, which
ultimately enhanced the power of the family. Lawyers and jurists set out to
strengthen their own family alliances and transform the well-born family into a
more effective political force. They did so by creating a body of civil law on marriage that favored patriarchal power. Women were the losers; the new legal context favored paternal rights over those of mothers and children.

Reformation thought and practice, along with the opportunities for wealth and
independence unleashed by ongoing capitalist development, promoted new sentiments about ideal family forms. The changes began first among the well born, predominantly in the urban, literate, business and professional communities, but also
among some of Europe's landed aristocrats. Their experiences gradually became
normative (that is, set an ideal for family living) for the rest of society. The transformations in family structures, roles, and norms had important consequences for
women, as we will see in more detail in Parts II and III of this book. But in our
period, three major changes affected the early modern family in the well-off
classes—the "discovery of childhood," a new discourse of love in marriage, and
the beginning of the use of birth control practices within marriage.

By placing responsibility for salvation on the individual, the Reformation
opened up new possibilities in parent/child relationships. Childhood was defined by
Catholic moralists and pedagogues as God's innocent age, "to which we must all
return . . . the age when hatred is unknown, when nothing can cause distress; the
golden age of human life, the age which defies Hell, the age when life is easy and
death holds no terrors."[24] Puritans held more to the idea of "original sin," but the
conclusion for both groups of reformers and educators was clear: children needed
to be segregated from adult (corrupt) society, carefully supervised, molded, and
strengthened so that later as adults they would be strong enough to withstand the
temptations of the devil and evil ways. Thus began a campaign to separate children
from servants, and, for the sake of "decency," boys from girls; to expurgate the historic texts deemed inappropriate for children's minds; and to develop toys and games
suitable for young people.

With this "discovery" of childhood as a separate stage of life would come the
social "invention" of motherhood, the definition of the woman as primarily responsible for the care and nurturance of children, which reached its apotheosis in the
nineteenth century. Much earlier, however, after the Council of Trent, manuals written for confessors began to stress parents' duties to their children. Between 1578
and 1687, catechisms were revised to place increasing stress on love between parents and children. Similarly, love between husband and wife was admitted into the
marriage sanctuary, first by the Puritans who were insistent that love was a prime
duty, and later, in the eighteenth century, by members of the elites in France. Sex
within marriage was seen to strengthen the conjugal bond. This is not to imply the

absence of intimacy or emotional connection in the past, however. Recent research, using innovative sources such as coroner reports of deaths of children or spouses, reveal deep emotional attachments and expressions of genuine grief. Women's historians now acknowledge fundamental continuity in human emotions; but such "structures" should not obscure what is new in this period. The self-conscious elevation of love in marriage created new subjectivities, expectations, and ideals. At the same time, however, the institution of marriage remained male-dominated.[25]

It was in this period, too, for reasons debated by historians, that some men and women began to undertake conscious control of family size. The fact that in France and England after the mid-seventeenth century, the fertility rate of the upper classes fell below that of the lower—despite the better nutrition and earlier marriages of the former—suggests the appearance of new attitudes. Perhaps couples realized the financial drain of numerous progeny on the family economy that, among the upper classes, no longer was dependent on the offsprings' labor. Parents, admonished more than before to assure the well-being of individual children, came to recognize that economic resources stretched further for fewer people. Primarily by means of *coitus interruptus,* termed by indignant clergy and "populationists" the "new Onans," some couples began to place their material welfare above religious stricture. The poorer classes, however, continued to beget many offspring, though infant mortality, through natural causes, neglect, and infanticide, often claimed 50 percent or more. If more survived than the family could feed or profitably put to work, excess children either died of malnutrition or left at an early age to live as servants or apprentices with another family.

Whatever the motive, birth control was of real benefit to women, who were burdened in former times with perpetual pregnancies. Alice Thornton, a seventeenth-century Englishwoman, recording her experiences in the context of a growing market for women's writings, has left us a graphic portrayal of the significance of childbearing in a woman's life. Daughter of a high-ranking public official, Thornton married at the age of twenty-four, stoically bore nine children (seven fewer than her sister) in eleven years and watched six of them die. She was continuously sick or suffering from pregnancy until she was widowed. Faced with an indebted estate and advised to marry an illiterate man "of indifferent parts or honesty," rather than struggle to administer it herself, she declined. Her countrywoman and contemporary, Jane Constable Josselin, married at twenty years to a country clergyman of comfortable estate, gave birth to ten children in twenty-one years, of whom five survived their parents. She also suffered three miscarriages. Since she weaned her infants between twelve and nineteen months, she was "with child" or nursing one almost continuously for more than two decades.[26] While Jane Josselin lived to be eighty-two, such intensive childbearing would have consumed the entire adult life of a woman of average life expectancy—about thirty-seven years in the seventeenth century. No wonder that the letters and diaries of Europe's well-off women increasingly contained references to their desire and endeavors to limit pregnancies. Let us stress that these efforts affected only a very small proportion of Europe's families in the early modern period, so small that family limitation did not yet show up in the aggregate demographic statistics of the European states.

"New Worlds" and Women's Roles

European explorers and colonizers as well as the administrators and settlers of the territories of the Americas started a new phase of global interaction that helps to define the early modern era. The twin development of European colonial domination and the evolving slave plantation systems created a wider Atlantic community, drawing peoples across the ocean into an intricate web of interdependency. The wealth of the Americas was staggering: to illustrate, between 1551 and 1560 forty-three tons of gold landed officially in Seville alone, opening the European continent to a massive influx of precious metals. It was the burgeoning protocapitalist classes of Europe—the merchants, manufacturers, landlords, rulers, and bureaucrats—who garnered the first fruits of colonialism. They promoted commercial agriculture at home, invested in shipbuilding and sugar refining, and redesigned the urban landscape by constructing town squares with elaborate fountains and new city halls in a baroque style.

In time, plantation agriculture in the Caribbean and the Americas more and more turned to slave labor from Africa. By careful estimates, the slave population of the Americas stood at 330,000 in 1700, at nearly three million by 1800, and reached over six million by 1850.[27] Wealth increasingly was expressed in colonial goods, which entered European markets on a growing scale. Sugar, tobacco, and indigo products fueled a "consumer revolution" that spread deeply into society. In return, new protoindustrial production burgeoned in the European countryside, providing the colonies with needed textiles, hemp, and manufactured goods. An "Atlantic world" was born, resting on colonial state rule and economic exchange in civil society. Europe, Africa, and the Americas became interconnected in new ways. At the same time, trade expanded with the Ottoman Empire, which exported coffee and tulips to European consumers who also had ready access to silks and spices from China and the East Indies.

These interdependencies had profound consequences for European society and politics as well as consciousness, just as the European colonial powers inexorably transformed the lives of women and men under their rule. The wealth and prestige of the colonies played directly into the political struggles among territorial states for power and influence. For example, Charles V, the Holy Roman Emperor, who was simultaneously Charles I of Spain (r. 1516–56), used the wealth and symbols of the Spanish Americas to promote Hapsburg territorial interests in the Old World. Similarly, colonial markets provided an increasingly important source of sales for European goods, helping to stimulate European economic development. In the late seventeenth century, exports of manufactured goods from England went primarily to continental Europe; by 1772–74, exports to America and Africa had increased by seven times, while those to the Continent were stagnating.

Importantly, the early encounters across the ocean were largely filtered through the lens of gender ideologies. Projections about masculinity and femininity—about the proper behavior of men and women—helped make what was, in essence, strange and foreign seemingly familiar. Already during the second voyage of Christopher Columbus, the explorers divided the Caribbean population into "masculine" and "feminine" types. Adapting the language of chivalry, the Spanish depicted themselves as protecting the so-called feminine Arawaks from their enemies, the Caribs, in effect rendering them "passive" victims of both the colonizers and their masculine adversaries. In contrast, the Caribs were acknowledged as equal—indeed as rivals for the possession of women—but were demonized as "savages" and cannibals, and turned into the quintessential "other." Gender and race concepts were essential accompaniments to the establishment of European domination.

Similarly, the encounters with distinct cultures of indigenous peoples heightened the sense of European identity through the logic of contrast. Columbus himself wrote of the natives that he met that "[t]hey are the color of Canarians, neither black nor white," implicitly defining Spanish—and the wider European identity—as white, and introducing color as a new category of identity.[28] Of course, until recently, "white" represented an unspoken sign of superiority and not a constructed race in its own right.

The historian Natalie Z. Davis demonstrates other mechanisms of identity-construction in these contacts. She follows French Jesuits and other travelers who worked among the Iroquois and Huron of North America in the sixteenth and seventeenth centuries. All manner of differences elicited commentary, but particular attention was paid to specific observations about native gender and sexual relations. "Women work without comparison more than men," noted Jacques Cartier in 1536.[29] The absence of private property—for the Indians held land and wealth communally—affected marriage, divorce, and family authority, all themes that were concurrently being debated in Europe, as we have seen. It meant that there was no inheritance to speak of in indigenous society and, thus no issues of "legitimacy" or questions of "legitimate" heirs. Indeed, unsuccessful marriages simply ended in divorce, with the children usually staying with the mothers. While on both sides of the ocean, women had little role in "politics" proper, among the Iroquois there were some "women of quality" who participated in local council meetings. By the eighteenth century, apparently, these women attended treaty councils of the Iroquois nations. Their European counterparts, perhaps, were the powerful dynastic women and court ladies who figured in the early modern debates about women. Through comparisons and contrasts with peoples of other cultures, then, Europeans were defining themselves as well.

Empire building abroad and state building in Europe were overlapping processes which drew European developments into the colonies and in turn reshaped European patterns of life and consciousness. Mary Elizabeth Perry (chapter 2) returns to the intersection of gender and race in her exploration of women's roles in sixteenth-century Seville, then undergoing the social dislocations of religious reform and colonial expansion. In this island port, where the presence of many African slaves destined for the Canaries, the Caribbean, and the Americas heightened preoccupation with inherited differences, inquisitors turned "purity of the blood" concerns with particular force against Jewish and Muslim converts at home. As Perry notes, "They became subject to a system of internal colonization that paralleled Spanish imperialism in other parts of the world." Indeed, the government simultaneously restricted the rights of anyone "stained" to migrate to the New World, just as it favored Old Christians (those untainted by Jewish or Moorish blood) for work back home. In time, family laws reflected these preoccupations, encouraging endogamic marriages with their premium on legitimacy and women's chastity. In a struggle similar to the case Sarah Hanley describes for France (chapter 1), the Spanish state increasingly assumed jurisdiction over marriage. Significantly, by 1778 it had exported the new family laws into its colonies. In principle, the laws suppressed free choice in favor of parental consent or disheritance, and required that the nobility and others of "pure blood" obtain special permission to marry "Negroes" or mulattos. Family interests and the social and racial hierarchy coincided to make marriages a "matter of state." As Verna Stolcke puts it, "Blood [was] a vehicle for family prestige."[30]

The Spanish exported not only their laws, but they brought the whole Christian cosmology, including belief in devils and witches, to the peoples of the Americas, whom they were determined to convert. Amid the very contradictions of imperial rule, in spaces opened for women outside the established male religious hierarchy, some Andean women took on the mantle of "witch," but ironically, they turned it into a voice of opposition and resistance. The Andean witch emerged as an advocate for village rights, customs, and society.[31] Popular beliefs defied ready control by European authority.

Women's Work in the Peasant Household

For the Jesuit missionaries in the "New" World, the male-headed household perpetuated through an orderly pattern of inheritance was the ideological norm of social life; its absence elicited considerable commentary. For a majority of the common people in Europe, the household, indeed, still functioned as it had earlier: as the basic economic unit of society. In preindustrial times individuals survived only as a part of a family economy to which everyone contributed labor. As Olwen Hufton shows, a few women might live in "spinster clusters" (convents and the like), pooling resources and skills, but most people of both sexes depended for food, clothing, and shelter on a household. Work typically was organized in the setting of the family—to be more exact, in the household—for, as we have seen, household members included servants and apprentices along with husbands, wives, children, kinfolk, and friends.

It was once accepted without question that the preindustrial peasant household was a large, extended family embracing multiple generations that ensured stability and deference to age and gender hierarchies. It was only with the industrial revolution and urbanization in the nineteenth century, so the argument ran, that the lower-class family became "nuclear," composed solely of father, mother, and children. This interpretation, however, has been relegated in large measure to myth. Marriage, baptismal, and funeral records and early census data show that households of peasants, laborers, and poor people in reality were small, consisting of four to six persons on average throughout much of western Europe in preindustrial times. Multigenerational living was not typical. Yet, given the prevalence of servants in the past, a majority of the total population lived in much larger households than the average size. For example, in Kent, England, in 1676 the small households of tradesmen, laborers, and the poor accounted for a majority of dwellings but only one-third of the population. Two-thirds of the population lived in more complex households of better-off yeomen and gentry. The higher the social status of the head of household, the greater the numbers under his roof. Furthermore, counting persons does not tell anything about relationships among family members and peer groups or about their ties to kin outside the place of residence. Finally, the once prevailing simplistic image of family evolution from extended to nuclear has been shattered by other demographic evidence. It was only with improved longevity in the nineteenth and twentieth centuries that demographic conditions became more favorable to the existence of multigenerational families. Multigenerational living also became relatively more prevalent in industrial societies.[32] These debates aside, it is incontrovertible that the labor of each member of the peasant household was indispensable for the survival of the whole; and the birth of too many children or the death of either spouse put intolerable strain on the family economy.

The vast majority of people in the early modern period were peasants, tilling the land or caring for livestock and eking out a bare subsistence, producing essential foodstuffs, clothing, a roof to cover their heads, and securing fuel. In western Europe, peasants had become free as to their persons, although the land they tilled was still encumbered with rents, dues, and labor services—vestiges of the older feudal system. In eastern Europe, popularly demarcated by the Elbe River that ran through Prussia, and in Russia, most peasants were serfs, obliged to provide labor services to the lord. They could neither work outside the lord's estate nor marry without his consent. Early modern society was divided into estates or orders, legal categories that assigned rights and obligations. A person's legal status was determined at birth. Peasants were the largest social group—well over 85 percent of the total population of most countries of Europe—and had the fewest rights. The social historian Pierre Goubert captures well the rhythm of rural life in France.

> Inside France there was a small annual movement of servant-girls, apprentices, and once more adventurers from country to town, the migrations of some tens of thousands of beggars, and a small number of soldiers. . . . [But most] people remained bound to the land, plot, hut, cottage, or *quartier* [neighborhood] where they grew up. Old France is characterized not by unrest, social mobility, and popular migration, but by sedentariness. Except for the perennial adventurers, people only became mobile when driven by necessity, which usually meant destitution.[33]

Women's productive work was extensive in this preindustrial world. In the countryside they might be seen caring for dairy animals and poultry, planting and tending the garden, and on occasion even hoeing and threshing, the latter two tasks generally regarded as men's work. They procured, processed, preserved, and prepared the family's food and took action—sometimes direct action through riot—if bad harvests, inflated prices, or other forces threatened their subsistence. The first responsibility of married women was to feed household members. For the most part, they produced goods for the family's immediate use rather than for exchange—although it was typically women who marketed eggs, vegetables, and other surplus foodstuffs and brought into the peasant economy the little cash it had. Women regularly made butter, cheese, and bread and brewed beer as well. After food production their most urgent duty was garment making, manufacturing items of clothing for the entire household. They spun yarn and wove coarse cloth for linens as well as clothing, made soap, washed, bleached, and dyed fabric, gathered feathers to make pillows, and managed their small enterprise and its family labor force. Work in the households of the more wealthy peasants, those who had property, was typically sex- as well as age-specific. There was men's work and there was women's work, adult work and children's work; but only together could the household economy manage to survive.

Urban Women, the Guilds, and Professionalization

Urban women also produced many of the goods that the family used on a daily basis. In addition, as wives and daughters of guildsmen, they participated in the processes of goods manufacture and they often supervised the work of apprentices and journeymen, too. Much of the daily organizing and running of the shops fell to them. So time-consuming and disruptive to their daily routine was the care of infants that many urban women regularly employed wet nurses. Wet-nursing was common practice from the sixteenth through the nineteenth centuries; gradually, a separate occupation, called in France *meneur,* the intermediary, emerged to facilitate the exchange of infants and arrange that urban babies be sent out to the countryside to peasant women who also had recently given birth. In earlier times, the practice of turning infants over to nursemaids was largely confined to upper-class women who wanted to free themselves for court life and aristocratic entertainment. Now the growth of the urban middle classes created a new market for women of meager means but with a "full breast of milk." The rural bourgeoisie also often placed their children with wet nurses. By the mid-nineteenth century, the commerce in infants had increased so much that a wet-nursing "business" and a government bureau, handling tens of thousands of exchanges, developed in France.

In the early modern period, religious views on the purposes of marriage also played a role in the promotion of wet-nursing. As long as sexual attraction and physical love were not primary motives for marriage, and sexual intercourse served (ideally at least) only the purpose of procreation, the sanction against sex during lactation could be maintained. Since it was commonly accepted medical wisdom that sexual arousal of a nursing mother ruined her milk, and that pregnancy dried her breasts, intercourse was frowned on until the suckling was weaned, usually a period of one or two years. As the sexual bond between marital partners loomed larger among the ideal purposes of marriage, a conflict arose between the needs of parents and infants. According to the historian Lawrence Stone, "moral theologians . . . thought it better for the wife and mother to satisfy the sexual demands of their husbands, with possible danger to the health of their infants, rather than to risk driving their husbands to adultery by refusing intercourse."[34] Wet nurses were the beneficiaries of this shift in sentiment. Wet-nursing continued to be condemned by the fledgling medical community (it was feared the child would imbibe the mental and moral characteristics of the nurse, and mothers were warned particularly against employing redheaded nurses), but it flourished because it met crucial economic and emotional needs. Yet death rates among infants put out to nurse were extremely high: 90 percent among foundlings in Rouen in the late eighteenth century, compared to 38.1 percent of the merely indigent. Nursed by their mothers, only 18.7 percent perished. Wet-nursing thus helps account for the extremely high infant mortality rate in urban centers in the early modern period.

The evolving Atlantic economy that was stimulating large-scale production for export while boosting the wet-nursing business, placed barriers on women's chances to be independent entrepreneurs, large-scale shopkeepers, and artisans. Increasing reliance on private property, and the growing use of cash and credit disadvantaged women, who were losing legal control over money and other resources. Capitalist advances meant a shift in the nature and character of women's work—although it tended to remain low-skilled and poorly paid. At one time, in the heyday of the medieval commune and guild production, women had been admitted as master craftsmen. Not all guilds did so, apparently, but thirteenth-century Paris had eighty mixed craft guilds of men and women and fifteen female-dominated guilds for such trades as dressmaking, gold thread, yarn, and silk manufacture. Central European guild statutes mentioned female participants in the thirteenth century. A policy of admitting women to a variety of nonagricultural occupations was compatible with a society that needed to use fully the productive capacities of all its members. But increasingly, as commercial capitalism expanded, merchant-capitalists had sufficient funds to stimulate production outside of and in competition with the guilds. Guilds responded by restricting their own membership and removing women from independent artisanship. Merry Wiesner-Hanks (chapter 3) provides in rich detail an example of this process and of other changes affecting women in the urban economy between 1500 and 1650.

By the seventeenth century, in urban centers of Europe it had become more and more difficult for women to work as artisans in their own right. Furthermore, men tended to monopolize the lucrative urban export industries. For example, when watchmaking became a successful export craft in Geneva, guild statutes changed and prohibited masters from teaching the skills to any woman, including their own wives and daughters. Silk manufacturing in Lyons was arranged as "free labor," that is, outside guild monopoly, and until 1561 access to the occupation had been unrestricted. At that time, however, the market began to look uncertain and about "158 merchants and masters engaged in various kinds of silkmaking met before a notary to set up 'good order' among them, prevent 'ruin,' and 'obviate disturbance, debates, and disputes.'" They limited the number of male apprentices to two per master and eliminated women apprentices altogether. Even in spinning, that female art par excellence, men began to replace women as masters. In Rouen, in the late eighteenth century, a new government policy of fiscalization—the selling of patents by the Crown—replaced the traditional practice that permitted women to transfer guild membership to their children and thus to maintain control of the industry. While recent research shows that in urban areas, the minority of skilled women workers who owned masterships continued into the eighteenth century to enjoy the privileges accorded to guild masters and mistresses—even administering public discipline to protect their advantages—increasingly, women heads of shops gave way to better-financed men. Indeed, in eighteenth-century Paris, public opinion turned against the women retailers of luxury boutiques while at the same time, it redefined femininity to include all manner of shopping for purposes of domestic happiness.[35]

Similar transformations occurred in brewing, once an important occupation for women in the local economy. However, by the beginning of the eighteenth century, those sectors of brewing that were incorporated into the burgeoning international markets were monopolized by men. The change required large capital investments and technical training, which were unavailable to women.

Capitalist advances paralleled a process of professionalization, which also worked to the disadvantage of women's economic autonomy. An examination of changes affecting the job of midwife is illustrative. This important female occupation was transformed in the early modern period because of new professional standards that were increasingly attached to medicine. Professionalization was achieved at the price of first, bypassing, and later, outlawing women, who once had been centrally involved in the healing process. The desire of physicians, surgeons, and apothecaries to monopolize the new science of medicine coincided with the objective of government officials to oversee the study of medicine so as to check witchcraft. In London as early as the time of Henry VIII, for example, anyone discovered practicing medicine without proper training or licensing might be declared a witch. Because of the long-standing beliefs in women's irrationality and inferiority, the schools of medicine and anatomy were closed to them.

The disadvantages of not obtaining the latest scientific knowledge were recognized by several mid-seventeenth century Englishwomen, who tried to extend training to midwives. Jane Sharp, for one, wrote a manual entitled *Complete Midwife's Companion; or, The Art of Midwifery Improved* (1671), in which she translated and made available to English readers many new practices and ideas from France, Holland, and Italy; these she combined with her own considerable experience of forty years. Sharp defended the long-standing practice of midwifery by women and admitted only one deficiency. Women were having trouble obtaining "Knowledge of Things as Men may, who are bred up in Universities . . . where Anatomy Lectures being frequently read, the situation of the Parts of both Men and Women, and other things of great Consequence are often made plain to them." Her book was designed to rectify the shortcoming. In 1687, as a preliminary step to making scientific training available to women, Elizabeth Cellier petitioned the king to form a midwives' "corporation," to be run by the "most able and matron-like woman among them."[36] Her goal remained unrealized and by the end of the century the trend was irreversible: male midwives and later doctors of obstetrics took over the services needed at birth and the birthing chair gave way to the delivery table.

Already in the seventeenth century, people were enamored with science and were impressed with the male doctors' aura, training, and technical vocabulary. Madame du Coudray (1714/15–94), who, a century later, invented an obstetrical mannequin that could simulate the birthing process as she trained rural midwives, was a rare exception.[37] Wealthy families showed a distinct preference for educated male midwives; they cost more and conferred status on the families that could afford them. Doctors took advantage of their monopoly over formal learning. Hugh Chamberlain, for example, in his midwife's manual pointed out that "it [cannot] be so great a discredit to a Midwife . . . to have a Woman or Child saved by a Man's assistance, as to suffer either to die under her own hand." But it took several more centuries at least for the benefits of science to outweigh completely those of tradition. In hospitals, women attended by doctors died of infection more frequently than those served by midwives at home. Only in the mid-nineteenth century did the Austrian physician Ignaz Semmelweis diagnose the causes of puerperal fever and require doctors, who also treated the ill, to wash their hands in chlorinated lime before each pelvic examination and birth of a child.

Let us stress that, as a general trend, when work became publicly controlled—whether by specifying the various steps in apprenticeship training or by requiring secondary and university education for professional opportunities—women were placed at a distinct disadvantage. Nonetheless, women continued to facilitate many of the day-to-day economic exchanges in the cities. The local market was filled with licensed stands run by women. In Nuremberg, for example, they sold citrus fruits that came from southern Italy, spices from the East Indies, and salted fish from Scandinavia.[38] Clearly, the local urban economy continued to rely heavily on women's work.

Protoindustrialization and Women's Work

Similarly, the burgeoning rural home or cottage manufacture for export rested on women's important labor contributions. In the sixteenth and seventeenth centuries in western and central Europe, manufacture of goods for the Atlantic markets mushroomed in the countryside when urban guilds no longer could meet the demand for their products. Extending beyond the urban setting described by Wiesner-Hanks (chapter 2), this was *rural* manufacture or "protoindustry," as it is often called. This activity was based on hand technology and it predated both mechanization and factory production. That the work took place outside the jurisdiction of the guilds was a distinct advantage to women because, as we have just seen, guilds increasingly curtailed female labor.

In the countryside extending from Flanders, Normandy, the Rhineland, and Bavaria to the Saxon-Bohemian borderland, Silesia, and the Zurich uplands, a wide range of products such as yarn, cloth, nails, and scythes, as well as pins, pots, and clogs came to be made in rural households. Production was organized by commercial capitalists who provided the workers with the raw materials and undertook to sell the finished goods, but the manufacturing itself was dispersed over thousands of workers' homes. Through this household form of manufacturing, men and women made their livelihood combining industrial and agricultural activities. In the course of time the income from cottage production became not just supplemental but essential to the survival of the rural homestead.

The spread of industry in the countryside drew the households into a distinct sociocultural world. New social rules came to influence inheritance patterns, fertility rates, and family formation as well as gender work roles. Before the appearance of rural industry, a peasant with several sons customarily left his lands to only one and the others remained single or sought their livelihood elsewhere. But listen to the calculations of a villager recorded in 1792 in the Zurich uplands after the advent of weaving and spinning in the area.

> I [might] have three or four sons, and [now] each will get some meadowland, at least one cow, a small amount of arable land, etc. This should yield some good

things to help see the household through and working the small plot would leave enough time to provide the rest from industrial wages. It is enough even if one has but a small corner to set up a spinning rod and loom and space for a little garden to grow vegetables.[39]

In this way, rural industry altered the rules by which families were formed and helped to fragment landholding. As owners of small cottages, sons and daughters of peasants and former day or migrant laborers could marry and start their own families. In areas of protoindustry, the incidence of marriage was high and couples married earlier than was true among the peasantries. Populations became exceptionally dense. In addition, in this rural household setting, men and women shared productive tasks and, in contrast to the peasant family economy, work patterns broke the bonds of gender role divisions.

It is difficult, however, to generalize about the extent of job sharing among men and women in cottage industry. The French plateau of Normandy—the pays de Caux—offers one example. There spinning and weaving were introduced into the countryside in the early eighteenth century. The growth of cottage textile work initially did not signify a major change in the sexual or seasonal division of labor, at least when seen from the perspective of an individual's primary occupation. It did, however, open up new supplementary employment opportunities for villagers. Men and women worked the fields during the harvest time, and women went into spinning yarn and men into weaving cloth during the rest of the year. Traditionally in the region, spinning had been considered women's work and weaving men's work and sex-typing of tasks continued through most of the eighteenth century. The sex division of labor loosened at the end of the century. Male labor could no longer meet the growing demand for weavers, because of the continuing need for their involvement in agriculture, crafts, and merchant trades. At that point, women went into weaving as well as agricultural day labor (which also began to require more hands), and the former two male occupations became sexually integrated.[40]

By contrast, evidence from the Rhineland and the Saxon Oberlausitz reveals a relative absence of division of labor by sex in protoindustrial households engaged in weaving. In central Europe, it is clear that the fusing of industrial activities and subsistence farming within a single residence forced its members to forego tradition and seek out flexible social alternatives. Within the weaving household, jobs tended to be fluid and exchangeable and not gender- or age-specific. At times, adult male weavers engaged in so-called "children's work," winding the bobbins (spools for yarn) along with young children present in the household; at other times, they commissioned an adult neighbor. Wives might prepare the warp, but so would husbands, and often husband and wife wove on one piece alternately. The means of production for these family operations were contributed by both partners as part of their marriage agreement. Alarmed middle-class commentators traveling in protoindustrial areas of the Rhineland described a world that in their eyes was topsy-turvy. Men were seen "cooking, cleaning, and sweeping" when their wives were busy meeting work orders.[41] These industrial households were integrated into the wider market economy and from the start worked for cash. Cash income was increased when both partners wove and family members probably thought of time as money. To save time, they readily helped one another out by sharing the nonpaid labor tasks as well. Shared work in weaving stands in contrast to agriculture, where older customs and the complexities of tasks had led to a gender-based division of labor.

The Scientific Revolution and Renewed "Arguments About Women"

The forces of change pervaded all aspects of European life. By the seventeenth century, the "Argument About Women" had become an important subject of public debate. As Maryanne Horowitz shows (chapter 5), debates among embryologists about women's formative role in conception were part of the scientific revolution. Accurate understanding of female biology, however, was long delayed by the tenacity of inherited ideas. Ironically, at the very time when new microscopic studies began to reveal women's equally active contribution to the embryological process, male medical practitioners were taking control of its conclusion, childbirth. Nonetheless, like Jane Sharp and Elizabeth Cellier, who tried to use medical science to benefit women, a group of well-born Englishwomen in the mid-seventeenth century turned the age's commitment to reason and critical thinking to their own advantage. In the process, they carried the prowoman tradition one step further. Their ranks included the Quaker Margaret Fell Fox (1614–1702), the philosophers Anne Conway and Margaret Cavendish, the duchess of Newcastle (1623–73), the playwright Aphra Behn, and Mary Astell, an early self-identified feminist writer in English. In all, in the 1650s alone, 130 texts were published by more than seventy women.[42]

These activists and scholars differed from the earlier "feminist" writers and thinkers. They thought of women as a group and defined their symbol as the "female pen," and they were less inclined to hail the exploits of exceptional individuals. Through their own work, they sought to demonstrate the intellectual potential of the female sex as a whole, which they constructed in their own image. Although they did not speak with one overarching "female voice," for much of their intellectual ammunition they adopted the ideas and methods of the great French philosopher and mathematician, René Descartes (1596–1650). Like other Cartesians, in questioning authority they relied on reason and critical observation. Unlike most Cartesians, they did not confine their investigations to the natural world but applied their analytic skills to the social world, including the condition of women.

Mary Astell, for example, was a devoted Cartesian who was deeply religious as well. She began her inquiry by doubting all knowledge except that of a perfect God. Like Descartes, she then established human existence by unfolding each step that demonstrated God's plan on earth. Using reason and logical argument, she "proved" how custom and inherited prejudice interfered with women's chances to employ and develop their God-given rational capabilities. Astell recognized that women were in a terrible bind. They were kept ignorant and their ignorance was used to dismiss efforts to improve their training. Her fundamental insight has been the foundation of recurring waves of feminism: the alleged nature and the behavior of the female sex are not something "natural" but reflect years of conditioning and the social environment. Women's defects, Astell felt, grew out of this faulty early education, which subsequently exercised a powerful influence over the course of their lives. To reverse this situation she developed a rigorous program of study that owed its inspiration to Descartes and to the epistemology of the influential British philosopher of liberalism, John Locke (1632–1704). Locke's theories of knowledge had turned attention to the environment and social circumstances in determining life's chances. Unlike most of her predecessors who had addressed the question of educational reform for women, Astell did not prescribe a series of books for women to read but emphasized method—how to think critically and how, in the search for truth, to move from the simple and sure to the complex and problematic. She called for opening vocations through higher education for spinsters who like herself chose not to marry. Similarly, Margaret Cavendish offered decidedly feminist analyses of the social circumstances at the root of female subordination.

Mary Astell and Margaret Cavendish were part of a group of professional women writers responding to the new commercial opportunities of a growing literary market. Their themes transcended the borders of England and participated in colonial discourses. In this fashion they helped to complicate definitions of Englishness to include notions of gender and race. The noted author of plays, poems, novellas, and epistolary fiction, Aphra Behn is a case in point. Personally involved in colonial projects in Surinam (her adoptive father had died en route to the colony), in her effort to negotiate multiple identities she wrote from a number of perspectives. Her "self" at times spoke for all women against cruel and powerful white men in blistering critiques of marriage; at other times her "I" stood for the property-owning English who profited by slave labor; and, as in her antislavery play set in Surinam, *Oroonoko* (1688), it could also forge an alliance between white females and black (male) slaves as one community united in consciousness of its oppression. She provides a complex picture of the ways in which English society marked itself as different. It was not simply through a binary opposition but through a paradox in which the "civilized" ideal could speak simultaneously of assimilation of well-bred and educated noble savages and of their essential alienation, since savages could never be truly equal under colonial rule. This provided, indeed, the justification for slavery. Furthermore, in this work, the narrator's alliance with the black male noble slave rested on irreconcilable rivalry with the black African female slave, who is destroyed in the end.[43]

"Arguments about Women" also played an important role in France, where they became a cultural metaphor for advocacy of social as well as political change. Parallel with the development of the absolutist state arose a so-called Republic of Letters, which both complemented and contested state legitimacy. In Paris, states Dena Goodman, this "new public sphere was structured by the salon, the press, and other institutions of sociability and publicity which were developed to counter the courtly institutions of the absolutist state."[44] Because women played a central role in the intellectual discourse and social manners of this emerging public sphere, as we will discuss more fully in Part II, the cause of women henceforth was often linked with movements for fundamental reordering of society.

In France, in the early seventeenth century, a new nobility had been created by the monarch, who sold public offices that were passed on as family property to the next generation. These men and women were called the *noblesse de robe* (nobility of the office, literally, of dress) and their presence in French upper society was regarded with hostility by the older titular nobility, the *noblesse d'épée* (nobility of the sword). While the new nobility was resented by the old, special criticism was directed at the social gatherings of men—and women—of unequal position in salons in Paris and other urban centers in the first half of the century. Salons were organized, run, and directed by women of the new nobility, who set the standards of civility—proper behavior, values, and manners—for aristocratic society, and brought together writers and their patrons and other members of the elite. As the old and new elites met in the salons, many people brought into question, through example as well as discussion, the proper stratification of French society. The controversy often centered on the public role that women had assumed in overseeing salon life, for women were the real light of the salons. For many in French society, gender equality became a marker of civilization.

In the rhetoric of the day, the advocates of change were known as the *moderns.* In contrast, the opponents of women's roles in salon life, known as the *ancients* or *traditionalists,* sought to restrict the entry of wealthy upstarts, the bourgeoisie, into the social elite and to keep it small, homogeneous, and aristocratic. In seventeenth-century France, the moderns included a variety of women and men including Marie de Gournay, François Poulain de la Barre, Michel de Pure, and Jacquette Guillaume, all of whom supported new social roles for women. Poulain de la Barre, who published treatises "On the Equality of the Sexes" (1673) and "The Woman as Good as the Man" (1677), asserted that "the mind has no sex." Recognizing, as did Mary Astell, that the condition of women reflected a "one-sided education that begins in early infancy," he challenged conventional understandings of "nature" of those who grounded men's dominance over women as part of the natural world. He also criticized Europeans for using the term *savage* to describe people with different customs. Beliefs in masculine and European superiority were not uncontested by the men and women who were social Cartesians.

The moderns took it as their task both to argue vigorously against prejudices of custom, tradition, and religious authority and to defend the women of the salons. They advocated a whole new foundation for marriage that they labeled, in its present form, an "institution of slavery," and claimed for well-born women as for aristocratic men the choice of whether or not to marry and the freedom to find affection and meaningful companionship outside of marriage. In some cases, they chose as a model England, where ladies termed "bluestockings" had emerged as cultural leaders, praising the apparent greater freedom of movement and of marriage enjoyed by English women—and men. The "companionate marriage" among Puritan business classes seemed to promise greater happiness.

The ancients, who opposed women's public roles, sometimes shunned salon life altogether; they preferred all-male literary gatherings. Their ranks included several doctors at the Sorbonne and lawyers, as well as the well-known philosopher and advocate of aristocratic reform, François Fénelon. Fénelon's views, particularly his treatise entitled *The Education of Girls* (1687), illustrate well the underlying motives of these men. He constructed an educational program that would not promote aristocratic women's participation in salon life. It purposely failed to include the requisite social and intellectual tools needed to run a salon. Thus, Fénelon excluded humanistic study because of its orientation toward the civic life and public leadership roles, which he considered inappropriate for women. But he also bypassed much literature—comedies, novels, books on the art of proper conversation, classical mythology, and poetry. The ideas in these works would turn girls' attention away from their important domestic functions. "All is lost," he warned, "if your daughter becomes infatuated with *bel esprit* and disgusted with domestic cares."[45]

Fénelon did not stop with his objection to women's prominence in the urban salons and at the French court in Versailles. Embedded in his protest was deep concern with the successes of monarchical absolutism and centralization in France and the fact that the nobility spent its days in endless pursuit of luxury, prestige, and empty power at the Bourbon court. Fénelon saw proper education for girls as a means to regenerate the titular aristocracy and keep it pure. He planned to revitalize the old nobility's domestic and agricultural life in the provinces by turning the aristocratic girl into a competent wife and mother who could oversee the family estate and manage family life. Girls were to learn bookkeeping, the demands of agricultural labor, the local customs and laws of their lands, as well as the more standard domestic arts of sewing, cooking, and supervising servants. Fénelon saw very clearly that carefully delineated gender roles were instrumental in the perpetuation of social hierarchy and inequality.

In France, then, the "Argument About Women" emerged as a key issue of controversy because the social structure was being strained by economic changes, the spread of wealth to merchants and professional people, and their subsequent legal ennoblement. The debate harks back to the old *Querelle* over women's roles that Christine de Pizan had launched in the fifteenth century. That it reemerged so centrally in seventeenth-century France reveals how alterations in the social structure created an intellectual climate in which social and sexual relationships needed to be redefined. It demonstrates as well that "ideas are not of a different order from the practices and institutions that constitute them."[46] Arguments about women assumed a materiality that drove social change in directions that confound any simple notion of linear progress.

Political Liberalism and Its Contradictions

A similar reassessment of the foundation of political authority took place across the Channel. Between 1640 and 1660, England had experienced a disastrous civil war over the question of the king's rights as against the prerogatives of the people's representatives in Parliament. We have already seen how opposition to the efforts by Europe's kings and princes to centralize authority was part of religious struggles over confessional identity. These tensions accounted for the *Fronde* in France (a mid-seventeenth-century aristocratic uprising after the death of Louis XIII), for Fénelon's backward-looking critique, and for the English civil war. The war itself and the Restoration that followed in England generated heated discussion over the basis of legitimate authority, in the course of which the liberal political theory of "natural rights" was formulated. This notion of the natural rights of individual human beings as the basis of justice and social organization may be the most important legacy of Enlightenment thought. It serves as a moral yardstick against which to measure actual rights on the ground at precise moments in time.

Implementation of the abstract principles that comprise liberal political theory, however, has been partial and contradictory. The theory later became the ideological basis for the American and French Revolutions, reinforcing bourgeois economic, social, and political power. In arguing the theory of natural rights, interestingly, the royalists and the parliamentarians in England employed an analogy with the marriage bond. In time, the arguments developed around the example of marriage were elevated to independent principles and became the basis of the liberal position on marriage and female status. What is less well known is the extent to which marital relations furnished the basis for the formulation of liberal political principles governing the state. Sarah Hanley, bridging the disciplinary borders of history and political theory, has shown how political practices followed the "social logic" contained in such maxims as "the husband is king in his household." In a striking example, she asserts that Montesquieu, who had served as a judge, drew on legal briefs prepared for marital litigation to formulate the foundational principle of separation of powers. "This defining principle of modern government—separation of powers—should be repositioned in its early social site: the marital legal briefs . . . that first publicly posited the principle in league with liberty, life, and property held hostage by despotic government." Hanley also draws the spheres of domestic and political life together by showing how the Salic law, invented in the 1400s to exclude women from royal succession, was premised on the false belief that only males contributed formative material to human reproduction.[47]

Under the influence of John Locke, contractual thinking had become widely popular in British political thought, so that both royalists and parliamentarians spoke in contractual terms. Royalists believed they had found the ideal defense of kingly authority in drawing an analogy with the marriage contract. Marriage, they said, was a contract that created an unequal relationship between the two consenting parties. Both the man and the women freely entered into marriage but God had established the husband's rule over his wife, and consent, once given, was irrevocable. As the royalist Dudley Digges developed it, drawing on scripture and a reading of family behavior, "There is a contract between Husband and Wife, the violation of which on the man's part doth not bereave him of his dominion over the woman." Similarly, once men freely had joined together to form a monarchy, royal authority was as fixed as that of husbands and there was no right of rebellion.

Parliamentarians were forced to debate the royalist conception of marriage in making their case. Initially, they took advantage of the right of divorce, which was recognized by both Luther and Calvin, and instituted in England by Henry VIII. If God had provided the remedy of separation in establishing marriage, so, too, He must have provided the remedy of resistance in creating government. But it was John Locke who advanced the liberal argument by abandoning scripture altogether in favor of natural law theory. As Locke stated it, if all beings were free and equal in the state of nature, and endowed with inalienable rights, then, when they agreed to marry they were free to set whatever terms to their relationship they wished as long as they met the needs of child care, which Locke posited as the only natural requirement of marriage. Conjugal society, he believed, was created by "a voluntary Compact between Man and Woman"; marriage, thus, did not mean consenting to preexisting rules and rights. Couples who agreed to marry could set some of the terms of their relationship. "Community of Goods and the Power over them, mutual Assistance, and Maintenance, and other things belonging to Conjugal Society might be varied and regulated by that Contract, which unites Man and Woman in that Society, as far as may be consistent with Procreation and the bringing up of Children. . . ."[48] Locke went even further and argued that the contract could be terminated. The concept of natural rights introduced the novel proposition of limited authority—and the right of resistance to authority—into Western thought.

As we have seen, the seventeenth century was an innovative period, setting the stage for an Age of Enlightenment. The scientific discoveries and philosophical propositions of great thinkers like René Descartes and John Locke as well as those of the physicist and mathematician Isaac Newton and the scientist and essayist Francis Bacon, transformed the understanding of the physical and human world. The age saw important advances in scientific methods of inquiry, in the development of new theories of knowledge, and in the emergence of the school of natural law. Significantly, the theorists, philosophers, and men of letters described their own work through the metaphors of exploration: marching into uncharted territory, they were embarking on a discovery of new worlds. These images fed renewed interest in methodologies of comparison, which were reinforced by ongoing explorations in the Pacific, as in the travels of James Cook (1728–79) and Louis-Antoine de Bougainville (1729–1811) to Hawaii and Tahiti in the 1760s and 1770s. Taken together, the developments added up to an intellectual revolution that challenged the inherited world view of Aristotle, the classical writers, and the scholastics, and constructed a new one in its place—but one that historians now recognize had its own shadows. If the next century popularized these theories and applied them to human society, it did so in ways that reveal multiple contradictions.[49]

For the position of women, of slaves in the colonial world, and of the growing ranks of the poor in Europe, the legacy of the seventeenth- and eighteenth-century Enlightenment was ambiguous. The philosophy of natural rights—the proposition that all men (and women) are free and equal in the state of nature—was potentially liberating for those on the margins. But the inclusion of property as an inalienable right and the emphasis on its efficient use for the common good perpetuated the actual institution of slavery, even if John Locke himself had railed against the notion that Englishmen were slaves to royal power. In the *Second Treatise of Government* (1690), he wrote, "Slavery is so vile and miserable an estate of Man, and so directly opposite to the generous Temper and Courage of our Nation; that 'tis hardly to be conceived, that an *Englishman,* much less a *Gentleman,* should plead for it."[50] But inconsistently, he nevertheless sanctioned slave labor and colonial appropriation of native lands in the Americas because of the apparent economic benefits for the "general good." Furthermore, the explicit linkage of property and citizenship—the merging of natural law and social organization at the heart of the liberal polity—narrowed the ranks of potential citizens to property-owning (white) males on both sides of the Atlantic. It excluded all women, people of color, and initially, those men with little property. However, where political liberalism triumphed, as in England, France, and North America, women had—in the natural rights philosophy—a ready-made argument for equality. They also could appeal to the Lockean view of marriage in expanding the rights of the married woman.

As we will see in Parts II and III, however, it nonetheless was difficult for women to appropriate this liberal version of individual autonomy in light of what was increasingly seen as their proper role in society—as mothers, responsible for the home and for safeguarding family and collective values. Women were defined, and for the most part defined themselves, primarily as social beings, not as autonomous individuals exercising rights. Yet, industrial class society and racial hierarchies rearranged needs, subjectivities, and visions of change, and set in motion forces that would complicate the universal category, "female."

The two realms of individual and social action were recast by political liberalism, which distinguished between the worlds of civic and family life to a much greater extent than was true in early modern political practice. The liberal notions rested on the idea of two separate spheres: the public and the private. In the course of time, each sex would be assigned, ideally, to a different sphere. Locke had rejected the older belief that the family was analogous to civil society and that the basis of authority in one realm was, by extension, the same in the other. Locke knew clearly what was meant by political power—that of a magistrate over a subject—and it was different from the father's authority over his children, or the husband's over his wife. A political ruler was not the same as a father in the family or a captain of a ship. The family was a private institution in liberal political thinking, preceding civil society. It was a haven and the state had no right to intrude into its affairs.

These distinct spheres—the ideological power of which we as authors both recognize and seek to transcend—expressed a paradox that shaped feminist struggles in the next century. The call for civil equality, for ending the legal obstacles to women's formal entry into political life, foundered on real and imagined differences—sexual differences, maternal and familial ties, and ascribed or perceived identities. Attention to gender differences, which often served to justify women's claims, could implicitly serve as well to undercut their call for equality, as feminist theorists now recognize. Part II begins the examination of how different women confronted these issues and Part III explores their implications for feminist politics until the present day.

The theoretical formulations of *political liberalism*, then, constitute a new context for women's efforts to become part of the political community in the West, itself being redefined by new notions of nationalism and the civic obligations of the male citizen-soldier. We will also see the wide-ranging social transformations that accompanied its corollary, *economic liberalism*. The workings of history are never simple. Massive disjunctures between the old and new, the ideal and the real, led from an "age of reason" to an "age of revolution," which brought into dispute once again understanding of the state, civil society, and the relations between the sexes.

NOTES

1. Verena Stolcke, "Invaded Women: Gender, Race and Class in the Formation of Colonial Society," in Margo Hendricks and Patricia Parker, eds., *Women, "Race," and Writing in the Early Modern Period* (London and New York: Routledge, 1995), p. 173.
2. Neil McKendrick, John Brewer, and J. H. Plumb, *The Birth of a Consumer Society: The*

Commercialization of Eighteenth-Century England (Bloomington, Ind.: Indiana University Press, 1982), p. 113.

3. Joan Kelly, "Early Feminist Theory and the *Querelle des Femmes,* 1400–1789," *Signs* 8, no. 1 (1982):21.

4. Ibid., p. 13.

5. Margaret Brabant and Michael Brint, "Identity and Difference in Christine de Pizan's *Cité des Dames,*" in Margaret Brabant, ed., *Politics, Gender, and Genre: The Political Thought of Christine de Pizan* (Boulder, Colo.: Westview, 1992), pp. 206–222.

6. In Ian Maclean, *The Renaissance Notion of Woman: A Study in the Fortunes of Scholasticism and Medical Science in European Intellectual Life* (Cambridge: Cambridge University Press, 1980), p. 92.

7. Ibid., pp. 8–9.

8. Nancy L. Roelker, "The Appeal of Calvinism to French Noblewomen in the Sixteenth Century, *Journal of Interdisciplinary History* 11, no. 4 (Spring 1972): 404.

9. In J. O'Faolain and L. Martines, eds., *Not in God's Image: Women in History from the Greeks to the Victorians* (New York: Harper and Row, 1973), p. 182.

10. For Thomas More, see Lawrence Stone, *The Family, Sex and Marriage in England 1500–1800,* abr. ed., (New York: Harper and Row, 1979), p. 142.

11. Natalie Z. Davis, "City Women and Religious Change," in her *Society and Culture in Early Modern France* (Stanford: Stanford University Press, 1975), pp. 65–95.

12. Judith C. Brown, *Immodest Acts: The Life of a Lesbian Nun in Renaissance Italy* (New York: Oxford University Press, 1986).

13. Mary Elizabeth Perry, *Gender and Disorder in Early Modern Seville* (Princeton: Princeton University Press, 1990), p. 25.

14. Joanne M. Ferraro, "The Power to Decide: Battered Wives in Early Modern Venice," *Renaissance Quarterly* XLVIII, no. 3 (1995): 492–512.

15. R. Po-Chia-Hsia, *Social Discipline in the Reformation: Central Europe, 1550–1750* (London and New York: Routledge, 1989), pp. 122, 125.

16. E. William Monter, "Women in Calvinist Geneva (1550–1800)," *Signs* 6, no. 2 (1980): 191–193; Susan C. Karant-Nunn, "Continuity and Change: Some Effects of the Reformation on the Women of Zwickau," *Sixteenth Century Journal* XII, no. 2 (1982): 21–26; and Mary Elizabeth Perry, "Deviant Insiders: Legalized Prostitutes and a Consciousness of Women in Early Modern Seville," *Comparative Studies in Society and History* 27, no. 1 (January 1985): 138–158.

17. In Karant-Nunn, "Continuity and Change," p. 39.

18. The following discussion of witchcraft draws heavily on the innovative study by Christina Larner, *Enemies of God: The Witch-Hunt in Scotland* (Baltimore: Johns Hopkins University Press, 1981).

19. Alfred Soman, "The Parlement of Paris and the Great Witch Hunt (1565–1640)," *Sixteenth Century Journal* IX, no. 2 (1978): 31–44. For James I, Larner, *Enemies of God,* p. 93.

20. Elizabeth Reis, *Damned Women: Sinners and Witches in Puritan New England* (Ithaca, N.Y.: Cornell University Press, 1997).

21. Sally Scully, "Marriage or a Career? Witchcraft as an Alternative in Seventeenth-Century Venice," *Journal of Social History* 28, no. 4 (summer 1995): 857–876.

22. Jean-Louis Flandrin, *Families in Former Times: Kinship, Household, and Sexuality* (Cambridge: Cambridge University Press, 1979), p. 118; also Stone, *The Family, Sex and Marriage,* p. 138.

23. In Robin Blackburn, *The Making of New World Slavery: From the Baroque to the Modern, 1492–1800* (London and New York: Verso, 1997), p. 291.

24. Philippe Ariès, *Centuries of Childhood: A Social History of Family Life*, trans. Robert Baldick (New York: Vintage, 1962), p. 110.

25. Barbara A. Hanawalt, *The Ties That Bound: Peasant Families in Medieval England* (New York and Oxford: Oxford University Press, 1986).

26. "From the Autobiography of Mrs. Alice Thorton," in Joan Goulianos, ed., *By a Woman Writt* (Baltimore: Penguin, 1974), pp. 30–53, quotation p. 51; Alan Macfarlane, *The Family Life of Ralph Josselin* (New York: W.W. Norton, 1970), pp. 81–91, 199–204.

27. Blackburn, *Making of New World Slavery*, p. 3.

28. Peter Hulme, "Tales of Distinction: European Ethnography and the Caribbean," in Stuart B. Schwartz, ed., *Implicit Understanding: Observing, Reporting, and Reflecting on the Encounters between Europeans and Other Peoples in the Early Modern Era* (Cambridge: Cambridge University Press, 1994), p. 164.

29. Natalie Zemon Davis, "Iroquois Women, European Women," in Hendricks and Parker, eds., *Women, "Race," and Writing*, pp. 243–258.

30. Stolcke, "Invaded Women," p. 285.

31. Irene Silverblatt, "Andean Witches and Virgins: Seventeenth-Century Nativism and Subversive Gender Ideologies," in Hendricks and Parker, eds., *Women, "Race," and Writing*, pp. 259–271.

32. On the evolution of the family, see John R. Gillis, *For Better, For Worse: British Marriages, 1600 to the Present* (New York: Oxford University Press, 1985) and Michael Mitterauer and Reinhard Sieder, *The European Family: Patriarchy to Partnership from the Middle Ages to the Present*, trans. Karla Oosterveen and Manfred Herzinger (Chicago: University of Chicago Press, 1982).

33. Pierre Goubert, *The Ancien Régime: French Society, 1600–1750*, trans. Steve Cox (New York: Harper and Row, 1973), p. 43.

34. Lawrence Stone, *The Family, Sex, and Marriage in England in England, 1500–1800* (New York: Harper and Row, 1977), p. 496.

35. Monter, "Women in Calvinist Geneva," p. 203; Natalie Z. Davis, "Women in the Crafts in Sixteenth-Century Lyon," *Feminist Studies* 8, no. 1 (Spring 1982): 68; Daryl M. Hafter, "Power vs. Privilege: A Case Study of the Spinners' Guild in Eighteenth Century Rouen," (Paper presented to the Social Science History Association, Bloomington, Ind., November 1982); and id., "Female Masters in the Ribbonmaking Guild of Eighteenth-Century Rouen," *French Historical Studies* 20, no. 1 (Winter 1997): 1–14. Jennifer Jones, "Coquettes and Grisettes: Women Buying and Selling in Ancien Régime Paris," in Victoria de Grazia with Ellen Furlough, eds., *The Sex of Things: Gender and Consumption in Historical Perspective* (Berkeley: University of California Press, 1996), pp. 25–53.

36. Hilda L. Smith, *Reason's Disciples: Seventeenth Century English Feminists* (Urbana, Ill.: University of Illinois Press, 1982), pp. 97–98; Alice Clark, *Working Life of Women in the Seventeenth Century* (New York: A. M. Kelley, 1968), p. 274; Moira Ferguson, ed., *First Feminists: British Women Writers 1578–1799* (Bloomington, Ind.: Indiana University Press; Old Westbury, N.Y.: Feminist Press, 1985).

37. Nina Rattner Gelbart, *The King's Midwife: A History and Mystery of Madame du Coudray* (Berkeley: University of California Press, 1998).

38. Merry E. Wiesner, "Paltry Peddlers or Essential Merchants? Women in the Distributive Trades in Early Modern Nuremberg," *Sixteenth Century Journal* XII, no. 2 (1981): 3–13.

39. Rudolf Braun, *Industrialisierung und Volksleben* [Industrialization and Everyday Life] (Erlenbach-Zurich: Eugen-Rensch, 1965), pp. 60–61.

40. Gay Gullickson, "The Sexual Division of Labor in Cottage Industry and Agriculture in the Pays de Caux: Auffay, 1750–1850, *French Historical Studies* 12, no. 2 (Fall, 1981): 177–199.

41. Douglas R. Holmes and Jean H. Quataert, "An Approach to Modern Labor: Worker Peasantries in Historic Saxony and the Friuli Region over Three Centuries," *Comparative Studies in Society and History* 28, no. 2 (April 1986): 191–216; also, Jean H. Quataert, "Combining Agrarian and Industrial Livelihoods: Rural Households in the Saxon Oberlausitz in the Nineteenth Century," *Journal of Family History* 10, no. 2 (Summer 1985): 145–162; id., "The Shaping of Women's Work in Manufacturing: Guilds, Households, and the State in Central Europe, 1648–1870," *American Historical Review* 90, no. 5 (December 1985): 1122–1148.

42. Elaine Hobby, " 'Discourse So Unsavoury': Women's Published Writings of the 1650s" in Isobel Grundy and Susan Wiseman, eds., *Women, Writing, History, 1640–1740* (Athens, Ga.: University of Georgia Press, 1992), pp. 16–32; Clare Brant and Diane Purkiss, eds., *Women, Texts and Histories, 1517–1760* (London and New York: Routledge, 1992).

43. Margaret W. Ferguson, "Juggling Race, Class, and Gender," and Margo Hendricks, "Civility, Barbarism, and Aphra Behn's *The Widow Ranter*," in Hendricks and Parker, pp. 209–224 and 225–239; Ros Ballaster, "Seizing the Means of Seduction: Fiction and Feminine Identity in Aphra Behn and Delarivier Manley," in Grundy and Wiseman, eds., *Women, Writing, History*, pp. 93–108.

44. Dena Goodman, *The Republic of Letters: A Cultural History of the French Enlightenment* (Ithaca, N.Y. and London: Cornell University Press, 1994), p. 14.

45. Quoted in Carolyn C. Lougee, *Le Paradis des Femmes: Women, Salons, and Social Stratification in Seventeenth-Century France* (Princeton: Princeton University Press, 1976), p. 176.

46. Goodman, *Republic of Letters*, p. 2.

47. Sarah Hanley, "Social Sites of Political Practice in France: Lawsuits, Civil Rights, and the Separation of Powers in Domestic and State Government, 1500–1800," *American Historical Review* 102, no. 1 (February 1997): 27–52, quotation on p. 50. See also Maryanne Horowitz's study in chapter 5.

48. Mary Lyndon Shanley, "Marriage Contract and Social Contract in Seventeenth-Century English Political Thought," *Western Political Quarterly* 32, no. 1 (March 1979): 80.

49. See Peter Hulme and Ludmilla Jordanova, eds., *The Enlightenment and Its Shadows* (London and New York: Routledge, 1990).

50. Quoted in Blackburn, *Making of New World Slavery*, p. 263.

CHAPTER ONE

Family and State in Early Modern France: The Marital Law Compact

Sarah Hanley

In the early modern period, the interests of the family and the state intersected in the public arena, where the family played an important political role. Through marriage alliances, inheritance practices, and patronage, family members exercised decisive power and influence. Because these power networks were built through family alliances, parents increasingly demanded the right to determine marriage decisions of their offspring. The marriage act, however, was subject to the jurisdiction of the ecclesiastical courts of the Catholic church, which maintained that at least nominal consent of the couple was necessary for a valid marriage. A serious conflict arose when the family practiced coercion and the church held fast to the ecclesiastical principle of consent.

As Sarah Hanley shows in this innovative study of early modern France, the balance in the struggle was tipped by the process of centralization, or state-building, that expanded secular jurisdiction over marriage arrangements. As members of potentially powerful families, jurists strengthened their own family networks by rewriting the laws governing marriage; in this case, family priorities coincided with those of the monarchical state. But the family is not an undifferentiated unit, and the laws promulgated between 1556 and 1639 effectively enhanced the power of men over the women and children in the family. Hanley offers five court cases, what she calls "dreadful family dramas," which graphically reveal the sex-specific consequences that these legal changes wrought for women's lives. To be sure, while family patriarchs did not always move against female cohorts, they certainly had the legal power to do so. Hanley bases this study on changes in the marriage laws and on court cases heard before the Parlement of Paris, the supreme court in France, where cases could be appealed from the ecclesiastical courts of the Catholic church. Her work illustrates the impact of political centralization on the personal lives of women.

In the history of Western civilization one institution has been transformed beyond recognition—the family. The social structure and function of the modern family (nineteenth through the twentieth centuries) bears little resemblance to that of its

early modern counterpart (sixteenth through the eighteenth centuries), and the difference between the two types of units reflects varied stages in the development of
the state. In the West, modern states are characterized politically by the separation
of public (state) and private (individual) interests, and economically by sustained
industrial growth, which supports large populations. Citizenship in a state under-
writes the life chances of individuals by guaranteeing basic social services (education, social security, welfare, etc.); therefore, citizens collectively maintain the
state bureaucracy over time. To the contrary, early modern monarchies were characterized politically by intertwined private–public (family–state) relations, and
economically by subsistence economies which could support only small populations. Membership in a family provided the only means of human survival through
networks of influence (marriage alliances, inheritance practices, patronage, and
apprentice systems); consequently, relatives planned strategies to perpetuate, or
reproduce, family lines across generations. The most pressing business of early
modern times was the maintenance and extension of family networks, which were
agencies of both social reproduction and economic production; and the negotiation
of proper marriage alliances, critical to that endeavor, depended on effective
parental authority. This essay traces the alliance of patriarchs and politicians for
the express purpose of controlling the formation of marriage in France between
1556 and 1789.

In very early times, prior to the year 1000, the marriage act involved a secular
legal contract negotiated by parents with little concern for the personal consent of
either bride or groom. From around the year 1000, however, marriage gradually
shifted from its secular base to one religious and ecclesiastical in orientation. Marriage became subject to the law of the Catholic church (canon law) and problems regulating it were judged in ecclesiastical (church) courts. During this shift from secular to ecclesiastical realms, the nature of the marriage contract also changed. Whereas
the earlier secular legal contract was coercive, that is, it did not consider the consent
of the couple, the new ecclesiastical marriage act, subject to canon law, came to
require at least nominal consent. This change of tenor from coercion to consent
reflected general concern over mounting cases of marriage litigation in ecclesiastical
courts. Besieged with requests for annulments and separations, many of them brought
on behalf of women, troubled canon lawyers sought remedies. Around the year 1140
the lawyer Gratian (in his *Decretum)* posed the thorny question, "May a daughter be
given in marriage against her will?" and answered in the negative based on the opinion that "A father's oath [in the contract] cannot compel a girl to marry one to whom
she has not assented." In his argument Gratian alluded to a psychological factor in
the making of a marriage. "Consent makes a marriage," he said, because of the "marital affection" involved between two people. Neither the church nor a feudal lord nor
a family could supply that element of affection, so there could be no proper marriage
when consent was absent. Gratian's argument was innovative, because it undermined
the traditional teachings of the Old Testament [Deut. 22:16], the early church fathers,
popes, and other received sources. By introducing the notion of individual consent
or choice into canon law, Gratian's rubric challenged parental authority: nominally,
at least, children might refuse the commands of parents in contracting marriage. In
the wake of that challenge, a contest developed between two institutions for control

over the connubial fate of children—the church (as the guarantor of choice) and the family (as the agent of coercion).

Between the twelfth and fifteenth centuries the contestants effected an uneasy balance of power: the church supported the precept of consent in marriage, but the family, eminent in its own domain, often ignored the directive. Over the next two centuries, however, this balance of power was disrupted, and the scales tipped heavily to the side of parental authority. During the sixteenth, seventeenth, and eighteenth centuries family power overwhelmed church influence in marriage arrangements. How did the power of families to control marriages advance dramatically at the expense of church authority? The story is best told by reference to early modern France, where family and state closed ranks against women, children, and church between 1556 and 1789.

In early modern times, state-building required the support of a political-professional elite that was loyal to the monarch and capable of staffing administrative and judicial offices in the kingdom. That elite emerged in France during the sixteenth and seventeenth centuries from the ranks of the bourgeois gentlemen who were trained in the famous law schools. Participating in the peculiar French system of venality (sale of office), these legists purchased royal offices from the monarchy and then legalized the hereditary transmission of offices (as family property) to the next generation. The partnership proved mutually agreeable: through the sale of offices king and state obtained financial assistance and professional service; through the acquisition of hereditary rights, office-holders augmented family fortunes and prestige. This welding of public and private interests gave rise to a new *noblesse de robe* (nobility of the robe, named for their judicial gowns), which thenceforth vied for status with the old *noblesse d'épée* (nobility of the sword, named for their military garb). Following the tradition of French legal humanism, these learned and patriotic legists of the *noblesse de robe* guarded French public (i.e., constitutional) law and French private (i.e., civil) law against the encroachment of church prerogatives and canon law. Practicing as judges and councillors in the Parlement of Paris (a supreme court), they applied the law to specific cases, amended it on occasion, and shaped the law over time to suit their own priorities. Since the consolidation of familial networks headed the priority list, the question of parental authority loomed large. The political bargain struck between family and state placed the ultimate power over the formation of marriage in the hands of the family.

The terms of the bargain reflected the sociopolitical and sexual ideology propagated by leading jurists. In the 1550s Jean de Coras complained about the problem of clandestine marriage (made secretly without parental consent). He labeled those unions as "polluted conjunctions" that disturbed the public good. Supposedly based on individual free choice and mutual affection, they really were products of reckless human passion. Since such liaisons were against divine law, natural law, and human reason, French laws should be enacted to prevent them. In the 1580s Pierre Ayrault sounded the same note. He emphasized the separation of political and religious authority. God had divided his empire with Caesar, so popes had no right to interfere with public affairs in France. In fact, the "Sorbonnists" (canon lawyers and theologians at the University of Paris) were predators who allowed the church to steal children from mothers and fathers and ruin families in the process.

The monarchical state should make its own laws to maintain families and disallow church interference. Others abhorred clandestine marriages that were conducted by Huguenot (Protestant) ministers. They viewed French law as the vehicle for assuring the public character of marriage in a time beset by religious strife. In the 1600s the jurists Barnabé Brisson, Jérôme Bignon, Pierre Séguier, and others followed suit. They too denied church cognizance over secular matters and placed marriage contracts under French civil jurisdiction. At stake here was the success or failure of state-building, which depended in some measure on the ability of the new *noblesse de robe* to form powerful family networks through marriage alliances.

At the international Council of Trent, the French delegates challenged church authority during the debates over marriage regulations. The French bishops repeatedly demanded that the church authorize parental control of marriage, but the other church prelates stood fast and denied that a valid marriage required parental consent. The church regulations governing marriage were quite minimal: first, they required the publication of banns announcing a marriage (in order to discover impediments, such as bigamy, incest, or *rapt* [abduction]); second, they required the presence of two witnesses (in order to prove the ritual took place). Actually the crux of the dispute between church and state lay in the definition of a clandestine marriage. For the church prelates the term "clandestine" signified a union that was invalid because it lacked requisite publicity (banns and witnesses); for the French legists the term signified a union that was invalid because it denied natural and legal propriety (parental consent). When the French delegates failed to reform marriage law at the Council of Trent, the legists at home picked up the standard in the courts.

To effect French hegemony over marriage law, the legists in the Parlement of Paris initiated a legislative reform movement that lasted for a century. Straightaway they promulgated laws against clandestine marriage; then they secured legal jurisdiction over disputed cases. At the outset, the discourse extolled the familial rights of mothers and fathers vis-à-vis children. The arguments of Coras and Ayrault raised philosophical and biblical standards of filial piety to sway opinion. Recounting the sighs, tears, and lamentations of parents who were perversely deceived by ingrates, they held that divine and natural law obliged children to honor mothers and fathers and that French law should follow suit. Evidently their colleagues agreed. In 1556 the Parlement of Paris registered a civil statute that overruled canon law. First, the statute decreed that persons who married without parental consent could be deprived of family support and disinherited. Second, it lengthened the age of minority (requiring parental consent) from twenty to thirty years for males, from seventeen to twenty-five years for females. At the same time the Parlement registered a companion statute that forbade women to hide a pregnancy or to deliver a newborn baby secretly. Following this extraordinary statute women were required to declare a pregnancy officially and to birth a child before witnesses. Those who failed to do so and delivered a dead child, or said they delivered a dead child, would be charged with the crime of murder and punished by death as an example to others. That was not the end of it. In 1578 the Parlement registered the Ordinance of Blois which made the publication of marriage banns stricter, demanded the presence of four witnesses instead of two, and required the officiating priest to have proof of the ages of the couple and the consent of their parents. Even more draconian, the ordinance decreed that persons who married without parental approval (and their accomplices) would be charged with the crime of *rapt de violence* (forced abduction) or *rapt de séduction* (willing elopement), and worse, it declared the crime of *rapt* a capital offense punishable by death. Clearly, the new laws supported parental authority, not individual choice.

Toward the end of the century, the tone of this discourse struck a new note as the legists turned to strengthen paternal rights. The seventeenth-century shift of emphasis from parental authority to paternal power accompanied the move from legal theory to judicial practice. Whereas the earlier generations had promulgated the new marriage laws in the Parlement of Paris, the later ones actually prosecuted cases of *rapt* brought to the Parlements. Determined to punish transgressors, legists such as Bignon and Séguier invoked severe Roman law notions of paternal power (*paterfamilias*), which strengthened the legal position of fathers at the expense of minors and women. According to Bignon and cohorts, families should be headed by authoritarian male figures who commanded obedience from children and wives. Since paternal authority proceeded directly from God, children and women (including widows and unmarried daughters) owed obedience to fathers and husbands. Disturbed by the rising number of *rapt* cases on the dockets, the later generation of legists closed remaining loopholes. In 1629 the Parlement of Paris registered the Code Michaud, which again expanded the definition of a minor (who must attain parental consent) to include widows age twenty-five and under, and decreed that priests could perform marriages only for known members of the parish who produced proof of parental consent. Finally, in 1639 the Parlement registered a decree that summarized all these provisions of 1556, 1578, and 1629, and added still others. This statute required parental consent (on pain of disinheritance) regardless of the age of the parties, making majority age irrelevant. Thus members of the older generation for their entire lifetimes could control members of the younger generation even into their middle age. In addition to promulgating legislation against clandestine marriage, the Parlement of Paris subjected marriage law to state jurisdiction.

Once the monarchical state created its own body of civil law on marriage, a clash between the state and church authority arose. Who had jurisdiction over these cases, the Parlements or the ecclesiastical courts? In fact, the judges in the Parlement of Paris steadily assumed jurisdictional supremacy through an appeal procedure, which allowed disputed decisions from ecclesiastical courts to be appealed in the Parlement of Paris. As the decades wore on the Parlements encroached at every opportunity. Marriage was a civil contract, not a religious one, the legists argued, because it involved transfers of family property (lands, valuables, offices) that were subject to the jurisdiction of Parlements. Furthermore, trials for the capital crime of *rapt* belonged in Parlements, because the crime in French law entailed the death penalty, which ecclesiastical courts could not impose. Although the Parlements rarely invoked the death penalty for cases of *rapt*, preferring to levy fines, the ingenious inclusion of capital punishment automatically placed such cases in their bailiwick. Indeed, the crime of *rapt* came to be regarded as a kind of treason against family and state. In the early seventeenth century the supremacy of Parlements over church courts was sealed when the French clergy finally acquiesced to the change of venue. In a decree of 1634, the Parlement of Paris directly assumed judicial competence over

marriage arrangements, and the French Assembly of the Clergy, when polled by the
king, concurred. All along the French prelates, caught between two masters, played
a waiting game. Many of them belonged to the same families as the legists and shared
in common family strategies and patriotic sentiments.

French laws governing the formation of marriage had come to reflect the
sociopolitical and sexual ideology of the *noblesse de robe* and its supporters. Clandestine marriage was outlawed and punished. A binding marriage required public
notice and parental, that is, paternal consent; nonconformists (regardless of age)
could be excised from the family unit and disinherited, which jeopardized chances
for survival; and they could be prosecuted in the Parlement for the crime of *rapt*.
Furthermore, the concealment of a pregnancy or the delivery of a child in secret
was enough to convict a woman of murder if that child were born dead. Illicit sexual conjunction was a risky business.

Set in this patriarchal context, a series of dreadful family dramas were played
and replayed on the public stages of Parlements. Armed with the law, some parents singlemindedly tracked down errant children involved in clandestine marriages
and sued them in the courts; others brazenly manipulated the laws to release children from earlier marriages when better opportunities appeared; some fought clandestine marriages for so many decades that their children had no lives left to live;
and still others brought family secrets out of coffers 150 years later to the ruin of
innocent descendants. The court cases tell the human tale.

Case Study 1

In 1587 Pierre Houlbronne (age seventeen) left Boulogne-sur-mer (with parental
permission) and sought employment in Paris at the *Palais de Justice* (law courts).
In Paris the same year he met a widow, Elisabeth Pallier, and moved into her house.
The two cohabited for eight years and children were born from the union. When
Pierre decided to leave Elisabeth in 1595, she filed a complaint with the ecclesiastical judge, who imprisoned Pierre pending investigation. In the hearing Elisabeth
testified that they had been married secretly by a Huguenot minister (Pierre's preference) and that the children had been baptized in the Catholic church (her preference). Although Pierre could not deny cohabitation or paternity, he testified there
had been no valid marriage. Since there were good reasons to presume that a marriage existed between the two, the ecclesiastical judge ordered them to regularize
the union. Pierre acquiesced and was released from prison. They signed a marriage
contract before two notaries and solemnized the marriage in the Church of Saint
Jacques.

But Pierre's parents, Valleran Houlbronne and Jeanne Deschamps, challenged
the marriage. They appealed the decision of the ecclesiastical judge to the Parlement
of Paris and charged Elisabeth with *rapt de séduction* and *rapt de violence*. The
alleged marriage was invalid, they argued, on two counts: first, in 1587 Pierre had
been seduced by Elisabeth while a minor (seventeen years old) and still subject to
his parents; second, in 1595 Pierre had been forced by Elisabeth and the ecclesiastical judge to solemnize a marriage while still a minor (twenty-five years old) and
through extortion, the threat of continued imprisonment. Pierre corroborated the

charges: he was forced to marry Elisabeth in 1595 or remain in prison; he could not have assented freely to a marriage at any time because he was a minor and lacked parental consent. Elisabeth countered the charges. She insisted that Pierre had freely assented to cohabitation from 1587 and to solemnize the marriage in 1595. She also noted that Pierre had lived on her assets in the early years and suggested that the Houlbronne parents wished to dissolve the marriage to arrange a better match for Pierre with a Marie Michel. Elisabeth stated in no uncertain terms that "What God hath joined together, no man can put asunder." The Parlement of Paris overruled the church verdict and found for the parents. The court declared the Houlbronne-Pallier marriage null and void, ordered Pierre to pay Elisabeth a sum of money, and allowed both parties to contract future marriages. Pierre married Marie Michel two years later. For Elisabeth and the church her marriage was valid because it followed long cohabitation freely chosen, the birth of children, and a belated public church wedding. For the Houlbronne family and the legists that marriage was invalid because it lacked parental consent. The Houlbronnes manipulated the law to make a better match for Pierre at the expense of Elisabeth Pallier and the Houlbronne-Pallier children (now legally illegitimate).

Case Study 2

In 1619 César Brochard (already a lawyer in Parlement) and Susanne Guy (a woman of lower social status) eloped and married without parental approval. César's father, Jean Brochard (a royal councillor), sued his son to invalidate the marriage. The Parlement of Paris ruled for the father and judged the alleged marriage null and void. The court found César guilty of evading parental authority, ordered him to beg parental forgiveness for such impropriety, and required him to enter the monastery of Saint Victor and remain there until released by parental declaration. The court declared Susanne guilty of *rapt (de séduction)*, forced her to renounce the marriage before the Brochard parents and four witnesses and to beg pardon from the king for the crime, and banished her from Paris for a decade. Jean Brochard had asserted parental rights over individual choice and won. He sued his own son in court to prevent a marriage not suited to family priorities, and he made use of a monastery as a short-term detention center for the errant son. The real victim, however, was Susanne, exiled for ten years from her own home and lacking marriage prospects.

Case Study 3

In 1636 Marc de Brion and Louise Gaudart (both eighteen years old) married with the consent of the Gaudart family. Charles de Brion (seigneur de Hautefontaine), father of Marc, promptly sued Jacques Gaudart, father of Louise, for *rapt (de séduction)*. The Gaudart family aided and abetted Marc's seduction, he argued, by condoning the courtship and the marriage. As a result, Marc's reckless passion for Louise interfered with his university studies and threatened his future career. The Parlement of Paris found for Marc's father, Brion. The court declared Louise's father, Gaudart, guilty of *rapt* (of Marc) and ordered him to pay Brion forty-six thousand livres (damages). The court found Marc guilty of acting without parental consent, fined him twenty-four thousand livres (to pay for the bread of prisoners), and confined him to the monastery of Saint Victor until released by his parents. The Brions no doubt had better marriage prospects in mind for Marc; the Gaudarts would find few good prospects for Louise in the aftermath of such scandal and with a depleted dowry.

Case Study 4

In 1647 the Duke of Attichy sued his daughter following her announced intention to live independently. She had spent several miserable years in a convent, left without taking solemn vows, and refused to return. In secular life she rejected all marriage plans and wished to live on her own inheritance (perhaps bequeathed by her mother or a relative). The Parlement of Paris ruled for the father: although unwed daughters could not be forced to marry or to enter convents, they were obliged by divine law, natural law, and French law to obey the will of fathers. Tied to paternal households in this manner, unwed daughters could never achieve independence regardless of age, disposition, or financial condition. They remained subject to paternal power until death did them part.

Case Study 5

In 1732 Louis-Henri de Saulx de Tavannes (marquis de Mirabel) and Ferdinande-Henriette-Gabrielle de Brun, who had known each other for years, wished to marry. Ferdinande's parents, Agathange-Ferdinand de Brun (marquis de Roches) and the marquise de Roches, who could not abide each other, fought a mortal battle over her future: the mother favored a union with Louis and encouraged the courtship; the father opposed the union and arranged a marriage with someone else. In May of 1732 after much plotting, Louis helped Ferdinande (accompanied by four servants) to flee from the family château. Apparently they did not plan to marry secretly but intended to install Ferdinande in a convent, where she could attempt to resist the impending marriage free of paternal pressure. Ferdinande tried to gain admission to three convents but was turned away because there was no one (i.e., parents, relatives) to vouch for her. The convents no doubt thought that the entourage looked suspicious and feared legal liability as accomplices. Caught in this limbo and short of funds, the desperate couple was tracked down by Ferdinande's father, the marquis de Roches, who filed a complaint of *rapt (de séduction)* against Louis (and the servants) and obtained a royal order *(lettre de cachet)* to retrieve Ferdinande. The marquis de Roches ordered his daughter to enter a convent in Metz; then he transferred her to Paris, first to the Convent of Saint Elisabeth, then to the dreaded Convent of Saint Pélagie. Although Louis and Ferdinande formally begged pardon of the marquis for their precipitous action, he turned to the law. Consumed by fury at Ferdinande's presumed "betrayal," the marquis de Roches accused his daughter of "odious treason," refused to see her, and severed financial support. Supportive to the end, the marquise de Roches visited her daughter at Saint Elisabeth's, took her word that no clandestine marriage had been contracted, treated her with loving kindness, and supported her financially. When the marquis transferred Ferdinande to the Convent of Saint Pélagie, the marquise rented an apartment for both of them at the Convent of Les Dames de la Croix.

Doubly enraged by this mother-daughter solidarity, the marquis refused to see either of them and drew the sword of paternal power. He obtained a royal order that separated mother and daughter, forced the marquise back into the paternal household, and transferred Ferdinande into the austere Convent of La Madeleine, which housed "sexually promiscuous" women under severe rule. For the first four years there she was forbidden to speak to anyone or to write letters to her mother. Ferdinande remained virtually imprisoned in convents for fourteen years, ten of them at La Madeleine, where she eventually took simple (not final) vows and served as superior of the house. Whereas monasteries served families as short-term detention centers for errant sons, convents provided long-term prisons for errant daughters.

In the meantime, Louis went to court. In 1738, a couple of years after Ferdinande was incarcerated in La Madeleine, the court convicted Louis of *rapt* and sentenced him to death. Since women could not bear witness in the Burgundy court without a husband's consent, the marquise de Roches could not testify for Louis, even though she separated from her husband in the same year. Given the severe sentence, Louis fled from France and lived in exile for eight years. Crushed by the legal weight of paternal power, the three (Louis, Ferdinande, and the marquise) must have welcomed the death of the marquis in 1746. Mercifully freed from paternal authority, Ferdinande left the convent for secular life, while Louis returned to France and obtained a pardon. But the terrible story does not end there. Just when rejoicing might have been in order, Louis died in 1747 and the marquise died in 1748. At this point Ferdinande, quite alone in the world, suffered a further blow upon finding herself disinherited by her beloved mother. Astonished and bewildered by the terms of the testament, Ferdinande brought suit in court against the next of kin. Apparently the aged marquise, bereft of her only child and separated from her husband, fell prey to the avarice of relatives. For years Charles-Paul Bureau de la Rivière (count de Montal) and Marie-Anne de Monsaulnin (countess de Montal) played upon the emotions of the lonely old woman. Ferdinande deserved disinheritance, they convinced her, because the daughter had lied to her mother when she denied having contracted a clandestine marriage with Louis in 1732. Ferdinande had already been disinherited by her spiteful father (she received only a *légitime*, a small portion of his estate); now she had to spend another decade fighting a brutal battle for survival, which depended upon her right to the maternal inheritance. Before this case was settled, the principal parties, young and old, had wasted their lives away. The marquis' display of paternal power shows how complete the subjection of children (especially females) and women in the family could be if taken to extremes under the laws governing the formation of marriage in the old regime.

In early modern France the eminent *noblesse de robe* controlled the formation of marriage and policed childbearing in concert with the state. The legal reforms promulgated by this family-state coalition subjected the interests of children and women to a patriarchal and familial *raison d'état* that promoted state-building. The human effects of this tenacious marital law compact seem clear: when paternal consent became the touchstone of a valid marriage, patriarchs and politicians triumphed over children, women, and church. Looking back from his vantage point in the mid-nineteenth century, Alexis de Tocqueville discussed the ascendance of paternal power over the formation of marriage and lamented the unnatural juxtaposition of human passion and legal statute, which placed such a heavy burden on the young. Yet for all his acuity in judging the old regime, de Tocqueville failed to grasp an essential point. The human effects of the marital law compact cannot be assessed without resort to the gender component. In any analysis of marriage formation within familial networks, women must be considered independently of men. One must perforce recast the question and ask: What were the effects of the marital law compact on women? At first glance the obvious can be stated. In early modern times, the less privileged groups in society in terms of access to status, wealth, and power were young people and women. On second glance, however, a corollary appears that is not so obvious. Across the board, the effects of the marital law compact were gender-specific. As young male members of families aged in this society, they usually had the opportunity to assume power over family resources; whereas females tended to remain less privileged whatever their age and often permanently so.

There is no doubt as to the public nature of the marital law compact. The peculiar rituals of pardon exacted from young people and the parental use of detention centers highlight the quasi-public nature of the family—a familial state within a political state, where family rules, written into law, were enforced. Some monasteries and convents served as official detention centers for errant members of families just as the Châtelet supplied an official prison for criminal subjects of the state. Yet in the case of males, detention was short-time; whereas in the case of females, detention could be quite long-term. Despite the fact that the French marital law compact legally undermined the church's principle of consent, many convents ignored the conflict of interest and gave institutional support to the new laws by helping to enforce family regulations. In this peculiar system, which required such support for the marital law compact to work, women policed women, sometimes in a moderate manner, other times with frightening severity. For the women forcibly held in these institutions, the sentences must have seemed, and often were, interminable. Young men like César Brochard and Marc de Brion could not remain long in the monastery of Saint Victor, because the patriarchal system required that they fulfill public offices and guard family interests in generational turn. But the young women fared less well. Once placed in a convent for contracting a clandestine marriage, it was not easy to return to secular life. Susanne Guy was actually forced into exile for a decade, and Ferdinande de Brun remained in the especially penitential austere environment of the Convent of La Madeleine for fourteen years with incarceration lifted only on the death of her father. Others shared similar fates.

To make matters worse, the same system attempted to regulate childbearing in order to prevent abortion and infanticide, obvious byproducts of clandestine marriage, too. Gradually the professional midwives, a licensed corporate group, policed the actions of pregnant women, in particular those without husbands. Thus clandestine childbearing fell under the same rubric, as midwives became the official witnesses for live and dead births, women policing women in the service of family-state priorities.

In the wake of the patriarchal marital law compact, access to paths of social mobility were also restricted for women. In the female ranks widows (even young widows) enjoyed considerable room to maneuver before the family-state marriage pact was forged. It was not uncommon for widows, especially those who ran small businesses, to marry young men, as Elisabeth Pallier wed Pierre Houlbronne, and facilitate their rise in the world. Whereas earlier church law regulating marriage protected widows like Elisabeth, following the marital law compact in 1556 Pierre could live off of Elisabeth's assets long enough to get a start in life, then abandon wife and children with near impunity, and finally fashion a better marriage opportunity for himself. Likewise, before the pact Susanne Guy and Louise Gaudart could bring decent dowries to unions and contract upwardly mobile marriages to young men like César Brochard and Marc de Brion. But after the pact outlawing clandestine marriages, young women caught in this vise were ruined morally, often confined to convents, left with dowries severely depleted by fines, and denied future marriage prospects.

Finally, the marital law compact, combined with the statute forbidding concealment of pregnancy or secret birthing, fashioned a world for women wherein human passion, illicitly indulged in terms of these social mores, spelled social, economic, and emotional ruin. To be sure, the young as a whole bore the brunt of the costs of state-building, but women in particular paid the highest price for contracting clandestine marriages in early modern France. The slow process of reversing such inequities began during the violent revolution in 1789, when militant women took their grievances to the streets, but it took another century of strife and the revolutions of 1830 and 1848 before the reversal began to take hold.

SUGGESTIONS FOR FURTHER READING

Davis, Natalie Zemon. *The Return of Martin Guerre*. Cambridge: Harvard University Press, 1983.

Donzelot, Jacques. *The Policing of Families*. New York: Pantheon, 1979.

Forster, Robert, and Orest Ranum, eds. *Family and Society: Selections from the Annales*. Baltimore: Johns Hopkins University Press, 1976.

Goody, Jack. *The Development of Family and Marriage in Europe*. Cambridge: Cambridge University Press, 1983.

Hanley, Sarah. "Engendering the State: Family Formation and State Building in Early Modern France," *French Historical Studies* 16, no. 1 (Spring 1989).

————. "Identity Politics and Rulership in France: Female Political Place and the Fraudulent Salic Law in Christine de Pizan versus Jean de Montreuil." In *Changing Identities in Early Modern France*, edited by Michael Wolfe. Durham, N.C.: Duke University Press, 1997.

————. *The Lit de Justice of the Kings of France: Constitutional Ideology in Legend, Ritual, and Discourse*. Princeton: Princeton University Press, 1983.

————. "The Monarchic State: Marital Regime Governance and Male Right." In *Politics, Ideology and the Law in Early Modern Europe*, edited by Adrianna Bakos. Rochester, N.Y.: University of Rochester Press, 1994.

————. "Social Sites of Political Practice in France: Lawsuits, Civil Rights, and the Separation of Powers, 1500–1800," *American Historical Review* 102, no. 1 (February 1997).

Hardwick, Julie. *The Practice of Patriarchy: Gender and the Politics of Household Authority in Early Modern France*. University Park, Pa.: Pennsylvania State University Press, 1998.

Rabb, Theodore K., and Robert I. Rotberg, eds. *The Family in History: Interdisciplinary Essays*. New York: Octagon Books, 1975.

Rosenberg, Charles E., ed. *The Family in History*. Philadelphia: University of Pennsylvania Press, 1975.

Wheaton, Robert, and Tamara K. Hareven, eds. *Family and Sexuality in French History*. Philadelphia: University of Pennsylvania Press, 1980.

CHAPTER TWO
_____

A Different New World:
Women of Seville in the Age
of Exploration

Mary Elizabeth Perry

Mary Elizabeth Perry's case of the women of Seville in the sixteenth century graphically demonstrates a fruitful new perspective on Europe and empire, reinterpreting their histories through their interaction. For a time, Seville was the hub of the Spanish Empire, containing a population of decidedly mixed ethno-religious groups, including African slaves destined for the colonies. The social and economic dislocations of colonial conquest took place in the context of Catholic revival and the patterns of exploitation and control "establish[ed] a vast system of imperialism that extended into the Pacific and doubled back to colonize women and minorities within Spain, itself." Perry draws careful attention to the importance of difference in assessing the broad impact of the changes on Seville's many diverse women. In response to instability, political and religious authorities sought to strengthen the gender order. Reassertion of patriarchal control, however, was refracted through class, marital status, religious and racial variables: the gender hierarchy took multiple forms. If, in the early modern era, furthermore, race remained an unstable category disconnected from biology, Perry shows that Spanish preoccupation with "purity of the blood" drew powerful markers between Christian, Jewish, and Muslim women, with implications for marriage, inheritance, sexuality, mobility, job opportunities, and public spaces.

The number of European ships exploring other parts of the world increased dramatically in the fifteenth century, and the voyages of Columbus across the Atlantic brought into European consciousness a New World to be conquered, colonized, explored, and exploited. Men turned their ships to the rich trade in gold and slaves in Africa and to the lucrative outlets of spices in the lands of the Indian Ocean. In Africa, Asia, and the Western Hemisphere they claimed distant lands for their rulers, took the Christian Gospel to countless "pagans," and drew up rules for the division of land and peoples. And what did the women do?

Seville offers an excellent case study of women in the Age of Exploration, for the Spanish monarchy designated this inland seaport as official port for all ships sailing between Europe and Spanish-claimed lands in the Western Hemisphere. Here commercial capitalism developed alongside the vast landed estates of local nobles, and here Europeans first felt the impact of the sixteenth-century "Price Revolution," a dramatic rise in prices that developed out of a growing population and increased circulation of gold and silver. Thousands of men sailed from this city into adventure and misfortune, riches and hardships; women, for the most part, remained in port. They did more than watch the horizon for signs of returning ships, however, for they found themselves in their own "new world"—a society of absent men and new challenges. In fact, women had to take care of so much of the day-to-day business during the absence of men that the Venetian ambassador to Spain described Seville in 1525 as a city "in the hands of women." Despite the greater visibility of women in the public sphere, however, the patriarchal order remained firmly in place. Women developed informal power through home, church, and work; but men continued to fill positions of authority in church, guild, and secular government to dominate a system in which religious beliefs legitimated both political authority and gender prescriptions. As commerce with newly discovered lands brought about economic and social dislocations, male authorities increased their efforts to preserve political and economic privilege. From the centuries-long wars of "Reconquest" against Muslim rulers, they maintained a warrior ethic that extolled the man of action, scorned the different, and exploited women and children. Soldiers, merchants, and clerics took this ethic with them across the Atlantic to establish a vast system of imperialism that extended into the Pacific and doubled back to colonize women and minorities within Spain, itself.

In Seville experiences of women varied greatly, according to class, marital status, and religious identity or race. Some wives of nobles, merchants, and wealthier artisans followed their husbands to the colonized lands of the Western Hemisphere, but more remained at home to direct the family business and act as household heads for months and even years at a time. Francisca de Carvajal, "wife of Pedro Alvarez, who is in the Indies," signed a rental agreement, for example, and Costanza López signed a statement that while her husband was away, she would pay her daughter's dowry in installments following an initial payment of ten thousand maravedís. Such activity did not automatically lead to the creation of a new and more independent woman, however, for frequently the notarized documents recording these transactions added that the woman took this action "with license of my husband." And sometimes the woman designated another man to act on her behalf in receiving, selling, or renting property.

Despite these gestures that seemed to preserve male authority even in the absence of husbands and fathers, concern that this absence gave women the potential power to overturn an entire social order prompted the publication of many books in the sixteenth century that prescribed correct behavior for women. In 1583, for example, friar Luis de León published a book that described the perfect wife and the ideal marriage that could bridle the independence of women and harness their energies for their God-given "natural place" in an economy of domestic production. Criticizing wealthy women who sought a life of leisure and luxury, friar Luis urged wives to be the first ones to rise in the morning, to supervise servants as captains oversee an infantry, and to work with their own hands throughout the day. Less wealthy women had learned very early this work ethic that valorized unpaid female domestic labor, for their parents had apprenticed them as servants from ages as young as seven years. From their masters, these girls learned female comportment as well as necessary domestic skills. They received board and room and, at the end of their apprenticeship, a payment that was to become part or the whole of their dowry.

Such an apprenticeship system might prepare girls for friar Luis's ideal marriage, but it did little to help them cope with marriages in which husbands disappeared. Repeatedly, male authorities complained that foreign men entered Spain and married Spanish women simply to profit in the economic system. Once they had made enough money, critics asserted, the men abandoned their wives and left Spain. Spanish men also left their wives, sometimes taking another, easily moving as soldiers sent throughout the vast Spanish Empire or as sailors on ships that sailed from the port of Seville. Attempting to enforce the Council of Trent's decision that marriage must be treated as a sacrament, the Inquisition prosecuted some of these men for bigamy. The galley service to which inquisitors sentenced convicted bigamists did nothing to restore their already disrupted marriages, nor to help support the abandoned wives.

Death also disrupted marriages, and the deaths of husbands and sons so far distant in the Western Hemisphere seemed especially poignant. Yet women who expected to inherit property had to interrupt any grieving to take legal action to protect their inheritance. For example, María de Silva, already widowed, signed an agreement giving power to a resident of Mexico City to represent her as heir of her son who had died in Mexico. Beatriz Martínez, widow of a merchant who had died in Mexico, filed two letters of power to claim her inheritance—one for her brother-in-law to represent her in New Spain, and another for a nephew to collect anything sent to her from her husband's estate. Widows also filed papers so they could act as legal guardians of their minor children, and many continued the business enterprises of their deceased husbands. Yet women of this social class rarely made investments in their own name; instead, they maintained the appearance of male authority, empowering sons, nephews, male servants, or agents to represent them in the commercial world.

Such deferential appearances mattered less to widows who had married with small dowries and received little inheritance from their husbands, for they had to work in order to survive. Many continued the occupation of the husband, since guild regulations traditionally provided that members' widows should be permitted to inherit their husbands' shops, tools, and guild membership, even when they prohibited membership for other women. The guild for carpenters and wood-carvers allowed widows to keep their husbands' shops as long as they did not remarry, but the women would forfeit this property if they married a man outside the profession. Wives of silk-weavers who had died or were simply absent could have their husbands' looms and cloths for a year, but after that time they would have to submit their work for guild examination. If the woman passed this test, guild rules permitted her to keep only one loom to sustain herself and no apprentices other than her children.

Women of little property had to work regardless of their marital status or the presence of a husband, but they faced a growing number of prohibitions that frustrated their attempts to survive. The silk-weaving that supported many women in the sixteenth century had become an occupation of piecework and female sweated labor by the mid-seventeenth century, as the guild redoubled its efforts to prevent women from becoming master silk-weavers. Female food-sellers had to contend with local ordinances that prevented them from selling food from their own homes, or in boarding houses, or as keepers or employees of taverns. Sumptuary laws, which limited the wearing of silk and brocade clothing and gold and silver embroidery, compounded the problems that women weavers and seamstresses already faced in foreign competition. This declining market also hurt the economic welfare of convents, for many nuns worked in silk-weaving and embroidery.

For centuries women had worked as healers and midwives, but in the sixteenth century their work came under increasing suspicion from inquisitors and a developing medical profession restricted to men. Women carried out the great part of the healing work of Seville, preparing in their homes remedies of plants and herbs that they had learned from an oral tradition that had been passed down from generation to generation. They nursed not only members of their families, but also neighbors and travelers, beggars and abandoned children, the inmates of prisons and hospitals. Clerics, such as friar Martín de Córdoba, praised those women who emulated Saint Monica, the mother of Saint Augustine, in consoling the ill. Such men recognized, at least by implication, that women's sphere extended from the house to the hospital to the prison and even to the streets where the poor fell ill.

A few wealthy noblewomen attended the ill personally as an act of pious charity, but most healers had to regard their work as a livelihood that could bring them some compensation, either in money or in food. Catalina de Ribera, mother of the duke of Medina Sidonia, founded a hospital for poor women and inspired Queen Isabel to follow her example in personally ministering to the poor when she visited Seville. Male authorities used the shining example of Catalina de Ribera, known as "the mother of the poor," to criticize women who depended on healing as a livelihood and expected some payment for their services. These men agreed that the city should pay salaries to a few women who nursed inmates of the city prison, but the women sometimes had to petition the city government to receive their salary. Often these women presented themselves as deserving charity as well as compensation for their work. At the beginning of the seventeenth century, for example, María de la Cruz described herself as an impoverished "barefoot beata" who had to support herself and her daughter, and requested alms from the city because she had served in the hospital during the plague of 1599–1600.

Beatas, women who had dedicated their lives to God but did not live as nuns in a convent, became very active in the healing work of this city. During the sixteenth and seventeenth centuries, the visibility and numbers of these women increased. The absence of men provides one explanation for this increase, since it meant temporary disruptions in rates of marriage; however, economic dislocations brought a more permanent problem to young women who had to have a dowry for either marriage or convent. Whether they lived alone, with family members, or other beatas, many of them became renowned for their abilities to heal. Sor Tomasa de

Santo Domingo, for example, was said to have completely cured a kitchen maid by making the sign of the cross on her throat and praying an Ave Maria. Such stories preserved the legend of the holy woman through whom God worked miracles, but they did little to fortify the status of women as knowledgeable healers who deserved compensation for their labor.

Stories of healers' miracles attracted followers but also detractors resentful and suspicious of their actual power over life and death. Inquisitors arrested four women who practiced healing in the village of Ayamonte and convicted them of sorcery in 1648. Evidently part of a female network in their village, these women had healed through prayers in particular, but they also conjured spirits and attributed special power to materials such as men's hair. Moreover, they told others that they could find lost items and help them attract the person they loved. People believed in such supernatural powers in this period, but some resented women's requests for payment for their magical work. Others may have distrusted the power that such work seemed to give to women practitioners; and they may have felt special concern about love magic, which attributed to women an awesome power over men and sexuality.

Midwives also faced considerable suspicion during the sixteenth and seventeenth centuries, for many believed that they, too, held special powers. The midwife, after all, presided over the rites of birth, which must have seemed very mysterious to people who knew little about human reproduction. Some people associated midwives with the immorality and sorcery of Celestina, the fictional bawd of Fernando de Rojas's drama, who specialized in mending hymens and restoring the appearance of virginity for sexually active women. To these people, the midwife sinned most not through ignorance of anatomy, but through teaching women a medicine of deception, contraception, and abortion that allowed them to subvert prescriptions for female chastity. Literally holding in her hands the power of life and death for both mother and child, the midwife became subject to increasing regulation through a licensing system carried out by governmental officials and male physicians. These men examined midwives not only for their knowledge about birth, but also for their morals and religious faith.

The Inquisition, an institution established to defend orthodoxy and rid Spain of heresy, became very concerned with midwives of Jewish or Muslim ancestry. Although Christian monarchs during the medieval period had sought Jewish midwives to attend royal births, authorities in the sixteenth and seventeenth centuries suspected that Judeoconversas, or women who had converted to Christianity from Judaism, could subvert Christian beliefs through midwifery. Such women, they believed, would contaminate infant baptism and could allow some infants to escape baptism by pretending that it had already taken place at birth. In addition, Judeoconversas who worked as midwives could encourage Jewish celebrations of birth and even permit the circumcision of infant sons.

Christian authorities also attempted to prevent midwifery and healing carried out by Moriscas, that is, women or their descendants who had converted to Christianity from Islam. To have such women attend births or the ill could pollute Christian births and spread the dissolute sexual tradition that Christians associated with Muslims. In Granada, which had a large Morisco population, authorities decreed that Morisca midwives should only be used when an Old Christian midwife, that is, one without any Jewish or Muslim blood, was unavailable. The reputation of Muslim medicine declined during the sixteenth century when Christian authorities burned Arabic books and exiled most learned Muslims. Moriscas preserved some of the medical traditions of their culture, practicing a medicine of water baths and fumigations, and passing on to sons and daughters their knowledge of healing practices. The Inquisition prosecuted some Morisca healers for practicing sorcery, for using forbidden Arabic writings, and for instructing others in Muslim traditions.

In the new world for women in the Age of Exploration, converted Moriscas and Judeoconversas became disenfranchised groups that faced special prohibitions as they tried to survive. They became subject to a system of internal colonization that parallelled Spanish imperialism in other parts of the world, which confiscated their homes and property and restricted the work they could perform. Subject to persecution by inquisitors who strongly suspected the sincerity of their conversions to Christianity, these groups also faced the many purity of blood laws that prevented people of any Jewish or Muslim blood from holding certain offices, practicing particular occupations, or attending university. In their emphasis on blood and ancestry, these laws transformed ethnic and religious prejudice into a racism of biological determinism.

In the face of such oppression, some Judeoconversas and their families forged genealogies that disguised Jewish ancestors in order to obtain permission to sail for the Western Hemisphere where they could establish colonies. They settled especially in New Spain, that region now known as Mexico and the states of Texas and New Mexico. Here they lived with far more distance from Christian authorities, and some of these colonists were able to form settlements where they could practice their Judaic traditions openly. Unfortunately, the Inquisition soon established tribunals in New Spain and prosecuted a substantial number of Judaizers among the colonists.

Moriscas had much less success in obtaining permission to sail to the Western Hemisphere or anywhere else. Christian authorities suspected any Morisco who sought to leave Spain of wanting to renounce conversion to Christianity and return to Islam. They also believed that Moriscos leaving Spain would become informers and betray the Spanish to their great rivals, the Turks. Some Moriscos eluded authorities as they sailed between Spain and the nearby coast of North Africa, and Inquisition cases show that women continued to attempt this escape. But few women of this community had access to boats; usually they escaped Spain only in the company of family and at considerable risk as well as expense, sailing to other lands where they found little welcome and even outright hostility.

Marriage posed particular problems for Judeoconversas and Moriscas. Those with considerable dowries might marry Old Christian men and leave the communities and traditions of their birth families. Those with small or nonexisting dowries might marry within their ethnic communities if enough men of marriageable age were available. This problem hit Moriscas especially hard because so many males of their community were absent—not for adventures in the New World, but because they had been exiled, had voluntarily left Spain for their own safety, had become outlaws in the mountainous regions where authorities could never find them, or had been sentenced to galley service, from which few men ever returned alive. Lacking the tradition of lifetime chastity of those Christians who entered convents and monasteries, and also lacking the dowries required for convents and marriage to an Old Christian, some Moriscas turned to the centuries-old solution of polygamous marriage with men who already had one or more wives.

The lives of many Moriscas became even more difficult after 1570, when royal armies finally defeated a two-year-long rebellion of Moriscos that had begun in the mountains between Granada and Seville. Christians enslaved thousands of Moriscas and their children, along with Morisco soldiers. With the royal decree that some fifty thousand Moriscos from Granada must be uprooted and dispersed throughout the towns and cities of Castile, even the free Moriscos began a life of new hardship among Christian neighbors who resented their very presence and suspected everything they did as evidence of treachery and apostasy. Royal orders directed the city of Seville to receive four thousand uprooted Moriscos, who arrived crammed on board ships, ill and dying, in miserable condition with no belongings but the clothing they wore. In 1589 parish priests carried out a census of Moriscos living in Seville, which shows that many lived in female-headed households. It listed about 6 percent of these Moriscos as slaves.

Slave women faced particular problems, for they not only lost the few protections enjoyed by nonslave women; they also had to work to support a master. Most slaves in southern Spain lived and worked apart from their masters, bound only to turn over to them a certain amount of money they earned. Female slaves worked especially as domestic servants and also as spinners. If they saved enough money, slaves could purchase their own freedom; but they had to carry documentation to prove their free status, for no amount of money or official ritual could erase the brand that many of them wore on the face or arm. Children of slave women inherited their mother's slave status and could be sold at any time separately from their mother.

By the sixteenth century Seville had become a major center for the slave trade from Africa. When ships carrying slaves arrived at the port, traders marched the slaves to a large central plaza and sold them on the steps of the cathedral. By 1565 some six thousand slaves lived in Seville and its surrounding villages, most of them blacks from Africa. After the enslavement following the unsuccessful Morisco rebellion that ended in 1570, more Morisco slaves entered the city, but traders sold most of them and sent them to other places, particularly male slaves, whom they usually put into galley service. At the end of the sixteenth century slaves accounted for nearly 30 percent of the population of the Archbishopric of Seville, and many of these were of mixed blood, the progeny of slave mothers and unnamed white fathers or masters who expected the sexual services of these women.

For the poorest women, the racism and imperialism of this period interacted with the familiar constants of hunger and sexism to create a world of violence and vulnerability in which women turned to one another in order to survive. Some lived as registered prostitutes in the city's legal brothel, enduring together the periodical medical examinations carried out by city-appointed physicians, and also the sermons by visiting clerics who would urge them to leave their lives of sin for shelter in a Magdalene house. Other women rented beds from an older woman who would not seem to notice when they stayed out too late or brought a man to stay with them for a while. Regulations decreed by authorities who feared another Morisco uprising forbade Moriscas to live together, but these women nevertheless crowded with their children into tiny rooms around an outdoor courtyard where they could come together to wash, exchange news, whisper warnings, and share child care. Slaves, too, lived in these neighborhoods of crowded streets that narrowed into dark alleys, abruptly ending in broken down buildings. Priests who took a survey of the poor of Seville in 1667 found a pattern of women and children living together, often with nothing more than a straw mattress and the clothing they wore, a spindle their only means of support.

For women of all classes and conditions, the Age of Exploration brought many problems and challenges. Men, too, confronted serious problems, for the majority of them did not sail off to distant ports. Nevertheless, women had to survive the dilemma specific to their sex, which required on the one hand their taking decisive action, but on the other hand their deference to male domination. In the face of economic dislocations that followed in the wake of the ships sailing for the New World, women made decisions and acted for their own survival and that of their children. While they adjusted to the absence of fathers and husbands, they also adapted to a reaction of male authorities determined to maintain a veneer of control over the deep political, economic, and social changes of the period. Women of Spain—as women everywhere under the Spanish flag—participated actively in their communities, even as they lived subject to a gender order legitimated by religious teachings, a male-centered warrior ethic, and imperialist authority that denigrated difference at home as well as abroad.

Suggestions for Further Reading

Altman, Ida. *Emigrants and Society: Extremadura and Spanish America in the Sixteenth Century.* Berkeley: University of California Press, 1989.

Boxer, C. R. *Mary and Misogyny: Women in Iberian Expansion Overseas, 1415–1815, Some Facts, Fancies, and Personalities.* London: Duckworth, 1975.

Cook, Alexandra Parma, and David Noble Cook. *Good Faith and Truthful Ignorance: A Case of Transatlantic Bigamy.* Durham, N.C.: Duke University Press, 1991.

Cruz, Anne J., and Mary Elizabeth Perry, eds. *Culture and Control in Counter-Reformation Spain.* Minneapolis: University of Minnesota Press, 1992.

Melammed, Renée Levine. "Sephardi Women in the Medieval and Early Modern Periods." In *Jewish Women in Historical Perspective,* edited by Judith R. Baskin. Detroit: Wayne State University Press, 1991.

Perry, Mary Elizabeth. "Beatas and the Inquisition in Seville." In *The Inquisition and Society in Early Modern Europe,* edited by Stephen Haliczer. London: Croom-Helm, 1986.

———. "Deviant Insiders: Prostitution and a Consciousness of Women in Early Modern Seville." *Comparative Studies in Society and History* XXVII:1 (Jan. 1985).

———. *Gender and Disorder in Early Modern Seville.* Princeton: Princeton University Press, 1990.

Perry, Mary Elizabeth, and Anne J. Cruz, eds. *Cultural Encounters: The Inquisition in Spain and the New World.* Berkeley: University of California Press, 1991.

Saint-Saëns, Alain, and Magdalena S. Sánchez, eds. *The Spanish Woman in the Golden Age: Images and Realities.* Westport, Conn.: Greenwood Press, 1996.

CHAPTER THREE

Women's Work in the Changing City Economy, 1500–1650

Merry Wiesner-Hanks

It was once a common ideal among privileged classes in European society that women should not work for a living and should be protected from "economic worries." The ideal housewife cared for the home and children, wove, knit, and embroidered a little. Men earned wages. The historical record tells a different story. Merry Wiesner-Hanks's description of women's work in the city economy between 1500 and 1650 reveals just how important women's contributions were. Her study rests on archival materials for southern German cities, which include municipal ordinances, wills, tax records, concessions to run market stalls, and petitions by widows to town councils. The single-leaf woodcuts from the period offer an excellent supplement. These cumulative sources document how involved women were in goods production, in retail trade, and in domestic and medical services. The chapter makes a number of innovative points. First, Wiesner-Hanks broadens the standard definition of work by looking beyond the labor officially organized by guild statutes, which increasingly excluded women's participation. She describes the daily routine of the artisan's wife, who fed the apprentices, sewed for them, and kept records. So essential was this contribution that guilds insisted every master-craftsman be married. Second, she shows that the commercial changes, or "the advent of capitalism," opened up new jobs for women in urban home industries, particularly in cloth production, while closing them in others. Finally, Wiesner-Hanks raises the important issue of how women's work was perceived by urban magistrates and male workers. She demonstrates a subtle but significant shift in attitudes toward women's work. Whereas once a husband and wife who typically shared tasks in municipal employ would both be referred to as officials, by the end of the period, they customarily would be described as the "official and his wife" even if she continued her official functions. As Wiesner-Hanks concludes, the definition of women's work was not just a function of economic factors, but also reflected gender ideology.

The period from 1500 to 1650 is one of major economic change in Europe, change usually described as "the commercial revolution" or "the advent of capitalism." In the Middle Ages production of goods went on in towns and cities for local use. Other than a few luxury items such as spices and silk, goods were rarely shipped further than a few miles. In the cities, production of most items was carried out by craft guilds, which regulated the price and quality of manufactured items and limited the amount each workshop could make. Workshops were small, usually including no more than the master craftsman and his wife and children, one or two journeymen, and one or two apprentices.

Very gradually, however, these highly localized city economies became part of an international trading network. Merchants and bankers began to buy manufactured goods to be shipped long distances and engaged workshops to produce articles for the international market. They resented the limitations imposed by the guilds and often hired rural households to produce for them, particularly in the making of cloth and clothing. In some cities the guilds were not very strong, and so urban households as well as rural ones became part of the domestic industrial system.

The impact of these changes on the economy, on politics, on social classes, and on work itself has been analyzed and argued over for decades, and the rise of capitalism viewed as both a positive and negative development. Almost all of these discussions have focused on men, however, often without realizing it. The merchant-capitalists were men, most of the guild masters were men, as were most of the journeymen. Did the commercial revolution also affect women? Indeed, it did profoundly, changing the kinds of work opportunities available to women and ultimately transforming the functions of the family as well, as women, men, and children began to receive individual wages for their work, rather than producing goods as a family. But were economic factors the sole determinants of women's work choices?

In order to explore how women's lives were affected by the changing city economy, we will first look at the employment opportunities available to them in the traditional guild system, the system that prevailed in most parts of western Europe in 1500. Then we can examine the women's role in the new, capitalist cottage industries. We must also consider occupations that were not greatly affected by the development of capitalism, such as domestic service, hospital work, and retail sales, for these employed a great many women. I will be taking most of my examples from the cities of southern Germany, for these cities, which had well-organized guilds, provided great opportunities for merchant-investors, and had a wide range of service occupations available for women. They are also cities that have extensive records for the early modern period, which is important because it is much more difficult to find information about working women than about working men.

With the exception of a few female guilds in Cologne, Basel, Paris, and several other French cities, the guilds were male organizations, and their structure followed the male life cycle. A boy became an apprentice at about age ten to thirteen, and learned the craft for a set number of years, beginning with very simple tasks and working up to more complicated ones. When the master-craftsman for whom he worked felt he had mastered the skills needed, the boy received his apprenticeship papers and became a journeyman, working in the shops of several different masters for several years. When he had perfected his skills, he could apply to a guild in a town to become a master-craftsman. If the guild members determined there was enough demand for their product to allow another shop, they let the young man make his masterpiece; if this was judged worthy of acceptance, he paid a fee and could open his own workshop and take on apprentices and journeymen. The boys and young men who were apprentices and journeymen generally lived with the master-craftsman and his family, often in a house attached to the workshop.

Girls and women fit into the guild system in a much more informal way. In the high middle ages (the twelfth and thirteenth centuries) girls had been taken on as apprentices in some craft guilds, especially those which required delicate work and great manual dexterity, but by the late Middle Ages (fourteenth and fifteenth centuries) they no longer were formally accepted as apprentices. Generally there was not any specific prohibition against female apprentices, but references to them simply disappear from the records.

This did not mean, however, that there were no longer any women working in guild shops. The daughters of a master-craftsman could learn their father's trade alongside his journeymen and apprentices. Some master-craftsmen went so far as to adopt a number of young women so that they could have more workers in their shops. Master-craftsmen also hired women as maids and pieceworkers to do simple tasks like polishing, packing, and cleaning.

The most important woman in any shop was the master's wife. The guilds recognized how important she was, for they required that every master-craftsman be married. She had to feed and clothe not only her own family but also the apprentices, journeymen and any domestic servants that lived in. She also worked in the shop and often sold the products her husband had made, either from the shop or from a stand at the city marketplace. She was often responsible for keeping records and collecting debts and for purchasing raw materials. If her husband was away, she ran the shop in his absence, directing the journeymen and apprentices.

Because the master-craftsman's wife was familiar with everything involved in running the shop, she was generally allowed to continue the shop after her husband died. Masters' widows in many towns ran breweries, printing presses, bakeries, brickyards, and other shops for years after the death of their husbands. Workshops run by widows often made up as much as ten to fifteen percent in some crafts. City governments were willing to let widows continue in business, for this meant the family would be self-supporting and not need public financial assistance. Widows paid all guild fees, but they could not take part in the leadership of any guild, for they were women and had not made a masterpiece themselves. If a journeyman married a widow, he was usually charged a much lower fee to enter the guild, which made widows very attractive marriage partners. Marrying a widow also provided the journeyman with a fully equipped shop, and a wife who was experienced in production and sales, which made her even more attractive.

Thus there were girls and women working in many capacities in guild shops, but their ability to do so was not officially recognized or discussed in guild ordinances, except for that of masters' widows. Girls did not go through a formal apprenticeship, so their work in the guilds depended on their relationship to a guild master, not on their own level of training. A woman's work in the guilds changed when her status changed from daughter to wife to widow and followed the female life cycle. Because these changes—marriage, the death of a spouse, remarriage, the birth of children who needed care—happened at different points in each woman's life, women generally did not develop a strong sense of kinship with other women of their age group. Women frequently switched occupations on remarriage, carrying their skills at buying and selling with them and learning to make a new product; this kept them from developing a strong sense of occupational identity as well, unlike male craftsmen who stayed in one guild their whole lives.

Specific restrictions on women's work in the guilds began in the fifteenth century in southern Germany, with the first limitations those on widows' rights. The time a widow was allowed to keep operating a shop after her husband's death was limited, often to as little as three months. Frequently she could not hire any new apprentices or journeymen, or even keep the ones she had. In some cases, she was able to keep working only if she had a son who could inherit the shop. Tax records indicate that widows usually had the poorest households in the city, for with no apprentices or journeymen, they could not produce enough to escape poverty.

Along with restrictions on widows' work, other limitations of women's work in the guilds began in the sixteenth century. Under the pressure of commercial capitalism, guilds saw their markets shrinking and one response was to limit women's productive roles in goods manufacture. Masters were no longer allowed to hire female maids and pieceworkers, and even the number of their own daughters that they could employ in a shop was limited. Women were not taught new processes of production in crafts like brewing, bleaching, and dyeing, or allowed to use new tools or machinery, such as frames for knitting stockings or ribbon looms, so they could not work as fast or as efficiently as men.

Because women's participation in guild shops was not guaranteed by guild regulations and ordinances, and because widows had no political voice in running the guilds, women as a group were not able to protect their right to work. Individual women, especially widows, often requested that they be allowed to work despite the restrictions, appealing to the city council or other municipal authorities by stressing their poverty, old age, or number of dependent children and praising the mercy and "Christian charity" of the authorities. These requests were often successful, for city authorities felt it was "always better for someone to work than to receive public charity"; they never allowed women as a group to continue working, however, but limited the permission to the woman making the request. Thus authorities increasingly came to view women's work as a substitute for charity, and were suspicious of women who were too successful or were not needy enough.

As the opportunities for women in the guilds decreased, those in the new domestic industries increased, particularly in cloth production. Early modern techniques of cloth production necessitated at least twenty carders and spinners per weaver, so that cloth centers like Augsburg, Ulm, or Strasbourg could keep many urban and rural women employed. The women picked up their raw wool to be carded or carded wool to be spun from a cloth merchant, and were carefully checked when they brought it back to make sure they had not substituted inferior wool or wet the yarn to make it heavier, for they were paid by the weight of the yarn. So many women turned to spinning to supplement agricultural income, augment their husband's meager wages, or support themselves if they were not married (which is why in English an old unmarried woman is called a "spinster"), that wages were kept low.

Spinners could rarely support a family on their wages, and in some cases could not even support themselves. Nevertheless, spinning was seen as an essential part of being a woman. Women were expected to keep spinning when they were in jail, in the hospital, or had even lost a hand or foot.

No other occupation became quite as identified with women as spinning, but women worked in many other types of domestic production. In cities where weavers were hired by capitalist investors, women as well as men wove, although in cities where weavers were a strong independent craft, guild women were forbidden to weave or allowed to weave only coarse cloth for dishtowels and veils. Sewing and seamstressing were seen as proper female occupations, and wealthy women established small endowments to teach poor girls to become seamstresses. Along with cloth and clothing, women also made cheap, simple items such as brushes, combs, candles, soap, thimbles, brooms, needles and pins, wooden bowls and spoons. Such products required little training and no expensive raw materials, and could be sold locally or traded long distances. They had never been regulated by guilds and were free for anyone to make; men working in their spare time after their first job was over for the day, and women working as much as their family responsibilities permitted. Because these small items were not highly profitable and could be made by a woman working alone, the women making them were not seen as a threat to anyone's economic well-being or social status.

Despite their low wages and low social status, women involved in domestic industry were viewed somewhat suspiciously if they were not married or did not live in a male-headed household. This suspicion of masterless persons, both female and male, was evident throughout Europe during the early modern period. As more people worked for wages in their own homes or as day laborers in a shop, they were no longer part of a household headed by an older, male master-craftsman, as young people had been earlier when they were primarily maids, apprentices, and journeymen. Though their wages were low and their ability to support themselves precarious, they did have more freedom now to move from place to place, to congregate with others of their own age, to discuss religion and politics, to compare employers and experiences—all of which city and state authorities viewed with great alarm. Governments began to pass harsher laws against vagrancy and begging and ordered young people, especially women, to live in households that were headed by an older male relative or employer. Such laws were never very effective, however, because the number of young women was simply too great, and, as the Augsburg spinners commented, they were not so dumb as to work as spin-maids for the weavers when they could earn three times as much spinning on their own.

Even though they were unsuccessful, these attempts to force young women into male-headed households point out that the kind of work women did at any particular point was not dependent on economic factors alone. As the economy changed, authorities feared a breakdown in public order and tried to force people back into patriarchal households. This fear combined with religious ideas that marriage was the "natural" vocation for women—for all women in Protestant areas and for most women in Catholic areas—and with popular and scholarly notions about women's weaker nature and proper subservient role. All of these together meant an increase in hostility toward unmarried women, a hostility which may have played a role in the upsurge of witchcraft accusations and trials (see overview, Part I).

In terms of women's work, this suspicion of unmarried women led authorities to view their work always as temporary, just a stop-gap until the woman could attain her "natural," married state. This helped to keep women's wages low, which was also justified as a way of getting women back into male-headed households. It may have actually had the opposite effect, for women's low wages meant they were more attractive as wage- or pieceworkers than men, and their living independently meant the merchant-investor did not have to worry about feeding or clothing them.

It is tempting to look at this ever-increasing employment in the new capitalist industries as a victory for working women, for it was not dependent on their marital status or relationship to a master-craftsman. If we look at what this actually meant for women, however, we find a somewhat bleaker picture. In 1500, many women had been essential parts of household workshops, their status recognized by the community, with some authority over journeymen and apprentices as well as maids and children. By 1650, masters' wives and widows could no longer have an active role in production. The women who worked received lower wages than did men for similar work and had no supervisory authority. Their wages were so low they often had to work twelve to sixteen hours a day to support themselves and take whatever work was available, particularly if they had a family to support. Freedom to live and work independently also meant freedom to starve. The economic need for cheap labor and the values of public order and the patriarchal household all worked together to keep women's wages low, whether the woman was an independent spinner, a widowed pinmaker with a family to support, or half a married couple who wove for a merchant-investor.

So far we have been looking at one area of the economy—production—in which there were great changes during the early modern period. When we turn to other occupations in which there were a large number of women working, we find less dramatic changes. If we want an accurate picture of the entire spectrum of women's work, however, we must also look at these other occupations.

Domestic service was perhaps the largest employer of women throughout the period. It was a stage in life for many women, until they had reached the age of marriage and had earned a small dowry. A girl might leave her own home when she was as young as seven or eight to become a servant, sometimes in the home of a relative, but more likely in the household of a complete stranger. She might find employment in her own town, or travel to a nearby city where households were larger and employed more servants. Because most Europeans married quite late, often waiting until they were twenty-five or thirty, her career as a servant might be as long as twenty years before marriage.

Service was also a lifelong occupation for many women, who worked their way up in a large urban household from scullery maid to children's maid to chambermaid or cook, or more likely remained with a family as its single servant their whole lives. Employers often left things to their servants and maids when they drew up their wills, with comments such as "for her forty years of devoted service and care for my children." Servants were rarely paid more than room and board, so these gifts from employers were a welcome treat, as inventories taken at the death of maids indicate they usually owned no more than the clothes in which they were buried.

A young girl looking for her first position often depended on her older siblings or relatives to find one for her, or she might simply go house-to-house. In some parts of Europe there were hiring fairs at one or two specific times a year, where employers and servants could come together to find each other. Some cities in Germany also had licensed employment agents to whom a girl or boy could go to find what positions were available. These employment agents were generally older women, the wives or widows of craftsmen or city officials who possessed a good knowledge of the households in their neighborhood. They were paid both by the servant and by the employer and were expected to follow certain rules—not take gifts or bribes, or house any servants themselves or store their trunks, which might contain stolen goods.

The increasing suspicion of masterless persons in early modern Europe led to various laws regulating the conduct of maids and servants. They were not to change positions more than once a year or stay in a public inn between posts. They were not to speak out against any employer or leave a position unless they could prove an employer had mistreated them. They were not to wear fancy clothing or demand wages along with their room and board. These laws appear quite strict, but their effectiveness is doubtful, for they were repeated year after year in many cities, which is a good indication they were consistently being broken.

Despite problems people had with servants, domestic service was viewed as the most acceptable occupation for a young woman. She lived with her employer, who was responsible for her behavior and activities. Cities also legislated the conduct of employers; they were not to treat servants too harshly, but were to be sure they acted "decently, modestly, and industriously," and did not behave in a "disobedient, contrary, untrue or otherwise inappropriate manner." The advantages of service for a young woman were the security it offered, the training in running a household, and the opportunity to meet other young people, particularly if she worked in a large urban household. As opportunities for women in other occupations decreased, those in domestic service remained the same or increased as larger household staffs became more fashionable and maids were used for production-related tasks such as spinning. Despite the disadvantages, such as the lack of independence and low salary, a greater share of the women who worked outside their own homes were domestic servants in 1650 than in 1500.

Along with domestic service there were a number of other service occupations that provided employment for women throughout the period. Many of these were viewed as extensions of a woman's functions and tasks in the home—cleaning, cooking, caring for children and old people, nursing the sick. They often required no training beyond what a girl learned from her mother, and were generally poorly paid and had low status. Despite this, because a woman could work or not work as her financial situation or family responsibilities changed, they remained practical employment options for women who had no specialized skills.

Medical institutions such as hospitals, pest-houses, infirmaries, and orphanages employed women in a variety of ways. The day-to-day operations of many hospitals were handled by a hospital-mistress or keeper, who was responsible for the physical needs of the hospital and patients. She handled all purchases and payments, oversaw the kitchen, led the patients in prayer, and also examined patients when they were admitted and on a regular basis.

This diagnostic function might surprise us, as hospital keepers had no medical training, but hospitals in early modern cities were very different than modern hospitals. They were not refuges for people with contagious diseases, who were sent to small infirmaries or pest-houses outside the city walls. The hospitals themselves were for the infirm elderly, people with chronic, noncontagious diseases, poor expectant mothers, the handicapped, people recovering from injuries, foundling children, and mentally retarded or psychologically disturbed children or adults. It was important that those with contagious diseases be kept out of the hospitals so that the disease did not spread to those already weakened by injury or old age. Because the hospital keeper oversaw all patient admissions, it was her responsibility to prevent those with typhus, typhoid, leprosy, cholera, bubonic plague, or similar diseases from being admitted.

The hospital keeper was assisted by other women hired as cooks, nurses, laundresses, and children's maids, and men hired as shepherds, nurses, and servants. Very large hospitals also had a male hospital keeper. During the early modern period many cities combined smaller hospitals into one large hospital so that the city council would have more control over the hospital's policies and administration. They also secularized many institutions, taking them over from the church. Every employee, from the hospital keeper down to the goosegirls and shepherds, had to swear an oath of loyalty and promise to perform his or her job "faithfully and truly."

Women also cared for those with contagious diseases in the small pest-houses and infirmaries. Most of these institutions were opened only when an epidemic moved through the area and closed again when the disease had passed. Very little could be done for such patients except to keep them clean and fed. Physicians would rarely enter a pest-house, for they were afraid of catching the disease, though this was perhaps a blessing in disguise, for their only treatment of such illnesses was to bleed the patients, which only made them weaker.

In addition to their work in medical institutions women also worked independently as medical practitioners and as midwives, although growing professionalism increasingly pushed women out of practicing medicine. This professionalism also affected other service occupations. Older women traditionally ran small primary schools in their own homes, teaching young children to read; but during the sixteenth century they were forbidden to teach boys, for now this was only to be done by the official city schoolmaster. (This was an economic issue as well, for the schoolmaster was paid per pupil, and so lost money when female teachers "stole" pupils away from him.) During the medieval period couples had often shared positions as minor city officials, such as toll collectors, grain inspectors, and gatekeepers, with both husband and wife taking the oath and receiving a joint salary. Gradually the women's names disappeared from the records, as these minor city officials tried to emulate the higher officials, like notaries, lawyers, and judges. These higher positions all required university or professional training, and so were closed to women; gradually the lower positions were closed to them as well, even though no special training was required. In fact, the wife of a gatekeeper or toll collector kept on sharing her husband's work, but she was no longer considered an official in her own right.

Women had also been appraisers, for most cities required an inventory and appraisal of all property and goods whenever someone died or property was being divided. They appraised the value of everything from houses and fields to dishtowels and spoons, often writing up the list themselves. Thus these women were literate and knew the market value of every kind of household item. During the sixteenth century, however, cities began to require specific legal language in inventories, which was difficult for women who could not receive formal legal education. Appraisers gradually became city officials which meant women were excluded.

We might expect that the growth of merchant capitalism would have a great impact on women's work in sales, but this was not the case. Almost all long-distance merchants and traders in the Middle Ages had been men, and the merchant-capitalists who invested in production for the international market were also men. Carrying out long-distance trade required financial resources that were unavailable to most women, as well as freedom to travel that was limited for women both by family responsibilities and by the lack of places for female travelers to stay. Unaccompanied female travelers were often suspected of being prostitutes or thieves and some cities specifically forbade inns to take them in.

Though women were not active participants in the rise of international commerce, they continued to dominate retail sales in every city. The city marketplace, the economic as well as geographic center of most cities, was filled with women. They sold fruits and vegetables that had been grown locally; mushrooms, berries, and herbs they had gathered in the woods surrounding the city, oranges and spices brought into the city by long-distance merchants. Farmers' wives sold eggs, milk, butter, and cheese; fishermen's wives fresh and salted fish; hunters' wives game and fowl. Female brandy makers had their stands, as did sauerkraut makers, sausage makers, and pretzel bakers. Poor women sold simple wooden implements, cookies, candles, and soap, for which they had received permission from the city council, to keep them from needing public charity. Pawnbrokers sold used clothing and household articles, and female money-changers exchanged travelers' money for that which was accepted in the city. Because there was no way to preserve food easily, women had to shop every day, and the marketplace was where they met their neighbors, exchanged information, and talked over recent events.

Every city had laws that regulated what went on at the marketplace, but, unlike the guild regulations, these did not differentiate between women and men. Everyone who sold at the market was ordered to use correct weights and measures and to sell things at an appropriate price. No one was to sell stolen goods, booty received from soldiers, or merchandise that came into the city from areas suffering from the plague or other epidemics. City inspectors dumped out milk that had been mixed with chalk water, confiscated bread found to be "too coarse and rough," or ordered "stinking dead goose-bellies" taken out of the city whether the seller was a woman or a man. Husbands and wives often shared an occupation in food production, like butchering or baking, and both could be hauled into court and fined if something was wrong with their products or sales techniques. These occupations were organized into guilds, which unlike manufacturing guilds did not feel pressure from capitalist investors; food production remained local and small-scale, and masters' wives, widows, and daughters continued to be active workers in these shops.

In addition to selling at the marketplace, women also ran small retail establishments throughout the city. They made beer, mead, and hard cider, and ran taverns to dispense their beverages. They operated small inns and sleeping-houses for
poor people who could not pay to stay in the more expensive larger inns. They
pickled and smoked meat, washed innards and prepared tripe, working in their own
kitchens and selling from the market or directly from their home. Women also sold
food and other items house-to-house, carrying baskets and trays, though city governments tried to limit or prohibit this because it allowed questionable merchandise
to be sold more easily.

Women continued to play an important role in retail sales throughout the early
modern period. There was little opposition to them for economic or status reasons
because these were not high-paying, high-status occupations. During the late sixteenth century, however, the increasing suspicion of masterless persons and unmarried women did lead several cities to try to limit retail sales to widows and married women. "Young female persons who could easily do some other kind of work,
like being a maid," were ordered to quit selling but the law was difficult to enforce.
Whether it was enforced or not, though, it does point out again the mistrust of young
unmarried women working independently.

In conclusion, we have discovered that women's work was affected by concerns about status, worries about public order and propriety, and ideas about
women's nature and proper role. Economic and ideological factors together combined to determine which occupations would be closed, remain open, or offer
increased employment to women. Occupations that required formal education, large
initial capital, or extensive traveling were closed to women, either by explicit prohibition, legal restrictions, custom, or the impossibility of combining such occupations with family responsibilities. Women worked at jobs that required few tools,
short training or none at all, and limited supervisory duties—jobs that were poorly
paid and could be done part-time. They changed occupations much more frequently
than men and moved in and out of the labor force as their individual and family
needs changed. Because women often fitted their work around the life cycle of their
families, moving in and out of jobs as children were born and grew up or as their
husbands died and they remarried, they had to take whatever low-skilled, low-pay-
ing jobs were available. In fact, because women worked in the kinds of occupations they did, even major economic changes may not have made much of a difference in their actual experience. The working conditions of a spinner did not
change very much when the cloth industry changed from guild control to capitalist. We must always be careful of assuming that change affected women in the same
way it affected men.

Despite the increasing restrictions in many occupations and the low status and
low pay of most jobs open to them, women continued to work. They were much
less likely than men to worry about issues of status. Supporting themselves and
their families was their primary concern, and they were willing to use any arguments necessary to be allowed to continue working. Unfortunately for the long run,
the arguments that were successful stressed the stop-gap, temporary, emergency
nature of their work, that they should be allowed to work because of the authori-

ties' pity and charity, rather than that they had a right to work. Such arguments were successful in the short run, for these women continued to work, but were ultimately harmful as they devalued women's work, thus contributing to the idea that "women's work" was always less important than "men's work." We should not judge these early modern women too harshly, however, for the question for them was one of survival.

Note: Most of the material in this article comes from unprinted manuscripts found in the city archives of Nuremberg, Stuttgart, Strasbourg, Augsburg, Munich, Frankfurt, and Memmingen, the Bavarian state archives in Nuremberg and the Wuerttemberg state archives in Stuttgart. The exact references may be found in my 1986 book, listed in the suggested readings below. The translations are my own.

SUGGESTIONS FOR FURTHER READING

Brown, Judith. "A Woman's Place Was in the Home: Women's Work in Renaissance Tuscany." In *Rewriting the Renaissance: The Discourses of Sexual Difference in Early Modern Europe,* edited by Margaret W. Ferguson, Maureen Quilligan, and Nancy J. Vickers. Chicago: University of Chicago Press, 1986.

Brown, Judith C., and Robert C. Davis, eds. *Gender and Society in Renaissance Italy.* London: Longman, 1998.

Davis, Natalie Zemon. "Women in the Crafts in Sixteenth-Century Lyon." *Feminist Studies* 8 (Spring 1982): 46–80.

Eccles, Audrey. *Obstetrics and Gynecology in Tudor and Stuart England.* Kent, Ohio: Kent State University Press, 1982.

Fairchilds, Cissie. *Servants and Their Masters in Old Regime France.* Baltimore: Johns Hopkins University Press, 1984.

Goldberg, P. J. P. *Women, Work, and Life Cycle in a Medieval Economy: Women in York and Yorkshire c. 1300–1520.* Oxford: Clarendon Press, 1992.

Gullickson, Gay L. *Spinners and Weavers of Auffay: Rural Industry and the Sexual Division of Labor in a French Village, 1750–1850.* Cambridge: Cambridge University Press, 1986.

Hafter, Daryl M., ed. *European Women and Preindustrial Craft.* Bloomington, Ind.: Indiana University Press, 1995.

Hanawalt, Barbara A., ed. *Women and Work in Pre-Industrial Europe.* Bloomington, Ind.: Indiana University Press, 1986.

Howell, Martha. *Women, Production and Patriarchy in Late Medieval Cities.* Chicago: University of Chicago Press, 1986.

Jacobsen, Grethe. "Women's Work and Women's Role: Ideology and Reality in Danish Urban Society, 1300–1550." *Scandinavian Economic History Review* 31, no. 1 (1983): 2–20.

Marland, Hilary, ed. *The Art of Midwifery: Early Modern Midwives in Europe.* London and New York: Routledge, 1993.

Prior, Mary, ed. *Women in English Society, 1500–1800.* London and New York: Methuen, 1985.

Wiesner, Merry E. *Gender, Church and State in Early Modern Germany.* London and New York: Longman, 1997.

————. "Paltry Peddlers or Essential Merchants: Women in the Distributive Trades in Early Modern Nuremberg." *Sixteenth Century Journal* XII, no. 2 (1981): 3–13

————. *Women and Gender in Early Modern Europe.* Cambridge: Cambridge University Press, 1993.

————. *Working Women in Renaissance Germany.* New Brunswick, N.J.: Rutgers University Press, 1986.

Willen, Diane. "Guildswomen in the City of York, 1560–1700." *The Historian* 46, no. 2 (February 1984): 204–218.

CHAPTER FOUR

Communities of Women, the Religious Life, and Public Service in Eighteenth-Century France

Olwen Hufton and Frank Tallett

In the early modern period, it was extremely difficult for women to survive outside the household. As Merry Wiesner-Hanks shows (chapter 3), there was growing hostility to "masterless persons." Olwen Hufton and Frank Tallett look at a group of women who neither married nor lived with their families but who survived by pooling resources and skills and forming what was in essence a substitute family, what Hufton has elsewhere called a "spinster cluster." The nun in Catholic countries has been the subject of relatively little secular historical research. As this chapter demonstrates, research on nuns and sisters successfully combines a number of important themes. One concerns the organization of social and educational support in the early modern period. Women religious provided most of the social services in the past; they staffed the hospitals for the sick, ran charitable institutions providing shelter for the needy, worked in orphanages, and sought to rehabilitate "fallen women." Whatever the degree of female literacy among the popular classes at the end of the old Regime, it was due to the teaching by the women's orders. Second, the Catholic Reformation, with its practical orientation, gave rise to numerous new orders, congregations, and associations for females. As Hufton and Tallett note, women became "the executive arm of the social policy of the Counter-Reformation in spite of the [church] hierarchy, which concerned itself largely with controlling their activities." The older contemplative orders, to which wealthy women paid dowries for the privilege of joining, were on the decline, replaced by a whole range of new, socially oriented congregations. By providing social services, these orders created "challenging careers" for women outside marriage, at a time when alternative opportunities for fulfillment were few and far between. And this is the third theme stressed by the authors. The nun, protected by her habit, faced numerous hardships and challenges. "Such an adventurous and dangerous life was simply not open to a woman on any other terms."

We have three conflicting versions of the nun in traditional French society. One is the particular legacy of the Enlightenment, perhaps best encapsulated in Diderot's

La Religieuse (The Nun), and interprets the nun as the reluctant and unnatural product of parental greed, driven into a useless and possibly immoral life to prevent inroads into the family estate. She is thus cut off from the fulfillment of woman's natural role as wife and mother, and is, as Madame Roland describes, dead to the world. The second version draws upon an ancient hagiographical tradition, reinforced by the immense spiritual flowering during the Counter-Reformation with its attendant rhetoric, of the nun devoted to a life of social as well as spiritual service. This image emerged with particular clarity during the French Revolution. Faced with the abolition of monastic vows and given the possibility of leaving their communities in 1790, a majority of women demonstrated exemplary devotion to their vocation (in stark contrast to the men) and opted to remain under vows. In response to fervent popular demand many stayed at their posts as teachers, nurses, or in orphanages, establishments devoted to the elderly, the poor, or the morally aberrant. There is a third interpretation. This recognizes the nun's social commitment but devalues her services by insisting upon her ignorance and incompetence. This image is founded in the more pragmatic critique generated by doctors and educational and social theorists during the Enlightenment and perpetuated in the nineteenth century by a republican and anticlerical tradition. The doctors were cogent critics. They struggled in the course of the eighteenth century to apply new pharmacological and medical concepts to the treatment of the sick in the hospitals and encountered hostility from the nuns, who controlled funds and had a different interpretation of what was fitting (refusing to permit, for example, the dismemberment of corpses in the cause of medical analysis). Other critics stressed the limited educational content of the nun's teaching work; her emphasis, for example, on Catholic teaching and morality, rather than on useful or civic qualifications. Taken a step further, she was open to the charge of conditioning girls in particular to church dominance and perpetuating superstitious dogma and practice.

Victim, social martyr, ignorant incompetent: imagery of so contradictory a nature needs some explanation. The professional historian has generally given scant attention to the nun, a neglect all the more surprising given the profusion of research on the male clergy in the eighteenth century. This short study is intended to highlight issues which need consideration, to point to some general trends, and to suggest where further work needs to be done if we are to have an impartial assessment of the nun. An appreciation of her services is critical to an understanding of women's roles in traditional societies, and also to any attempt to highlight elements of continuity in professional organization into the contemporary period. Even in twentieth-century Britain the vocabulary of nursing, with "sisters" in starched uniforms ruled by a "matron" redolent of a mother superior, is striking, and this is not surprising given Florence Nightingale's overt emulation of the Daughters of Charity. Moreover, we might reasonably reflect upon the genesis of the lingering conviction that women with time on their hands—single women above all—should give themselves to unremunerated social or charitable work, a conviction that draws upon a deep-rooted tradition of women seeking an outlet in philanthropy and service.

We cannot be certain of the precise number of women who took religious vows in the eighteenth century. An estimate, based on a list of religious pensioners drawn up in 1817, suggests a total of approximately 80,000 regulars and *congréganistes* of both sexes in 1790—26,000 men and 55,000 women. It seems likely, however, that the estimate of 1817 is a chronic underrecording of the situation prevailing on the eve of the Revolution, and fails to take fully into account many who only took "simple" vows and were only loosely attached, or hardly attached at all, to a specific religious house. Nevertheless, the proportion of women to men (70 percent to 30 percent) indicates that more women than men sought a religious life in the eighteenth century. Less perhaps did so than a century before or a century later—by 1878 there were more than 125,000 women religious in France.

Such inadequate statistical material as we have suggests that the women who chose the religious life exercised specific options. There was no single standard nun, but a range of religious vocations, differing over the seventeenth and eighteenth centuries. At one end of the spectrum were the old religious orders, Benedictines, Augustinians, Bernardines, etc., characterized by the fact that the members, though individually committed to poverty, were corporately rich, paid considerable dowries for the privilege of entry (and hence were often aristocratic), swore solemn vows, wore religious dress, and were cloistered. They were primarily dedicated to the contemplative life, and their decline may plausibly be explained by the increasing hostility shown toward a life dedicated merely to prayer by educated elite circles, sensitive to Enlightenment criticism. Even before such criticism became manifest, however, the dynamic thrust of the female vocation was toward a religious life with a more clearly defined practical role. The Counter-Reformation, which reached its fullest flowering in France in the seventeenth century, gave rise to a spate of foundations with well-delineated social functions. The Ursulines, for example, founded in Italy in 1535 and introduced into France in the early seventeenth century with the help of Madame de Sainte Beuve, were the Church's oldest teaching order. The Filles de Notre Dame de Charité (Sisters of Our Lady of Charity), founded by Saint Jean Eudes, set themselves to rehabilitate fallen women. The Visitandines were established in 1610 by Saint François de Sales and Sainte Jeanne de Chantal, primarily to visit the sick.

These orders, a few of many, had a number of common traits. First, they sought to give practical expression to the social philosophy of the Counter-Reformation, which rearticulated the obligation of the Christian individual toward the poor and needy. Second, they owed much to the efforts of a number of extremely wealthy and pious widows who brought financial means, influence, and dedication, which provided the dynamic for establishment and expansion. Pauline teaching, which urged chastity and good works upon the widow, was reemphasized, and a series of cogent spiritual directors gave guidance to this reservoir of widow-power. These new establishments became magnets attracting a spectrum of educated and wealthy women, the daughters of nobles and financiers, as well as mobilizing others of less elevated social status for more menial services. To read Gueudré's account of the Ursulines, given the task of rearing generations of aristocratic girls in the Catholic faith, rescuing the daughters of newly converted fathers whose mothers remained attached to Protestantism, and of spreading Catholic education for girls to Canada, is to comprehend how challenging a career was offered to the nun, who, protected by her habit, faced innumerable hardships and challenges. Such an adventurous and dangerous life was simply not open to a woman on any other terms.

Yet the Ursulines, the Filles de Notre Dame de Charité, and the Visitandines were all to become monastic orders proper, with enclosure, the veil, and solemn vows, thus limiting their untrammeled powers of initiative for work in the community. The papacy and the episcopal hierarchy had a long tradition of hostility toward the uncontrolled presence of large numbers of women (and of men) circulating freely in the community, immune from control. Enclosure and a "rule" (code of discipline) resolved this dilemma. It had also some positive advantages. Institutionalization meant the perpetuation of the house, even when the individual initiative flagged, and establishment could attract funding and contribute to an *esprit de corps*. But the disadvantages were also apparent. The Visitandines, who tried to resist claustration, appreciated that they would be cut off from society. For the Ursulines, it meant restricting most of their teaching functions to boarders who had to pay for the privilege, though many of the houses used the funding from the school fees paid by the nobility to finance the teaching of selected poor girls. Above all, enclosure meant a certain loss of spontaneity, and a rule entailed ossifying in a certain mold.

The Ursulines and the Visitandines perhaps failed to escape conversion into enclosed orders because of their sheer size, which frightened the Catholic hierarchy. Indeed, it is tempting to posit that women became the executive arm of the social policy of the Counter-Reformation *in spite of* the hierarchy, which concerned itself largely with controlling their activities. Yet once enclosed, their numbers began to decline. Women looked elsewhere for a fulfilling practical life outside marriage. The trend in the seventeenth and early eighteenth centuries was toward the establishment of congregations (religious societies without permanent vows) rather than orders. Most of them were very small and their influence was circumscribed within certain localities. An exception in size, extent, and influence were the Filles de la Charité (Sisters of Charity), founded by Saint Vincent de Paul and a widow, Louise de Marillac. Vincent de Paul was insistent that he had not founded a religious order. "Your convent will be the house of the sick," he told the sisters, "your cell a hired room, your chapel the parish church, your cloister the city streets or the hospital wards, your enclosure obedience, your grill the fear of God, your veil modesty." Their function was to go into the villages and make domiciliary visits to the sick and poor, administer soup kitchens, care for the orphaned, prisoners, and wounded soldiers. In exchange for food, lodgings, care, and attention for themselves in illness and good treatment in old age, they contracted to serve in the *hôpitaux généraux* and *hôtels Dieu* (hospitals for the poor) and charitable institutions founded by ecclesiastics or municipalities. Known as *soeurs* (sisters) rather than *religieuses* (nuns), they swore only simple vows, which were renewed annually, and in the beginning had no distinctive dress. As Saint Vincent had intended, the harshness of the work attracted good village girls, rather than aristocratic women, and although dowries were later asked when the girls took their vows, they were modest enough to ensure wide entry.

The Counter-Reformation also produced confraternities of pious lay folk (of both sexes), many of them of solid social standing, dedicated to practical as well as spiritual ends. The Dames de la Charité (Ladies of Charity), for example, existed in many towns and larger parishes and had complemented, though they were no substitute for, the work of the Filles de la Charité. They visited needy families and distributed, possibly on no more than an annual basis, such scant relief funds as a parish possessed, or perhaps no more than cast-off clothing; or, they might help the daughter of a poor family to find a job in service. The women involved were sometimes married, were often widowed, with some social conscience, prepared to give a restricted number of hours per month to charitable endeavor, rather than dedicate their lives to the same. One of these associations, in the city of Besançon (see Figure 1), existed to provide layettes for poor mothers expecting babies and to give them some assistance in the months after the birth, when their earning power might be reduced by their physical debility and restrictions imposed by breast-feeding a baby. This association had a continuous history through the ancien régime, the Revolution, and the nineteenth century. Yet such associations have almost entirely escaped the historian's attention.

It is difficult to summarize in a few short paragraphs the extent of the services proferred to society by women in the various branches of the religious life. The type of work can be subsumed under short headings: health (work in the hospitals and domiciliary assistance in the form of food and medicaments); institutional relief for the orphaned and the aged poor; education, extending to girls of all classes and village boys as well; social welfare, embracing categories as diverse as informal soup kitchens in time of harvest failure and associations to rescue young prostitutes from a life of vice; services to promote community or individual self-sufficiency, which might range from pioneering industrial enterprises such as spinning schools to providing crèche-type services for working mothers. Such a list must also include miscellaneous enterprises, such as ancillary prison services, or running sheltered accommodation for genteel widow geriatrics who could afford to pay. To get an idea of the quality and importance of the work involved we shall have recourse to a number of specific examples: the nursing sister in an *hôtel Dieu;* the teacher in a parish school; the *béate* (devotée) in Le Puy and the villages of the Velay helping the lacemaker to live on pitiful wages; and the quasi-industrial, even "entrepreneurial," nun who responded as her group saw fit to local problems.

The *hôtel Dieu* was a hospital intended for the sick whose family could not provide care. Many were founded in the Middle Ages and were the precursors of the modern hospital. If *hôtels Dieu* and *hôpitaux généraux* are taken together there may have been far more than two thousand of them in 1789; certainly well over 100,000 people were hospitalized. Some catered to a mere handful of people, others to eighty to a hundred at any one time. In the course of the seventeenth century many *hôtels Dieu* were substantially overhauled, and as part of that process, the administrators or municipalities who had, or who gained control of them, invited or contracted with one of the new orders to fulfill nursing and (to a greater or lesser extent) administrative functions. The Filles de la Charité were often the first recourse of the hospital authorities unless there was a local alternative—though sometimes there were simply too few sisters to respond effectively. Hence, the Soeurs de Saint Charles de Nancy (est. 1652), or the Soeurs de Saint Thomas de Villeneuve (est. 1661), the Soeurs Hospitalières de Saint Joseph de Puy (est. 1686 and most common south of the Loire), or the Soeurs Chrétiennes de Nevers and innumerable other local groups might be called upon. The agreement between the sisters and the inviting administrators, often in formal contract, generally laid down provisions for

Figure 1. France in 1789

the upkeep of the women and conditions of entry into the institution, as well as the extent of their authority over all personnel and internees. Usually, the invitation recognized that the sisters were coming to introduce order and authority into the institution, and although some administrators sought to keep some control over financial matters, generally they were prepared to cede financial autonomy and management of the funds and scope of activities to the women.

The sisters had to be guaranteed food, warmth, and clothing. By 1789, an annual payment of 150 *livres* per head was reckoned for their subsistence, which ensured modest comfort. The insane, those suffering from incurable, recognizably contagious, or infamous disease (by which was meant sexually transmissible) were excluded from the *hôtels Dieu*. There was an element of sense in such provision.

The sisters were small in number and operating in a limited, sometimes medieval building, which would have made treatment of the violent mentally ill impossible. Contagious disease would have decimated sisters and patients alike, though a closer examination of what was understood by contagious reveals that whereas plague and smallpox victims were excluded from the institution, tuberculosis, typhus, typhoid, scabies, dysentery, and enteric fevers were accepted. The exclusion of venereal disease was on the grounds that the integrity, both of the institution and its personnel, needed to be preserved. Saint Vincent placed emphasis on the need to admit the indigent sick in which the condition of poverty was a substantial determinant. The sisters, however, were the arbiters of who should be admitted, and they gave a practical interpretation to the notion of poverty. They saw as eligible anyone who was not resident in his or her own home, for example, the migrant laborer en route to or from his place of seasonal work struck down with sunstroke, or the Lyonnais silk worker with tuberculosis. Such people were not without resources, but they were in conditions that precluded care. The rules applied more closely to the old with a terminal condition, requiring assistance beyond that which an *hôpital général* could give. Sometimes the nuns had to have an eye to the funds. Taking in sick or wounded (but not syphilitic) soldiers commanded fees from the war ministry. On the other hand, some of the *hôtels Dieu* had to receive foundlings, and the expense of these grew with the increased frequency of abandonment.

Once the patient had been admitted, diagnosis, surgery, and some treatment was the sphere of a surgeon, and sometimes a doctor, who were both paid fees for their services. Care, feeding, and medication were usually in the hands of the nursing staff. The pharmacy, its contents, and the mixing of medicines was one of the areas of contention between these medical men, intent on what they interpreted as medical progress, and the sisters. The latter were not trained in pharmacology nor to any extent were the doctors and surgeons. What the sisters disposed of was traditional lore that passed as a pharmacopeia: a limited range of medications, and a yet more limited budget. They had little faith in the power of medicine alone to cure, and in their thinking it ranked behind nourishment, rest, prayer, and cleanliness. Certainly they were not prepared to sacrifice the quality of their beef-tea to finance mere drugs. Indeed, the pharmacy-nun at the *Hôtel Dieu* of Saint Brieuc, an institution deeply in debt, believed that the first economy to be introduced to save the hospital was the abolition of all medication save rhubarb, a suggestion that looks more sensible if we take into account the other drugs at their disposal. They resented the doctors' assertions that they overfed patients. Fashionable medical thought believed the sick should be on a strict regimen, and deemed the seven cups of beef-tea provided by the sisters to be "overfeeding." Given the weakened physical state of some of the patients, and the need of those with dysentery and typhoid for salted sustenance to prevent dehydration, it is difficult to accept the case of the medical men in this instance. However, it is undeniable that the sisters did stand in the way of autopsies, and hence the advancement of knowledge, in some of the larger hospitals. Their vision of the dying man was that of a soul preparing itself for immortality and needing an intact body, a belief they shared with at least 90 percent of the population.

The nursing sister was but one role of the nun in eighteenth-century France. Many of the women's orders, congregations, and associations were concerned in some way with education, though what was understood by this term varied considerably. At the end of the ancien régime it is calculated that about 35 percent of French women could sign their own names. There was a considerable difference, however, between female literacy rates north of the Saint Malo-Geneva line and those below, with the highest levels found in Flanders and parts of northeastern France. The ability to read, however, is unmeasurable and it is generally, if speculatively, assumed that more could do so than could write. More positively, we can make two observations. First, whatever the degree of female literacy, it was largely achieved through the teaching of the women's orders. Second, much teaching, to a broad social spectrum, concentrated not on literacy, but on skills that could generate self-sufficiency such as spinning, sewing, lacemaking and embroidery, along with knowledge of the catechism to allow the girl in question to resist heresy. Hence, the teaching orders could have more extensive impact than a consideration of pure literacy skills would suggest. Orders such as the Ursulines and local congregations ran boarding schools for the daughters of the social elite. However, on closer examination such fees as were paid by wealthy families were used for a less elevated tier of schooling, aimed at teaching poor girls to read and perhaps to write, but above all to work. A poor girl fortunate enough to be received into one of these establishments came by a limited educational package but acquired skills that were equivalent to an apprenticeship. Paradoxically perhaps, the Enlightenment's views on the education of the poor concentrated on the purely vocational and deemed literacy an unnecessary, even dangerous, extra, and hence accorded well with the intentions of many of these religious associations. The point of contrast was the emphasis given by the nuns to purely spiritual considerations.

Many of the houses of the religious congregations, which had a dual educational and charitable purpose, had original, local, and particular features that almost preclude generalization. Take, for example, the house of the Sisters of Charity at Bayeux. Invited to Bayeux in 1650 by the bishop to help care for the domiciled sick, to distribute relief during years of hardship, and to mobilize the wealthy women of the town to organize soup kitchens when food was scarce, the entrepreneurial activity of the next two generations of sisters proved quite remarkable. By the mid-eighteenth century they had introduced onto their premises or in hired adjacent buildings, the manufacture of soap, cloth, and lace. In the production of the first two items they could undercut any merchant in town. The profits allowed them to keep forty young girls of poor parentage between the ages of ten and seventeen, and to engage a further forty-five people in their miscellaneous productions and to help poor families with shoes for their children. Their enterprises flourished until the aftermath of the Seven Years' War (1756–63), when the demands of inflated numbers of poor, a slump in lace production, and the debts arising from building a small chapel saw them in financial difficulties. However, sanctioned in the sale of a little property by the Intendant, they survived and by 1789 expenditures and receipts just about balanced.

More modest, yet equally effective, were the *béates*. The *béate* of the Velay represents one of the most original manifestations of Counter-Reformation enterprise. She was one of a limited number of women, enjoying no communal life and taking no vows, who dedicated themselves to fulfilling the economic needs of an entire job sector, those who worked in the lace industry. The idea was that of a widow, Anne Marie Martel, who in 1665, with the encouragement of the Bishop of Le Puy, set herself to gather and train women to meet the peculiar requirements of lacemaking.

While being a highly skilled craft, taking many years to acquire and perfect, the remuneration of the lacemaker was slight. The young girl of the Velay, a region with little other absorption for its woman-power, who took to lacemaking, probably could not maintain self-sufficiency during the learning period. Certainly she could not put aside any small profits from her labor that would allow her to accumulate a dowry after ten or more years and with the dowry find a husband. If, however, the girl who came into Le Puy from the country around was given free accommodation in a dormitory, paid only for the costs of her food and shared heating expenses, was helped to market the finished product, and then helped to put aside some of her profits from the sale, something, if perhaps not very much, could be saved. A *béate* was a pious widow or spinster, perhaps an accomplished lacemaker herself, prepared to run such a dormitory (possibly in a building given by pious bequest) and serve as cook and organizing agent. Theoretically independent of the marketing process, which was done through merchants, she could however keep an eye on transactions and advise the girl of the commercial value of her activities.

The *béates* organized themselves to maximize the profits a lacemaker might make. At the invitation of the village community who had to provide a simple, one-roomed dwelling, crowned by a bell, a *béate* would establish herself and organize a daily routine. At the first light of day a bell would arouse the village, and the young children and girls up to the age of twelve would come to the *béate's* house. The service was partly that of a crèche to keep the fingers of the prying toddler away from the mother's lace bobbins. The children, however, were taught their catechism and to sing hymns and the girls were schooled in the first steps in lacemaking. As the natural light receded the children returned home, and after an early evening meal, the bell sounded again and the village lacemakers gathered for a long work session in the *béate's* cottage. Light was provided by sharing the cost of candles placed in reflective globes too expensive for the lacemaker to purchase alone. Heating was usually provided by boxes containing charcoal embers, placed under the skirts at one's feet. This prevented the discoloration of the lace. Each lacemaker contributed a few vegetables or a bit of bread to a communal soup pot, thus providing a kind of late supper. The *béate* had no direct role to play in the economic aspects of the trade. This was carried out by the lacemaker herself, who negotiated with the distributors who were employed by the merchants to visit the villages. However, her services in maximizing potential earning power from lacemaking were widely acknowledged and without these services the plight of many families in this stark, virtually resourceless area would have been bleak indeed. The *béate* did nothing for female literacy, but she did much to foster a work skill, and to instill traditions of piety through chanting hymns and devotions.

Even so cursory an examination of the eighteenth-century nun reveals an immense range of activity and energy. However, while the range of services was impressive, indeed almost boundless, it should not obscure the limitations, in terms of comprehensive coverage of all those in need. The women with whom we are concerned were the executive arm of a particular social philosophy, according to which help to the needy was the responsibility of the individual Christian, intent on securing entry to the kingdom of God. It was not the concern of a coercive state obliging its citizenry to contribute effectively to the succor of the poor. The women were donors of funds, or raisers of money, or givers of time and energy in putting such resources to work. They operated, however, within the restricted confines of voluntary charity that could not, and certainly did not, expand with the demands made upon it. Indeed, magnificent as the principles underlying the social philosophy of the Counter-Reformation undoubtedly were, they were to a considerable extent weakened by demographic movements that broadened the base of the social pyramid more extensively than ever before. The number of those seeking help increased dramatically.

The inadequacy of voluntary charity in the long term to provide any realistic solution to social problems perhaps tended to deter those with the means to give. Enlightenment philosophy certainly deemed the entire notion of private charity as the origin of a group of social parasites, and this critique, too, may have stemmed the flow of bequests upon which many of these religious and philanthropic associations depended. It is perhaps useful to draw an analogy between the efforts and intentions of a Sister of Charity in ancien régime France, and those of Mother Teresa and her associates in modern Calcutta, which are so widely publicized. In individual terms, their efforts were of critical worth. Viewed in more general terms, they were a frail panacea to the problems of poverty, touching only an infinitesimal proportion of those in need. Nevertheless, until the state deemed and proved itself in a position to assume responsibility for social welfare—which presupposed greater economic growth, an increase in state resources, and a simultaneous reduction in the demand factor—they represented all there was to be had in the way of help.

Their efforts, therefore, need to be assessed by criteria other than their impact on France's massive social problems; or put another way, we should recognize that, limited though that impact might be, when the Revolution dispensed with their nursing and welfare services, the loss was keenly felt and bitterly resented. The mayor of Toulouse in 1816 demanded of a protesting crowd whether they would like a return to "the charity of the *philosophes*," thus evoking a period in which the efforts of the religious orders, associations, and voluntary services had been removed. When a number of nuns fled from persecution to London during the Revolution, they were struck by the absence of any association or institution to help poor and orphaned children and promptly set themselves to organize one. The resources they could muster were puny and the effect of their presence on the generality of the deprived young can only have been minimal. When Napoleon reestablished the nursing and teaching sisters in poor houses and girls' schools, he consciously allowed the state to shelter behind their endeavors, minimizing state expenditure and transferring responsibility. The women accepted this because they interpreted their vocation as Christians as the solace of the poor and afflicted. For had God not made the poor the means whereby the wealthy might obtain salvation? The elimination of the problem remained in his hands, not theirs. They were his agents in his absence, and would be judged by what they did with what they had at their disposal, rather than by their total impact upon the situation. Such are the criteria whereby their work should be assessed.

The dismantling of their work by the Revolutionary assemblies, theoretically prepared to assume responsibility of the poor, and the ensuing chaos and dislocation, were to provide the incentive behind the rapid expansion of associations, congregations, and new religious orders characteristic of the nineteenth century. The executive arm of Catholic social policy, with its emphasis on patronal responsibility and Christian duty, again lay with "women religious." Their influence only began to recede as the state provided alternative services, staffed by salaried female nurses and teachers, and as the professionalization of both teaching and medicine gave careers to lay women endowed with qualifications laid down by the state. The process was far from swift or clear-cut and it must not obscure the fact that whether state- or church-organized, women were the personnel, and the notion of vocation remained attached to both teaching and nursing until perhaps the second half of the twentieth century. Only then did the vestigial notion that the teacher and nurse had dedicated their persons to social, not family, obligations, begin finally to disappear.

SUGGESTIONS FOR FURTHER READING

Fairchilds, Cissie. *Poverty and Charity in Aix-en-Provence, 1640–1789.* Baltimore: Johns Hopkins University Press, 1979.

Farmer, David H. *The Oxford Dictionary of Saints.* Oxford: Clarendon Press, 1978.

Gueudré, Marie de Chantal. *Histoire de l'ordre des Ursulines en France* [History of the Ursuline Order]. 2 vols. Paris: Editions Saint-Paul, 1957–1960.

Hufton, Olwen. *Bayeux in the Late Eighteenth Century.* Oxford: Clarendon Press, 1967.

———. *The Poor of Eighteenth-Century France, 1750–1789.* Oxford: Clarendon Press, 1974.

Jones, Colin. *Charity and Bienfaisance: The Treatment of the Poor in the Montpellier Region, 1740–1815.* Cambridge: Cambridge University Press, 1982.

LeGoff, T. J. A. *Vannes and Its Region: A Study of Town and Country in Eighteenth-Century France.* Oxford: Clarendon Press, 1981.

McManners, John. *French Ecclesiastical Society under the Ancien Régime: A Study of Angers in the XVIIIth Century.* Manchester: Manchester University Press, 1960.

CHAPTER FIVE

The "Science" of Embryology Before the Discovery of the Ovum

Maryanne Cline Horowitz

History textbooks rarely include studies of women's biological and physiological role in human reproduction. Yet scientific paradigms help shape fundamental assumptions about women's "nature" and social roles. When Aristotle defined woman as an "infertile male" and declared her "passive" because man contributed the formative influence in reproduction, he established a close link between presumed biological essence and social experience. It is ironic that although women were increasingly defined in terms of their biology, the learned scientific authorities misrepresented women's function in reproduction until the early nineteenth century. Maryanne Horowitz examines the biological controversies in the seventeenth and eighteenth centuries that pitted "spermaticists," who were inspired by Aristotle's views, against "ovists," who attributed generativity to the ovaries. The debates centered on a range of issues. Did females produce semen? Were they a distinct sex or merely imperfect males? What were the means by which the sex of a child was determined?

Drawing on scientific treatises, anatomical illustrations, and instructional manuals of the day, Horowitz analyzes the debate among male scientists during the great era of scientific experimentation. She includes William Harvey, who pioneered research on the human ovum; Anton Leeuwenhoek, whose microscopic studies only confirmed his belief that the sperm was the true source for the embryonic form; and Albrecht von Haller, representative of an opposite, ovist position. Scientific "progress" had to wait until Karl von Baer's discoveries of 1827 and even these were not incorporated into the scientific corpus for twenty-five more years. The lag was so great that well into the nineteenth century Aristotelian views still showed up in vernacular treatises on midwifery. This chapter demonstrates how gender preconceptions intrude into scientific research.

No one knew for certain that the female ovum existed until Karl Ernst von Baer's microscopic studies of 1827. From ancient through early modern times the subject of female contribution to the formation of the embryo in its mother's womb was misrepresented. Aristotle and Galen, whose rival theories of embryology both attributed to the father's seed the major contribution to the characteristics of the offspring, were the dominant authorities on reproduction quoted by theological, philosophical, and medical writers throughout the Middle Ages and Renaissance. The Renaissance publication of the classics and the proliferation of books to a wider and wider readership of men and women expanded public knowledge of the ancient "science" of embryology. Concurrently, the exclusively male scientific community, through animal dissections and experiments, had finally reached a serious intellectual quandary concerning the process of human reproduction. This chapter presents the conflicting scientific hypotheses that preceded von Baer's important discovery of the ovum and the consequent recognition of woman's role in embryonic development.

This debate parallels the well-known "Scientific Revolution" in physics and astronomy, in which the Ptolemaic theory of an earth-centered planetary system was overthrown by the scientists Copernicus, Galileo, Kepler, and Newton. From the sixteenth through the nineteenth centuries, the Aristotelian–Galenic theory of a sperm-centered embryological process, too, was overthrown by scientists investigating the capacities of the female reproductive organs. We shall follow this scientific revolution through its five major stages: the Aristotelian–Galenic tradition, William Harvey (1578–1657), Anton Leeuwenhoek (1632–1723), Albrecht von Haller (1708–77), and Karl Ernst von Baer (1792–1876).

Despite the advancement of knowledge within the scientific community, the Aristotelian and Galenic theories continued to dominate the popular vernacular treatises on midwifery that proliferated from the sixteenth through the nineteenth centuries. The simple confusion in popular manuals parallels the much more erudite confusion among scientists in the seventeenth and eighteenth centuries. Aristotle believed that the childbearing woman provided only the location and the sustenance for the reproduction of the human child. The father was the true parent in that his semen provided the form, impetus, and direction of the embryo's growth. On account of woman's lack of semen, Aristotle defined her as an "infertile male." Assuming the exclusively material nature of her contribution to reproduction, he viewed femaleness as "material" and "bodily." Due to the inability of the female to bear young without the efficient, formative, and telic influence of male semen, he defined females as "passive." Unaware of anything as minuscule as an ovum and unwilling to hypothesize a human equivalent to animal eggs, he attributed to the visible male semen the sole source of human generation.

Aristotle's negative stereotypes of the female, which were still current in the early modern period, had an appearance of "scientific" respectability. Perhaps most disturbing of all was his presentation of the female body as a variant of the model of the male body. Women's menstrual fluid he viewed as a stunted form of semen. He defined the birth of a female child as the birth of a child whose surplus blood was distorted in development, leading to the later production of menstrual fluid instead of semen. The same semen, depending on conditions in the mother's womb, might produce a male or a female child: thus, by definition, a female child was a "mutilated male." At least, however, Aristotle's belief that the same seed, depending on circumstances, could grow to be either a male or a female laid the foundation for his very important metaphysical conclusion that men and women are of the same species.

The competing theory emanating from classical sources was the theory of Galen. He had accepted Hippocrates' view that both the males and females produce seed, both stronger seeds (source of males) and weaker seeds (source of females). If strong seeds came from both the mother and father, the child would be male; if weaker seeds came from both the mother and father, the child would be female; if a stronger one came from one parent than the other, the child's sex would depend on which seed prevailed. The stereotype of the female as "weaker" pervaded the Galenic writings as well as the Aristotelian. Like Aristotle, Galen utilized a male model for the female body. What we now call "ovaries," Galen called "testes." Going beyond Aristotle's observations, he discovered vessels within the female body. His illustrations of them showed the "testes" to be internal organs resembling the male's external testicles in the same way as, in his view, the uterus was an inverted penis.

Galen's major advance over Aristotle, while attributing generative power to women, nevertheless perpetuated many of the same stereotypes of inferiority. Both Aristotle and Galen viewed females as colder than males and designated their embryonic location as the colder, left side of the womb. Warmth was superior to coldness, and the male, produced in a superabundance of warmth, was viewed as biologically superior to the female. For Galen, as well as for Aristotle, man provided the "active" component in the formation of the embryo. A major difference between the two theorists, however, was that for Aristotle no material part of the embryo came from the male seed, whereas for Galen both the male seed and the female seed contributed materially to the embryo. This distinction opened up paths to further hierarchies: for example, the male semen was thought to produce the important heart of the embryo while the female semen produced the nutritive umbilical cord.

Galenic embryology, which utilized many Aristotelian principles, pervaded the textbooks in the medical schools of early modern universities and served as the starting-point for the seventeenth-century biological controversies. The issues included the classical question of whether or not females, as well as males, produce semen and the means by which the sex of the child is determined. By the turn of the seventeenth century a minority of medical writers, influenced by the experimental anatomists, expanded the debate to ask whether the male and female sex organs are comparable or are distinct, and whether woman is an imperfect version of the male or is equally perfect in her distinct sex. Answers were diverse and were often eclectic in their sources. Renaissance scholars had made available full editions of the classics of Aristotle, Hippocrates, Pliny, and Galen, as well as modern volumes of the anatomists such as Andreas Vesalius (*Humani corporis fabrica,* 1543), whose illustration of the male human body has been reprinted in textbooks as representative of the Renaissance discovery of human nature, and Gabriele Fallopio (*Observations anatomicae,* 1561), who discovered the "Fallopian tubes" which bear his name.

Fallopio's descriptions of female anatomy were a major source for medical authorities who defended the new view that both sexes in their specific functioning are distinct and perfect. While Fallopio himself continued to compare male and female genitalia under the Galenic assumption that the organs were the inverse of one another, André Du Laurens (1558–1609) in 1593 represented the dominant modern trend in the medical profession with a functionalist argument. Du Laurens argued that the male sex organs and the female sex organs are distinct and perfect; and by the seventeenth century, medical textbooks no longer assumed that the genitalia exist on one continuum upon which the female version might be judged an imperfect version of the male.

On the issue of whether the female secreted semen, there was diverse opinion surprisingly among both Galenists and neo-Aristotelians. The dominant view was the Galenic one that women secrete semen which is colder and less active than the male's and that both seeds contribute to both the form and the matter of the embryo. While research proceeded on the way in which menstrual blood provided the matter for the developing embryo, traditional religious associations of menstruation with the curse on Eve and uncleanliness continued to appear in medical books. The dominant new trend, however, was to view menstruation as a harmless, natural flow from the body.

The debate over what caused an embryo to be male or female was a medical topic with clinical implications. The natural curiosity of parents to know the sex of their future child opened up a market for midwives and doctors, as well as for charlatans and diviners. The Pythagorean theory that attributed a male child to location on the right side of the woman's womb and to a secretion from the right testicle might be combined with either Galen's theory, which stressed temperature and the conjunction of distinct male or female seeds, or with Aristotle's theory, which stressed the diet, climate, and strength of mother and father at the time of conception. Not until 1956 was a test devised that was truly scientific, namely amniocentesis; but predictors of sex have always had a market and some credibility, for, unless stricken with terribly bad luck, about half the time their prediction was accurate.

Prediction of the sex of a child in early modern times often relied on the left-right continuum, on the timing of the first fetal movement (the warmer males moved earlier than the cooler females), the relationship of the time of conception or the time of the last birth to the movements of the moon, or a variety of Hippocratic tests of the mother's urine, saliva, or blood. There was steady demand for help in ensuring a male offspring. A popular treatise, *The Compleat Midwife's Practice Enlarged* (1659), helped both to predict the sex of an offspring and, more importantly, to prescribe recipes for copulation that would lead to a male offspring. Recommendations included eating hot and dry meats, holding back from intercourse until the seed was well-developed, and positioning oneself so that the seed fell in the right side of the womb. It is a gross misnomer to call these "old wives' tales," for most of the theories were established and promulgated by male medical authorities, and even when utilized by a midwife at the request of a wife, often were catering to the societal pressure for male offspring.

Proof of the continuing negative influence of Aristotelian authority was the eighteenth-century forgery known as *Aristotle's Masterpiece*. It is a good example of how Aristotle's name continued to grant legitimacy to an array of ideas, some of which directly contradicted his own biology. The editions produced in the eighteenth and nineteenth centuries varied, showing some impact of rival modern theories of reproduction on the dominant traditional phraseology coming from Aristotle and Galen. The ancient theory that the seed of man is the efficient cause of generation runs into problems with the observation of seminal vessels in the female.

However, the tract describes the testicles of woman as two eggs that are there merely to receive man's seed, and then presents another view that the testicles of woman are for the generation of seed. Fallopio's discovery and the work of later scientists, such as William Harvey, in no way ended the debate in the lagging popular literature between the Aristotelian one-seed theory and the Galenic two-seed theory.

Harvey's *De Generatione Animalium* of 1651 reported on his research on hens and deer and made some extrapolations to the human species. In his modification of Aristotle, he was influenced by Hieronymus Fabricius (1537–1619), who held that the female organs were stimulated by the semen of the male to produce eggs. In drawings such as those of Jacob Rueff's popular *The Expert Midwife,* the Aristotelian amalgam of semen and menstrual blood appears in oval shape as an egg; the succession of drawings shows the human embryo in formation. Harvey modified those illustrations by denying that the semen is physically in the egg, and suggesting that the embryonic egg derived from a minuscule egg not yet observed in the ovaries. Both Fabricius and Harvey wanted to explain how a hen, without any contact with a rooster, might produce unfertilized eggs. Harvey posited that parallel circumstances existed in the human womb. He observed the production of the eggs of hens in their ovaries, and could find no trace of semen in the uterus. He rejected the view that the egg was a mass of material produced after copulation; rather he attributed to the female organs the capacity to produce eggs. For Harvey, as for Fabricius, the sperm never reached the uterus physically, but rather acted from afar to determine embryonic development. In dissecting deer that had recently mated, he found no semen in the uterus, and concluded that there was no physical contact of female egg and male seed. In metaphoric language he compared the male semen to a magnet that attracts from a distance, like a star that exerts a "spiritual" influence on earthly beings.

Recently, Carolyn Merchant has argued that the dichotomy between active/passive and spiritual/material in Harvey's descriptions of male semen and female egg reflected and perpetuated both an Aristotelian mental framework and the sexual biases of his English society. Harvey's popularization of the adage "Ex ovo omnia" ("All beings come from eggs") in his frontispiece gave some recognition to the female generativity in the ovaries and inspired some scientists to become "ovists"; but overall, his work further accentuated the amazing power of the male semen to form an embryo without material contact.

Experimentation on mammalian ovaries in the 1660s and 1670s led several researchers to further substantiate the production of female ova before fertilization, while experimentation on semen led to the observation of the spermatozoon. What we now call the Graafian follicles were mistaken by some scientists as the true eggs, an error that delayed the true discovery of the ovum for well over a century. The more detailed illustrations of embryonic development, produced with the aid of a simple microscope, that appeared in the 1673 book of Marcello Malpighi (1628–94), ushered in the preformationist viewpoint: "So admirable is every Organ of this Machine of ours framed, that every part within us is entirely made, when the whole Organ seems too little to have any parts at all." In the 1680s, Leeuwenhoek, who also did microscopic study of the Graafian follicles, denied that they were ova. He believed that the ovum provided only nourishment for the sperm, which was the true source of the embryonic form. His examination of human semen in the 1670s led him to observe what he called "animalcules," tiny organisms that moved with a swish of their tails.

Leeuwenhoek's detailed descriptions of what, since von Baer, we have called "spermatozoa," combined with his lack of observation of an ovum, confirmed his belief that each "animalcule" in the semen contained the full formative structure of the embryo. While hesitating at first on preformationism, in 1718 he described the spermatozoon of a sheep that contained a full description of the organs of the adult within it. In a letter to the German philosopher Leibniz in 1716, he suggested the following source of sex distinction:

> Moreover, all the animalcules of male semina [of all animals, it seems] agree not only in size but also in shape or conformation; except that some years ago I thought I observed some difference at the tail of a number of animalcules, near the body itself. This observation aroused in me the suspicion that the animalcules too differ in sex and are distinguished as male and female. Whence it would follow that if after marital copulation a male animalcule should reach that place in the matrix provided for the reception of these animalcules, a male would be born; but if a female should have taken possession of that place, a female would be born. By this explanation, the received view would fall to the ground; namely, that if the male semen has prevailed over the female, male offspring will be born; if the female semen has prevailed over the male, female offspring will be born.

This "scientific" description aroused hilarity among the community of scientists, and was used to ridicule Leeuwenhoek's spermaticist position. Nevertheless, his view served to undercut existing assumptions. He challenged the Galenic two-seed theory completely, by allowing for the production of both female and male beings from the male's seed alone. His belief that the animalcules are material embryos in miniature also discredited Harvey's modified Aristotelian theory of the spiritual, not material, formative impact of the male seed. Furthermore, his spermaticist position encouraged analogous but inverted claims to be made by ovists studying the so-called miniature egg, the Graafian follicles.

An exemplar of the ovist position is the Swiss physiologist Albrecht von Haller (1708–77). Like Leeuwenhoek, he came to reject epigenesis in favor of preformationism, but von Haller believed the embryo-in-miniature to exist in the prefertilized ovum. In 1766 he wrote, "No part of the animal body is created after another and all are created and appear at the same time." His faith in no way inhibited his remarkably accurate narrative of embryonic growth. The semen in fertilizing the ovum calls up nourishment from the female body to bring about embryonic development. The goal and form of the embryo, which in the Aristotelian system were derived from the male's seed, and in the Galenic system were derived from the seed which had prevailed, are in this ovist position present fully and completely in the female egg. Von Haller's views gained wide distribution in Diderot's *Encyclopedia of the Arts and Sciences* (1751), an influential enterprise of the French Enlightenment.

One of the problems with the ovist, as with the spermaticist, position was the necessity to admit that if the full human being exists in miniature within one seed or egg, then the embryo's future children are likewise there in miniature ad infinitum. The theory of a box within a box corresponded in painting to the portraiture of a mirror reflecting a mirror reflecting a mirror ad infinitum in miniature. Antonio Valisnieri (1661–1730) suggested that the entire human race was within the ovary of Eve; Nicolaus Hartsoeker (1656–1725) made light of the controversy by attempting to calculate when the store of minuscule human beings that might have been contained within Eve's ovaries would be depleted.

Of the positions that allowed for only one sex to be the true "parent," the ovist position was obviously more disturbing to the male medical profession, and the satires of ovism far exceed those on spermaticism. Some historians, such as Joseph Needham, have been reluctant to conclude that the emergence of the ovist position corresponded with the greater visibility of women in Enlightenment society and the increased appearance of feminist tracts. Others, such as Ian Maclean, see anti-Aristotelianism and attention to the ovaries as feminist. Must we thank only the chickens under the scientists' observations for the openness of the ovists to consider accrediting to women the major impact on embryology? The ovist position, much like Jean-Jacques Rousseau's *Discourse on the Arts and the Sciences* (1749), questioned the glib assumption of scientific progress by viewing the post-Aristotelian versions of embryology as myths. The ovist position came closest to the natural notions of primitive peoples who identify the female as the life-producing force in the universe. Trobriander Islanders observed by the anthropologist Bronislaw Malinowski in the twentieth century went even further in their unawareness of a connection between the sex act and procreation, attributing to the female the sole role in reproduction. The ovists who initiated the preformationist position in the seventeenth century were met by a backlash of spermaticists, and out of this dialectic emerged the "egalitarian" epigenesist embryological paradigm of the modern period.

While scientific societies were offering prizes for the discovery of the ovum, the German scientist von Baer reported in a famous letter of 1827 that his own lack of interest in prize-seeking had deterred him from directly seeking to find the ovum by an examination of the ovary. Instead, he claimed to have accidentally noticed a yellowish little body in every Graafian follicle of the ovaries of a pregnant dog, that later he identified more fully through a microscope. He emphasized that the embryo derives its origins from an ovum formed in the ovary long before fertilization. Von Baer's observation and proper identification of the ovum were not noticed at first, but some years later received significant recognition through a prize from the Paris Academy and translations of some of his writings into French and English.

The elaboration of the roles of the ovum and the spermatozoon in embryology was the cumulative effort of nineteenth-century investigators. Three years before von Baer's discovery, Jean-Louis Prévost (1790–1850) and Jean-Baptiste A. Dumas (1800–84), investigating the mammalian ovum, concluded that fertilization follows coitus by some days, and that the "animalcules" in semen were responsible for fertilization. It took another half-century of research for the modern view of conception to be fully established. Von Baer's discovery of the ovum ushered in comparative studies revealing the variation in the relative size of these eggs in different animals. In 1854 George Newport (1803–54) made a significant breakthrough with his observation of a spermatozoon entering a frog's egg. At first it was believed that larger eggs were multicellular, but in 1861 Karl Gegenbaur (1826–1903) gave evidence that each egg was one cell. At first it was not known how many spermatozoa were necessary for the fertilization of an egg. In 1876 Oskar Hertwig (1849–1922) observed the actual fusion of the male and female nucleii within the egg of a sea urchin, and by 1879 he showed that only one spermatozoon entered the ovum of a starfish. Parallel investigation by botanists in the sexual reproduction in plants affirmed the basic similarity at the cellular level of all life and the essential features of the reproductive process. Ovism and spermaticism were overthrown, and embryology was placed on a modern scientific basis.

Von Baer's discovery of the ovum led to the consequent recognition of the combined contribution of the mother's ovum and the father's sperm to the conception of a human embryo. Nineteenth-century research on the ovaries encouraged woman's active, formative role in the embryological process to be taken seriously; and as experimentation proceeded on a sound scientific basis, the debate between the eighteenth-century spermaticists and ovists was forgotten. By the mid-twentieth century ideas derived from the Aristotelian-Galenic "science" of embryology were disparaged as "old wives' tales"; in that misnomer, the general public lost knowledge of the significant scientific revolution in embryology that took place between the sixteenth and the nineteenth centuries, among the international community of scientists. Through the work of women's historians, a significant episode in the history of embryology will enter the mainstream of Western history.

SUGGESTIONS FOR FURTHER READING

Barkai, Ron. *A History of Jewish Gynaecological Texts in the Middle Ages.* Leiden, The Netherlands: Brill, 1998.

Bullough, Vern. "An Early American Sex Manual, Or, Aristotle Who?" *Early American Literature* (Winter 1973): 236–246.

Dean-Jones, Lesley. *Women's Bodies in Classical Greek Science.* Oxford: Clarendon Press, 1994.

Duden, Barbara. *The Woman beneath the Skin: A Doctor's Patients in Eighteenth-Century Germany.* Translated by Thomas Dunlap. Cambridge: Harvard University Press, 1991.

Farley, John. *Gametes and Spores: Ideas about Sexual Reproduction, 1750–1914.* Baltimore: Johns Hopkins University Press, 1982.

Freeland, Cynthia A., ed. *Feminist Interpretations of Aristotle.* University Park, Pa.: Pennsylvania State University Press, 1998.

Horowitz, Maryanne C. "Aristotle and Woman." *Journal of the History of Biology* 9, no. 2 (Fall 1976): 183–213.

———. "The Image of God in Man: Is Woman Included?" *Harvard Theological Review* 72 (1979): 175–206.

———. *Seeds of Virtue and Knowledge.* Princeton: Princeton University Press, 1998.

———. "The Woman Question in Renaissance Texts." In Karen Offen, ed., Special Issue on Women's History, *History of European Ideas* 8, nos. 4–5 (1987): 587–595.

———. "Women's Studies in Its Third Decade: Integrating Women's Studies into the College Curriculum." In *The State of the Art in Women's Studies,* edited by Suzanne W. Hull. Huntington Library Seminar on Women's Studies, 1986.

Irwin, Joyce. "Embryology and the Incarnation: A Sixteenth-Century Debate." *Sixteenth Century Journal* IX, no. 3 (1978): 93–104.

Jordan, Constance. *Renaissance Feminism: Literary Texts and Political Models.* Ithaca, N.Y.: Cornell University Press, 1990.

Keeble, N. H., ed. *The Cultural Identity of Seventeenth-Century Woman.* London: Routledge, 1994.

King, Margaret L. *Women of the Renaissance.* Chicago: University of Chicago Press, 1991.

McLaren, Angus. *A History of Contraception: From Antiquity to the Present Day.* Cambridge, Mass.: Blackwell, 1990.

———. *Reproductive Rituals: The Perception of Fertility in England from the Sixteenth to the Nineteenth Centuries.* London: Methuen, 1984.

Maclean, Ian. *The Renaissance Notion of Woman: A Study in the Fortunes of Scholasticism and Medical Science in European Intellectual Life.* Cambridge: Cambridge University Press, 1980.

Merchant, Carolyn. *The Death of Nature: Women, Ecology, and the Scientific Revolution.* San Francisco: Harper and Row, 1980.

Meyer, Arthur William. *The Rise of Embryology.* Stanford: Stanford University Press, 1939.

Morsink, Johannes. "Was Aristotle's Biology Sexist?" *Journal of the History of Biology* 12, no. 1 (Spring 1979): 83–112.

Moscucci, Ornella. *The Science of Woman: Gynaecology and Gender in England, 1800–1929.* Cambridge: Cambridge University Press, 1990.

Needham, Joseph. *A History of Embryology.* New York: Abelard-Schuman, 1959.

Pinto-Correia, Clara. *The Ovary of Eve: Egg and Sperm and Preformation.* Chicago: University of Chicago Press, 1997.

Rich, Adrienne. *Of Woman Born.* New York: Norton, 1976.

Roe, Shirley A. *Matter, Life and Generation: Eighteenth-Century Embryology and the Haller-Wolff Debate.* Cambridge: Cambridge University Press, 1981.

Smith, Hilda. "Gynecology and Ideology in Seventeenth-Century England." In *Liberating Women's History: Theoretical and Critical Essays,* edited by Berenice A. Carroll. Urbana, Ill.: University of Illinois Press, 1976.

I I

WOMEN IN INDUSTRIALIZING, LIBERALIZING, AND IMPERIALIZING EUROPE

Overview, 1750–1890

Historians customarily divide the vast sweep of human experience they are charged with recording and interpreting into periods that are short enough to be manageable and that are framed by dates of significant events. Thus, the nineteenth century, which is the primary focus of Part II, is often dated 1789 to 1914, years that mark, respectively, the outbreaks of the French Revolution and of the First World War. Both events are assumed to have created, by the depth and extent of their impact on society, historical "watersheds" that changed the course of all that occurred thereafter. The traditional approach to history, as we pointed out in our original Introduction, focuses heavily on revolutions and wars, for it is concerned above all with sudden, dramatic, often violent, changes in political structure and authority, territorial boundaries and geopolitical power.

In considering the history of women in the modern era, we are faced with a more difficult problem of periodization. Standard markers of change may have affected women's lives little, if at all, and then only gradually, for women were all but excluded from the formal realm of politics and from the battlefields. Consigned ideologically to the unpaid sphere of family, women's outside employment remained poorly paid and generally low skilled, despite ongoing socioeconomic changes. Yet, by the mid-nineteenth century, the lives of many women began to differ profoundly from those of their foremothers, revealing the complex rhythms of social transformation. The "New Woman," who is sometimes, as we will see in Part III, greeted as a product of the First World War, appeared in Parisian circles in the 1830s and in Russian literature in 1862, when Vera, in Chernyshevsky's novel *What Is To Be Done?* demanded a room and an income of her own. Votes for women in national elections, often portrayed as a reward for women's contributions to the war effort, in fact capped a struggle waged over many decades, with notable victories as early as 1869 in the Wyoming Territory of the United States, 1893 in New Zealand, and 1906 in Finland.

Today women and men live in an increasingly interconnected and global world. In contrast, Europeans in the seventeenth and early eighteenth centuries typically lived in small, relatively static communities, rarely venturing more than a few miles from the place of their birth, or seeing a crowd larger than it took to fill a country church on Sunday—except perhaps during food or other riots. While the processes of change have been exceedingly uneven, nevertheless, as the social historian Peter Stearns puts it, "The basic fact of European history since 1750 has been an unprecedented social upheaval. . . . A new kind of society has been formed, as different from its predecessor as agricultural society was from the hunting culture with which man first began to fight for survival."[1] Conceived most broadly, this picture is, of course, correct: a so-called modern world has indeed replaced premodern society, but the change was neither sudden nor synchronized and there was much dynamism in the old that influenced the character of the new industrial world.

We offer a distinctive chronology to frame the diverse stories of women's lives that comprise Part II. We take as our convenient starting place 1750, and as a closing point, 1890. The year 1750 symbolizes the commencement in many areas of Europe of the types of economic, ideological, and social reconstruction that had the radical potential to transform the conditions of life for all European women and men. The cumulative impact of commercial exchanges in the Atlantic world accelerated economic transformation in Europe itself starting in the 1750s. The social dislocations called into question standards of justice, economic freedoms, and notions of the common good, which became objects of theoretical debate as well as practical reform. The date 1890 points to the closing of the era of laissez-faire principles, and the beginnings of a monumental move toward greater state intervention in social, familial, and personal affairs in Europe and in the new empires of Africa and Asia. It duplicates the process of reciprocity between Europe and its colonies that we have illustrated in Part I. Indeed, slum clearance in European urban settings was matched by new building projects in the heart of empire, reflecting the values of order and modernity—even progress itself—that transcended geographical borders. The emphasis in Part II, then, is on the complex, interrelated series of events that go under the headings of the Industrial and French Revolutions, as well as the attendant demographic, agrarian, transportation, and ideological changes that surround those two great transformations in Europe and in its system of empire.

Although some historians today consider the term *revolution* to be misleading because it obscures the many gradual changes that took place, it continues to call attention to the degree to which, undeniably, the transformation was accelerating. Although many of the changes were not apparent to ordinary Europeans as they lived their daily lives, the educated classes were struck by the new developments going on around them—whether transfixed with wonder or horror. Theirs was a language of novelty, innovation, and inexorable technological progress. But we must again stress the complex nature and the diversity of impact of these changes. They had various meanings for the lives and livelihoods of women and men, depending on their place in society and the degree of their involvement in commercial and imperial ventures.

The process termed the Industrial Revolution encompassed numerous innovations in the economic organization of production and distribution of goods. The

French Revolution, a subject of intensive investigation and analysis ever since 1789, was one of many "democratic revolutions" that, beginning in America in 1776 and culminating with the creation of the first free black nation-state in the world in Haiti in 1804, saw rights of political participation extended to ever-widening segments of the population. This "Dual Revolution," as the cumulative changes have been called, however, depended on the interaction of other socioeconomic and political factors. Historical demographers, charting population change over time, describe transitions from patterns of high mortality and high fertility to low fertility and low mortality. Beginning in the late eighteenth and early nineteenth century in western Europe, these shifts caused a "population explosion" because mortality declined more rapidly than fertility before ultimately settling into the relatively slow and stable growth patterns that today characterize advanced industrial nations. So profound are the effects of these changes that they are collectively designated a Demographic Revolution.

Inextricably intertwined with population size, agricultural production was also altered due to factors such as the consolidation of relatively unproductive small holdings, the extension of lands under cultivation, the application of new chemical fertilizers, and later the utilization of new machinery to supplement or even to replace animal power. Termed an Agricultural Revolution, forces of change in the countryside stood in a complex relationship to the processes of industrial growth. In geographic areas in which small landholdings had been consolidated (for example, in England and Prussia), more and more people were forced off the land. As "free labor," they had to find work in urbanizing areas where, especially after the development of the factory system, increased employment was available for landless people. In these cases, rural areas contributed workers for urban industry. In turn, the growing need for food in urban areas acted as an incentive for agricultural development. This meant that some regions, like Bavaria in central Europe, experienced a reruralization in the course of the nineteenth century, becoming actually *more* agrarian than they had been a century earlier. Furthermore, the unprecedented movement of goods and people was facilitated by another revolution—the so-called Transportation Revolution. Canals were dug, roads were paved, and increased numbers of steamships and locomotives were constructed, opening up new jobs in iron and steel works and spurring on the development of heavy industry.

Finally to our list of "revolutions," we must add the Ideological. The decline in the religious world view and loss of confidence in the church and the hereafter by some intellectuals that dates back to the Renaissance and Reformation produced, by the eighteenth century, a sense among the educated elite that society had progressed from the "dark ages" of the medieval period to an Age of Enlightenment. Many believed that through rational thought and the scientific method human intelligence could discover the laws of nature; and by applying them to social structures, could reform society for the greater good. Like the Renaissance humanists, the Enlightenment philosophers stressed the importance of education; in knowledge, not faith, lay the path to virtue. These philosophers sought to accumulate (and simultaneously produced much) knowledge about everything in the natural world. They also applied critical thought to human institutions. After centuries of repression of unpopular or heretical views, Voltaire (1694–1778), the best-known *philosophe* of the age, championed total freedom of thought and speech. His contemporaries, Diderot (1713–84) and d'Alembert (1717–83), set out to compile in their thirty-five volume *Encyclopedia* all useful philosophic and scientific knowledge. Social thinkers of the nineteenth century went further: they devised schemes for the reconstruction of all human institutions, including along with religious, political, legal, and economic structures, personal relations and the family as well. As we will see in more detail shortly, Robert Owen, Henri Saint-Simon, and Charles Fourier invented new ways for men and women to live and to govern themselves in harmonious communities, and they expected that, once convinced of the reasonableness of new ways, people would hasten to adopt them. Near midcentury, in 1845, Karl Marx established a new agenda for social critics by declaring that the point was not merely to understand the world, but to use scientific knowledge of historical laws to change it. These intellectual projects, no matter how different in purpose and scope, shared a commitment to progress and truth as well as the premise of a knowable, objective world and the power of human agency to create more perfect social institutions within it.

Reviewing the many "revolutions" in this period, we may ask if women's lives were revolutionized by the onset of the new industrial society? How did the agrarian changes affect women's roles as participants in rural marketing and manufacture? Did the industrial revolution transform "women's work?" What was the impact of new definitions of citizenship on women's public roles? To what extent did women confront the moral dilemmas of European society and empire? In what ways did wealth, age, marital status, and geographic location shape women's lives, fashion distinct identities, and forge common movements for feminist or other kinds of reform? And finally, for our understanding of historical processes, what are the linkages between what some analysts term the "macrostructures" that we have highlighted here and the individual subjectivities and identities of women? What kinds of evidence can historians draw on to demonstrate these connections?

Industrialization and Women's Work

The industrialization of western Europe was a long and complex process in the ways that human beings transformed raw materials into the commodities necessary for life. As we have seen in Part I, it began with increased trade and commercialization in the emerging Atlantic community of Europe, Africa, and the Americas. Supporting a growing market in colonial goods, it also stimulated the growth of cottage industry, rural manufacturing, and urban centers in Europe itself. By the end of the nineteenth century massive changes in population had taken place, both in numbers and in location. A European population of approximately 190 million in 1800 grew to 500 million by 1900—despite the emigration of over forty million Europeans, largely to North and South America. Furthermore, differences in birth and death rates shifted the relative size of population eastward from France, the most populous European nation at the dawn of the nineteenth century, to Russia, where the crude birth rate was the highest in Europe by its end (at 49.3, double that of France at 21.3).

These changes among nations were paralleled by movements of people within territories. Over the course of the century the number of people living in large cities (over one hundred thousand) increased tenfold, growing from 3 percent to 11 percent of the aggregate population. The growth of urban centers created social needs that governments provided only slowly, after long struggles between laissez-faire and interventionist forces. Ultimately, however, municipal, regional, and national authorities created and extended their police forces, mail and rail services, census bureaus and public health agencies. Political leaders also accepted new responsibilities for people's education, creating the extensive school systems necessary to produce a literate industrial work force.

Despite the many factors tending toward change, and the degree of alteration that, in the perspective of a century, appears so striking, on the scale of an individual life—on average very short (less than forty years) in our period—most change came in small steps. Ordinarily people who left the land migrated first to villages and small towns. Most workers who entered factories followed along the path of their kinfolk who had preceded them and who helped them to find jobs and housing. Many families who turned to wage-earning endeavors in the early phases of industrial capitalism continued to farm small plots. The processes of proletarianization (the dispossession of peasants of their lands and artisans of their tools and workshops) were matched by the development of new individual and collective identities which highlighted the category of class. A powerful rhetoric of class consciousness and solidarity rooted in labor emerged as work and family life was evolving into new patterns of living.

Although James Watt's invention of the modern steam engine in 1769, which was adapted to railroads half a century later, is sometimes used to mark the beginning of the Industrial Revolution, the early developments that most affected the lives and work of ordinary people came in textile manufacturing, the first major industry to be reorganized. Inventions such as the "flying shuttle" in 1733 and the "spinning jenny" in 1764 raised productivity drastically, quickly doubling, then multiplying by factors of twenty, thirty, and one hundred, the output of a single worker. While woolen cloth had long constituted the most important product of textile manufacturers, the new methods were first applied to production of cotton cloth—for which there was a vast latent demand because of its cheapness and versatility—in England, on the continent, and indeed, increasingly around the world. Early in the eighteenth century fashionable ladies had begun to add variety to their silk, linen, and woolen wardrobes by importing fine chintzes and calicoes from India. But ordinary people wore "homespun," coarse cloth that was usually made of wool and was in short supply. One costume usually sufficed for everyday use until it wore out; another "Sunday-best" might be set aside for church. Europe's mushrooming population, already geared to consumer purchases of colonial goods, provided a ready market for new, cheaper fabrics.

For a time, the first workers to adopt the new speedier methods of production in spinning and weaving enjoyed greater earnings while continuing to work in their homes. Within a few years, however, as increased wages attracted new workers to spinning, competition for work drove down profits; and the introduction of new machines, too large for workers' cottages and too expensive for their resources, impelled textile workers to seek employment in the new factories that began to dot the countryside. Located alongside rivers that provided water power, the first factories were often small, dark, and poorly ventilated. Later, steam power permitted

construction of still larger and more complex machines and bigger factories with
more specialized operations, which could be built at some distance from the older
sources of power and labor.

The earliest factory labor forces were dominated by girls and young women, and
it was in female-typed occupations that the fastest and greatest gains in productivity
took place. Historians now point out that "gender shaped the industrial revolution."
Beginning in the cotton factories but also in other crafts such as garment-making and
shoemaking, manufacturers found they could turn out cheaper products by reorganizing work processes in ways that took advantage of the availability of female and
child labor. By subdividing the process of production into smaller components and
separating those that required specialized skill and training from those that untrained
women and children could perform, they were able to employ the cheapest labor
available. By using the "putting out" system of subcontracting portions of the work
to workers' homes, they could also save on overhead costs. Even skilled women
workers often preferred to work at home.[2]

Not only were spinning and cloth production traditionally "women's work";
young females constituted a reserve that was relatively underused in agriculture and
that could be hired for about half of a man's wage. By the 1830s, textile centers,
such as Lowell, Massachusetts; Lyons, France; and Manchester, England, employed
tens of thousands of women. In many cases working conditions were poor. The
women who extracted silk from cocoons in the factories of Lyons for fourteen to
sixteen hours six days a week, had to thrust their hands into near boiling water and
suffered from pain and sores that formed under their fingernails. Silk dust penetrated their pores and lungs, producing high rates of skin disease and tuberculosis.
Cotton mills likewise were filled with dust; and in cases where production required
processing with water or steam, workers were compelled to spend hours in damp
clothing and humid air. Machinery sometimes required uncomfortable or dangerous manipulations. A young English woman, who had started factory work at age
nine, complained about

> always having to stop the flies [cylinders] with my knee. I could stop it with
> my hand, but I had to hold it with my knee while I piecened [spliced] it. It was
> having to crook my knee to stop the spindle that lamed me as much as anything
> else.

An older woman, who worked in one of the coal mines that provided cheap fuel to
industrial change, described graphically the physical hardships she endured.

> I have a belt round my waist and a chain passing between my legs, and I go on
> my hands and feet. The road is very steep, and we have to hold by a rope, and
> when there is no rope, by anything we can catch hold of. There are six women
> and about six boys in the pit I work in: it is very hard work for a woman. The
> pit is very wet where I work, and the water comes over our clogs always, and I
> have seen it up to my thighs: it rains in at the roof terribly; my clothes are wet
> through almost all day long. . . . I have drawn till I have had the skin off me; the
> belt and chain is worse when we are in the family way. My feller [husband] has

beaten me many a time for not being ready. I were not used to it at first, and he had little patience. I have known many a man beat his drawer.

Young workers also suffered from factory discipline. Zealous overseers used leather straps to apply frequent "lickings" to children who fell asleep on the job.[3]

The employment of women and children in English factories gave rise to demands for protective action by the state. Though doctrinaire liberals and some industrialists opposed all intervention, by the 1830s legislation was passed limiting the employment of young children, and the Factory Acts of 1842 and 1844 also prescribed a maximum work day for women. French leaders likewise sounded the bell of alarm. After Dr. Louis Villermé's famous report on the physical and "moral" costs of unbridled industrial labor, French leaders of many political views began to call for "English legislation." However, laws comparable to the British legislation of the 1840s would not be passed until the 1880s and early 1890s in France and Germany, and until the early twentieth century in the United States.

Some countries took avenues other than legislation for the protection of their girls and women. For example, in Lowell, Massachusetts, cotton mill owners who wanted to attract a labor force of young women from the New England countryside built dormitories where their workers could be housed and fed at reasonable cost and receive suitable familial and moral support. In France, where many poor women who migrated alone to cities for work could afford only the most miserable of accommodations—often sleeping two or more to a bed of straw—*internats*, or boarding-houses, blended the Lowell plan with a conventlike regime to provide a kind of dormitory life and close supervision. By 1881 an estimated 1,110 of these establishments housed working-class children, of whom 80 percent were girls. Jules Simon, whose 1860 work *L'Ouvrière (Woman Worker)* was the most famous nineteenth-century account of the effects of industrialization on working women in France, estimated that these institutions produced 85 percent of the shirts sold in the Paris market. While the *internats* were highly profitable enterprises, they won praise for providing working-class girls with a substitute home from which they could, after some ten years' residence, leave with a sufficient dowry to found a new family. To critics they represented "nothing but commercial enterprises founded on the exploitation of children."[4]

Despite this evidence, research by social and women's historians has provided a needed corrective to the once-popular notion that working-class families were torn apart by the demands for factory labor. Not only did many textile-manufacturing families continue to work together as a unit in the early factories, but in cases where women did take factory employment apart from kin, they were most often young and single. The nursing mother separated all day from her infant, forced to tend machines while "the milk pours from her breasts, so that her clothing drips with it"; and the babies quieted at home by opium-laced cordials, described so passionately by Friedrich Engels in 1844, were not typical of women workers' experiences or of family life. In textile cities, however, there was indeed a great demand for female labor, for it was cheap. A family endowed with daughters might, at least during their prime years as mill workers, become relatively prosperous. For a time in the second quarter of the nineteenth century, women workers enjoyed improved earnings and new job opportunities.

The increasing employment of women, which in the view of Engels "unsexes the man and takes from the woman all womanliness," scarcely turned the workers' world topsy-turvy. Such images were overdrawn, often created by social reformers who used the authority of so-called natural gender distinctions to press lawmakers to abandon their laissez-faire principles and pass protective legislation. Joan W. Scott and Louise A. Tilly, in an important study that draws upon occupational and demographic data from systematic samples of urban households in England and France, demonstrate that throughout the nineteenth century, traditional forms of female employment continued to dominate women's wage-earning activity. In 1851, the largest group of female wage-earners in England, fully 40 percent, worked as domestic servants. In 1866, 40 percent of the female labor force in France was employed in agriculture. Moreover, no more than one-fifth of the total female labor force in England, and one-tenth in France, worked in textile manufacturing. Outside of textiles, tobacco, and food processing, relatively few women worked in factories at all. Furthermore, in the major cloth-manufacturing centers such as Roubaix, France, where in 1872 over half the labor force worked in textiles, relatively few *married* women were employed outside their homes—about 17 percent. In the textile center of Lancashire, England, three-quarters of women workers were single.[5]

Although factory work, then, was not *typical* female employment in the nineteenth century, women's lives were altered by the processes that reorganized their work, whether removing the work to factories or, as Barbara Franzoi Bari shows (chapter 6), providing increased opportunities for wage-earning employment at home. In the first place, the symbiosis of married women's labor in production and reproduction, whereby women provided the daily necessities for family survival and gave birth to new generations of producers as well, was distorted by the redefinition of work that spread with the growing dominance of factory production. Work was recognized solely as "paid labor" and much of women's work remained unpaid. This enhanced the economic value and increased the autonomy of single women who found work outside the home, but it marginalized married women's work at home, even that done for wages. Second, factory manufacturing increasingly displaced much of the production done at home for the family's own use. In the course of time, mass production of soaps, yarns, and cloth, for example, encouraged their consumption "ready-made." In many instances, old industries based on highly skilled handwork declined drastically. For example, commercial lace embroidery, which in Britain employed four hundred thousand handworkers in 1780 offered work for only fourteen thousand a century later. Elsewhere, as in the rural Lorraine district of France where embroiderers successfully resisted introduction of a frame invented in Switzerland, old hand methods—as implied in the word "manufacturing"—persisted, along with dispersed production. In this case, urban embroiderers, generally older, married, and more exclusively dependent on wages from their work, accepted the new method, which decreased the cost of production while, in the workers' view, making their labor physically more demanding.[6]

New industries for ready-made goods proliferated in all European cities. In late nineteenth-century Britain and Germany, hundreds of thousands of women did "slop work" (low-skilled, repetitive piecework) in "sweatshops." In France, half of the female industrial labor force remained "isolated," that is, homeworkers. Domestic industry allowed women to continue contributing to family survival, but even in these households, family schedules were increasingly regulated by the factory whistle. Berlin home industry garment-makers in the last third of the nineteenth century organized the rhythm of family life according to their husbands' work schedules, ensuring men leisure time even if it meant for themselves sewing for pay well into the wee hours of the morning. But women working at home avoided the stigma borne by the "factory girl."

Agricultural and industrial reorganization, with its increasing scale of production and growth in market economies and market mentalities, restructured family roles by shifting the location of much traditional women's work out of the home. These developments created a conflict between the two primary facets of women's lives—one that remains today as a problem for working mothers. Furthermore, as early as the eighteenth century, men had begun to encroach on the domain of women's work. In textile factories a roomful of female operatives might be supervised by one or two men. Even in the countryside, the shift to market-oriented production narrowed the traditional female economy. In Bavaria, for instance, to the extent that dairy farming centered on the needs of the household, women obtained the necessary know-how on the farm. But market production required the mastery of new knowledge not necessarily related to the work processes. And this was acquired by men from trade associations and agricultural institutes that were set up in rural areas.

In sum, the nineteenth century was a critical period in the redefinition of women's work. In the "struggle for the breeches" women were unable to win recognition as skilled workers. Nor did they obtain the resources and status accorded the "labor aristocracy." Industrialization and commodification exaggerated the process whereby the labor of women, both paid and unpaid, became subsidiary to that of men, even in work traditionally deemed feminine. Rather, the right to gainful employment became an undisputed attribute of manhood.[7]

Women, Political Culture, and the "Rights of Men"

Before, during, and after the French Revolution, women's primary role was support for their families. For the leaders of all parties that contended for power through the protracted period of struggle in France—the aristocrats, the radical Jacobins, the moderate Girondins and the *sans-culottes* (without breeches, or common people)—politics was the province of men. But politics cannot be separated from the culture and social arrangements in which it is grounded and which in turn it shapes and reshapes. Revolutionary leaders in late eighteenth-century France indeed intended to reconstruct society and create a new "man." They drew on ideas that contained powerful notions not only about the division of public political power but also about individual rights and responsibilities that were pertinent to the lives of all people—men and women, free and slave. As we saw in the overview to Part I, the seeds of "enlightened" thought about inalienable human rights were planted by English political liberalism (natural rights philosophy) in the seventeenth century. While the association of political rights with property ownership worked against married women, and perpetuated the institution of slavery, the concept of natural rights contained the powerful germ of equality. Indeed, John Locke, to strengthen his argument against patriarchal government and its logical extension, absolute monarchy, went so far in theory as to grant mothers "equal Title" to their children.[8]

Locke's ambivalence regarding women's rights echoed through the work of eighteenth-century philosophers. The "Age of Reason" saw a magnificent flowering of new secular thought that, embodied in the American Declaration of Independence as well as the French Declaration of the Rights of Man and Citizen, has shaped liberal political democracy in the world. Sometimes also called the Age of Ideas, the Age of Humanism, or the Age of Neo-Classicism, the century that culminated in the French Revolution is most popularly called the "Age of Light," or The Enlightenment, to signify the illumination produced when ancient Greek and Renaissance ideas were rekindled in the context of the seventeenth-century scientific revolution. More popularizers than original thinkers, the *philosophes,* supported by educated women who managed and participated in salon discussions, spread the ideas of Bacon, Descartes, Newton, and Locke deep into literate society. With full confidence in the power of human reason, they defined as "natural law" the principles that governed animal and human life, including "laws of justice and equity." Distinct from the "positive law" of nations, natural law was held to be perpetual and immutable, either given by God (according to some), or inherent in the material universe (according to others). Opposed to the church, to monarchy, and to all arbitrary forms of hierarchy and rule, the *philosophes* set as their goal to bring the laws of the state and the structure of social institutions into agreement with nature. Who was to remake the laws and institutions? "The only true sovereign is the nation," wrote Diderot. "There can be no true legislator except the people." For Jean-Jacques Rousseau (1712–78), "sovereignty" resided in the "general will," a collective being created by a "social contract" with "absolute power over all its members."

The extent to which such ideas influenced the revolutionaries of 1789 (and other political leaders) has long been the subject of lively debate among historians and political scientists. From the publication in 1790 of Edmund Burke's *Reflections on the Revolution in France,* conservatives have held the political rationalism of the *philosophes* responsible for rending the organic fabric of traditional society and letting loose the twin demons of disorder and destruction—often portrayed by female images. Liberals have emphasized, on the contrary, the *philosophes'* contributions toward development of the democratic institutions which promise political liberty and economic mobility for the "common man." Even Marxists, who deny the possibility of freedom in bourgeois class society, credit the *philosophes'* ideas for replacing prejudice and privilege with a "kingdom of reason" designed to usher in a "democratic bourgeois" republican regime. Other analysts de-emphasize the role of ideas, and stress the economic background of the French Revolution: bankruptcy of the royal treasury due to the expense of supporting the American Revolution; bad harvests, a bitter winter, widespread unemployment, high bread prices; resentment by various classes of high taxes or seigneurial dues; the ambitions of merchant or professional groups for greater economic as well as political power. The many perspectives on causes are matched by multiple interpretations of outcomes, showing the complexity of the relationship between politics and society, metropole and colony.

The political facts are simpler. In 1787 the Parlement of Paris rejected the King's proposals for new taxes, demanding that the Estates-General, a representative body that had not met since 1614, be summoned. It was composed of three bodies: the First the clergy, the Second the nobility, and the Third everyone else. Following traditional procedural rules, each Estate would cast one collective vote in the assembly; the vast majority, over 90 percent of the population, could then be outvoted, two to one. When denied their petition to vote by head rather than by order, the Third Estate proclaimed itself a National Assembly and voted to establish a new constitution for the country. As King Louis XVI tried to mobilize enough strength to regain his prerogatives, rumors of an aristocratic conspiracy fed on political and economic tensions to produce a "Great Fear" throughout the countryside. Dismissal of a reform-minded minister sparked riots in Paris, establishment by its populace of its own government and militia, and on July 14, the famous destruction of the Bastille, a prison that symbolized royal despotism.

The events in France, which began as attempts at reform, quickly progressed into social revolution. Every class played a role. Lawyers, officeholders, and members of the liberal professions led the creation of a new and masculine political culture, but market women and artisans from the streets and shops of Paris emerged at critical junctures to accelerate the pace of revolution. In the French colonies of the West Indies, free blacks and mulattos and eventually slaves rose in rebellion as well. Clergy who resisted secularization, loyalist peasants and aristocratic émigrés who sought foreign intervention against the revolutionary government constituted counterrevolutionary forces. Regicide and war, at home and abroad, military conscription, scarcity of food and inflation, all intensified the level of conflict. Although revolutionary fervor peaked during the so-called Reign of Terror, between October 1793 and July 1794, constitutional changes, popular uprisings, and disorder continued until, in 1799, Napoleon Bonaparte assumed power by military coup. He, of course, carried the revolution with his Grand Army all the way to the steppes of Russia, and to the shores of Hispaniola.

In a brief summary it is impossible to do justice to the constructive aspects of the revolutionary experience. These include the ending of feudal remnants that oppressed peasants and stymied economic development; the creation of a constitutional government balancing executive and legislative powers; the adoption of the Declaration of the Rights of Man and Citizen, establishing civil equality among men (including Jews and Protestants); the enactment of new (though temporary) family laws allowing for civil divorce and inheritance rights by women; the defense of equality against inherited privilege; and by 1793, the abolition of slavery in Saint Domingue (Haiti). Most significantly, the revolutionaries in France replaced an absolute monarchy grounded in divine right with a republic based on the consent of the governed. The flames of the French Revolution lit a beacon for oppressed peoples everywhere—and cast a shadow of revolution over the entire nineteenth century.

It created a new political vocabulary and established a new agenda for rearranging social and economic relationships. Henceforth many people would imagine the world anew and seek to close the gap between what was and what could be. The revolutions in North America, France, and Haiti were followed by numerous others in countries and city-states across Europe: the Chartist movement in England, led by workers demanding universal manhood suffrage, abolition of property qualifications for membership in Parliament, and other political reforms; the revolutions of 1848 and subsequent nation-building in central Europe; and the experiments with liberalization in Russia—these events ultimately brought political emancipation to most classes of *men*. The abolition of absolutism in relations between kings and subjects and between masters and servants might be expected to facilitate liberalization of social relations between the sexes. For women's rights, however, separate battles had to be fought. The Declaration of the Rights of Man did not encompass the female half of "mankind." It was, however, soon challenged.

During the past two decades, historians of women have reexamined the work of both the Enlightenment philosophers and the French revolutionaries. Mme. de Pompadour, Mme. Geoffrin, Mlle. de Lespinasse, and other Parisian *salonières* contributed moral and financial support to the Encyclopedists; and a few joined their opponents. While historians debate the overall impact of Enlightenment thinkers on subsequent events, what emerges clearly from their writings is that the topic of "women," played a central role in their thought, conversation, and writings. They criticized the institution of marriage, women's education, women's role in public affairs, and gender relations. Karen Offen has recently pointed out that Rousseau's patron Mme. d'Epinay in the 1770s used the terms *genre masculin* and *genre féminin* and "insisted that she was not speaking only about grammar but about socialization."[9]

The Encyclopedists themselves, however, divided on the question of women's rights—the Huguenot nobleman Jaucourt penning entries in support of equality of the sexes in marriage; Desmahis, the dramatist protégé of Voltaire, reemphasizing misogynist views of women as vain, deceitful, and empty-headed. The thirty-one entries on "woman" or topics beginning with that word include many contradictory opinions, some of which themselves cannot easily be categorized as "for" or "against" improvement in women's status. Overall, the Encyclopedists, like the *philosophes* more broadly, tended to see women as physically delicate, psychologically timid though passionate (a potentially dangerous combination), and socially destined for motherhood. Interestingly, the *Encyclopedia's* seventeen volumes of text and eleven volumes of plates offer no reference to the salons, an institution of significance as we have seen, both to women of the seventeenth and eighteenth centuries and to the philosophers themselves. Although female workers in dozens of occupations are mentioned in passing, and some illustrations of the workplace indeed depict women workers, there is little discussion in the text of women at work. "Only an abstract hint of [women's] extraordinary influence on eighteenth-century France can be divined from the *Encyclopédie*" remarks Terry Smiley Dock.[10]

In the more fundamental task of defining natural law—the purported basis of social institutions—eighteenth-century philosophers were divided in their assessments of the nature of women. The *philosophe* perhaps most famous for his support of enhanced women's rights is the marquis de Condorcet (1743–94) while, for his recasting of traditionally restrictive roles, the best known is Rousseau. Condorcet, a mathematician and philosopher, was a leading member of the liberal nobility who supported the goals of the American Revolution and later of the Third Estate in his own country. Influenced perhaps by his experiences in America as well as by his relationships with educated women, he dealt with women's rights in several works. Writing even from prison in a society torn apart by social conflict, he envisioned a basis for reconstruction that included the "admission of women to rights of citizenship." Condorcet recognized the incompleteness of the revolution. The revolutionaries had:

> violated the principle of equality of rights, in tranquilly depriving the half of the human race of that of assisting in the making of laws; in excluding women from the right of citizenship. . . . Either no individual of the human race has genuine rights, or else all have the same; and he who votes against the right of another, whatever the religion, colour, or sex of that other, has henceforth adjured his own.

Alleged conditions of female disability, such as "pregnancy and passing indispositions," he rejected as a justification for denying women rights, since "nobody ever dreamt of depriving people who have the gout every winter, or who easily catch cold." Because he believed that the perfection of human life required the elimination of all types of inequality, Condorcet also argued eloquently for the abolition of slavery, declaring that "the time will therefore come when the sun will shine only on free men who know no other master but their reason; when tyrants and slaves, priests and their stupid or hypocritical instruments will exist only in works of history."[11]

Despite the harmony of Condorcet's position on women's roles with the basic principles of the Enlightenment and the Revolution, he gained few allies. Rousseau, on the other hand, won widespread support. He tapped several strong currents: traditional misogyny; distrust of the power of royal mistresses and the artifices of aristocratic ladies (dressed fashionably in tall, elaborate coiffures so that as they passed "you could see nothing but a forest of feathers, rising high above the heads and nodding to and fro") who symbolized the corruption of the old order; and the romanticism that envisioned "natural woman" as the companion of "natural man." Defining the female role narrowly, for purposes of reproduction, Rousseau assigned women to their "proper" calling of childbearing and childrearing. Perhaps because he celebrated women's domestic role and made mothers feel important, Rousseau attracted an immense following among women. But Rousseau added a new language to the discourse on women's subordination, because for him their differences entailed disabilities that precluded their membership in the "general will." Since participation in the general will required the transcendence of personal interest, and women, by Rousseau's definition as well as by custom and law, were dependent on personal relations, they could not exercise the highest duties of citizenship.

Rousseau's theory reflected the political reality of eighteenth-century Europe. Although exceptional women such as the Hapsburg Empress Maria Theresa of Austria (1717–80) and Catherine II of Russia (1729–96) exercised power over great countries, they owed their prerogatives to their inherited, dynastic status. Both women tempered their power with Enlightenment ideals; but neither effected any change in attitudes, customs, or laws regarding the female sex as a whole any more than had Elizabeth I of England two centuries before. Indeed, the laws codified by Catherine—one of the notable achievements of this "Enlightened Despot"—subjected women to the authority of men. Empowered by the laws of every European country to prescribe and enforce rules for their families and households, men also represented their dependents in the political world. However, if most women had few formal political rights, they could exercise certain customary rights. Because the obligation to feed their families fell heavily on women, they might, during times of economic distress, participate in direct and highly political action such as bread riots and resistance to taxation. During the revolutionary upheaval in France, women were active politically in old as well as new ways. Some women took their demands into the marketplace and streets. Others wrote political tracts, formed political clubs, and called into question the very basis of male political power.

Consciously responding to the revolutionaries in France whose political double standard, like Rousseau's, violated their own principles, two unusual women quickly penned eloquent defenses of women's right to equality in the newly emerging society. In 1791, Olympe de Gouges, a butcher's daughter whose writings had gained her access to the French court, paraphrased the famous *Declaration of the Rights of Man and Citizen* in a radical manifesto that called on women, as "mothers, daughters, and sisters, representatives of the nation," to constitute themselves a national assembly. Asserting in terms also resonant of Rousseau that "woman is born free and remains equal in rights to man," she redefined the general will explicitly to include female citizens. Like her antagonists, she catalogued women's defects but blamed them on their state of subjection to men. She prescribed "an invincible means of elevating the soul of women; it is for them to join in all the activities of men." Despite Olympe de Gouges's stirring call to her sisters, which was rediscovered in the 1860s and the 1890s, her voice went largely unheard for the next century and a half. Perhaps because she soon paid with her life for her unfeminine political activity, guillotined in 1793 at least partially "for having forgotten the virtues that suited her sex," her work remained outside most history texts until recuperated by women's historians in the 1970s.

Across the Channel, Mary Wollstonecraft, an Englishwoman who first answered Burke's *Reflections* with her *A Vindication of the Rights of Men* (1790), was similarly indignant that revolutionary republican heroes who set out to reconstruct society instead reinforced patriarchal patterns of the past. She challenged the French leaders to examine the causes and consequences of women's situation. In the preface to her *A Vindication of the Rights of Woman* (1792), Wollstonecraft stated that

> If women are to be excluded, without having a voice, from a participation of the natural rights of mankind, prove first, to ward off the charge of injustice and inconsistency, that they [lack] reason—else this flaw in your NEW CONSTITUTION will ever shew that man must, in some shape, act like a tyrant, and tyranny, in whatever part of society it rears its brazen front, will ever undermine morality.

Wollstonecraft, a former governess and teacher whose wit and pen won her a place among the Enlightenment-inspired Philosophical Radicals in Britain, issued a stinging, point-by-point critique of Rousseau's treatise on female education, extending his blueprint for men's education to women, in the common interest. For, she wrote, "Till women are more rationally educated, the progress of human virtue and improvement in knowledge must receive continual checks. . . . Let woman share the rights and she will emulate the virtues of man."[12] Quickly moving through several editions and translations, the *Vindication* came to be considered by Anglo-American historians as the beginning of the modern women's rights movement, though Wollstonecraft herself, after dying in childbirth, was vilified for her unconventional life. Known to the leaders of the nineteenth-century struggle for women's rights in several nations, by mid-twentieth century she, too, was largely absent from the historical record, to be recovered for us also by feminist historians in the late 1960s and the 1970s. Between 1970 and 1975 alone, five new biographies of Wollstonecraft appeared in the United States; her collected works have since been published—a rarity for feminist writers.

In recent years, feminist analysts have noted the limitations of Wollstonecraft's vision. While arguing eloquently against some of the privileges of gender and class, and attributing the flaws she found in women's character to their faulty education, she failed to transcend many assumptions of her day. Given the very real burdens imposed by female biology in her own life and the lives of many women in an era lacking effective contraception, she downplayed the positive values for women of sexuality and family; and she did not think beyond the male-dominated bourgeois family model. She also absorbed her society's "orientalist" views of the inferiority of non-Europeans even while repeatedly lambasting defenders of the "abominable traffick" in slaves. Her work, nevertheless, served to inspire feminist advocacy even in regions far beyond western Europe.[13]

Many others, before and after Condorcet, de Gouges, and Wollstonecraft, enjoined the leaders of society to include women in the new rights of citizenship. Abigail Adams is now well known for rebuking John Adams and his fellow "Founding Fathers" of the United States for ignoring women's rights. In Germany, Theodor von Hippel, in the same year that Wollstonecraft's second *Vindication* appeared, revised his popular treatise on marriage to reproach the revolutionaries in France who, in their new constitution, had "opted to forget one half of the nation. . . . All human beings have equal rights—all French men and women should be citizens and free." Agreeing with the German philosopher Immanuel Kant that no human being should be used merely as a means, he challenged Rousseauean principles. "Men, do you really believe that half the world exists merely for your pleasure, for your own desires, to satisfy your selfishness? Animals function; human beings act. Why should a woman not be allowed to pronounce the word I?"[14]

The challenge of revolutionary reconstruction not only inspired renewed debates about women's rights and abilities. Many women participated directly in the political events in France, and they played many roles. Women of the popular classes formed part of the crowd that attacked the Bastille on July 14, 1789, and they marched by the thousands to Versailles in October of that year to demand bread—the famous march which resulted in the royal family's being brought back to Paris. An obscure lacemaker named Louise Chabry served as spokesperson for the forty women who had gained an audience with the king at the palace, rushing to Paris to tell the tale to the mayor of the city. Other unnamed women served as soldiers, and a female delegation approached the National Assembly demanding weapons. "Yes, Gentlemen, we need arms, . . . and we come to ask your permission to procure them." Women joined men also in submitting *cahiers de doléances,* or lists of grievances, to be delivered to the king. Merchant flower sellers petitioned for protection of their craft from untrained competitors. Fishwives saluted their "brothers" on the new venture "in the interest of the people." Women artists and silversmiths pledged both their moral support and their goods—a "widow's mite"— to sustain the new government. Still others of modest means called for "free schools where we can learn the principles of our language, religion, and ethics," although they explicitly rejected instruction in science, for it might, they said, "inspire us with a foolish pride and lead us toward pedantry." They also asked for paid midwives in the countryside.

Women joined the political clubs which sprang up around the city, and in some instances formed separate women's clubs, the most famous being the Revolutionary Republican Women Citizens led by Pauline Léon, a chocolate maker, and Claire Lacombe, an actress. In 1793 during debate over the new constitution in one of the sections of Paris, a woman announced, "Women are not taken into account in the political system. We request primary assemblies, and since the Constitution is based on the rights of man, we demand full participation in them right away." None of the specifically feminist proposals submitted to the Assembly received serious consideration.[15]

The women's political clubs were short-lived, dissolved by the Jacobins in the fall of 1793, possibly for their support of the *enragés.* who demanded extreme price control measures, or because the women transgressed social conventions of feminine behavior, donning the red cap of the revolution, debating politics in public, and attacking women in the marketplace who failed to wear the republican tricolor. The leader of the Paris Commune greeted a delegation of women with the admonition:

> Since when have people been allowed to renounce their sex? Since when has it been acceptable to see women abandon the *pious* duties of their households, their children's cradles, to appear in public, to take the floor and to make speeches, to come before the senate?

Robespierre's Committee of Public Safety counseled women who wanted to be republicans to dress simply, work hard at home—and give only moral support to the revolution.

The Jacobin's prescriptions for women, like Rousseau's, were perhaps in tune with the material and emotional needs of most people, for whom radical changes in gender roles were disquieting. Faced with conditions that threatened the sustenance of their families, most women have always utilized every means at hand to find food and the revolutionary decade was no exception. Whether subject or citizen, their first concern was assuring subsistence. Thus, the marketwomen, housewives, and working women who marched to Versailles in search of bread in October 1789 ("Let them eat cake" was Marie Antoinette's famous reputed reply), were far more typical of women engaged in political action than those who spoke in political clubs or signed petitions. The march to Versailles exemplifies a characteristic form of women's collective action, the "bread riot." During the eighteenth and nineteenth centuries, as national markets prevailed over local needs and authorities ceased to control foodstuff prices, angry women, sometimes armed with knives and sticks, used their informal communal networks to help assemble crowds, and they led mobs to attack mills, millers, machinery, or other ostensibly appropriate targets. "The bread riot," Olwen Hufton points out, "was female, or rather, maternal, terrain," especially if it occurred in the marketplace.[16] Otherwise, women probably played a role subsidiary to men, and increasingly so if violence erupted.

Female militancy over the shortage of foodstuffs during the winter of 1793, however, helped propel the revolution toward its bloody climax. Recognizing the force of women's intervention on the course of politics, one Jacobin warned,

> It is these counterrevolutionary *bougresses* [sluts] who cause all the riotous outbreaks, above all over bread. They made a revolution over coffee and sugar, and they will make others if we don't watch out.[17]

Since coffee and sugar were colonial goods, this reaction may illustrate suspicion of women's new consumption patterns and their easy slippage toward female militancy. After the Thermidorian coup in July 1794, autonomous public activity by women was forbidden. In May 1795, the National Convention decreed further that women be excluded from its meetings and allowed to watch from a gallery only if accompanied by a man.

In the mid-nineteenth century, the famous French historian and man of letters Jules Michelet laid the foundation for a long-lasting myth about women's roles in the French Revolution. Depicting women as more violent than men, Michelet, for whom the revolution itself represented the triumph of reason over religion, asserted that women embodied the worst excesses of emotionalism and religious fanaticism. Although liberty was symbolized by a goddess and France itself represented by the figure of Marianne, flesh and blood women were excluded from political life. Throughout the century, with the triumphs of the nation-state, law codes in France, Prussia, and elsewhere made active citizenship a privilege of maleness. Historian Geneviève Fraisse finds "a necessary link" between the founding of democracy and the exclusion of women. "Women's rights were not inadvertently overlooked but were denied," based on assumptions about sexual difference. Women's role in the new democratic regimes would be as "republican mother." In French republican parlance, contractual marriage implied a kind of domestic government in which "the husband [was] minister of foreign affairs, the wife the minister of the interior." The simple and sweet Cosette, in *Les Misérables,* exemplified the kind of wife idealized by Michelet and many of his contemporaries, although the famous republican, romantic author, Victor Hugo, was a staunch defender of women's rights. The notion of woman as the creator of "sons-of-the-fatherland" stretched across the continent to Russia, where "citizen-mothers" were expected to devote themselves to this patriotic mission.[18]

Despite being excluded by definition from "active" citizenship and relegated to "passive" citizenship on grounds of their sex, women of the revolutionary era, as we have seen, participated actively in the "practices" of citizenship.[19] In the decades following the Revolution, men with political power continued to deny women access to equal rights, and the double standard enacted into law by the Napoleonic Code constituted a significant setback. However, women persisted in contesting their relegation to second-class status. Furthermore, revolutionary legislation that gave women increased inheritance rights and established special tribunals to adjudicate disputes over legacies, custody rights and other family conflicts continued to facilitate women's quest for equality.

The many conflicting visions of women's capacities and appropriate roles that had been expressed during the centuries-long "argument about women," which was recapitulated by Enlightenment philosophers, were played out continuously in both theory and practice in succeeding decades. Although political theorist Joan Landes asserts that "the republic was constructed against women, not just without them," other scholars stress the positive. Throughout the nineteenth century women and men inserted feminist arguments into the developing public sphere that women had helped to create preceding and during the Revolution, and would revisit in later periods of reform and revolution.[20] When the leading architects of post-revolutionary France sought to diminish the public roles that some aristocratic women had played in prerevolutionary salons and that more ordinary women had assumed during the revolution, they found their efforts repeatedly and strenuously contested.

Reconstructing Society: Utopian Socialism and Antislavery Movements

The reaction against revolutionary change in women's formal social and political roles that began in France in the mid-1790s—the drive to construct a public arena only for men—was strengthened by the accession to power of a great military leader, Napoleon Bonaparte. For the Corsican-born conqueror turned emperor, women contributed to the nation above all future soldiers. Indeed, the justification for male political privilege was the duty to serve as citizen-soldier. Often praised by champions of democracy for having "opened careers to talent," that is, for replacing inherited status with merit as the criterion for selection of army officers and other leaders, Napoleon became infamous among nineteenth-century feminists for several provisions of the influential Napoleonic Code of 1804, once lauded for having established civic equality among "all men." Feminist critics objected strenuously to many of the articles that served to establish a new double standard based on a gendered ideal of citizenship and to create a polarity between public and private acts, particularly those provisions that required married women to "obey" their husbands, to take on their spouse's nationality and accept his domicile, and those that denied them legal status in court. They criticized regulations that prohibited lawsuits by unwed mothers to establish paternity of their children, thus denying them recourse for child support; that gave fathers exclusive authority to administer their minor children's affairs and to withhold consent to their marriage, even to imprison them for "correction," without the mother's consent. They rejected as well the provision that decreed adultery a crime only if committed by wives. For these laws, individually and collectively, made women second-class citizens, rather than full-

fledged participating members of the new French nation. Moreover, during the ensuing decade, Napoleon's victorious armies carried his code of laws across the Rhine
into the German lands and southward into the Italian peninsula. Its influence persisted; in the 1860s, after the unification of Italy, the new government drew on
Napoleon's Code. Napoleonic laws concerning women affected even the Louisiana
Territory of the United States, purchased from Napoleon in 1803, and the statutes
of subsequent state governments in the United States. In France, although feminists
condemned the Code for a century and a half and publicly burned it during solemn
events celebrating its centennial in 1904, French people escaped its influence very
slowly, beginning with married women's control of their own earnings in 1907, and
the right to initiate paternity suits in 1912.

Napoleon was overthrown by the combined armies of Europe in 1815. The
ensuing two decades, following on twenty-five years of upheaval, were largely ones
of conservative reaction, of attempted "restoration." Revolution had bred war; and
as Olwen Hufton points out, "war strikes at the family; it takes fathers and sons
and what death does not destroy can be left to the effect of long separation. This
was certainly the hard lesson of the French Revolution." Regardless of class, most
women who left a record of their experiences in revolutionary times felt themselves
to be victims.[21] In the end, women looked forward to more settled times and many
renewed their fervor for the church. The church not only symbolized stability and
continuity, it centered around the family. "The church," Hufton notes, "stood for
[the family's] integrity, its sanctity; the hallowing of birth, marriage, death; the
cement of something much more intrinsic than the social system." Even Napoleon
had recognized the power of the church and had come to terms with it in his Con-
cordat of 1802. During the ensuing century middle-class women in both Catholic
and Protestant countries increased their participation in religious observances. The
feminization of religion was a notable accompaniment to an increasingly commercial and industrial society.

The old regime, however, was never to be restored. Although England, Austria,
and Russia, among other European countries, guarded against renewed revolutionary outbreaks by enforcement of repressive laws—for instance, in England the "Six
Acts" of 1819 restricted mass public meetings and the Metternich Carlsbad decrees
of the same year imposed censorship of the press and of university life in all the German states—industrial development continued apace and new ideas continued to be
generated. Not all the agents and armies of the Holy Alliance and the Concert of
Europe (formed by the victors of Waterloo to maintain order on the continent) could
stamp out the spirit of revolution that spread across Europe in the early nineteenth
century. Popular movements that gained impetus in early nineteenth-century Europe
sought to change the lives of the "working classes" and "women," helping to constitute new identities through the linkages. They also worked to transform religious
practices and national boundaries, to emancipate slaves, and to remove civic disabilities imposed on minority religious groups.

Prominent among the thinkers promoting change whose ideas had been shaped
in the French revolutionary upheaval and the developing industrial system were the
Frenchmen Henri Saint-Simon (1760–1825) and Charles Fourier (1772–1837), and
the Englishman Robert Owen (1771–1858). Believers in a universal (natural) law

of progress, these men, known as "utopian socialists," went beyond criticism of existing privilege and exploitation to invent new systems of social organization. Most important for our concerns, they and their followers included in their contemplated reconstruction of society profound changes in women's roles and in gender relations. Saint-Simon, who proposed that the rulers of his new order be scientists, intended to base a rationalized utilitarian social structure on the ethos of early Christianity. But, he said, "The true Christianity must render men happy on earth as well as in heaven." His key to the future would be "moral science"; his vision illustrates the new power of "science" to authorize action.

Acknowledging that human beings were not identical in capacity, Saint-Simon considered their differences to be beneficial, for society was an organism of many parts, all functioning, ideally, in harmony. Work appropriate to capacity was the first law of Saint-Simon's "New Christianity." Furthermore, since "love was the fluid which coursed through the body social," the followers of Saint-Simon, who after his death set about proselytizing throughout Europe, envisioned a critical role for women. "Who else throughout the common ages," they said, rhetorically constituting their subject, "stained with blood, rust, and tears, has won man over to peace and love, if it is not woman?" Indeed, one of their primary goals became the reversal of centuries of Christian repression of sexual love and its concomitant degradation of women. Following Saint-Simon in his denial of the Christian dichotomy between body and soul, Saint-Simonians proposed to liberate the instincts, to "rehabilitate the flesh." Led by Prosper Enfantin, a former engineering student who later turned banker, they organized expeditions to Egypt to search for a lost "Female Messiah" who would emancipate not only "women" but indeed the whole human race. An interesting if unintended result of the Saint-Simonians' foreign adventures was their turn to industrial development, including plans for creation of the Suez Canal. Enfantin stated, "I ask you to regard my participation in the building of the dam [on the Nile] as an *ordinary* industrial act, in which there is only a distant relationship to the human regeneration that we have been announcing. . . ."[22]

Not all Saint-Simonians accepted Enfantin's conception of complete equality of the sexes, which was based in a rejection of the "politics of individualism" that he considered the cause of greed and inequality. This perspective led to one of his most controversial propositions—a denial of monogamy—labeled by its opponents (who eventually sent Enfantin to prison) as "free love." It also caused schisms among the Saint-Simonians. But Enfantin's ideas attracted women, initially bourgeois friends and relatives of the leaders, and later working women, some of whom were attracted by Saint-Simonian outreach programs that provided medical services, free vaccinations for children, and a cooperative workshop for seamstresses. Some two hundred women regularly attended the lectures that were given almost daily by the Saint-Simonians after the July Revolution of 1830. In 1831, 110 working-class women enrolled as "faithful adherents." Although they were perhaps attracted originally less by consciousness of themselves as women than by interest in the emancipation of workers, some of these women developed a new gender awareness and eventually founded an autonomous women's movement. They published a newspaper, which in successive issues announced in its title the advent of "The Free Woman," "The Apostolate of Woman," "The Woman of the Future," "The

New Woman," and "The Emancipation of Woman," before finally becoming *The Tribune of Women*. Its editors and contributors used only first names, declaring, "If we continue to take men's names we shall [continue to] be slaves." While some of them put the new sexual emancipation into practice, and others left the movement in disagreement with Enfantin's radicalism on this issue, most of the "new women" simply rejected ideas that conflicted with the reality of their lives. As historian Claire Moses points out, they recognized that the "love without marriage" advocated by Enfantin posed far greater dangers to them than to the Saint-Simonian men, most of whom would find places as industrialists, scientists, and managers in the new economic order, while they continued to labor as seamstresses for wages inadequate to maintain themselves, let alone their children. Rejecting abstract formulations of equality, the Saint-Simonian women used their differences from men to argue for practical measures to improve their lives.

Eventually many Saint-Simonian men became leaders in the development of new railways or invention of credit banks and other commercial or industrial ventures that multiplied during the heyday of economic liberalism. During the second quarter of the nineteenth century, the rich got richer, perhaps following the advice of the French minister Guizot, who asserted that a country's political power belonged of right to the men of fortune who owned and exploited its resources. Meanwhile, as urban slums mushroomed and worker rebellions led to violent clashes, some intellectuals began to assert that social peace could be achieved in industrial society only by reconstructing its economic and social foundations. They shared an optimistic belief in the power of human beings to shape their own societies, and hoped voluntarily to draw people into new communities carefully planned to ensure a total harmony of interests.

One of the earliest social, or "socialist" thinkers, Charles Fourier, an eccentric bachelor banking clerk, proposed a new order composed of "phalansteries," where men and women, carefully selected to assure a full complement of 1,620 different naturally occurring personalities, would be assigned to perform work so perfectly matched to their passions that socially useful labor would be perceived as play. A change of task every two hours or less would relieve workers of the "torment" of their present twelve- to fifteen-hour days spent at tedious jobs, and allow them freedom to express their "butterfly" and other passions. Thus work would bring pleasure, even dirty work such as spreading manure, which would fall to youngsters because of the "natural penchant of children for filth." A potential murderer would be reformed by assignment to work in the slaughter house. Fourier was so confident that a wealthy benefactor would appear to endow his scheme that for twelve years he went home every day at the announced hour of noon to wait. Although he died unrewarded, even before his death and for decades afterward, Fourierist communities were established in Europe and North America. Examples of the thirty-seven "phalansteries" founded in the latter include Brook Farm in Massachusetts (1841–47), famous for its association with American transcendentalism, and the North American Phalanx in New Jersey (1843–56).

To Fourier, the phalansteries, governed according to purported laws of harmony, represented an evolutionary improvement over societies based on individualistic competition, which he considered "the mother of all social crimes." From earlier chaotic stages of "savagery," "patriarchalism," "barbarism," and "civilization," human beings would progress through "simple association" to the highest stage of perfect harmony, called "compound convergent association." A measure of the level of progress in all societies was, he proclaimed, the status of women, a criterion later adopted by Karl Marx and other important thinkers. Thus like the Saint-Simonians, Fourier looked to a future world in which gender equality would prevail. Fourier's own passion for equality extended to the provision of identical clothing, education, and employment opportunities for both sexes. Individual families would give way to more efficient forms of collective living, with communal responsibility for child care and housework. Anticipating Freud, Fourier also developed an extensive analysis of human motivation and called for sexual liberation.[23]

If Fourier's scheme for social progress represented the vision of a lonely genius, an English utopian who set out to reorganize society, Robert Owen, was just the opposite, a successful businessman respected for his economic contributions to the community. After a spectacular rise from draper's apprentice to manager of a cotton mill employing five hundred workers by the age of eighteen, Owen bought the largest mill in Scotland and embarked on an experiment to disprove the myth of competitive individualism that his own career might have reinforced. Paying higher wages and providing better working conditions than his rivals, furnishing good homes and schools for his work force, he made New Lanark more productive and profitable than competing enterprises. Workers themselves adopted his ideas, later replacing Owen's paternalistic management with their own cooperative direction. Like Fourier, he also inspired experiments in communal living in the United States and elsewhere. New Harmony in Indiana (1825–27) and Nashoba in Tennessee (1826–29), which included as equal members former slaves (who moved to Haiti when the commune failed), are two of the thirteen Owenite communities established in the United States.[24]

Like the Saint-Simonians, the Owenites attracted considerable female interest. Mutually reinforcing contacts between the groups included the translation of articles from *The Tribune of Women* for publication in Robert Owen's journal, *The Crisis,* by an Irish Saint-Simonian turned Owenite, Anna Wheeler (1785–1848). Wheeler was closely associated with yet another "utopian," William Thompson (1775–1833), an Irishman who reorganized his seven hundred-peasant estate into a model scientific farming community. He also left his body to medical research, and his skeleton, library, and estate to the cooperative movement he founded. In concert with Wheeler, Thompson worked out the ideas he published in 1825 as the *Appeal of One-Half of the Human Race, Women, against the Pretensions of the Other Half, Men, to Retain Them in Political, and Thence in Civil and Domestic Slavery.* The Thompson-Wheeler *Appeal* was an attack on James Mill, the famous Utilitarian who, with Jeremy Bentham, adapted the ideas of the French *philosophes* to English society, calling for government by an educated middle class to procure "the greatest good for the greatest number." While proposing "universal suffrage," Mill had nevertheless rejected female enfranchisement, arguing that the "rights of men" included the interests of women. Thompson and Wheeler exposed the fallacies of Mill's position and protested his "pretensions," as indeed did his son, John Stuart Mill, whose own eloquent defense of women's rights, *The Subjection of*

Women, co-authored with Harriet Taylor and published in 1869, eclipsed the *Appeal* in fame and far-reaching influence.[25]

Another woman of the "utopian" era, Flora Tristan (1803–44) also drew on Saint-Simonian and Fourierist ideas, to become a major contributor to socialist and feminist thought. Daughter of a Peruvian army officer and a bourgeois French mother, Tristan learned only in adulthood that she would be denied social status and inherited wealth because her parents' religious marriage had not been paralleled by the civil ceremony required to establish its legality in France; that is, she was considered before the law an "illegitimate" child of an irregular union. Furthermore, she was twice a pariah, for she also had deserted an abusive husband, whom she could not, under the law of France (from 1816 until 1884), divorce. Traveling alone to Peru, where she vainly sought an inheritance from her father's substantial estate, and to England, where she met Owen and Wheeler and studied the social circumstances of women and urban workers, she used her uncommon experience as the basis of what Joan Moon has termed a "utopian synthesis of socialism and feminism." Feeling herself to be Mary Wollstonecraft reincarnated, she also used her pen to make a living writing passionate accounts of her experiences that established her reputation as a novelist and social critic. She felt herself called to tour France, bringing to "workers" and "women" her scheme for their liberation. The first to call for a universal workers' association, in 1843 she published her *Workers' Union,* proposing to reorganize both work and family along Fourierist lines. The "absolute equality" of men and women, she believed, was essential to the emancipation of the working classes and the moral transformation of human society. For every community she planned education for the children of the working classes and refuge for the old and homeless. No one should henceforth suffer the ostracism and poverty she had endured.[26]

During the first half of the nineteenth century, currents of romanticism inspired an intense concentration on the self that resulted in both "dandyism," or extreme elegance in men's fashions, and the poetry of Byron, Shelley, and Keats. The literary *Sturm und Drang* period in Germany, the Jewish Hasidism of eastern Europe, the Gothic revival in architecture, and the music of Chopin and Liszt all reflected rejection of the extreme rationalism of the eighteenth century. At the same time, romanticism also affected the more socially oriented founders of the new science, the "social science" defined by Thompson and Wheeler as "the science of promoting human happiness." All of the progressive political ideologies of the nineteenth century—utilitarianism, liberalism, anarchism, socialism, feminism, Saint-Simonianism, Fourierism, Marxism—shared the conviction that human beings could perfect the social world. Common to many of these systems of thought and political movements was the belief that (in words taken from the conclusion of the Thompson-Wheeler *Appeal*) men could and must be persuaded to take "the most certain step towards the regeneration of degraded humanity, by opening a free course for justice and benevolence, for intellectual and social enjoyments, by no colour, by no sex to be restrained."

Three decades before the founding of the first organized feminist group in Britain, women in England and the German Confederation, inspired by evangelical religion, created thousands of "female societies" dedicated to social improvement.

Quaker and other evangelical women drew on a tradition of female engagement in moral reform and religious philanthropy to organize for the abolition of slavery in the British colonies. For example, the Birmingham Ladies' Society for the Relief of Negro Slaves, founded in 1825 before a "general" anti-slavery group existed in that city, held regular meetings, raised extensive funds, and distributed thousands of pieces of abolitionist literature. Their campaign techniques included organizing by neighborhood, recruiting members to visit households to pass out literature and solicit donations, and collecting hundreds of thousands of signatures on petitions to parliament. They also called for avoiding use of slave-produced commodities. While their propaganda drew heavily on the religious principle that all people are children of God, it assumed as a corollary that blacks were "younger brothers and sisters who must be educated and led by their older white siblings." This attitude provided an inadvertent justification for imperialism. Englishwomen would be educators as well as liberators, providing the colonies with models of respectability against which to measure native behavior. Historian Catherine Hall describes the Christian mission of abolitionists as a " 'contest for empire' between Christianity and slavery" in which the battle against sin drew on a "faith rooted in an ethnic superiority." Christianity was equated with civilization; freedom depended on accepting the Christian God.[27]

After the emancipation act of 1833 ended slavery throughout the British Empire, some British women turned toward North America to continue the fight for abolition. Members of ladies' antislavery societies in English cities also worked actively to end the "apprenticeship" system which allowed planters in the British West Indies to maintain black servitude. One petition they sent to Queen Victoria in 1837 bore over half a million signatures; a group of fourteen women in Darlington alone had collected 5,315 signatures. Through the efforts of women such as the Quakers Elizabeth Pease and Anne Knight and the Unitarian journalist Harriet Martineau, the tactics pioneered by British women were conveyed across the Atlantic, where Quaker women also played a vital role in the antislavery movement. Political skills honed in these campaigns proved useful later in the century when women organized to redefine gendered roles and rights of citizenship. Female antislavery work was also responsible for the formation of international networks through which radical movements in Europe and America were linked. The English anti-slavery activist Anne Knight attributed the inspiration for her subsequent feminist work with women of several nations to the famous rebuff suffered when the American antislavery activists Lucretia Mott and Elizabeth Cady Stanton were denied seats at the World Anti-Slavery Conference held in London in 1840, on grounds of sex.[28] The evangelical movement that produced both women "cottage preachers" in rural England and antislavery activists was followed later in the century by other campaigns inspired by religion, including the project of taking Christianity to "primitive" peoples in the British colonies.[29] As Antoinette Burton shows in chapter 7, British women's lives in the Victorian era were profoundly affected by empire, both the ideology that supported it and the commodities it produced. By the 1860s and 1870s, British women found the colonies a source of food, clothing, and interesting reading, as well as—especially for single women—employment as missionaries. "Empire," Burton concludes, "was, in short, not just a phenomenon 'out there,' but a fundamental part of domestic culture and national identity." Women reformers linked Christian and liberal ideology to women's traditional role as moral educator to create new opportunities at home and abroad. This linkage also served as a foundation for "imperial feminism." The founding of the Society for the Propagation of Female Education in the East in London in 1834 was the first of many steps justified "on the grounds that because of the 'Asiatic' practice of secluding women . . . only 'ladies' had any chance of 'being welcomed to their seclusion.' " The ladies' charge was to spread the ideal of Christian family life. Antislavery activists, missionaries, and feminists all drew comparisons between women in England and the colonies to further their aims; but they shifted from suggesting similarities in women's subservient condition in the early feminist arguments to emphasizing the superiority of European women as a normative model in the later period.[30] Indeed, French women seeking admission to medical education in the 1860s used this cultural assumption to justify their quest.

Until its last decades, the nineteenth century was dominated by a passion for progress, by an Enlightenment-inspired belief in a law of progress that would spread its benefits from Europe to the world. The French sociologist Emile Durkheim spoke for Saint-Simon and generations of his spiritual descendants when he declared, "The supreme law of progress of the human spirit carries along and dominates everything; men are but its instruments." Women were both the agents and the beneficiaries of this historical current. But the experiences of women and men of all classes were more problematic than such formulaic pronouncements suggest.

The "Woman Question"

Amid the forces for revolution and the countervailing movements toward reaction, the "woman question," as debate over women's roles was called expressively in the nineteenth century, captured attention as never before. Intertwined with the "social question," or the debate about class relations and the condition of the poor, as well as with the slavery issue, it led to an unprecedented outpouring in all the languages of the Western world, and later in Europe's colonies as well, of articles, books, sermons, theses, poetry, and painting concerned with the "place" of women and the political and social consequences of changing gender relations. Changes in household functions that altered the productive, educative, and caretaking roles of the family had enormous impact on society. The reorganization of men's and women's work within and beyond familial boundaries created a split between reproduction and production that affected virtually everyone. Most men adapted by increasingly withdrawing from shared domestic labor to take on paid employment outside the household. Indeed, by the middle decades of the nineteenth century, some workingmen, principally tailors and other craftsmen, organized against work for wages at home, for they could obtain better working conditions and higher pay in workshop and factory employment. They developed a new work identity based on a nondomestic workshop, using concepts of gender to create also a novel feminine work identity that emphasized not the specific professional skills of the dressmaker or seamstress but instead the association of these skills with domesticity. The notion of skill itself became linked to the location of the workplace rather than the occupational capacities of the worker.[31]

The emergence of a new commercial and industrial economy seemed to make old questions about women's proper pursuits more acute. Tension developed between normative expectations and lived experience. Even though the ideology of domesticity, which had been expounded and popularized by Rousseau, attracted adherents throughout society, the needs of working-class and some middle-class families for additional income made the gainful employment of women still imperative. Thus, the ongoing productive activities for the home or for exchange by wives and daughters defied the new normative divisions of work and home life inherent in the ideology of domesticity. Furthermore, while the theory of natural rights led to new emphasis on individual liberty, equality, and self-fulfillment, the accelerating preoccupation with childhood, seen for example in new regulations restricting child labor and mandating schooling, led to increased demands for nurturance over longer periods by mothers. As a result, although the reality of women's lives defied any simple normative standard, discussions of women's roles and rights contained contradictory prescriptions for women. At stake were answers to such questions as whether women should be educated and if so, why and how; whether women had a "right to work" and if so, where and when; whether married women should enjoy rights to individual ownership of property or income; whether femaleness should entail permanent political disability.

As work was redefined in the nineteenth century, so, too, was education. Basic to the Enlightenment spirit and the liberal thought of the eighteenth and nineteenth centuries was a belief in the power of education to create a better world. Faith in education was fundamental to the belief in progress. Echoing the work of Fénelon in the 1670s, in the 1760s, the French physiocrat Nicholas Baudeau (1730–92?) pointed out that "national education [would be] imperfect in every respect if we were to abandon half the State to prejudice, routine, and abuse." Alluding to the example of ancient Sparta, where girls received rigorous training, he concluded that "Daughters of the Nation," would make "worthy wives for the Great Men" of France only if properly educated. The importance of an educated mother was linked to nation-building across the continent.[32]

During the nineteenth century, movements to establish public schools and to increase access to them by children of all classes were established in England, France, Germany, the United States, and many other countries. The motives of the founders were mixed. Some were compelled by new theories on child development (such as Rousseau's and Pestalozzi's) and moved to found child-oriented programs, such as the first kindergarten, founded in Germany in 1837 by Friedrich Froebel.[33] Others were concerned primarily with the need of representative governments for an educated citizenry. Some advocates of public education represented privileged groups who, fearing the potential of illiterate and untrained people for crime and social unrest, considered the terms *working classes* and *dangerous classes* virtually synonymous. A "penny press" brought new information and expectations to the expanding and increasingly literate populace, making it seem imperative for the ruling classes to create a "schooled society" committed to emergent national norms in language, manners, and morals, and especially to the values of hard work and self-discipline (the "work ethic").

The education of women could hardly be ignored in this effort although the push for female education, like so many responses to the situation of women in a changing society, contained contradictory elements. Educational reformers sometimes assumed that women, as mothers and the first educators of the young, were naturally disposed toward conservatism and patriotism. Educated women through their moral presence would exert a "calming influence" on men and hence promote social stability. Others, primarily anticlericals, hoped that improved public education would free women from the sway of the Catholic church, which continued in many countries to monopolize classroom teaching for girls.

Overall, education for girls changed little until the late decades of the century. Formal education for girls was not always deemed essential. In France, for example, only after 1850 were primary schools for girls required by the government. Few girls could aspire to formal education beyond elementary school; secondary schools were opened to girls only in the 1870s and later. Not only did conservatives such as Joseph de Maistre, a leading French conservative of the Restoration period, argue that female schools were unnecessary because girls were meant for "a life of retreat and shall be solely concerned with familial needs," the question of girls' schools was caught up in many countries with the struggle for dominance of education by church or state. Major improvement in female education depended upon acceptance of new ideas about women's roles and about female intellectual capacities. Ultimately, following revolutionary political, economic, and social change, the significance of women's roles as the first educator of their children, and an important source of influence on men as well as social life, led to new attitudes about schooling for girls. But the question of educating girls was also closely tied to the availability of female teachers and of funds to pay them.

If girls were to be educated, it was assumed that they should be taught by women, and the first female colleges were teacher training institutes. As Kreszenz Rapp, a German teaching candidate, wrote in 1807 in her qualifying exam, girls

> require a softer, gentler treatment than boys, because nature plants in the girls' hearts the seeds of gentleness and timidity, a noble gift of their sex. . . . Who can understand/manage these feminine feelings, whose delicacy envelopes the entire being of the girls, better than one of their own sex? . . . Male teachers are less effective because their knowledge of female delicacy only comes from books.

Careers for women in teaching were thus justified as an expression of femininity and an extension of domesticity—women's "natural"nurturing role performed in another setting for a worthy public purpose. The teacher's role was "social motherhood."[34]

As early as 1814, the southern German state of Bavaria created a teacher training institute for women—a so-called normal school. However, widespread employment of women as teachers in public elementary schools generally began later, for example, in the Netherlands, Sweden, Denmark, and Italy in the 1850s and 1860s. Women won acceptance as secondary school teachers still later and more slowly, at first mostly in subjects such as music, drawing, and sewing.[35]

In Catholic countries such as France, the dominance of the church in educating girls meant that many teachers were trained by religious congregations. Nuns, with moral support from the church, tended to obtain more lucrative positions than lay teachers. "Most of the female lay instructors languish in poverty; the female instructors from religious orders lack for nothing," declared a school inspector in 1839. An inspector in another region noted that male teachers earned an average of 487 francs, women 380. In addition, while other teachers were required to pass an examination to be eligible for employment, those educated by Catholic congregations needed only a "letter of obedience" from the church to be qualified. After 1886, however, when the republican government intent on separation of church and state passed a law prohibiting employment of religious teachers in public schools, the Catholic influence over girls' education gradually diminished.[36]

Because teachers' pay was closely linked to their qualifications as well as sex, most women teachers earned very little. Women's salaries supported only the most frugal existence, and some lay teachers faced destitution. Sometimes paid less than subsistence wages, although expected to remain celibate, they might be forced to depend on aid or gifts from the parents of their students. Historian Anne Quartararo notes that male teachers in rural France also were poorly paid and could expect to earn about 600 francs annually, a sum hardly sufficient to maintain a family. Graduates of a normal school earned from about 15 percent to as much as 60 percent more (based on years of service) than other teachers. The disparity between women's and men's salaries diminished between 1875 and 1905, since wages increased about 40 percent for women, 25 percent for men. However, "to ask for parity with the male profession never occurred to women teachers in this period," states Jo Mardagant, author of a study of the first generation of French teachers who challenged the male monopoly of secondary education in France.[37]

Ultimately, the increase in public schools, even for boys alone, created a new demand for large numbers of literate teachers, and the teaching profession was opened to large numbers of women. Especially in rural areas, these lay teachers played an important role in educating a peasantry sometimes hostile to secular and republican values. In the north and west of France, sometimes at the behest of the local priest, villagers and peasants boycotted lay teachers—men as well as women— and encouraged children in disobedience. "Lay women teachers," declares Quartararo, "needed to demonstrate strong character at their village posts." The first profession opened for women, teaching provided an excellent school for self-reliance, and teachers constituted an important constituency for both labor union organizers and for feminists.[38]

The motivation for change was different in England. The first colleges for women, Queen's and Bedford, date from the late 1840s. Established to elevate the status of governesses and other "ladies," they opened the teaching profession to women in order to meet an urgent need for "respectable" employment for impecunious middle-class spinsters. It was said that "every lady is and must be a teacher— of some person or other, of children, sisters, the poor." One of the pioneers of female education in England was Barbara Bodichon (1827–91), whose father had founded a "Ragged School" for the education of poor children, where he employed a teacher trained at Robert Owen's New Lanark School. He gave his own children an Owenist education as well as an early introduction to the work of Mary Wollstonecraft. In her own school, established in 1854, Bodichon drew also on the ideas of the educational reformers Froebel, Pestalozzi, and Emanuel Swedenborg to apply the latest theories in child development. She carried the argument for female education well beyond a utilitarian standard of preparation for domesticity, however, to insist on the importance of training for economic independence.

Women want work both for the health of their minds and their bodies. They want it often because they must eat and because they have children and others dependent on them—for all the reasons that men want work.[39]

Thus the question of female access to education and to employment as teachers shaded into a developing controversy over women's "right to work." Physicians and professors debated the purported deleterious effects on the female reproductive system of intense, sustained mental exertion, some alleging that highly educated women would suffer sterility. The underlying ideology of domesticity also affected attitudes toward the roles of working-class women, for whom hard physical labor and early death remained the common experience. In the 1860s and for the rest of the century, organized workingmen's groups repeatedly placed "the woman question," or its variant, "the industrialization of women," high on the agenda at their trade union and political party conferences. Often their goal was to eliminate women from industrial work. Largely artisans in threatened handicrafts, they faced new competition from national and international markets of the evolving world economy, reduced wages and unemployment due to the mechanization and centralization of their industries, and, in some cases, for the first time they began to see women other than family members entering their workshops. They could draw on an older guild tradition of sex role divisions that reserved the production of goods for exchange to artisans alone (or their widows) and assigned women housework or service in other peoples' households. Perhaps also partly because, as skilled workers, they could better afford to support families than could the untrained day laborers who rarely participated in workers' councils, these workingmen called for the elimination of industrial work by women. By a large majority in 1866, members of the International Workingmen's Association, largely English, French, and Swiss artisans, passed resolutions declaring that women's place was at home, and that man's role was to support her. Furthermore, they declared that women should give birth to numerous offspring (ideally four children at two-year intervals) and remain at home to raise them. Every good woman, they insisted to a protesting minority, would find a husband.

Working-class men who condemned industrial work for women argued that they intended thereby to improve the moral and physical condition of families, class, and nation. They supported gainful labor by married women at home in the traditional ways that Barbara Franzoi Bari depicts (chapter 6). This marginalization of women workers, however, often led to their exploitation as pieceworkers in sweatshops. In other cases, as Donna Gabaccia shows among the Italian peasantry (chapter 9), domesticity represented not a new cultural norm for ladies but a measure of decline in wage-earning opportunities. In rural populations such as Sicily, families required female contributions to move "beyond subsistence." When rural entrepreneurs responding to shifting markets reorganized the structure of agricultural industry and women lost cash-generating labor, they became fully dependent on inadequate male wages. Some of the women thus "unemployed" into full-time housewifery faced male hostility; others emigrated to the United States.

The developing feminine ideal, articulated at midcentury by numbers of working-class men, also denied women access to full membership in a society where labor was increasingly becoming the prime criterion of social value and the signature of personal identity. Paule Mink (1839–1901), a young Polish-French woman later active in the Paris Commune of 1871 and in the founding of the French Workers' Party, responded to the workers' delegates of the First International:

> By denying woman the right to work, you degrade her, you put her under man's yoke and deliver her over to man's good pleasure. By ceasing to make her a worker, you deprive her of her liberty and, thereby, of her responsibility. . . . Certainly there will come a time—and I hope it is not too far off when our honor will come primarily from our work, where no one will be worth more than he produces. Then what will woman's role be if, inert and passive, she is entirely at the disposal of her husband? If she is forbidden to think of work? If she has no future apart from marriage? And if she is deprived forever of liberty and a life of her own?[40]

Some of these debates pitted the men who followed the Frenchman Pierre-Joseph Proudhon (1809–65), the father of philosophical anarchism, against the supporters of Karl Marx (1818–83), the founder of "scientific socialism." Proudhon defended the family centered ideal of the peasant-proprietor and artisan-merchant that rejected concentrated, capitalist industry, credit and exchange banking, centralized government, and female emancipation. Marx alternatively looked toward increasing industrialization and centralization as means to greater abundance and more equitable distribution of work and wealth. He saw the participation of women in "social production," or work outside the home, as a necessary step toward achievement of a just and "classless" society. According to Marx, in *Capital* (1867), despite its evils in the short run, under capitalism, ultimately,

> modern industry, by assigning as it does an important part in the process of production outside the domestic sphere to women, to young persons, and to children of both sexes, creates a new economical foundation for a higher form of the family and of the relations between the sexes.

Although Marx went beyond the utopian socialists to develop a more sophisticated historical and philosophical analysis of political economy and the "social question," he unfortunately narrowed his vision to exclude serious attention to the "woman question." Shortly after his death, however, his close colleague, Friedrich Engels, extended the analysis and directly shaped the emerging European social democratic interpretation of the woman question. In *The Origin of the Family, Private Property and the State* (1884), Engels traced the subordination of women to the institution of private property and men's concern for accumulating and preserving wealth. Only through participation in "social production" could women escape subjugation; the key lay in abolition of the monogamous family and restoration of a higher form of early communalism in which women were no longer economically dependent on men. Engels's work was widely read, translated, and serialized in the international socialist press. Today, aided by the new feminist theorizing, we can see the limits of Engels's monocausal interpretation of women's subordination. By anchoring the issue of sex-based, social asymmetry in the material fact of private property, he failed to appreciate the complex links among women's roles—in sexual relationships, in the family, in religious institutions, as well as in political and economic activities—and their subordination to men. He also failed to recognize the significance of race and ethnicity in formulating the bases of women's identity. This made him and his followers, many of whom truly expected the emancipation of women to follow directly upon socialist revolution, unduly optimistic about the possibility of change.

Following Marx and Engels, most other Marxists ignored the unpaid household labor of women as productive activity, and they neglected the effect of family values and experiences on workers' consciousness. Nonetheless, social democrats (as the followers of Marx were known) gave the woman question more attention than most other developing political parties of the day. The exploitation of working-class women by capitalist employers was a recurrent theme in socialist literature and socialists gave strong support to protective legislation for women workers. Ambivalent about women's right to work, they nevertheless inscribed women's rights on their banners and at least in theory—and to a limited degree in practice—opened their ranks to all, "without distinction by sex." In nineteenth-century Europe, the woman question and the social question were entwined. But the "marriage" of two social movements for reform, feminism and socialism, was stormy and the anticipated partnership unequal, as we shall see below.

Efforts to obtain advanced education and improved employment opportunities for women were largely the work of a small group of mostly middle-class women who recognized the contradictions between Victorian ideals and the circumstances of women's lives. Although the self-educated scientist Mary Somerville (1780–1872)—the first person to sign John Stuart Mill's 1868 petition for women's voting rights—had in 1862 petitioned the University of London to open its examinations to women, colleges and universities continued to offer liberal, scientific, and professional education only to men. Access to advanced studies to prepare women for teaching in secondary schools required further battles, such as those faced by the graduates of the school founded in 1881 at Sèvres near Paris, to train women for teaching in the lycées of France.[41]

While daughters of the middle classes pioneered a new role for women as members of this "exalted profession," professionalization itself, which required creation of new schools for training and new and formal standards of admission to practice, generally served to exclude women, as we saw also in Part I. According to the historian of science David Noble,

Just as the leaders of the orthodox clergy of the fourth century or the founders of the scientific academies of the seventeenth anxiously strove to formalize their position and legitimize their authority through a process of exclusion, distancing themselves from any and all who might jeopardize their elite respectability, the professionals of the nineteenth century strove nervously to forge for themselves a similarly exclusive, exalted, and unassailable social identity. As in the earlier episodes, this entailed, among other things, a renewed distance from the undisciplined enthusiasm, impassioned iconoclasm, and supposed latent hysteria of women.[42]

Fears of the effects of admitting women to the universities persisted in some cases well into the twentieth century.

Nowhere was the incongruence between assumptions about women's nature and women's experiences greater than in the simultaneous apotheosis of the married woman and mother as the moral guardian of the family and her exclusion from legal authority in marital and parental matters. If men had "rights" and women only "duties," as the title of an English pamphlet suggested, how could the latter ensure family welfare in the event of masculine malfeasance? Did women's invisible contributions to material and social success merit no reward? What would become of the increasing numbers of "redundant women" destined not for the blessings of matrimony but for enduring spinsterhood? The "woman question" defied simple answers.[43]

Domesticity and Demography: Women and the Family

Western feminists today may look back to Charles Fourier, John Stuart Mill, and Karl Marx, as well as to Mary Wollstonecraft, Flora Tristan, Barbara Bodichon, or Paule Mink as defenders of the "second sex" and women's rights as individuals. But middle-class women of the nineteenth century, who perceived themselves primarily as members of families, more likely aspired to achieve the new kind of femininity expressed in the work of the poets Coventry Patmore, whose poem "The Angel in the House" gave the ideology of domesticity a new symbolic expression, and Alfred Lord Tennyson, whose verses perfectly captured the doctrine of "separate spheres":

> Man for the field and woman for the hearth:
> Man for the sword and for the needle she:
> Man with the head and woman with the heart:
> Man to command and woman to obey;
> All else confusion.

Tennyson's dichotomous presentation of the sexes illustrates the phenomenon analyzed by a historian of German women, Karin Hausen, who suggests that in the nineteenth century the "character of the sexes" previously defined by particular household duties—field and hearth, sword and needle—came to be understood in terms of essential and universal attributes of male and female.

We should not overestimate the newness of Hausen's formulation, for Aristotle long before spoke of woman's essentially weak character mirroring her imperfect nature; but she correctly points to the continuous process of constructing sex differences at distinct historical moments. Now, however, as economic changes spurred the evolution of the European family toward a unit bound more by desires for affection and consumption than by production, the doctrine of separate spheres became largely normative. Concerted efforts were made to impose it on the working classes, and especially "to educate the women of the lower strata of society for their 'destiny as wife, housekeeper, and mother' . . . as the best solution to the social question." Artisanal workers such as printers and metalworkers demanded a "family wage" sufficient to support their wives and families. In 1891, the Catholic church added its endorsement with the influential papal encyclical *Rerum Novarum* (On New Things). The separation of work from home life idealized in the concept of domesticity served to establish a family's "respectability." Both women and men aspired to this elevated status. Later this norm was exported to colonial territories through women's emigration schemes. "Respectable" family living became one way colonists could set themselves off from "native" populations.

Sibylle Meyer's study of "conspicuous leisure" among the wives of civil servants in the German Empire (chapter 8) provides a telling example of the tensions posed by the new ideal feminine role. Meyer shows that perfect housewives who "determined the atmosphere of the household through their character, not their work," existed only in imagination. In reality middle-class wives led active, productive lives that paralleled and supported their husbands' increasingly routinized and disciplined labor. Yet they strove to maintain an *appearance* of ladylike idleness commensurate with their husbands' status. Indeed the leisure of its women, even more than the occupation of its men, served to validate a family's claim to middle-class standing. Increasingly the desire for respectability made work outside the home unacceptable for working-class women as well. Concepts of proper gender behavior played an important role in constructing a class society. They also contributed in colonial settings to the ongoing identification of white Europeans with a set of class-specific gender behaviors.[44]

For most women of all classes, marriage continued to be the only honorable—indeed often the only available—career throughout the nineteenth century. But slowly its purposes and significance changed. Facing the fateful decision of choosing a mate—a decision that would determine, in a real sense, her life course, a twenty-one-year-old Frenchwoman, Stéphanie Jullien, wrote to her brother in 1833, "This is not child's play, this is a matter of my whole life, of my future, of my happiness. . . . To decide my fate once and for all, my whole destiny! I don't dare do it." She worried lest her prospective young husband fail to establish himself sufficiently and she questioned the nature of *his* character and *his* commitment. "Who can assure me that he will succeed? And if he loves me now, how do I know that he will always love me in the same way? Perhaps I'll be paving the way for lots of trouble if I accept, but if I refuse, what will I do? . . . I don't have any calling, nor could I have one."[45] Like most women of all but the wealthiest classes, Jullien found marriage essential for economic security.

But men also were concerned with making good marriages, for marriage was a ticket required for inclusion in middle-class culture. Leonore Davidoff and Catherine Hall, studying "family fortunes" in the late eighteenth and first half of the nineteenth centuries, assert that "the significance of marriage for middle-class men cannot be overestimated." The "manly man" was expected to maintain a religious and respectable, sober and stable family life; with his wife, he oversaw well-mannered children and managed a "properly ordered" household. Every aspect of home design, even the garden, had to meet specific gendered standards considered essential to middle-class status.[46]

For the urban poorer classes, often kept from legal wedlock by poverty (as well as state intervention where laws prohibited the marriage of indigents), "common-law" marriage was commonplace in the nineteenth century. Middle-class moralists, however, disapproved, and some philanthropic groups, such as the Society of Saint Vincent de Paul in France, actively encouraged poor people to marry and to "legit-imize" their offspring. And marriage rates increased as the century progressed. For the spinsters, however, who were destined by an increasing demographic imbal-ance or the lack of a sufficient dowry, and sometimes by choice, never to marry, other solutions were required. No longer able for the most part to retire to convents, less likely than single men to emigrate to the Americas or the colonies, unable to find respectable or remunerative employment, single women sought alternative forms of domesticity. Large numbers entered domestic service. A study of spinsters in mid-Victorian England shows that about 25 percent of single women of all ages up to the midforties were employed as live-in servants. Older spinsters tended to live with siblings, especially spinster sisters and bachelor brothers. Sometimes spin-sters formed what we today call "surrogate families," or cooperative living groups.

The difficulties of earning a living continued to make life alone precarious for single women. In addition, they faced the societal disdain that Charlotte Brontë illustrates in her mid-nineteenth-century novel *Shirley:* "Old maids, like the house-less and unemployed poor, should not ask for a place and an occupation in the world." They were not wanted by married relatives. Furthermore, much of social life was closed to unescorted women. Jules Michelet felt that "the worst fate for a woman was to live alone. She could hardly go out in the evening; she would be taken for a prostitute. If she were late, far from home, and became hungry, she would not dare enter a restaurant. . . . She would make a spectacle of herself." As single women and widows in the nineteenth century led efforts to provide aid to unwed mothers, to care for foundlings, to rehabilitate prostitutes, to improve oppor-tunities for education and employment for their sex, they also created new social roles for themselves. Some women, moreover, chose spinsterhood because they pre-ferred the company of their own sex. Lifelong, emotionally as well as economi-cally supportive, relationships among women provided them a not uncommon alter-native to marriage. These "romantic friendships" also offered an important outlet for their emotional or erotic impulses.[47]

Women's desire to marry and their chances of finding a suitable partner depended on many factors, including notably the ratio of women to men in appro-priate age groups. Unlike earlier periods when differential death rates due to aban-donment or neglect of female infants or disproportionate female mortality in plague epidemics might have caused a deficit of eligible women, the seventeenth and later centuries were marked generally by a surplus of girl babies and overall of women. Sex ratios varied locally and regionally, however, as migration between rural and urban areas, employment expansion or stagnation, and laws determining inheritance rights all served to affect demographic patterns. According to historical demographer Anne-Lise Head-König, "Only when there is a large surplus of women combined with an expanding labour market can any significant degree of female economic and social independence be achieved."[48]

Most women, however, preferred to marry. Typically, they entered matrimony later than we might expect, usually only well into their twenties, on average about twenty-four or twenty-five, though with many specific variations. In rural areas, where young people still often had to await both parental permission and economic resources, women might not marry until their intended groom could convince his father to deed him a share of the family plot. Some parents resisted their children's marriages because the departure of grown children from the household meant the loss of labor power or wages essential to family survival. In 1835, when Villermé, while investigating working conditions visited cottage workers in the region of Tarare (near Lyons), he found that men married on average at the age of thirty, women at twenty-seven. Not only age at marriage but even the chance to marry at all depended on occupation. Thus, at midcentury in the textile cities of Roubaix, France (1861) and Preston, England (1851), all but 12 percent and 10 percent, respectively, of women married. But in the artisanal and commercial cities of Amiens, France, and York, England, 24 percent and 16 percent of women remained unmarried at fifty years of age. Some women, of course, formed long-lasting "free unions," also called "concubinage" and "Parisian marriages," and contributed to the rising number of "illegitimate" children. Burgeoning rates of illegitimacy reflected the vulnerability of young women attracted to new urban centers by opportunities for employment. Particularly if they came from communities where premarital pregnancy had routinely led to a wedding, they were very susceptible to promises of love and marriage. Separated from family and community, which in earlier times exerted pressure on reluctant bridegrooms, they might find themselves "with child" and deserted by their partner who, in an urban setting with considerable occupational mobility, could easily evade his responsibility.

Marital fertility, illegitimacy, and infant mortality have been the subject of extensive research by historical demographers. Social historians, including historians of women, find these records pregnant with meaning for the quality of women's lives. Using crude birthrates (births per 1,000 inhabitants), fertility ratios (number of children under five per number of married women, aged fifteen to forty-four), and infant mortality rates (deaths of infants under one year per 1,000 live births), they have reconstructed a world of reproduction in which women gave birth to numerous offspring and—especially in the working classes—saw half of them die. Birthrates and fertility rates declined steadily throughout the nineteenth century, a token perhaps of new attitudes about human control over their lives. Infant mortality, however, diminished only after the development of public health measures such as the purification of water and pasteurization of milk in the early twentieth century. The latter was particularly significant in reducing recourse to wet-nursing. The sending of the newborn to a rural cottage to be breast-fed diminished among the upper classes after the eighteenth century—at least partly because of the admonitions of Enlightenment philosophers. During the nineteenth century, however, this custom spread among the urban lower-middle classes. Wet nurses were also used by officials charged with the care of foundlings, the thousands of infants abandoned by their unwed, or married but impoverished, mothers. Many destitute women preferred abandoning their children to watching them suffer or die of hunger. This measure was in earlier ages a common recourse of poor families. "Abandonment," states Rachel Fuchs, "was a socially acceptable means to cope with an unwelcome child in an era without safe birth control or abortion, and without an effective program of aid to dependent children." Twenty percent of all babies born in Paris in the early nineteenth century (and over half of the "illegitimate") were abandoned.

If the care of abandoned children created a widespread social problem, in France wet-nursing became so prevalent that it constituted a major "business," subject to regulation by law and government agency. Because mortality among nurslings reached scandalous heights—over 50 percent in some cases, up to 80 percent among foundlings—the government in 1874 adopted the Roussel Law, which put all infants nursed outside their homes for pay under state protection. Across the Channel, in 1871, an Infant Life Protection Society was formed to combat the similar practice of "baby-farming." In 1911, legislation prohibited employment of mothers within four weeks of delivery—but enforcement was lax. These responses of the state offer early examples of a new role for government in family matters.[49]

In the development of the modern family perhaps the most significant change has been the deliberate reduction of the number of children born to the average woman and a concurrent intensification of emotional ties between generations. Beginning with France in the late eighteenth century, followed by Sweden at mid-nineteenth century and much of Europe after the 1870s, most populations in the Western world have employed deliberate means to limit their fertility. The ability to limit births, and hence to reduce economic obligations, has contributed to earlier as well as to increased rates of marriage. The source of these changes was not a new technology, as is sometimes assumed. Effective artificial contraceptive devices were not available until the twentieth century. Large-scale production of the condom, which was known in the sixteenth century, and the pessary and diaphragm, both invented in the nineteenth, was indeed possible after the discovery of the vulcanization of rubber in the 1840s, but widespread distribution came many decades later, during World War I. Therefore, some historians have assumed an increased practice of *coitus interruptus,* or withdrawal before ejaculation, a male-controlled method known since biblical days but not employed earlier on a scale large enough to affect overall population growth. More recently, historians such as Angus McLaren have pointed to female agency in control of family size, through abortion as well as infanticide and abandonment or neglect. In the nineteenth century, it appears, the mainspring of change was a new secularized attitude justifying human intervention in events previously attributed to nature or to God.

A movement to promote the new ideas and to spread knowledge of birth control practices began in the 1830s. Following an overture by William Thompson, who was concerned about potential population problems in his Mutual Cooperative societies, in 1823 the Utilitarian Francis Place published a handbill addressed "To the married of both sexes," which offered instructions in the use of a vaginal sponge as the means to avoid the "evil consequences of too large a family." It was distributed by a very young John Stuart Mill among others. In 1832 in the United

States and in 1834 in England, an American doctor, Charles Knowlton, published his *Fruits of Philosophy, or the Private Companion of Young Married People.* Knowlton was fined and sentenced to jail but gained a considerable following in both countries. The impact on British popular opinion was most noticeable after 1877, when Charles Bradlaugh and Annie Besant reissued the Knowlton pamphlet, deliberately challenging the law that censored such material as "lewd, filthy, bawdry and obscene," definitely not fit "to be talked about among Christians." Publicity surrounding their trial made the subject headline news in the daily newspapers. As a result, hundreds of thousands of people learned about possibilities for fertility control; and many women wrote Besant begging for useful information. The jurors were "unanimously of the opinion that the book in question is calculated to deprave public morals," and found the defendants guilty. Although they escaped penalty on a technicality, Besant nevertheless was deprived of custody of her daughter, the judge fearing Besant's influence on the child's morality. Criminal prosecution of advocates of contraception continued for decades in all the states of Europe and in North America. Nevertheless, many women demonstrated their support. In Amsterdam in 1882, when Dr. Aletta Jacobs opened the world's first birth control clinic, hundreds of women lined up for help.[50]

In Europe the movement for birth control was called Neo-Malthusianism, in recognition that the limitation of births, deemed by the economist Malthus as the only way the working classes could avoid starvation, might be achieved by means other than the abstinence that he had recommended. "Family planning" was thus originally proposed as a solution to the "social question," as a means to reduce poverty by limiting the numbers of children to be fed. It would also, in this view, raise the bargaining power, and hence wages, of workers through reduction of the ratio of labor supply to demand. While its usage spread less quickly among the impoverished than among the propertied classes, in urban centers, poor women could draw on informal female networks for knowledge and assistance. In a subculture linked by midwives, laundresses, and concierges, friends, and neighbors, sometimes employers and charitable ladies as well, all helped poor women to survive. In some textile areas of East Saxony, Germany, in the early twentieth century, generally apolitical village women fired off petitions to the government supporting the work of "natural" healers. They were registering deep dissatisfaction with the unwillingness of the male medical profession to dispense birth control information and devices to women hungry for such knowledge.[51]

The deliberate reduction of fertility, by separating sexuality and reproduction, allowed for a new attitude toward sexual pleasure. But it is unclear what this meant to women. A widely publicized medical opinion of the era, notably in England, asserted that women were essentially "passionless." Lacking in spontaneous sexual urges, they would, if protected from corrupting influences, remain chaste. Without lust of their own, they could easily refrain from sexual activity and indeed would so prefer, except for their naturally occurring desires to please their husbands and to experience maternity. Believing ignorance the means to preserving innocence, parents should—according to the custodians of Victorian morality—insulate their daughters from all suggestive sights and sounds. Hence the euphemisms "bosom" and "bust" for breast, "limb" for leg (and the leggings once installed on piano posts), "second joint" (of a chicken) for thigh, and such circumlocutions as "private parts" and "down there" for vulva and vagina.

While no one will ever know, of course, how many women were so well brought up by Victorian mothers that they went to their bridal beds ignorant of where babies came from (a Victorian ideal), the views of female sexual passivity expressed by the English physician Lord William Acton found their way into many medical texts and sex manuals in both England and the United States.

> There can be no doubt [he wrote] that sexual feeling in the female is in the major-
> ity of cases in abeyance, and that it requires positive and considerable excitement
> to be roused at all; and even if roused (which in many instances it never can be)
> it is very moderate compared with that of the male.

This opinion constituted a virtual reversal of the long-standing view of women as sexually lascivious, which as we noted in Part I helped to explain the dominance of witchcraft by the female sex. It also reflected, however, something new: the discovery by biologists that women's reproductive organs were not, albeit in inverted and lesser form, morphological duplicates of men's but different and incommensurate. Biologists learned only in the 1840s that unlike men, women did not require orgasm to release fluids containing their reproductive cells. The way was now clear—without supporting scientific evidence—to construct a human female with little if any "natural" sexual drive. Drawing on the Darwinian theory that natural selection favored the advancement of males over females (and of whites over all other "races"), "the differences between the sexes bec[a]me the product of the grand and inevitable process of selection that governs all life." The concept of separate spheres became grounded in assumptions of biologically determined bodily differences. This belief exemplifies not only the tendency of nineteenth-century scientists to group all women and men into the abstract categories female and male but also to naturalize as biological much behavior that reflected social conditioning. Scientific ideas buttressed the social inequality of women and of so-called races deemed inferior on the basis of reported differences in brain weight and skeletal structures. Criminals and Jews were also said by some physical anthropologists to constitute avatars, "savage[s] in the midst of civilization." By the turn of the century, empirical studies had disproved brain-weight theories. But science continued to be employed by publicists for race and gender prejudice.[52]

Elizabeth Blackwell, however, who in 1849 became the first woman to earn a medical degree in the United States, saw clearly that the views of Lord Acton and others who traced women's supposed lack of passion to biological foundations were flawed. Stressing the psychological component of women's experiences, she pointed out that not only had women been taught to consider sexual passion as sinful, they also feared continual childbearing, with its inevitable companions, pain, uterine injury, or death from toxemia, hemorrhage, and "childbed fever." Blackwell maintained that sexual urges were just as strong in women as in men. The consequences of sexual expression, however, differed greatly.

To understand female sexuality and the body in any period or place, it is essential to examine a complex set of circumstances—economic, social, legal, medical, and religious—which affect each woman's life. The overriding factors for most women in the modern period have been their economic dependency on men; their social subjection to a double standard that demands chastity of females while condoning, even encouraging, promiscuity in males; their liability before legal codes enacted and interpreted exclusively by men; their vulnerability to pregnancy and lack of control over related medical interventions such as contraception and abortion as well as parturition; their exposure to religious doctrines that deny female spiritual authority and preach submission to men as obedience to God. Most women experienced marriage, sexuality, and reproduction as a unitary phenomenon that dominated their lives. Neither the material conditions nor the theoretical perspectives of the Victorians encouraged any distinction or fluidity between gender, understood as culturally constructed differences, and biologically determined characteristics. The social systems that controlled people's lives made it difficult for most women to claim possession of their bodies and to define their own sexuality. On the contrary, it was through motherhood that most women established their social position and as mothers that they claimed a larger role in public life. As Part III shows, in the early decades of the twentieth century, a few pioneers began to articulate new views on these issues.

Feminist Reform, Nationalism, and Empire

If the first half of the nineteenth century is associated with a rising swell of democratic political reform, economic liberalism (laissez-faire), and romantic individualism, the second half is often viewed retrospectively through a cloud dark with belligerent nationalism, rampant materialism, and class conflict. While the advance of commercial and industrial capitalism continued throughout the century, creating an era of overall prosperity that lasted until the depression of 1873–96, the tide of laissez-faire liberalism began to ebb much earlier. Throughout Europe, emerging nationalist movements had formed, some in reaction to Napoleon's conquests, with the goal of liberation from foreign domination, others bent on creation of unified nation-states from numbers of smaller, dynastic territories. For many of the early nationalists, the idea of "country" embodied the expression of a glorious unifying and humanitarian spirit. A spontaneous "rising of the people," or reasoned argument and compromise, would achieve the aims of restructuring the state to reflect national sovereignty safeguarded by the people-in-arms. While the movements toward nationalism in central Europe originated in an idealistic desire for liberation and liberal government, the achievement of national liberation and unification fell to the force of military might. It was not the heroic poet Giuseppe Mazzini (1805–72) of the Young Italy Movement, but the shrewd manipulator C. B. di Cavour (1810–61) who, aided by French arms, brought success in the Italian peninsula; and the antiliberal diplomat and chancellor, Otto von Bismarck (1815–98), who used the "blood and iron" of the Prussian-led army to forge a unified German state in the wars of unification (1864–71). Nationalism turned more aggressive in the international arena in Europe and in imperial rivalries abroad.

Increasingly, too, nation-states began to intervene in people's lives, moved by concern for maintenance of social order and military power. Late nineteenth-century discussions of the social question and the woman question were never far removed from concerns about patriotic goals. Whether analyzing the French defeat by Prussia in the war of 1870–71 or the bloody end to the Paris Commune, Frenchmen were likely to point to national "decadence" or "degeneracy" as a cause. This sense of national decline was closely related to fears about the reduced population growth termed "depopulation." While some blamed the population decline on the pattern of land inheritance that emerged from the revolutionary period (which ended primogeniture and reduced patriarchal power), others, as Karen Offen shows persuasively (chapter 10), looked pointedly at the changing roles of women and pronounced feminism as the guilty factor. Late-century women's movements were profoundly shaped by the population debate and the rising tide of nationalism. The rhetoric of nationalism and patriotism often slipped into a discourse on empire which charged women with a burden of "imperious maternity." Female emigrants to the empire responded by using maternalist language to portray their mission as a form of female philanthropy. "The right sort of women, fitted to be the wives of a sturdy band of settlers and the mothers of loyal subjects . . . [should emigrate] to help us make the future of South Africa an era of Civilisation, of Progress, and of Illumination, where semi-barbarism, Retrogression and Ignorance for years have reigned supreme," wrote Susan, Countess of Malmesbury.[53]

Feminist thinking was integrally related to the social question and the intensifying class conflict of the late nineteenth century as well as to national rivalries. The first phase of modern, organized European feminism, as we have seen, developed in response to social upheaval during the French Revolution and called for equality for women on the basis of natural rights. The first successful reforms targeted sex-based inequities in the law. They date from the 1830s, when the British writer Caroline Sheridan Norton turned her pen against injustice wrought by marriage and family law. Perhaps because of the nineteenth-century apotheosis of "the family," the feminist "politics of the breach" (limited, step-by-step reform), focused first on improvement of women's status and enhancement of their authority in marriage and family.

Norton brought the most notable case of the century before a wide public. Granddaughter of a famous writer, she was an accomplished novelist, wife of a successful political figure, and mother of three children. Estranged from her husband, who falsely accused her of adultery, she could not, under the laws of England, obtain a divorce. She was legally deprived of custody of her children, visiting rights, and the income from property she had inherited from her family and brought to the marriage. Forced to support herself by writing, she struck back by publishing pamphlets attacking the laws—although the copyrights to her work, of course, belonged to her husband. Norton's work is credited with helping to win passage of statutes in England that, in 1839, allowed courts to give mothers some rights to their children; and in 1857, permitted courts to dissolve marriages in cases of adultery by wives or adultery coupled with incest, bigamy, rape, sodomy, bestiality, or extreme cruelty by husbands.[54] Tolerance for wife-beating and husbandly adultery diminished and, at first very slowly, divorce began to join desertion and death as ways that marriages might end. Englishwomen, who were plaintiffs in only 1 percent of divorce cases between 1670 and 1857, comprised 42 percent between 1859 and 1909.[55]

In the nineteenth century, however, far more women benefited from feminist reforms in property rights than in divorce. In the same year that divorce was liberalized in England (1857), a married woman's property bill was introduced into Parliament; it was to be passed only in 1870. German wives waited for redress until 1900, and married Frenchwomen gained legal rights to their own earnings only in 1907. Although socialists sometimes expressed disdain for the feminist demands for property rights, from this campaign married women of all classes, increasingly drawn into the paid labor force, obtained the potential for greater power within their families as well as an increasing measure of independence.

Most feminists of nineteenth-century Europe sought to enhance women's familial roles and to broaden their traditional powers. By organizing and agitating for custody and property rights, women gained experience and built a base from which to launch other drives. As middle- and upper-class women won access to secondary and university education, they also sought admittance to occupations monopolized by men. After securing a foothold in teaching, they moved into other white-collar employment. For a small, pioneering minority of women access to the "liberal professions" became a focal point. Indeed, as the healing professions developed new standards and required advanced education in medical schools closed to female students, some women created opportunities by encouraging the new profession of nursing. One early leader was Amalie Sieveking, an upper-class German spinster who, as she rejected marriage, vowed to be "If not a happy wife and mother, then founder of an order of Sisters of Charity!" When with twelve other women she founded the Female Association for the Care of the Poor and the Sick in Hamburg in 1832, she renewed opportunities for her sex, which had diminished with the decline of religious orders. "To me," she told an audience a decade later,

At least as important were the benefits which [work with the poor] seemed to promise for those of my sisters who would join me in such a work of charity. The higher interests of my sex were close to my heart.[56]

Sieveking's more famous successors, the Englishwoman Florence Nightingale and the American Clara Barton, organized nursing services on the battlefields of the Crimean War (1854–56) and American Civil War (1861–65) respectively, and likewise set out to promote the interests of women. Nightingale, who transformed nursing from a menial occupation of lower-class, untrained, and sometimes dissolute servants into a profession of respectable, educated, middle-class "women in white," was deliberately seeking a means to escape the narrow limits of her own life as a proper spinster daughter in a well-to-do Victorian family. Feeling herself called by God to treat the bodies of soldiers fallen in a distant land, she broke the bounds of Victorian femininity. Like Barton, she proved that women could overcome not only hard physical labor but also the sight of blood and death.

After 1864, through Red Cross service that combined notions of patriotism and femininity, conservative women began to participate in a wide range of war preparation activities. In Germany these efforts were organized by patriotic women's associations under dynastic patronage and sanction; these groups were also active in all manner of philanthropic work in local communities. This highly publicized work in the municipalities was justified as a training ground for women's future medical war services in the "home front." Similar patriotic nursing fields opened for women in England, when its territorial defense system was reorganized in the early twentieth century. Indeed, in this way some aristocratic and middle-class women (or even poorer rural women who became Red Cross nursing sisters in the state of Baden, Germany) were directly involved in promoting nationalist causes. In Norway, during the tense years surrounding the separation of their country from Sweden, conservative women aided the cause of national defense by raising funds for a warship, appropriately named *Valkyrien* for a northern war goddess. Some more radical women used the "women's warship" project to justify their call for extending the electoral franchise to their sex. "From the day women all over the civilized world enjoyed political rights with men—from that day war would be banished from the earth," declared one anonymous voice. According to historian Ida Blom, "Female responses to defence policy and activity during the final national crisis in 1905, earned women a sympathetic reaction when the question of the vote was discussed in Parliament and contributed to victory in 1907."[57]

Other, more reform-minded women engaged men directly on another battlefield, one that pitted them against the double standard of moral behavior and the male license for extramarital sexual behavior that it allowed. Beginning as early as the Jacksonian period in the United States, Victorian women drew on the age's increasing differentiation of sexual "character" to justify female intervention against prostitution. In 1834, women met in a Presbyterian church to form the New York Moral Reform Society. Resolving that "the licentious man is no less guilty than his victim, and ought, therefore, to be excluded from all virtuous female society," they launched a crusade against prostitution in New York City. It was, they declared, the "imperious duty of ladies everywhere . . . to cooperate in the great work of moral reform." In England, Josephine Butler led the Ladies' National Association to campaign successfully for repeal of the Contagious Diseases Acts, and to extend its mission to India as well. Butler's example directly inspired a Continental Federation based in Switzerland to abolish all state-regulated prostitution. The British legislation of the 1860s, which was intended to control the spread of venereal disease among soldiers, subjected suspect women to pelvic examination and possible involuntary hospital confinement, while ignoring male participants. French women also organized in the cause of "abolition"; that is, for elimination of a state-sanctioned system of "public women" who were required to undergo periodic examination and to obey regulations regarding their dress, housing, and social behavior. Many reform-minded women agreed with Flora Tristan, who labeled English brothels "temples that English materialism has raised to its gods!—the *male* guests who come there to exchange their gold for debauchery." While most women of her era preserved their respectability by disdain for "fallen women," Tristan had laid the onus directly on men.[58]

Most abolitionists, as the activists against regulated prostitution were called, believed that the male sexual drive, on which the maintenance of prostitution had long been justified as a "necessary evil," was not immutable. But they found less support for reforming men's sexual behavior in the Catholic countries such as Italy than in Britain, where Protestant sects typically called for male continence. In most of Europe, regulationists, who called for the registration and regular examination of prostitutes, rather than abolitionists prevailed. Prostitutes, who were increasingly visible in rapidly growing urban centers, were deemed immoral sexual deviants, even criminals, to be isolated from respectable society. They would be confined in legally tolerated brothels, controlled by police, military, and public health authorities. Weekly inspection of prostitutes in England dates from 1828. Regulation was one of the supposedly progressive reforms introduced by new governments in Russia in 1843 and in Italy in 1860.[59]

Historians of prostitution in countries as different as England and Italy have found that prostitutes were not only victims of men or society. "Far from being passive victims, nineteenth-century prostitutes exhibited a surprising vitality, flexibility, and ingenuity," says historian Mary Gibson of Italian women. Judith Walkowitz, studying English women, comments that "their lives were a piece with the larger body of laboring women who had to eke out a precarious living in the urban job market, for whom sexual coercion was but one form of exploitation to which they were subjected." Luise White (chapter 11) also finds economic motivation driving prostitution in the British colony of Kenya. Prostitution with all its drawbacks and dangers was most of all a means for women to survive.[60]

While many women worked as "clandestine" practitioners of their trade, registered prostitutes have left their traces in the records. Studies show that most were young, single, and uneducated. In Italy one survey found that in 1875 their level of illiteracy reached as high as 86 percent, 95 percent, and 100 percent in Rome, Naples, and Palermo, respectively, far above the average for all women in those cities. A noticeably high percentage also lacked the economic security and social support of their native families. While not all prostitutes were poor, few came from the middle or upper classes. It was middle-class women who set out to rescue their "fallen sisters," for motives sometimes self-serving as well as altruistic.

Besides taking on the cause of prostitution, middle-class feminists also turned to educational, employment, and social rights. Others decided, as early as the 1840s in the United States and England, that equal participation in the political arena was prerequisite to all other reform. The English and American women's rights movements began at midcentury to organize for the conquest of the suffrage, although as we point out in Part III, without great success before World War I. In most countries, however, women and men whom we today call feminist for their advocacy of improvement in women's condition, avoided both rhetoric and action that smacked of strictly individual rights. They tended to focus on issues designed to enhance women's performance of their traditional familial duties. In the American context, this strategy has been called "womanly," since it purported to strengthen women's power in the home. Karen Offen, in an important study of historical variations in feminism, traces this "relational" or "familial" feminism, which was very pronounced in France but influenced women's movements elsewhere, in Ernest Legouvé's concept of "equality in difference." One of the most influential writers on the woman question in nineteenth-century Europe, Legouvé blended Enlightenment thought on "natural" or biological law with appreciation of the historical contributions of women to human culture. Arguing for reforms in law and customs that would allow both sexes to fulfill their unique and complementary responsibilities,

Legouvé posed a doctrine of separate but equal spheres in family and social life that promoted women's interests against the power of patriarchy.[61]

For still others, who followed in the tradition of Tristan, Marx, and Engels, the woman question was subsumed within the social question; that is, they traced the oppression of all groups to the power of states organized primarily to protect private property and to preserve class inequality. Believing that the problems of women would disappear once the conflict of classes was resolved, they devoted their lives to movements for radical social and political change. In the 1870s, young Russians of both sexes formed study circles to prepare for social revolution. Sofya Perovskaya (1854–81), one of the assassins of Tsar Alexander II in 1881, launched her career as a revolutionary with a quest for personal autonomy along with nine other women in the "Chaikovskii circle," a study group of idealistic, radical young men and women. For her, emancipation for women was part of a broader attack on authoritarianism in personal life and despotism in political affairs. Her contemporary, Anna Kuliscioff (1854–1925), cofounder of the Italian socialist party, believed socialism to be pre-requisite to the "perfectibility" of all "whom the present order of things compromises materially or morally . . . workers, youth, and women." The French Marxist Aline Valette (1850–99) headed her weekly journal, *L'Harmonie sociale,* with the slogan "The Emancipation of Women Lies in Emancipated Labor." In the last decades of the nineteenth century, as socialists and feminists organized to contend for political power, socialist parties possessed greater resources and appeared to some working-class women to be more congenial than feminist organizations dominated by mid-dle- and upper-class women. When they attempted, however, to introduce "women's issues" into socialist programs for action (as distinct from party platforms), typically they were ignored, rejected, or labeled "deviationists."

As socialist victories at the polls accelerated throughout most western and cen-tral European states and put impressive power into the hands of male-dominated social democratic parties in several nations, it became essentially impossible for socialist women to maintain alliances with so-called bourgeois feminists, who had been officially declared as their class enemies, or to support reforms deemed inade-quate to promote the class struggle. The problem is exemplified by the conflict between two German socialists, Lily Braun and Clara Zetkin, over establishing household cooperatives to reduce women's domestic duties. For Braun, such arrangements would not only relieve the conflict between home and work created by female entrance into the industrial labor force, they would also establish an institu-tional basis for the transition from capitalism to socialism. To Zetkin, the acknowl-edged leader of European socialist women, they represented nothing but "bourgeois reformism," Band-Aids for festering wounds. For Zetkin, as for most socialist men, alteration of the domestic division of labor could only follow, not precede, the revo-lution. Committed to the practice of class conflict, they soft-peddled issues such as domestic arrangements, family power, or family planning that might pit working-class women against working-class men, even as they sought to improve women's position in the work force and to win for them basic individual rights. If nineteenth-century socialist feminists found their theories often compromised in practice by socialist resistance to new roles for women and to issues defined as "feminist," they continued to believe first and foremost that fundamental transformation of family and society was prerequisite to the emancipation of women. Therefore, their emphasis remained on social revolution; the rest, they believed, would follow.

The importance of solving class conflict loomed large also for reformers who hoped to avoid the revolutionary confrontation envisioned by many Marxists. The French Solidarists, the English Fabians, the Catholic Center Party in Germany, and other political groups inspired by religious values sought solutions to the social question that were geared toward class and familial harmony, to "solidarity" rather than to conflict. A common ground among political factions (including, in fact, socialist parties) that adopted irreconcilable positions on most other matters was the need to safeguard the reproductive potential of the working classes by "protecting" women. Catholics and socialists stood together in the interest of family stability and maternal fecundity. Despite the protests of feminists concerned to enlarge, not to restrict, women's right to work and of some employers and laissez-faire liberals, politicians of the left, center, and right joined to pass labor legislation restricting women's employment in certain industries and limiting their hours. Through these protective laws the state intervened to act, as it were, as guardian of female health and family welfare. Assuming that women's health and endurance were more fragile than men's, and their ability to organize for self-protection less developed, it enacted statutes deemed philosophically or constitutionally unacceptable when applied to men. Parliamentary speeches in favor of protective laws often evoked nostalgic images of idyllic family centered domestic industries falsely assumed to have prevailed in earlier times. Indeed, in many areas the new laws operated to revitalize home industries, but as we have noted, the working conditions in these late-century "sweatshops" were far from idyllic. By applying restrictions only to factory-type employment, protective legislation served to marginalize women workers further and to contain them within the least advanced, often home-based, industries where piecework and long hours prevailed and no inspectors intruded.

Nevertheless, for many lawmakers the passage of protective legislation was the ideal solution to the woman question: it would "protect" those "mothers" whose families (now or in the future) would require their active financial contributions. It would also strengthen the "race," it was said, in the ongoing struggle for national dominance. As Karen Offen points out (chapter 10), national politics and family politics were "inextricably intertwined." The century-long campaign for a wide range of women's rights was, at least for a time, partially eclipsed by "reason of state," especially in the interest of national strength and military defense. This debate was also transformed by the new context of the welfare state. Even middle-class women who consistently fought as feminists for their sex felt compelled to emphasize familial, and often national, rather than personal needs. The power of the nationalist rhetoric was so strong that in the last decades of the nineteenth century, they even began to narrow their scope to the vote in the interest of "social housekeeping" or "imperial motherhood," a topic involving Europe and its colonies that will be discussed further in Part III. When the idealistic optimism with which the century began turned toward cultural despair at its end, "women" would be called on to rehabilitate society in an idealized role as moralizing mothers.

NOTES

1. Peter N. Stearns, *European Society in Upheaval,* 2d ed. (New York: Macmillan, 1975), p. 1.

2. Anna Clark, *The Struggle for the Breeches: Gender and the Making of the British Working Class* (Berkeley: University of California Press, 1995), p. 5; also Maxine Berg, "What Difference Did Women's Work Make to the Industrial Revolution?" *History Workshop Journal* 35 (1993): 22–44. See also Judith G. Coffin, *The Politics of Women's Work: The Parisian Garment Trades, 1750–1915* (Princeton: Princeton University Press, 1996).

3. Thomas Dublin, *Women at Work: The Transformation of Work and Community in Lowell, Massachusetts, 1826–1860* (New York: Columbia University Press, 1979); Laura S. Strumingher, *Women and the Making of the Working Class: Lyon 1830–1870* (Montreal: Eden Press, 1979), especially pp. 21–22. For younger Englishwomen, see excerpt from Parliamentary Factory Inquiry Commission (1833) in Erna O. Hellerstein, Leslie P. Hume, and Karen M. Offen, eds., *Victorian Women: A Documentary Account of Women's Lives in Nineteenth Century England, France, and the United States* (Stanford: Stanford University Press, 1981), p. 389. For older Englishwomen, Wanda Fraiken Neff, *Victorian Working Women: An Historical and Literary Study of Women in British Industries* (London: Cass, 1966), p. 72.

4. Bettina Berch, "Industrialization and Working Women in the Nineteenth Century: England, France and the United States," (Ph.D. dissertation [economics], University of Wisconsin, Madison, 1976), especially pp. 157–159.

5. Friedrich Engels, *The Condition of the Working Class in England,* trans. and ed. W. O. Henderson and W. H. Chaloner (Oxford: Blackwell, 1958; German first edition, 1845). Louise A. Tilly and Joan W. Scott, *Women, Work, and Family* (New York: Holt, Rinehart, Winston, 1978).

6. Pamela Sharpe and Stanley D. Chapman, "Women's Employment and Industrial Organization: Commercial Lace Embroidery in Early Nineteenth-Century Ireland and England," *Women's History Review* 5, no. 3 (1996): 341; Whitney Walton, "Working Women, Gender, and Industrialization in Nineteenth-Century France: The Case of Lorraine Embroidery Manufacturing," in Daryl M. Hafter, ed., *European Women and Preindustrial Craft* (Bloomington, Ind.: Indiana University Press, 1995) pp. 87–107.

7. Clark, *Struggle for the Breeches.*

8. On Locke's "equal Title," see Susan Moller Okin, *Women in Western Political Thought* (Princeton: Princeton University Press, 1979), p. 200.

9. Karen Offen, "Reclaiming the European Enlightenment for Feminism; or Prologomena to Any Future History of Eighteenth Century Europe," in Tjiske Akkerman and Siep Stuurman, eds., *Perspectives on Feminist Political Thought in European History: From the Middle Ages to the Present* (London: Routledge, 1997), pp. 85–103, quotation on pp. 85–86.

10 Terry Smiley Dock, *Woman in the Encyclopédie: A Compendium* (Potomac, Md.: Studia Humanitatis, 1983), quotation on p. 167.

11. Our summary of the Encyclopedists' views draws heavily on Abby R. Kleinbaum, "Women in the Age of Light," in Renate Bridenthal and Claudia Koonz, eds., *Becoming Visible: Women in European History* (Boston: Houghton Mifflin, 1977), pp. 217–235; and Sara Ellen Procious Malueg, "Women and the *Encyclopedie,*" in Samia I. Spencer, ed., *French Women and the Age of Enlightenment* (Bloomington, Ind.: Indiana University Press, 1984), pp. 259–271. Excerpts from the works of several of the philosophers appear in Susan Groag Bell and Karen M. Offen, eds., *Women, the Fam-*

ily, and Freedom: The Debate in Documents I: 1750–1880 (Stanford: Stanford University Press, 1983). Condorcet on slavery quoted in Marvin Perry, *An Intellectual History of Modern Europe* (Boston: Houghton Mifflin, 1992), p. 155.

12. Mary Wollstonecraft, *A Vindication of the Rights of Woman,* Norton Critical Edition (New York: W.W. Norton, 1975), pp. 5, 40, 194.

13. For example, Wollstonecraft was evoked in the first issue of a feminist journal, *Filipina,* published in Manila in 1909. For criticism of Wollstonecraft, see, e.g., Joan B. Landes, *Women and the Public Sphere in the Age of the French Revolution* (Ithaca, N.Y.: Cornell University Press, 1988), pp. 127–138; and Susan Gubar, "Feminist Misogyny: Mary Wollstonecraft and the Paradox of 'It Takes One to Know One,' " in Diane Elam and Robyn Wiegman, eds., *Feminism Beside Itself* (New York: Routledge, 1995), pp. 133–154.

14. For Hippel, see Bell and Offen, eds., *Women, the Family, and Freedom* I, pp. 116–118.

15. On Chabry, see Darline Gay Levy and Harriet B. Applewhite, "A Political Revolution for Women? The Case of Paris," in Renate Bridenthal, Susan Mosher Stuard, and Merry E. Wiesner, eds., *Becoming Visible: Women in European History,* 3d ed., (Boston: Houghton Mifflin, 1998), pp. 265–292, especially p. 272; for *cahiers* and petitions, see *Women in Revolutionary Paris, 1789–1795: Selected Documents,* trans. and ed. Darline Gay Levy, Harriet Branson Applewhite, and Mary Durham Johnson (Urbana, Ill.: University of Illinois Press, 1979), pp. 22–33, 72–74.

16. Olwen Hufton, "Women in Revolution, 1789–1796," *Past and Present* 53 (November 1971): 94.

17. Chabot, *Journal historique et politique,* no. 69 (September 18, 1793), quoted by Olwen Hufton, *Women and the Limits of Citizenship in the French Revolution* (Toronto: University of Toronto Press, 1992), p. 35.

18. Geneviève Fraisse, *Reason's Muse: Sexual Difference and the Birth of Democracy,* trans. Jane Marie Todd (Chicago: University of Chicago Press, 1994), pp. xv, 2. On domestic government, Eugene Pelletan quoted by Judith F. Stone, "Republican Ideology, Gender and Class: France, 1860s–1914," in Laura L. Frader and Sonya O. Rose, eds., *Gender and Class in Modern Europe* (Ithaca, N.Y.: Cornell University Press, 1996), pp. 239–259, quotation on p. 244; on Cosette ibid., p. 242. Richard Stites, *The Women's Liberation Movement in Russia: Feminism, Nihilism, and Bolshevism, 1860–1930* (Princeton: Princeton University Press, 1991), p. 16.

19. On the distinction between the "natural and civil rights" defined as *passive* and the "political rights" of those designated *active,* see Abbé Sieyès, "Preliminary to the French Constitution" (August 1789) in Lynn Hunt, ed., *The French Revolution and Human Rights: A Brief Documentary History* (Boston: Bedford Books, 1996), p. 81.

20. Landes, *Women and the Public Sphere,* p. 171. On women's political practices, see Dominique Godineau, "Masculine and Feminine Political Practice during the French Revolution, 1793-Year III," in Harriet B. Applewhite and Darline G. Levy, eds., *Women and Politics in the Age of the French Revolution* (Ann Arbor: University of Michigan Press, 1990), pp. 61–80; and Harriet B. Applewhite and Darline G. Levy, "Women, Radicalization, and the Fall of the French Monarchy," in ibid., pp. 81–107. On gender and the public sphere, including a critique of Landes, see Dena Goodman, "Public Sphere and Private Life: Toward a Synthesis of Current Historiographical Approaches to the Old Regime," *History and Theory* 31, no. 1 (1992): 1–20.

21. See Marilyn Yalom, *Blood Sisters: The French Revolution in Women's Memory* (New York: BasicBooks, 1993).

22. On women and the utopian socialists, see Susan K. Grogan, *French Socialism and Sexual Difference: Women and the New Society, 1803–44* (New York: St. Martin's Press,

1992), Frank E. Manuel, *The Prophets of Paris* (New York: Harper and Row, 1962), pp. 122, 127, 186–187, 229, 231, 241; Claire Goldberg Moses, *French Feminism in the Nineteenth Century* (Albany, N.Y.: State University of New York Press, 1984), pp. 10, 47–48, 52, 65, 92, and id., "'Difference' in Historical Perspective: Saint-Simonian Feminism," in Claire Goldberg Moses and Leslie Wahl Rabine, *Feminism, Socialism, and French Romanticism* (Bloomington, Ind.: Indiana University Press, 1993), 17–84; and Mark Poster, ed., *Harmonian Man: Selected Writings of Charles Fourier* (Garden City, N.Y. Doubleday, 1971), p. 258.

23. For an outstanding study of Fourier's life and work, see Jonathan Beecher, *Charles Fourier: The Visionary and His World* (Berkeley: University of California Press, 1986).

24. For a history of the commune movement in the United States, see Yaacov Oved, *Two Hundred Years of American Communes* (New Brunswick, N.J.: Transaction Books, 1988).

25. For the latest reprint, with an introduction by Richard Pankhurst, see Thompson's *Appeal . . .* (London: Virago, 1983). Also Barbara Taylor, *Eve and the New Jerusalem: Socialism and Feminism in the Nineteenth Century* (New York: Pantheon, 1983).

26. S. Joan Moon, "Feminism and Socialism: The Utopian Synthesis of Flora Tristan," in Marilyn J. Boxer and Jean H. Quataert, eds., *Socialist Women: European Socialist Feminism in the Nineteenth and Twentieth Centuries* (New York: Elsevier, 1978), pp. 19–50.

27. Catherine Hall, *White, Male and Middle Class: Explorations in Feminism and History* (New York: Routledge, 1992), p. 225.

28. Louis Billington and Rosamund Billington, "'A Burning Zeal for Righteousness': Women in the British Anti-Slavery Movement, 1820–1860," in Jane Rendall, ed., *Equal or Different: Women's Politics, 1800–1914* (Oxford: Basil Blackwell, 1987), pp. 82–111; Bonnie Anderson, "The Lid Comes Off: International Radical Feminism and the Revolutions of 1848," *National Women's Studies Association Journal* 10, no. 2 (Summer 1998): 1–12.

29. Deborah M. Valenze, *Prophetic Sons and Daughters: Female Preaching and Popular Religion in Industrial England* (Princeton: Princeton University Press, 1985).

30. Jane Haggis, in "White Women and Colonialism: Towards a Non-recuperative History," in Clare Midgley, ed., *Gender and Imperialism* (Manchester and New York: Manchester University Press, 1998), pp. 45–75, quotation on p. 53; Clare Midgley, "Anti-slavery and the Roots of 'Imperial Feminism'" in id., ed., *Gender and Imperialism*, pp. 161–179.

31. Joan Wallach Scott, "Work Identities for Men and Women: The Politics of Work and Family in the Parisian Garment Trades in 1848," in id., *Gender and the Politics of History* (New York: Columbia University Press, 1988), pp. 93–112.

32. In Bell and Offen, eds., *Women, Family, Freedom* I, pp. 73–74.

33. On the work of Swiss educator, Johann Pestalozzi, see Ann Taylor Allen, *Feminism and Motherhood in Germany, 1800–1914* (New Brunswick, N.J.: Rutgers University Press, 1991), pp. 22–26.

34. De Maistre in Moses, *French Feminism*, p. 241, n. 20 and p. 6, respectively; Joanne Schneider, "Enlightened Reforms and Bavarian Girls' Education: Tradition through Innovation," in John C. Fout, ed., *German Women in the Nineteenth Century: A Social History* (New York: Holmes and Meier 1984), p. 58; Persis Hunt, "Teachers and Workers: Problems of Feminist Organizing in the Early Third Republic," in *Third Republic/Troisième République* 3–4 (1977): 180. Also Mary Jo Maynes, *Schooling in Western Europe: A Social History* (Albany, N.Y.: State University of New York Press, 1985).

35. James C. Albisetti, *Schooling German Girls and Women: Secondary and Higher Edu-

cation in the Nineteenth Century (Princeton: Princeton University Press, 1988), pp. 87–89, 292–301.

36. Laura Strumingher, *What Were Little Girls and Boys Made Of?: Primary Education in Rural France, 1830–1880* (Albany, N.Y.: State University of New York Press, 1983), p. 17; Linda L. Clark, *Schooling the Daughters of Marianne* (Albany, N.Y.: State University of New York Press, 1984), pp. 13–18.

37. Jo Burr Mardagant, *Madame le Professeur: Women Educators in the Third Republic* (Princeton: Princeton University Press, 1990), p. 258.

38. Anne T. Quartararo, *Women Teachers and Popular Education in Nineteenth-Century France: Social Values and Corporate Identity at the Normal School Institution* (Newark: University of Delaware Press, 1995), p. 150.

39. M. Jeanne Peterson, "The Victorian Governess: Status Incongruence in Family and Society," in Martha Vicinus, ed., *Suffer and Be Still: Women in the Victorian Age* (Bloomington, Ind.: Indiana University Press, 1973), pp. 17–18; Jacquie Matthews, "Barbara Bodichon: Integrity in Diversity (1827–1891)," in Dale Spender, ed., *Feminist Theorists: Three Centuries of Key Women Thinkers* (New York: Pantheon, 1983), pp. 90–123, quotation on p. 100.

40. In Hellerstein, Hume, and Offen, eds., *Victorian Women*, pp. 398–400.

41. Mardagant, *Madame le professeur*, p. 4.

42. David F. Noble, *A World without Women: The Christian Clerical Culture of Western Science* (New York: Oxford University Press, 1992), p. 276.

43. Rita McWilliams-Tullberg, "Women and Degrees at Cambridge University 1862–1897," in Martha Vicinus, ed., *A Widening Sphere: Changing Roles of Women* (Bloomington, Ind.: Indiana University Press, 1977), pp. 120, 294 n. 11.

44. Karin Hausen, "Family and Role-Division: The Polarisation of Sexual Stereotypes in the Nineteenth Century—An Aspect of the Dissociation of Work and Family Life," in Richard J. Evans and W. R. Lee, eds., *The German Family: Essays on the Social History of the Family in Nineteenth- and Twentieth-Century Germany* (London: Croom Helm, 1981), pp. 67–68; Leonore Davidoff, "The Rationalization of Housework," in Diana Leonard Barker and Sheila Allen, eds., *Dependence and Exploitation in Work and Marriage* (London and New York: Longman, 1976), p. 136; Sonya O. Rose, *Limited Livelihoods: Gender and Class in Nineteenth-Century England* (Berkeley: University of California Press, 1992), p. 99.

45. In Hellerstein, Hume, and Offen, eds., *Victorian Women*, pp. 144–149.

46. Leonore Davidoff and Catherine Hall, *Family Fortunes: Men and Women of the English Middle Class, 1780–1850* (Chicago: University of Chicago Press, 1987).

47. Michael Anderson, "The Social Position of Spinsters in Mid-Victorian Britain," pp. 377–393 and Olwen Hufton, "Women without Men: Widows and Spinsters in Britain and France in the Eighteenth Century," pp. 355–376, in *Journal of Family History* 9, no. 4 (Winter 1984); Lillian Faderman, *Surpassing the Love of Men* (New York: Morrow, 1981). See also Martha Vicinus, *Independent Women: Work and Community for Single Women, 1850–1920* (Chicago: University of Chicago Press, 1985).

48. Anne-Lise Head-König, "Demographic History and Its Perception of Women from the Seventeenth to the Nineteenth Century," in Karen Offen, Ruth Roach Pierson, and Jane Rendall, eds., *Writing Women's History: International Perspectives* (Bloomington, Ind.: Indiana University Press, 1991), pp. 25–44, quotation on p. 40.

49. Rachel Ginnis Fuchs, *Abandoned Children: Foundlings and Child Welfare in Nineteenth-Century France* (Albany, N.Y.: State University of New York Press, 1984), especially pp. 72–73, 277; George Sussman, *Selling Mothers' Milk: The Wet-Nursing Business in France, 1715–1914* (Urbana, Ill.: University of Illinois Press, 1982).

50. Norman Himes, *Medical History of Contraception* (1936; reprint, New York: Schocken, 1970); Linda Gordon, *Woman's Body, Woman's Right: A Social History of Birth Control in America* (New York: Penguin, 1977); Angus McLaren, *Birth Control in Nineteenth-Century England* (London: Holmes and Meier, 1978); J. A. and Olive Banks, *Feminism and Family Planning in Victorian England* (New York: Schocken, 1964). On Aletta Jacobs' career as the first female university graduate and physician in the Netherlands, see her *Memories: My Life as an International Leader in Health, Suffrage, and Peace,* ed. Harriet Feinberg, trans. Annie Wright (New York: Feminist Press, 1996).

51. Leslie Page Moch and Rachel G. Fuchs, "Getting Along: Poor Women's Networks in Nineteenth-Century Paris," *French Historical Studies* 18, no. 1 (Spring 1993) 34–49; Jean H. Quataert, "The Politics of Rural Industrialization: Class, Gender, and Collective Protest in the Saxon Oberlausitz of the Late Nineteenth Century," *Central European History* 20, no. 2 (June 1987): 91–124, especially pp. 121–122.

52. Thomas Laqueur, *The Making of Sex: Body and Gender from the Greeks to Freud* (Cambridge: Harvard University Press, 1990), p. 208. It was only in the 1930s that the process of ovulation in the human female was fully understood. On anthropologists, Cynthia Eagle Russett, *Sexual Science: The Victorian Construction of Womanhood* (Cambridge: Harvard University Press, 1989), quotation on p. 71.

53. See also Karen Offen, "Depopulation, Nationalism, and Feminism in Fin-de-Siècle France," *American Historical Review* 89, no. 3 (June 1984): 648–676. On emigrants to empire, Julia Bush, "'The Right Sort of Woman': Female Emigrators and Emigration to the British Empire, 1890–1910," *Women's History Review* 3, no. 3 (1994): 385–409, quotations on pp. 385, 400.

54. Lee Holcombe, "Victorian Wives and Property: Reform of the Married Woman's Property Law, 1857–1882," in Vicinus, ed., *Widening Sphere,* pp. 3–28, and Lee Holcombe, *Wives and Property: Reform of the Married Women's Property Law in Nineteenth-Century England* (Toronto: University of Toronto Press, 1983), pp. 50–58; also excerpt from Caroline Sheridan Norton, *The Separation of Mother and Child by the Law of "Custody of Infants," Considered* (London: 1838) in Bell and Offen, eds., *Women, Family, Freedom* I, pp. 161–163. Also Moses, *French Feminism* and Patrick Kay Bidelman, *Pariahs Stand Up! The Founding of the Liberal Feminist Movement in France, 1858–1889* (Westport, Conn.: Greenwood Press, 1982).

55. Roderick Phillips, *Putting Asunder: A History of Divorce in Western Society* (Cambridge: Cambridge University Press, 1988); see especially Ch. 11, "Nineteenth-Century Divorce Laws: Liberalization and Reaction, 1815–1914," pp. 403–478.

56. Catherine M. Prelinger, "Prelude to Consciousness: Amalie Sieveking and the Female Association for the Care of the Poor and the Sick," in Fout, ed., *German Women,* pp. 118–132.

57. Catherine M. Prelinger, *Charity, Challenge, and Change: Religious Dimensions of the Mid-Nineteenth Century Women's Movement in Germany* (New York: Greenwood Press, 1987); Jean H. Quataert, *Staging Philanthropy: Patriotic Women and the National Imagination in Dynastic Germany, 1813–1916* (Ann Arbor: University of Michigan Press, 2000); and Ida Blom, "Equality and the Threat of War in Scandinavia, 1884–1905," in T. G. Fraser and Keith Jeffery, eds., *Men, Women, and War* (Dublin: Lilliput Press, 1993), pp. 100–118, quotations on pp. 105, 114.

58. Carroll Smith-Rosenberg, "Beauty, the Beast, and the Militant Woman," *American Quarterly* 23 (1971): 562–584; Judith R. Walkowitz, *Prostitution and Victorian Society: Women, Class, and the State* (Cambridge: Cambridge University Press, 1980);

Tristan in Hellerstein, Hume and Offen, eds., *Victorian Women*, pp. 419–421, and *Flora Tristan's London Journal: A Survey of London Life in the 1830s*, trans. Dennis Palmer and Giselle Pincetl (Boston: Charles River Books, 1980).

59. Mary Gibson, *Prostitution and the State in Italy, 1860–1915* (New Brunswick, N.J.: Rutgers University Press, 1986), pp. 63–64, and Laurie Bernstein, *Sonia's Daughters: Prostitutes and Their Regulation in Imperial Russia* (Berkeley: University of California Press, 1995).

60. Gibson, *Prostitution and the State in Italy*, p. 8; Walkowitz, *Prostitution in Victorian Society*, p. 31. On the historiography of prostitution, see Timothy J. Gilfoyle, "Prostitutes in History: From Parables of Pornography to Metaphors of Modernity," *American Historical Review* 104, no. 1 (February 1999):117–141.

61. Karen Offen, "Ernest Legouvé and the Doctrine of 'Equality in Difference' for Women: A Case Study of Male Feminism in Nineteenth-Century Thought," *Journal of Modern History* 58, no. 2 (June 1986): 452–484.

CHAPTER SIX

"...with the wolf always at the door...": Women's Work in Domestic Industry in Britain and Germany

Barbara Franzoi Bari

The transformation of women's work has been hailed as one of the most significant results of the Industrial Revolution. Many nineteenth-century observers such
as Friedrich Engels (in his 1844 book, *On the Condition of the Working Class in
England*) decried the reorganization that "tore" women from their families, confined them to factories, and turned thriving artisanal communities into "she-
towns." Historians, however, now know that this was an exaggerated, even erroneous, portrayal. Most women, especially married women, continued to labor at
traditional tasks in domestic settings. A more pervasive and permanent effect of
industrial development was the marginalization of women's work and the feminization of domestic industry. In this study, Barbara Franzoi Bari illustrates vividly
the role of paid homework in the daily lives of working-class women. She draws
attention to the phenomenon of "sweatshops" and the close fit between the pressures on women exerted by their need for income, the imperatives of the ideology of domesticity as it spread to the working classes, and the demands of industrial capital for cheap and seasonal labor. Along with traditional sources, such as
contemporary portraits of working-class life, Franzoi employs statistics taken from
occupational censuses in England and Germany to analyze the changing sexual
division of labor in trade and industry. Occupational census data, while often
understating women's work, nonetheless contain useful demographic information
on age and marital status of workers and indices of industrial organization. By
focusing on women's work in industries that are labor—rather than capital—intensive and require little skill or training, Franzoi Bari illustrates how household production in an industrializing economy plays an essential role in the complex
processes of capitalist development. Her work on nineteenth-century Britain and
Germany provides insights into the persistence of industrial homework by women
in the global economy today.

The term "industrial revolution" is one of those catchwords that conjures up a host of vivid images, most typically of factories, machines, and overheated, overcrowded workrooms. Among Western economies, Britain and Germany often are singled out as models of industrial transformation. Britain, after all, was the home of the first industrial revolution and for a century was the mightiest industrial power in Europe. As the end of the nineteenth century, its economic supremacy was challenged by the newly unified German Empire. Too often, the spread of industrialization appears as a monolithic occurrence and the labor force is depicted solely as factory workers who are predominantly male. This is only half the story, for it neglects an integral component of industrial capitalism—domestic industry or work done in the home, in the main by women. Less visible than factories or smokestacks and the throngs that came and went through the factory gates, the industrialized economies of both Britain and Germany housed thousands of women and children who worked in kitchens, attics, and tenement basements at the fragmented tasks of industrial homework.

Emphasis on factory production and mechanization conceals the complexity of capitalist economic development. In the nineteenth century, capitalist expansion used both machine and hand labor. If the factory symbolized industrialization, it is important to understand that large groups of workers remained outside it, carrying on essentially traditional tasks in old industries and performing the new jobs created by industrial expansion. Capitalism sought to maximize production and minimize costs. In selected work processes and in specific industries such as ribbonmaking, silkweaving, and lacemaking, these ends could best be achieved by keeping manufacturing in the home, or by locating it there, as was the case with the clothing trades and tobacco products. Mechanization—the introduction of machinery—in one part of the work process often generated expansion of homework in another. Growth of large factories was frequently accompanied by a proliferation of small production units in homes and workshops where capital-saving, labor-intensive methods prevailed. Subdivision of labor separated the work process into tasks that could be performed easily by hand at home.

In *Life and Labour of the People of London*, Charles Booth, a British shipowner and social reformer of the late nineteenth century, described the intricate processes of subdivision in the paper industry and the resultant gender segregation of the work force.

> The men who cut the paper and cardboard for the boxes make use of machines, worked some by steam and others by hand. . . . Boys tend the scoring machines, which make cuts in the cardboard along the lines on which the card has to be folded. . . . Women and girls make the boxes from the materials prepared by the men and boys. . . . The material is cut and prepared, and then given out, usually to married women who have worked in one of the factories before marriage.

Booth's narrative also points up the close connection between the factory and domestic industry in the paper trade and suggests a high degree of interaction as women moved from one work setting to another. In needlemaking, too, centered in Worcestershire, England, an observer estimated that the production process was so finely subdivided that a single needle was worked on by 120 different people.

A second characteristic of industries that expanded into homework was irregular market demand. Factories and machinery saved costs only if they were geared for large-scale production most of the year. While many industries in both Germany and Britain experienced periodic uncertainties, consumer goods were especially prone to the vagaries of the market. Production runs varied from season to season, even from day to day. An elastic market required a flexible labor supply. A widow in London remarked:

> The slacks in the cloak business occur twice a year—that is to say, at the end of the winter and the summer season. . . . Now I shall have nothing from the warehouse not before next March; so I shall have to seek some other employment till then.

Whether this particular woman was available the following March did not really matter to the employer. The important consideration was a labor supply that was ready on short notice, that could be hired when needed, and did not have to be maintained when there was no work. There was always a flurry of activity in season or when rush orders forced workers to stay at their tasks for fourteen and fifteen hours a day.

Countless women were present in the industrial labor force, albeit employed irregularly, often in their homes. The basic reason was the fit between capitalism's search for abundant and cheap labor and women's need for wages. While society claimed that men were primary providers, in many instances men's wages were unreliable and inadequate for family support. Industry controlled women through the economic insecurity of men. Skilled men in heavy industry could earn a family wage, but that was the privilege of the minority. Unemployment and underemployment regularly depressed men's wages. Even if a man were steadily employed, his earnings alone were rarely enough to support a family. Women and children had to be available as compensatory labor. Because women worked from necessity, in many cases just managing subsistence, they were economically vulnerable. They accepted poor wages because there were no real alternatives.

The conditions of proletarian poverty forced women into waged work. In most laboring families women and children were expected to supplement total income. Women's involvement with paid labor traced a pattern of recurrent hardship "with the wolf always at the door." Working-class women could not evade the hazards of marginality, for women formed a large part of the surplus labor force primarily because of their roles and responsibilities in the family. Most women who could do factory work were young and single, but marriage did not mean transition out of the labor force. Family ties limited the options available to women and required considerable juggling of workplace and schedules. Women's choices were limited and they were disadvantaged, but they were not completely powerless. Wives and mothers resisted outside work when they could; they preferred ways of earning money that were compatible with household routine. Therefore, for many women, the constraints of economic need coupled with family responsibilities made domestic industry the only possible alternative to destitution. However, the fact that domestic industry was often the most exploited form of labor further perpetuated the desperate condition of the working population.

A glimpse at wage levels illustrates the depth of female poverty. Especially for those who relied on their own earnings, such as widows and single women, it was a terrible situation. Women's wages, depressed in comparison with men's, were further jeopardized by income interruptions and rate changes. Women usually prefaced responses to questions about what they earned with complaints about the lack of steady work. While a skilled male worker in the German machine industry, for example, could expect regular employment at about thirty-five marks a week, women homeworkers averaged less than twelve marks even when they had work.

Wage reduction was the most effective way for industry to increase profit. Because most homework was paid by the piece, wage adjustments were simple, direct, and disastrous. Women were forced to work harder just to stay even. The scramble among employers and middlemen to undercut prices worsened at the end of the century, and women homeworkers were the unfortunate victims of that competition. Since women's unskilled labor had no real scarcity value, too many women seeking work compelled all of them to take industry's meager offerings.

Women's economic activity at home was almost always augmented by the labor of children, a condition that further gave industry an abundant and cheap labor reserve. Henry Mayhew, who compiled detailed accounts of the London working classes in 1849–1850, was quick to see the connection between poverty and exploitation. He observed that families escaped destitution only by putting children to work as soon as they were able to do simple tasks.

> From people being obliged to work twice the hours they once did, a glut of hands was the consequence, and the masters were led to make reductions in the wages. They took advantage of our poverty and lowered wages, so as to undersell each other, and command business.

The prevailing pattern of women's work at home reflected the more pervasive gender division of industrial labor. Certain "women's jobs" were created in factory-based, mechanized industries, but the real volume of women's work was found in areas related to traditional work roles. Women workers were concentrated in large numbers in trades connected to household jobs and in occupations related to consumer goods and foods manufacture. In London at the turn of the twentieth century, women made up 68 percent of all workers in the clothing trades. They constituted about 40 percent of upholsterers, 90 percent of quill and feather dressers, 65 percent of textile workers, 80 percent of jam, preserves, and sweet makers, almost 75 percent of chocolate and cocoa makers, and 60 percent of tobacco workers. Similarly in Germany, a profile of domestic industry shows that women were concentrated in specific trades. It demonstrates clearly that between 1895 and 1907 domestic industry absorbed great numbers and high percentages of women. By the end of the century, every industry in Germany experienced an expansion of female labor in homework. Textiles was the only occupation that showed an overall decline

TABLE 1. Percentage of Female Domestic Workers in Selected Industries in Germany

Industry	Year	Percentage of Women
Metals	1895	7.2
	1907	13.5
Machines	1895	9.4
	1907	19.8
Chemicals	1895	68.6
	1907	86.6
Textiles	1895	46.0
	1907	59.2
Paper products	1895	38.3
	1907	54.3
Wood products	1895	17.4
	1907	42.4
Foods and tobacco	1895	44.6
	1907	62.6
Clothing	1895	56.2
	1907	68.6

Source: Occupational Census of the German Reich, 1907.

numerically, but here, too, the percentage of women employed at home expanded. The figures for Britain and Germany show that capitalist organization of work intensified the feminization of certain industries, principally textiles, clothing, and tobacco, and increased the feminization of domestic industry in all areas.

The clothing industry in both Germany and Britain encompassed all the defining features of women's work. The clothing trades were a prime example of the degree to which industrial capitalism penetrated the work experience of women, especially work done in the home. All kinds of sewing such as corsetmaking, hatmaking, the manufacture of ties, scarves, collars and cuffs, fine feather working, artificial flowermaking, even dolls' clothes fell into this category. While sewing was performed by women all over Germany and Britain, in its modern, capitalized form, it was really an urban industry concentrated in specific cities. In Britain the clothing center was London; in Germany, it was Berlin.

In Britain, the lineal descendants of the handicraft trades of tailoring and seamstressing were the "sweated" trades of plain sewers, shirtmakers, button-stitchers, and pelt sewers that were the refuge of women in dire need. It was largely manual labor, requiring minimal skills and little outlay in terms of space and materials. The clothing trades were ultimately flexible and goods could literally be picked up and put down as market demands dictated. The term, "sweating," was in use in England by the 1830s to describe a system of subcontracting in the tailoring trades that used agents for the distribution and collection of goods. Orders were obtained by offering the lowest possible prices and by undercutting competitors, which directly reduced wages paid to homeworkers. While the term was usually associated with sewing, it was not restricted to clothing. Any work done at home with little or no equipment, that used repetitive, manual labor, with simple or easily acquired skills could fall within this category. Descriptions of sweated workers tell the story of long hours for little pay, and the term conveys a graphic image of severe destitution and appalling exploitation. The poorest paid jobs and cheapest goods were called "slop work." Mayhew told his readers that he was saddened by what he saw in the rooms of London sloppers.

> I then directed my steps to the neighborhood of Drurylane, to see a poor woman who lived in an attic in one of the closest courts in that quarter. On the table was a quarter of an ounce of tea. Observing my eye to rest upon it, she told me it was all she took. "Sugar," she said, "I broke myself of long ago; I couldn't afford it. A cup of tea, a piece of bread, and an onion is generally all I have for my dinner, and sometimes I haven't even an onion, and then I sops my bread."

Decentralization in the clothing industry in Germany enforced the sexual division of labor and replicated the conditions of sweating chronicled in Britain. Not only did piece work and subdivision of tasks multiply the numbers of women working at home, but changing technology, especially the sewing machine, increased production and roughly evened out the quality of domestic-made goods. In Berlin, the prevailing method for handling work was the middleman system. Subcontractors either delivered goods directly to the homeworkers or distributed them at factories and workrooms. It was rare to find a clothing firm that did not employ countless numbers of persons working at home in addition to those in the factory. In 1906, in women's and children's clothes, 350 firms employed fifty-two thousand homeworkers; 210 establishments making boys' and men's wear utilized twenty-two thousand homeworkers; 320 firms making undergarments employed forty-seven thousand homeworkers; 150 hatmaking and flowermaking shops employed six thousand homeworkers; and 170 shoemaking establishments employed two thousand persons working at home.

By no means peripheral to the practical reasons for the expansion of home industry was the implicit and overt resistance of men toward women workers. Eliminating the competition of low-paid female labor was perceived as the best guarantee for a family wage. Thus the negativism contained both economic and ideological components. Caught in the powerlessness of their own economic uncertainty, men blamed poor wages and insecure jobs on women. Capitalist expansion pitted men against women, factory labor against homework, simultaneously as men, women, and families depended on the earnings supplied by domestic industry. The thousands of women in domestic production were not obviously visible because they were in their proper place—the home. But the appearance of women in previously male-dominated industries and the proliferation of jobs done by homework were both a real and a symbolic threat. Criticizing women workers because they were poorly skilled and cheap, all labor unions addressed the problem of domestic industry. Because domestic industry was indeed competition, trade unions sought to organize women homeworkers, while at the same time, they agitated for restrictions on homework and even demanded its abolition.

Hostility from male-dominated trade unions was only one facet of collective resistance to women's paid labor. The prevailing nineteenth-century image of woman as wife and mother formed the ideological context for the social anxiety about women's work. Women's factory work was never fully condoned. The view that woman's place was in the home caring for her husband and children set certain limits on the way women engaged in paid labor and made women's work into a public issue. Employment outside the home was an elemental threat to social values and summoned a call of alarm that generated debate in Germany and elsewhere. As working women entered the public arena, their roles were sharply defined and efforts were made to bring industrial work into conformity with patriarchal values. Elaborating the dangers of the factory while embellishing the merits of work done in the home was one approach to solving the dilemma. Another was the development of protective laws governing women's work. It is instructive to recognize that labor legislation in the nineteenth century virtually ignored domestic industry. "Going out to work" was the critical problem. Most public and private alternatives to women's employment were directed at keeping them at home. If women in the working classes were supposed to work, they were not to be conspicuously present in the labor force.

In Britain, legal restrictions on the hours of work and employment of women as a distinct occupational group dated from the Factories Amendment Act of 1844. Prior to that time, chief emphasis in the development of protective legislation had been on child labor. In the 1830s and 1840s, there was growing public concern about the physical and moral effects of factory employment on women. Several medical witnesses called by the Select Committee on the Labour of Children in Factories in 1832 (the Sadler Committee) said those abuses were the greatest evils of the factory system. Creating a new category of protected workers provided a way to deal with several interrelated problems simultaneously. Segregating women assured industry that male labor would not be tampered with legally. Not only did industry defend its prerogatives, but male workers perceived the real benefits from putting female labor at a competitive disadvantage. The Short-Time Movement achieved success in 1847 when the hours of factory work for women and children were reduced to a maximum of ten per day, but the Act applied only to textile mills. The desire to protect women because they were the mothers of future generations was an important component of factory legislation. Concern about women's labor generally focused on the effects of married women's labor on the family and on the health of the nation. Maternal breast-feeding became a metaphor for national strength: ". . . you cannot rear an imperial race on the bottle."

Charles Booth's investigations of the London poor brought to light important information about the marital composition of the labor force and the degree of destitution that drove women to seek paid work. Booth's narrative made it clear that not only single women and widows worked, but married women with children worked as well, and that most women were not in factories. In the 1890s, largely as a result of Booth's disclosure and the urging of his associate, Clara Collet, it was publicly acknowledged that there was special need for inquiry into home industry. The newly created Women's Industrial Council collected statistics and information. Domestic industry was officially "discovered." Ameliorative solutions stressed education, domestic skills, and self-improvement. Reform efforts were conventional middle-class remedies. Their implementation did little to relieve economic distress and in practice, actually limited chances for any real change. There was some reluctance to provide help because married women's work was thought to bring out latent male laziness and to erode the man's sense of responsibility. One observer commented that " . . . a dislocation of trade which throws the married woman out of work may even result in increased steadiness in the part of the husband." The problems and solutions of female labor were set in the context of women's "true role" and the damage that work outside the home was said to cause. It is no surprise that domestic industry was idealized as the appropriate way for women to earn.

The themes and social policy measures were much the same as Germany confronted women's industrial work at the end of the century. In the 1870s, the first official investigation of industry focused on factory work, child labor, and women. The report raised the question of whether the government should restrict or prohibit women's factory work, and at once responded with economic justification for female labor, moderated by proposals for protective measures. Conceptualization of the woman worker as a social problem was based on the premise that women had special moral and social responsibilities as wives and mothers. While protection was adopted by most major political parties in Germany, the Catholic Center Party was the most important source of agitation for prohibition and restriction. Catholic motivation was preservation of the family. A factory inspectorate, set up by the Imperial government, collected statistics on women's work and supplied much of the information for the development of protective laws. In 1891, major labor legislation stipulated general conditions for all factory workers and mandated specific regulations for children and women. Child labor under fourteen was prohibited and children were required to attend school until that age. Daily work time for all women workers, married and single, was limited to eleven hours a day. Married women with family responsibilities were allowed an extra half hour at midday break. Maternity leave of four weeks following delivery was provided unless the woman chose, with medical permission, to return sooner.

In Germany, there was no official investigation of domestic industry in the nineteenth century, although many studies analyzing its nature were published in economic journals and trade union reports. Domestic industry remained unregulated until 1911. Evidence suggests that a major effect of regulation of women's factory work and the prohibition of child labor was expansion of their labor in domestic industry. Employers used traditional work forms as a way to circumvent changes in the employment and education laws. And women moved away from regulated factory jobs into lightly restricted and uncontrolled industries because they could not afford the "cost" of protection.

Several brief comments about women's work in contemporary Third World countries will confirm that the effects of capitalist expansion are not bounded by time and geography. Remarkable parallels emerge as women are drawn into the developing economies of Africa, Asia, and Latin America. Asymmetrical growth, much of it directed by Western models and multinational corporations, structures an uneven economy. It results in a capital-intensive industrial core usually referred to as modern or the "formal" sector, and the "informal" sector that includes a large variety of activities based on the labor of women in a casual, intermittent, and marginal way. It was assumed by development planners that the informal sector would become redundant and would be absorbed as modernization progressed. This has not happened.

The activities in the informal sector are not traditional or transitional. They are essential responses to the capitalist system. The informal sector is labor-absorptive; it sustains large numbers of persons, mostly women, at low levels of living. The sector acts to maximize production at minimal cost. Handicrafts, cottage industry, trading, food preparation and sale, tasks closely related to agriculture in rural areas, small-scale manufacture in urban centers; these are the kinds of income-generating activities that fall into the informal sector. They require little capital outlay, low-level skills, few tools, little or no mechanization, and minimal technology. The jobs are flexible, fluid, and can be carried out individually or with family assistance. Where Third World women work in industry, they are usually concentrated in textiles, clothing, and electronics factories, many of which have a multinational connection. These industries actively seek out female labor because women are more docile, more dextrous, and less likely to organize. Ultimately, the basic reason for the prevalence of female labor is women's willingness to work for less pay. The ingredients are very familiar, indeed.

Domestic industry did not decline in the nineteenth century. It expanded. Homework was a nucleus for capitalist development. The pattern is replicated in contemporary Third World economies. Cheap, abundant labor in the form of women's work served important functions for economic growth. Romantic notions we may have about the family workshop do not fit the realities of industrial homework. Sweatshops and slop work comprise the dramatic testimony of hardship and inequity produced by capitalist transition. As societies moved from traditional to modern methods of production, women were forced into a condition of constant adjustment. They devised ways to survive that were adaptive, preservative, and flexible. Under the impact of industrialization, women seem to change less than men, but the continuity should not be read as an expansion of choices. Rather, it is the result of diminished options. Paradoxically, women's strategies for coping turned on the very hindrances that blocked escape from limited opportunity and economic constraint.

SUGGESTIONS FOR FURTHER READING

Alexander, Sally. "Women's Work in Nineteenth-Century London: A Study of the Years 1820–50." In *The Rights and Wrongs of Women,* edited by Juliet Mitchell and Ann Oakley. New York: Penguin, 1976.

Booth, Charles. *Life and Labour of the People in London.* 1889. Reprint. New York: A. M. Kelley, 1969.

Boserup, Ester. *Woman's Role in Economic Development.* New York: St. Martin's Press, 1970.

Franzoi, Barbara. *At the Very Least She Pays the Rent: Women and German Industrialization, 1871–1914.* Westport, Conn.: Greenwood Press, 1985.

Gillis, John R. *A World of Their Own Making: Myth, Ritual, and the Quest for Family Values.* New York: BasicBooks, 1996.

Hewitt, Margaret. *Wives and Mothers in Victorian Industry.* London: Rockliff, 1958.

Mayhew, Henry. "Labour and the Poor" (1849–1850). In *Voices of the Poor: Selections from the Morning Chronicle,* edited by Anne Humphreys. London: Cass, 1971.

Pinchbeck, Ivy. *Women Workers and the Industrial Revolution, 1750–1850.* London: Virago, 1981 (orig. 1930).

Quennell, Peter, ed. *Mayhew's London.* London: W. Kimber, 1951.

Safa, Helen I., and Eleanor Leacock, guest eds. "Development and the Sexual Division of Labor." *Signs* 7, no. 2 (Winter 1981).

Samuel, Raphael. "Workshop of the World: Steam Power and Hand Technology in Mid-Victorian Britain." *History Workshop* (Spring 1977).

Smith, Bonnie G. *Changing Lives: Women in European History since 1700.* Lexington, Mass.: D. C. Heath, 1989.

Tinker, Irene, Bo Bramsen, and Mayra Buvinic, eds. *Women and World Development.* New York: Praeger, 1976.

Yeo, Eileen, and E. P. Thompson. *The Unknown Mayhew.* New York: Schocken, 1971.

CHAPTER SEVEN

Women and "Domestic" Imperial Culture: The Case of Victorian Britain

Antoinette Burton

Antoinette Burton continues the fruitful perspective of Europe and empire introduced for the early modern era by Mary Elizabeth Perry in chapter 2. Burton takes us to the "heart of empire," Victorian Britain, connecting the spheres of "British society at home and the British empire in India, Africa and the dominions. . . ." Victorian society was infused with powerful imperial imagery and goods, helping shape British national identity. It is the women of nineteenth century Britain who are given particular focus, however, not only as consumers and producers but as pamphleteers, feminist activists, public speakers as well as professionals and missionaries in the colonies. Early in the century, immediate abolition was a woman's issue; the debates reveal, however, many of the ambiguities of white, middle-class women's politics in the context of European colonial domination; so, too, later in the century, the feminist demand for the vote relied on the ideology of "white woman's burden." Indeed, Burton explores the many ways evangelical ideology helped shape distinct women's politics: for example, working-class women's involvement in Chartism in the 1840s at home drew sustenance from an imagery of exploited African slaves. Later in the century, middle- and working-class women also went to the colonies, which, through the reports in cheap mission magazines read by countless women subscribers, came back into England as well. These connections opened up professional opportunities for work abroad that were closed to women physicians in England, for example; they later encouraged the training of Indian women physicians, preserving female specialties while at the same time challenging professional hierarchies based on race and gender. Burton demonstrates new configurations in the languages of race, gender and class in women's histories. The stories of Victorian Britain look profoundly different when refracted through the revealing lens of empire.

In 1782, Bridget Gibson was removed from the parish of Whitehaven, Cumberland, because she lacked a legitimate claim to residency there. Her first husband and the father of her baby daughter was a seaman who belonged to the ship *Violet*, which was part of the late eighteenth-century African slave trade. In his absence Bridget hired herself out as a wet-nurse, earning four guineas a year through an informal contract with her employer, who kept her on even after Gibson's own child passed away. When Gibson's husband died at sea, near Guinea, Bridget was able to lay claim to his unpaid wages, but despite remarriage and a newborn child she was unable to remain in Whitehaven. Thus "the commanding influence of a colonial empire intruded into . . . [the] otherwise restricted provincial life" of Bridget Gibson—shaping her destiny and with it, the lives and historical experiences of many other British women from the sixteenth century onward.

Although they have traditionally been seen as separate spheres, British society at home and the British empire in India, Africa, and the dominions were intimately connected, and had been since the sixteenth century. International slavery—which together with monopoly capitalism was "the spinal cord" of modern Western commercial prosperity—brought gold, ivory, pepper, and even some slaves to English shores. The Tudors and Stuarts had "blackamoors" at their courts, men and women of African and Indian descent populated the streets of Georgian London, and provincial lives like Bridget Gibson's were both full of and economically dependent on the raw materials extracted from Britain's colonies. During the Victorian era, evidence of Britain's imperial wealth and power continued to make its way to the heart of the empire in the form of both human and commercial capital, as the traffic in goods and people from the colonies became crucial to Britain's national and international preeminence in the modern period. One simple and commonplace example of the impact of empire on domestic British society is to be found in the word "guinea," which has a double bearing on Bridget Gibson's story. By the eighteenth century "guinea" was the popular name for the coin struck from gold in which Bridget was paid her servant's wages—gold that originated on the coast of Africa, where her husband perished at sea.

Even after the abolition of the slave trade in 1807 and the abolition of slavery as a legal institution in 1833, freed men and women, together with a variety of colonial people from all parts of the empire, continued to travel to Britain. They took up permanent or semipermanent residence, thereby guaranteeing that the United Kingdom would become not just an imperial nation but a multicultural one as well. Manufactures based on the raw materials produced from colonial plantations filled the marketplaces of this celebrated nation of shopkeepers. Meanwhile, newly liberated but hardly "free" colonial labor continued to provide sugar for the tea and coffee cups of British aristocrats. With the advent of mass production and the rise of an increasingly urbane middle class, more and more Britons partook of these delicacies as British housewives strove to reconcile the family appetite for colonial foodstuffs with the limits of the household budget. Nor was contact with empire limited to the privacy of the middle-class home. Displays of Britain's colonial influence and power were everywhere on offer in the British Isles—through missionary tracts, novels, public exhibitions, the decorative arts, political debates, and popular entertainments. If imperialism was a core ideology in Victorian domestic culture, its imagery was virtually ubiquitous in the nineteenth century as well. On biscuit tins, in museum displays, through the Girl Guides, and in commercial advertisements, Britain proclaimed its cultural superiority and encouraged Britons to identify with its power and its glories through imperial themes and visual images. Empire was, in short, not just a phenomenon "out there," but a fundamental part of domestic culture and national identity in modern Britain.

By the time Victoria came to the throne in 1837, the impact of British colonialism on British women of all classes was considerable, even while empire itself seemed like such a normal and natural part of English "civilization" that its influence at home would scarcely have been remarked on by Victorians. In economic terms, the fruits of empire were an everyday reality for women in Britain. Slavery and its related economic practices had perhaps the most significant impact on their lived experiences, in part because the commodities produced by colonial labor passed literally through women's hands, whether in the form of edibles or wearables. Sugar and cotton were chief among these. Girls and women who worked in factories were involved not just in consumption but also in the production of raw materials from the colonies into manufactured goods for Britain and the world. Whether they handled woolen goods, cotton pieces, or the more exotic "pacotille" (sundries produced in Bristol for export to Africa), mothers and daughters from Dublin to Dundee to Lancaster were connected to the West Indies, Asia, and India alike through the dependence of industrial capitalism on colonial materials and markets. Curry, shawls and rice were just a few of the colonial commodities that gained popularity and cachet in the 1860s and after, as English cookery and domestic culture more generally were gradually transformed by new ingredients and a variety of colonial influences. Slavery's impact on British women was by no means limited to their role as producers or consumers, however. In fact, the campaign for abolition arguably transformed middle-class and some working-class women into early Victorian feminists by appealing to their evangelical commitments and drawing them into public discussions about the morality of colonial capitalism and their complicity with its slaveocratic practices. As tract-writers, boycotters, organizers, and in some cases, public speakers, British women took up the abolitionist cause and in the process claimed a public, political voice for themselves in the imperial nation-state.

As work by recent feminist scholars has made clear, British women's involvement in abolition may have been a radical move into the public sphere but it was nonetheless conservative of traditional "feminine" values. Especially as poets and writers for the cause, British women "played an important part in harnessing . . . evangelical ideas about feminine sensitivity to the fashionable cult of sentimentalism"—a sentimentalism that romanticized Africans as pathetic creatures incapable of resisting slavery themselves and promoted English women as their helpmates and saviors. In fact, slaves often rebelled against the tyrannies of plantation life and many African- and Caribbean-born blacks were active in the abolitionist campaign from the 1780s onward. Freed men and women wrote antislavery tracts that were published in Britain; they spoke on abolitionist platforms; and they pressed for the equality of Africans when many if not most British activists preferred to avoid that question altogether and to work for the emancipation and education of slaves. Significantly, women active in the British campaign were more likely than their male counterparts to support immediate rather than gradual emancipation, and they organized an impressive array of local associations, national petitions, and fund-raising drives in support of their goals. As Elizabeth Heyrick, a Leicester-born Quaker and the foremost female antislavery pamphleteer of her generation, put it: "slavery is not an abstract question, to be settled between the Government and the Planters—it is a question in which we are *all* implicated."

For many, abolition became a household concern, especially when the call to "abstention" involved boycotting sugar, that staple of the family larder. Relationships with enslaved women were rare. Despite the fact that English women activists had contacts across the Atlantic with their American abolitionist sisters, few traveled to the West Indies and fewer still joined the political efforts of freed people in the metropole. In part because English women writers depended on the plight of their "slave sisters" for their abolitionist pamphlets and poetry, they found it hard to see black women as anything but victims. Thus when Mary Prince, a West Indian slave, published her autobiography in London in 1832 in order "to let the English people know the truth" about slavery, many doubted its veracity and were unable to see her as a fellow worker in the cause. She was not recruited as a member of any of the ladies' antislavery organizations (to which she remained a lifelong outsider) because, in the estimation of a recent feminist historian, "the voice of a black woman could not be allowed to displace the voices of white women speaking on behalf of their enslaved sisters."

Images of the exploited African slave gave also rhetorical force to Chartist demands in the 1830s and 1840s, drawing working-class women and their families into the struggle for better wages and encouraging some to articulate a connection between economic issues and British women's political rights. The combination of evangelical commitment and economic self-interest motivated women of all classes to seek their fortunes in the colonies, either through missionary work or emigration. British women initially went to Africa and India as missionary wives, just as Jane Eyre of Charlotte Brontë's 1847 novel would have done had she not rejected St. John Rivers' marriage proposal and chosen Edward Rochester instead. Lower-middle-class women like Jane, who faced a life of genteel poverty as governesses and domestic servants in Britain, were particularly vulnerable to the call of the mission field. By the 1870s single British women were making "the journey for Christ" under the auspices of female missionary auxiliaries and through the support of congregations throughout Britain, whose "pennies for the heathen" helped sustain a vast network of evangelical workers and activities in the nineteenth century. As it had in the antislavery campaign, evangelical ideology offered women an active role in the saving of Hindu and Muslim souls and in the promise of civilization and uplift that followed from conversion.

Although many British women undoubtedly did useful work in indigenous communities, for many missionaries, "the first ideological task was to revile local religions, cultural practices and social customs." British women missionaries ran schools in Ceylon, oversaw medical facilities in India, Africa, and China, and stayed connected to their metropolitan sponsors through periodicals like *The Indian Female Evangelist,* which often produced graphic images of "native" life for domestic consumption. Readership of mission magazines was largely female and subscriptions were cheap, so that even if most British women did not go to the colonies in their lifetimes, the colonies came to them—and not just through monthly magazines.

Missionaries returned to Britain with stories, lantern-shows, and native catechists (teachers in a mission church) as well. Indeed, by the 1880s, ordained Indian and African ministers came to Britain on their own, sometimes with their wives, to raise money for the missions which sponsored them and the local projects they themselves initiated. They traveled throughout the United Kingdom, advertising their accomplishments and recruiting British men and women in cities and in villages for that noblest of causes, "colonial Christendom."

If the promise of saving souls for Christ was a prime motivation for British women's travel to empire, unemployment at home was also an important impetus. The specter of "surplus women"—itself the result of a patriarchal economic system incapable of imagining a niche for the unmarried woman worker—haunted the Victorian era, driving many middle- and working-class women to South Africa, Canada, Australia, and New Zealand, mostly as domestics. Thanks to the concerted efforts of the British Women's Emigration Society, by the turn of the century the white settler colonies had attracted tens of thousands of British women immigrants. They were encouraged by the colonial state which, especially in South Africa, was eager to "swamp" the rebellious Boers through marriage to white English women. The majority of women sold their labor in the form of household service, while some who emigrated to the colonies sold sex as well. The white slave trade brought European women to India, South Africa, and Asia under duress or false pretenses or both. London was a central site for this traffic in bodies; and though social purity advocates and some feminists may have exaggerated the numbers, there is little doubt that English girls and women, many of whom may have already been at the margins of poverty or prostitution already, were caught up in the trade.

In India as in South Africa, British women sex-workers served a multiracial clientele, thus violating the contemporary proscriptions against interracial sexual contact that the British colonial government, its officials, and its legislative enactments, worked so hard to enforce. On the whole, Victorian feminists, who made female employment one of their chief political commitments, were not as nearly as concerned about English women prostitutes in colonial cantonments and bazaars as they were about the native women who serviced British military men of all ranks. And though some, like Josephine Butler, were genuinely outraged by the system of compulsory medical inspection for venereal disease to which local women in India, Hong Kong, Gibraltar, and the Straits Settlements were subject, chief among their concerns was that soldiers might contaminate English wives and daughters upon their return to the metropole. In this sense, the connections between the domestic and the colonial spheres were intimate indeed—an intimacy at once produced and policed by imperial ideology, which inscribed the boundaries of colonial rule on the body of the white Englishwoman.

Especially after 1857, when a mutiny against the British army in India resulted in the massacre of British women and children at Cawnpore, the English woman came to embody the purity and integrity of race, nation and empire in the Victorian cultural imagination. The fact that Queen Victoria was the titular head of the nation and, after 1877, the empress of India, helped to guarantee British women a special symbolic and material place at the heart of the empire. For middle-class women, Britain's colonial possessions were particularly attractive and, as it turns out, historically convenient as well. The Victorian empire provided newly trained professionals with a place to use their skills in a culturally acceptable cause—service to the Raj and its peoples—at the very moment when public opinion at home was hostile to women seeking to enter the professions at all. Medicine was the most carefully guarded masculine preserve, in part because women doctors were considered to be unsexed and unsexing. As one critic of the American doctor, Elizabeth Blackwell, put it, "It is impossible that a woman whose hands reek of gore can be possessed of the same nature or feelings as the generality of women." The first generation of British women doctors had to storm the battlements at Edinburgh in order to be admitted to medical school, and once they did, they were prevented from getting on the medical register in Britain and hence from practicing. Even after the law was amended, there were few institutions willing to train or qualify female doctors—a state of affairs that prompted several enterprising women (including Isabel Thorne, Sophia Jex-Blake, and Elizabeth Garrett Anderson) to found the London School of Medicine for Women in 1874.

From the beginning the London School of Medicine for Women viewed the empire, and India in particular, as a field ripe for colonization by English women doctors. Its founders focused on the *zenana* (the female-segregated area of the upper-caste Hindu, or wealthy Muslim, household) as a space to which Western female physicians could gain privileged access by virtue of being the same sex. Together with financial support from Lady Dufferin's Fund for Supplying Female Medical Aid to the Women of India (1885) and a variety of Victorian female reform associations committed to helping colonial women, the London School trained hundreds of women surgeons, midwives, and hospital assistants for employment in the Indian empire. Over time the London School and the Fund also trained Indian women; like their English counterparts, they tended to specialize in gynecology and "women's" ailments, thus preserving the sex-segregated status quo even as they challenged professional hierarchies based on race and gender. While some English women made the "voyage out" as secular doctors, others chose the medical missionary route because they believed that healing the body was crucial to saving the spirit of the heathen woman, who was in turn the key to converting entire native families. Fanny Butler, the first qualified British woman doctor to practice in India, took up medicine primarily because "it was a means of approach to many who were inclined to be hostile to [missionary] teaching, but could not resist it when it was expressed in acts of mercy." After a relatively short career, she died of dysentery at Srinagar in 1889. Her martyrdom inspired many British women to take up practice among "zenana patients."

Medicine was not the only professional avenue open to women seeking a career and a lifetime of useful work in the British empire. Education, and specifically teacher training, was a popular and a much more culturally acceptable occupation. Mary Carpenter's trip to India, made public by her travelogue *Six Months in India* (1866), exhorted British women readers to look to the colonies as the right and proper sphere of Western female influence. She detailed the conditions of girls' schools all over India, assured her audience that progressive Indian men wanted educated companions for wives, and founded the National Indian Association in Bristol upon her return to help guarantee an institutional framework through which

British women could seek support in their efforts to help Indian girl children. The NIA moved to London at Carpenter's death in 1877. There it was run by her successor, Elizabeth Adelaide Manning, who produced a monthly journal (*The Indian Magazine and Review*) for the organization until the early twentieth century. Manning had connections among educated natives, Anglo-Indian elites in India, and the official colonial establishment in Britain. She used the journal to advertise scholarships, raise money for the London School of Medicine for Women, and disseminate information, through the NIA's many branches in Britain and India, about the allegedly pathetic condition of Indian women.

Manning was well connected with women's suffrage groups and their periodicals, so that *The Indian Magazine and Review* became an important source of news and information for all kinds of British women reformers in India and in Britain who were interested in the status of colonial women. Despite the accomplishments of several Indian women, Pandita Ramabai and Cornelia Sorabji among them, who were seeking professional degrees and reform support in Britain in the 1880s and 1890s, "the Indian woman" was almost invariably represented in the metropolitan press as degraded, fallen, and in need of rescue by her British sisters. The connections between such colonial representations and middle-class British women's interest in the plight of England's working classes should not be underestimated, especially since the languages of class through which the "domestic" poor were apprehended were often managed by discourses of racial aberration and sexual pathology that had imperial resonances and traces. Whether these kinds of representations originated in the empire and were circuited back through domestic space, or whether they emerged in dialectic tension with the formation of the imperial nation-state itself, is still a matter of speculation and argument among historians. What remains clear is that bourgeois British women involved in all manner of reform projects during the nineteenth century invoked the racialized languages of social darwinism and emergent anthropology to justify their intervention in the lives not just of working-class men, women, and children, but of colonial peoples, and especially of Indian women, as well.

Nowhere was this reliance on images of "the Indian woman" more evident than in writing by British women seeking inclusion in the imperial nation by means of the vote. Pamphlets, periodicals, and speeches by suffragists from the 1880s until after World War I demonstrate how crucial the ideology of the "white woman's burden" was to suffrage arguments and how foundational convictions about the powerlessness of Indian women were to Victorian and Edwardian feminists' claims to self-representation. Despite the fact that most suffrage workers never went to India, the plight of Indian women preoccupied them and helped to make their feminism an imperial as well as a domestic concern. To be sure, British feminist women had to counter the polemics of antisuffragists, who ridiculed their quest for political rights and who conjured images of an empire in collapse if women were granted the vote. Nor should the availability of stereotypes of Indian womanhood as passive and in need of protection by the "daughters of empire" in Victorian culture be discounted—especially since such images were broadcast in part by Indian men seeking to realize their own nationalist claims on the British government by inviting British women to take up the cause of "India's daughters."

And yet feminists of the period readily appropriated such images, casting Indian women as a colonial clientele dependent on the goodwill and uplift of their British sisters, whose support of India's women in turn, it was argued, guaranteed the future stability of the British empire itself. Such arguments had considerable appeal in fin-de-siècle Britain, when fears of national degeneracy, especially in the wake of the Boer War, were rampant, and when doctors and other public health officials were invoking imperial degeneracy as a scare tactic to promote maternal welfare and infant health. But in the end such apocalyptic claims were as ineffective as the reasoned constitutional arguments suffragists had made since the 1860s; when British women over the age of thirty won the vote in 1918, it was granted by the government as much for service in the war as anything else. Ideals and rhetoric about international sisterhood notwithstanding, British feminists took for granted that the cultural superiority of English civilization—evidence of which surrounded them from their childhood to their graves, especially if they did not live to see the challenges to empire that accelerated after 1918—could and would guarantee them the vote so that they might more effectively represent their poor, "benighted" Indian sisters.

India had tremendous visibility at the century's end, not just because of the ways in which the women's movement appropriated it. Indian nationalism was emerging as a political force to be reckoned with after 1885. Indian reformers campaigned for and won seats in the House of Commons in the 1890s, while a variety of popular entertainments brought the Raj close home in the last decades of the nineteenth century, as when the Colonial and Indian Exhibition—with its mock Indian villages and regional courts—drew five million visitors to London in the summer of 1886. And yet it was Africa that was "on everybody's mind and in everybody's mouth" at the turn of the century. The defeat and inglorious death of General Gordon at Khartoum (1884), the raid on Benin (1897), and the Boer War (1899–1901) drew the British public's attention to the whole continent. Attention was thereby riveted on the fate of the empire and with it, on the stability of Victorian imperial culture as well. For during these the same two decades, the British government struggled to stake and to maintain its claims there in the face of the nationalist rivalry with France and Germany over territory, resources, and international reputation known as the "scramble for Africa." British women—reformers and feminists—involved in African questions found themselves in the headlines during these years. Many expressed opinions about the Boer War, albeit for different reasons. Some, like Josephine Butler, emerged as champions of the "native races" in South Africa. Millicent Garrett Fawcett identified more strongly with the government's position on the conflict: she acted as an official British delegate, traveling to the Transvaal to inspect the camps set up for Boer prisoners of war. Olive Schreiner, for her part, used colonial South Africa as the setting for popular novels and political tracts that linked the plight of the Boer woman to the "woman question" and the labor question as well. As with British feminists interested in Indian women, Schreiner's concern for the women of South Africa, both Boer and "native," was shaped in part by the domestic culture of imperialism, which encouraged even British women who traveled from Britain to empire and back again to view their colonial sisters as "others" rather than as equals.

Upper and middle-class women traveled to the colonies and, like Mary Carpenter had done after her trip to India, turned their experiences into authority about imperial matters and Britain's world-civilizing mission. The British reading public was treated to the adventures not just of men explorers like David Livingstone or Henry Stanley, whose images dominate fin-de-siècle ephemera, but to daring women like Mary Kingsley as well. Her reputation was made in Britain in the 1890s because of her books (*Travels in West Africa* in 1897 and *West African Studies*, 1899), her public lectures and her enthusiastic support of the Liverpool trading lobby. Women like Kingsley and Alexandra David-Neel "craved to go beyond the garden gate," but they did more than simply prove that British women were as fearless or as even as feckless as British men. They aimed to map the world, to delineate the full reach of Britain's imperial power, and to prove themselves as worthy of the term *imperialist* as any British man. As Kingsley wrote to her publisher in the fall of 1896 in an effort to persuade him to let her include a map in her forthcoming book: "it[']s not a question of where I have been—or rather where I say I have been [—] so much as a map to show the geographical facts I have stated." Other British women revealed that they did not have to go far from home to "discover" colonial peoples in their midst. Margaret Harkness's *In Darkest London* (1891), which followed on the heels of Henry Stanley's *In Darkest Africa* (1890) and William Booth's *In Darkest England and the Way Out* (1890), provided a more "local" travelogue, typical of late nineteenth-century urban investigative literature, which mapped a kingdom of street arabs, lascars and a variety of colonial "others" at home in Victorian society.

The British public's appetite for things African was whetted by these high-profile events and publications, and in their wake various images of Africa and its peoples were commodified for broad-based public consumption. Advertisements for Pear's Soap, which flooded the marketplace in the last quarter of the century, promised to wash the "savage" clean and to maintain that all-important boundary between white and black upon which empire and British civilization apparently depended. Given women's role as chief purchaser of household goods, it seems likely that they were influenced, however subtly and unconsciously, by these powerful signs linking domestic service with imperial pride in the cultural imagination. In the last decade of the nineteenth century and into the first decade of the twentieth, a number of the queen's subjects—ethnographers, missionaries, capitalists, and traders— orchestrated a variety of cultural encounters between "native" Britons and Africa on the home front, which helped to popularize such ideas about racial difference. The British raid on Benin, for example, resulted in the "acquisition" and display of the Benin bronzes and other African material culture in museums large and small throughout Britain; the Franco-British Exhibition in 1908 treated ticket-buyers to "native" villages, dancers, and other performers, thus working to consolidate notions about British national unity during an extended historical moment when presumptions about the supremacy of the imperial nation-state were being tested in arenas beyond the British Isles.

Images of Africa, and more specifically, notions of African degeneracy and inferiority, were circulated and managed in public spaces as diverse as the British Museum, the home mission movement, and the *Illustrated London News,* where they were on display for an avid English public to consume. British women and children were chief among these spectators: when the Education Act of 1902 made museum visits by schoolchildren an acceptable part of the educational curriculum, thousands of young Britons were brought into contact with ideas about Africa and into close physical proximity with Africans on British soil. Such encounters were not just contrived but also regulated and policed; fears of miscegenation made the presence of white women at exhibitions a matter of public scrutiny and outcry. As London drew more students and travelers from the empire and Britain's other port cities drew more labor from the West Indies and the Middle East, more and more English women—especially in working-class communities—took up with "colonial men" and in the process, contributed their share to the racially mixed and ethnically diverse populations of modern Britain.

Despite its geographical distance, the British empire reached into the lives and shaped the historical experiences of British women in tangible and equally intangible ways. For some it was the very distance of Britain's colonial possessions which offered the possibility of adventure and the opportunity for advancement; for others, empire was intimately connected with their daily work, entertainment, and religious practices. In any event, few Victorian women were untouched by empire, whether through personal experience, family connection, or collective cultural imagination. It behooves us to remember that the fact of empire was such a natural, unquestioned dimension of the Victorian experience that it scarcely impinged on the consciousness of most British women, even though it arguably shaped the ways in which they imagined themselves as British subjects. Some Britons were critical of the colonial government's policies and practices, but there were few in the nineteenth century, at any rate, who wished to dismantle the empire itself. And although British men and women may have had differently inflected experiences of Victorian imperial culture, for the most part they shared the conviction that it was a privilege to be a subject of the British empire in a world apparently "marked by nature for [rule by] the United Kingdom."

SUGGESTIONS FOR FURTHER READING

Burton, Antoinette. *Burdens of History: British Feminists, Indian Women, and Imperial Culture, 1865–1915.* Chapel Hill, N.C.: University of North Carolina Press, 1994.

Chaudhuri, Nupur, and Margaret Strobel, eds. *Western Women and Imperialism: Complicity and Resistance.* Bloomington, Ind.: Indiana University Press, 1992.

Coombes, Annie E. *Reinventing Africa: Museums, Material Culture and Popular Imagination.* New Haven: Yale University Press, 1994.

Fryer, Peter. *Staying Power: The History of Black People in Britain.* London: Pluto Press, 1987.

Hall, Catherine. *White, Male and Middle Class: Essays in Feminist History.* London: Routledge, 1992.

Jayawardena, Kumari. *The White Woman's Other Burden: Western Women and South Asia during British Rule.* New York: Routledge, 1995.

McClintock, Anne. *Imperial Leather: Race, Gender and Sexuality in the Colonial Context.* New York: Routledge, 1995.

Midgley, Clare. *Women against Slavery: The British Campaigns, 1780–1870.* London: Routledge, 1992.

Prince, Mary. *The History of Mary Prince, a West Indian Slave, Related by Herself.* Edited by Moira Ferguson. London: Pandora, 1987.
Sinha, Mrinalini. *Colonial Masculinity: The "Manly Englishman" and the "Effeminate Bengali" in the Late Nineteenth Century.* Manchester: Manchester University Press, 1990.
Ware, Vron. *Beyond the Pale: White Women, Racism and History.* London: Verso, 1992.

CHAPTER EIGHT

The Tiresome Work of Conspicuous Leisure: On the Domestic Duties of the Wives of Civil Servants in the German Empire (1871–1918)

Sibylle Meyer
*Translated by Lyndel Butler**

In the absence of historical research on women, image and myth long passed for factual description of women's lives. Among the most persistent misconceptions was the popular picture of the typical Victorian lady as a woman of leisure. Freed from demeaning physical labor and sustained mental effort, the model middle-class wife and mother supposedly passed her days in ornamental pursuits, indulging in piano playing, china painting, fancy dress, and lavish entertainment. With a legion of servants at hand to attend to every necessity including infant and child care, she herself became an ornament reflective of her husband's class status.

This familiar but false image may be traced to the confusion between prescriptive and descriptive literature. Victorian novels and advice manuals portrayed women's lives as their authors wanted them to be. Extensive research based on studies of occupation, household income, wage levels, and the like, now reveals that even in mid-Victorian England, relatively few families of the middle class could afford to hire a host of servants. Most often the mistress of the house had to make do with one servant, usually an early adolescent working-class or country girl who was unfamiliar with middle-class styles and standards of living, and required considerable training and supervision.

Similarly, as Sibylle Meyer shows in this study of the wives of midlevel government officials in Imperial Germany, the women at home worked hard to sat-

*This chapter first appeared in German under the title "Die mühsame Arbeit des demonstrativen Müssiggangs. Über die häuslichen Pflichten der Beamtenfrauen im Kaiserreich," in Karin Hausen, ed., *Frauen suchen Ihre Geschichte. Historische Studien zum 19. und 20. Jahrhundert* (Beck'sche Schwarze Reihe, Band 276) Munich, 1983, pp. 172–194. It has been translated by Lyndel Butler. We thank the Beck Publishing House for permission to translate and publish an abbreviated English version of the article. Consult the German version for the notes and sources; we have included only a few of the works in the list of suggested readings.

isfy the increasingly stringent requirements for the governance of a well-ordered household—all the while striving to maintain the appearance of domestic tranquillity. "Conspicuous leisure" required that housework be viewed as the expression of love and devotion rather than as labor. Yet this hidden work by women might be the key to their husbands' success in the bureaucratic order. The social and economic history of housework has been of particular interest to German historians as well as to British and American Marxists and feminists. Their work demonstrates the interdependency of private and public life even in the heyday of "separate spheres."

In historical research, bourgeois women appear most frequently as idle ladies of the drawing room who supposedly occupied their time with piano playing, literature, fine needlework, and the next social invitation. They are seen as persons who determined the atmosphere of the household through their character, not through their work, and who delegated all housework to servants, whom they merely supervised. This myth of the idle bourgeois lady of the salon indeed has little in common with the everyday reality of most bourgeois women in the last third of the nineteenth century.

The work of middle-class women was structured by specific obligations that bisected their lives and subjected the two parts to different rules. In the public eye, they were to appear idle and were, through their alleged freedom from housework, to symbolize the social status of their husbands. Within the family they had to fulfill their domestic duties following the principle of maximum thrift—housework recognizes no leisure. This study examines the complicated daily work of wives of the educated middle class of modest income using the example of domestic social relationships to bring clearly to light the pressures caused by the combination of bourgeois lifestyle and bourgeois housework. My evidence is based primarily on Berlin and there, above all, on the wives of civil servants; however, it appears to have general validity for the urban educated middle class of the German Empire.

The occupations of the educated middle classes—most especially civil service—required continuous allegiance to the government; not only was one's labor claimed by the state, but one's entire personality. Occupational duties embraced the entire life of persons in these professions. In every context, behavior worthy of the state was demanded of them. Every appearance in public—alone or accompanied by a spouse—was a test of respectability and social acceptability. Even the private sphere of bourgeois families was determined by professional pressures that found their expression in the family's considerable expenditures for keeping up appearances in public. Respectability required a correspondingly appropriate dwelling, whenever possible in a better quarter of the city. The annual summer trip to the seaside was obligatory for middle-class families. Sons had to receive an appropriate education; daughters, an adequate dowry to assure a marriage worthy of their class.

A special symbol of the socially respectable position, the "idleness of the wife" also expressed the wealth of the family. All housework was supposed to be taken care of by an army of servants. Every form of work was considered inappropriate for middle-class women and violated the rules of etiquette. Instead, the occupations prescribed for bourgeois women were obligatory piano playing, knowledge of French language, literature, and conversation. These required skills were to come into play on social occasions and were, therefore, functional for maintaining middle-class appearances. Bourgeois women in public were expected to sparkle and to maintain appearances in order to provide their husbands with a backdrop of education, respectability, and economic power. Idleness became a central component of the woman's obligation to keep up appearances.

The pressure to keep up appearances extended into the "private sphere" of the bourgeois family and objectified itself in the floor plan and partitioning of the middle-class residence. The arrangement and functioning of the rooms corresponded to the attempt, on the one hand, to establish the relationship to the public with the formal rooms near the street entrance and, on the other hand, to shield the private rooms from the outside world. The size of the individual rooms reflected the orientation of the residence to the requirement of keeping up appearances. The formal rooms frequently occupied four to five times as much floor space as the housekeeping rooms: kitchen, larder, and servants' chambers.

Occasions to demonstrate the respectability of the husband and the leisure of the wife were offered primarily by calling at the house or by private invitation. As soon as the family moved to another city—regular transfers were a permanent part of the careers of civil servants—it immediately initiated "social intercourse" by "paying calls." The domestic visits took place in the drawing room, which was not usually used by the family, but served only the purpose of keeping up appearances for guests and callers. The other rooms remained closed to strangers. From the splendor of the drawing room and the apparent worth of each individual piece of furniture, the wealth and social acceptability of the family could be ascertained.

In order to decorate the drawing room as a status symbol, corners were cut in furnishing the other rooms, so that there was a considerable disparity between the quality of the furnishings of the drawing room and the rest of the residence. Luise Otto-Peters (1819–95), a leading German feminist, late in the 1870s described this contrast between drawing room and other rooms: "In the one elegant furnishings were exposed to view, splendor and attempts to keep up the latest fashion; in the others shabbiness and anxious attempts to make do. . . ."

Social events underwent a formal patterning that was maintained through the inflexible constraints of norms to be meticulously heeded. As a rule, between twelve and sixteen persons were invited to festive soirées. The upper limit derived necessarily from the relatively small size of the middle-class residence. The sequence of events for the parties was prescribed in detail, and every guest was familiar with it. The company met in the drawing room, was introduced, chatted, and sat down together at the table for a festive dinner. After an elaborate bill of fare, at which everything was served that the family had to offer, coffee and tea were served, the group heard the hostess or the daughter of the house play the piano, and conversation continued.

The obligatory banquet always constituted the high point of the social evening. On the basis of the table decorations, the china and silver displayed, the menu, and the consummate service, the host family was scrutinized by its guests to determine its qualifications for membership in "polite society." For this reason the guests' eyes should be virtually blinded by the brilliance of the silver, the number of glasses, and the gleaming china. Along this line, homemaking manuals recommended: "The gleaming focal point of the dining room should always be the table; therefore, it demands plenty of light and brightness. To this end have all your treasures of silver chest and china cabinet polished as bright and clean as possible; let everything simply sparkle with cleanliness. . . ."

At that time an important attribute of prosperity was a complete and appropriately expensive tableware service that was the pride of every housewife, for china and silver were usually part of her dowry. In any case "society" must not notice if the family owned no such lavish table service and silverware. One possible way to hide the lack was to borrow dishes from parents and friends, and, if they also had none, then if worse came to worst, to turn to a rental agency. Hans Fallada (1893–1937), a popular German writer, describes this necessity at his parents' house: "We had to obtain glasses and silverware from a rental agency, but not the dishes, for we owned the Wedgewood service notorious among our acquaintances. . . ."

The service at a dinner party had to be faultless. The only servant of educated bourgeois families, the maid-of-all-work alone would have been overburdened with the preparation of foods, serving, pouring drinks, and cleaning up afterward. Besides, most of them were very young girls from the country and not familiar with the strict rules of serving. Difficult "incidents" could arise that would destroy the painstakingly contrived arrangements. Thus the manuals on housekeeping recommended: "Since few servants understand faultless service, one hires a temporary servant, one from northern Germany who is a very well-schooled in fashionable usage." The temporary servant, who was engaged for one evening and with the maid took over the service for the soirée, appears to have been the rule in the family of the civil servant of that period. A male servant, who could only be afforded by the wealthiest families in the final years of the nineteenth century, was considered to be a sign of greatest refinement. The temporary servant became a favorite theme of contemporary family periodicals, which cynically portrayed the picture of a servant who could not find his way around strange quarters, who exploited the dependency of the family on his services, and purloined the leftovers from the expensive menus.

Such images caricatured the secret fears of the housewife that the temporary servant might behave badly or that the other guests might recognize him. "Isn't that the same one as at the privy counsellor's?" The housewife had to live in constant fear of the discovery of the elaborately arranged deception. It is easy to imagine how the furtive glances of the housewife clashed with the critical ones of the guests searching for faux pas. "One feared for the success of the evening. The guests, to whom all these situations were all too well-known, followed the course of the evening with almost fearful suspense."

The same women who, during the official dinner parties had to appear idle in keeping with their husbands' social positions, were at the same time responsible for the events of the evening and the comprehensive preparations. The appearance of refinement and the social deception, which was supposed to hide the lack of wealth, had to be arranged by the housewives. Days ahead detailed plans were worked out and the difficult undertaking of a table arrangement was begun. Every wife tried to create a special table decor, yet the accessorizing of her table should not be more sumptuous and more impressive than at all the other parties. In this vein one author advised in 1897: "In short, everything is permitted that is pleasing and there is only one law: within the limits of good taste, give your table the most individual touch possible." This principle became obligatory for the women.

Over the spotless white damask tablecloth, hand-embroidered or hand-painted table runners were spread—or as an especially extravagant variation—"the new unusual runners out of printed crepe paper" were used. Also the women, for the most part, painted the placecards and found endless fresh ways of informing the guests of the courses, e.g., "in the shape of small musical instruments such as tambourines, harps, or zithers, or apples, oranges, and flowers, decorated with the names, lying on the napkins, or as tiny palettes with figures painted in water colors."

The actual dinner party menu meant just as much painstaking preparatory work for the women. The rules of etiquette prescribed at least six courses, and their combinations were to be elegant, original, and distinguished through the use of luxurious ingredients and excellent preparation. Recommended menus for festive dinner parties were found in every contemporary cookbook or housekeeping manual, frequently also in women's magazines. The suggestions varied according to the projected readership. A simpler dinner party menu consisted of a bouillon with pastries or sandwiches as hors d'oeuvres, after which the two obligatory main courses, normally fish and a roasted meat dish, were served. Afterward, butter and cheeses followed, and the meal ended with a dessert. In more elevated bourgeois circles, three or four main courses were considered appropriate. The exaggerated value placed on these dinner parties increased even more the painstaking efforts already made by the housewives.

Not only the abundant menus, the faultless service, and the smoothness of the evening determined its success, but also the correspondingly decorative spatial backdrop of the drawing room. For this, not only short-term efforts were required, such as thorough cleaning and possible rearrangement of the room, but also long-term work in which women made part of the fittings for the drawing room. Many pieces of furniture, which would have been too expensive if purchased, were made by the women themselves or their apparent value was increased through artful adornment. Having conclusions about the wealth of the family drawn directly from the magnificence of the drawing room required establishing for the guests the best possible appearances.

Following the principle of obtaining the most decorative effect possible at the least possible expense, the women went to work and made artful pieces of decorative furniture. Accessories, wall decorations, glass paintings, hooked rugs that looked like real Persian carpets, table covers, piano throws, lamps, screens, tassels, pulls, and draperies were hand-sewn, embroidered, crocheted, and knitted. Out of four old carpet-beaters, they fashioned little tables for the drawing room. The handles were crossed and bound so that the lower parts formed legs, the four upper parts formed a small basket that was covered with embroidered cloth. The table legs were upholstered with plush or knitted covers so that no one could know that this apparently fine piece had been made out of old carpet-beaters.

The tremendous amount of trouble involved in the outfitting of a drawing room and in the preparations for the party were not to be noticeable to the invited guests.

The more completely the housewife succeeded at this deception, the more certain appeared the professional promotion of the husband, assuring the material basis as well as the social reputation of the family. Guests of the house must not see the housewife engaged in physical work, or detect traces of this work on her. Thus soft, well-cared-for hands, on which one did not notice the daily work, were an attribute of class that women were concerned with keeping. As early as 1845 a housekeeping manual recommended:

> It often happens that even high-ranking ladies help at home with housework, and particularly with kitchen chores, scrubbing, etc., so that, above all the hands have good cause to become very rough, hard, and calloused. When these ladies appear in society, they are extremely upset at having such rough-looking hands. In order to perform the hardest and most ordinary chores, as for example, cooking, dishwashing, sweeping, and the like, and, at the same time, to keep a soft hand like those fine ladies who have no heavier work to do than embroidering and sewing, always keep a piece of fresh bacon, rub your hands with it just before bedtime, and you will fully achieve your goal. You will, as a result, have the inconvenience of having to sleep with gloves on, in order not to soil the bed.

The opposite pole to the elegance of the public facade was the meager everyday life of the family. Here everything had to be extremely economical in order, once or twice a year, to facilitate the contrived social appearances. The work fell to the housewife to carry out the strict requirement of compulsory, domestic thrift in all areas of housekeeping. Thrift here meant the reduction of expenditures required by the life of the family through the increase of unpaid work on the part of the wife—exploitation instead of expenditure.

The smaller the income of the husband, the more necessary to forego the work of servants; educated bourgeois families had to be content normally with one maid. The dominant interpretation since the period, that several maids could have carried out the entire work of the household on their own and the job of the wife consisted of overseeing the servants, misses the reality of most bourgeois women. It assumes a division of labor between the lady of the house and the housemaids corresponding to the separation of decision making from physical work. However, it is misleading and serves to buttress the dominant thesis of the "idleness" of the middle-class women. The housework to be accomplished was so comprehensive and so manifold that it could scarcely be completed by two women.

Housework required cooperation between all persons concerned, or at least required communication about the current task. This necessity was intensified when the normally very young maid-of-all-work brought no specific knowledge of housekeeping with her at the time she was hired and, therefore, had to be instructed by the housewife. In addition to the inhuman work pressure on the maid, which one cannot overestimate, the maid's arrival brought with it an increase in the work of the housewife. There was, indeed, a division of work between the two women, but it was not along previously assumed traditional lines of decision making and physical work. The division varied with the demands of the work to be accomplished at a given moment and was maintained through cooperation.

A generally ambivalent relationship resulted between the housewife and the maid. While the former worked out of "love," permanently and unpaid, the latter was poorly paid and could be let go at any time. On the other hand, both were required in the common work of the household and, in the process of accomplishing the everyday work of the family, depended on each other. They stood—although they belonged to different social classes—in a structurally comparable legal and material dependency on the man of the house. Subject to the familial, patriarchal power relationship, both of the women had to reach some mutual understanding in order to make their living and working situations as bearable as possible. Simultaneously the housewife served as mediator on behalf of the needs and interests of the man of the house. She had a concrete interest in maximizing the work accomplished by the maid; something that could only be achieved by applying continual pressure. Only the efficient functioning of the maid could ease the wife's schizophrenic life situation—appearing idle to the external world and not permitted, according to the rules of etiquette, to carry out any servants' work, such as she was, in reality, forced to do.

In those areas into which guests and callers could not peer, the housewives had to institute significant savings in order to free the means for keeping up external appearances. One very productive area for savings was the expenditures for physical care of the family, above all food, which, at the same time, was considered to be the foremost obligation of the housewife. How she dealt with groceries demonstrates the determining principles of housework in the bourgeois family. On the one hand, the woman must be extremely economical and satisfy the family with the cheapest ingredients; only by doing so could she cover the high costs of keeping up appearances. This demanded exact budgeting of household funds, shopping for the most reasonable items, differentiated food storage, and, above all, very economical cooking. On the other hand, the housewife was supposed to provide lovingly for the wishes of the husband and children. Their wishes also had to be taken into account in shopping and laying in foods, and special wishes were to be fulfilled by cooking. The housekeeping manuals emphasized the duties of the women to take the needs of the men as their highest goal; if they did not satisfy these needs, then an unhappy marriage was the result because "the way to a man's heart is through his stomach."

A festive roast appeared on the middle-class table only on Sundays and holidays, for roasts were "aristocrat's food." On workdays middle-class families had to content themselves with mixed dishes. Soups, which satisfied hunger and were inexpensive and quick to prepare, were the main component of the scanty everyday fare. Cookbook authors and manuals advised to thrifty wives simple fare which depended on the cooking of vegetables and meats in combination. For meat, the cheaper small cuts and internal organs of the animal such as feet, tongue, jowl, lungs, liver, heart, kidney, brain, and tripe were used. According to a popular author, even "in better houses the entrails were not scorned." As a consequence, cookbooks, which were aimed at a bourgeois class constrained by extreme thrift, abounded with recipes for dishes from cheaper cuts of meat.

Also crucial for cheap cooking was the reuse of all leftover ingredients and dishes. The leftover roast from Sunday was warmed up on Tuesday or Wednesday;

leftover vegetables together with their liquids produced the next day's soup; sausage and pancake leftovers provided additions to the soup; dried bread became a new main dish as bread casserole. Tasty soups were cooked from the ribs of rabbits and poultry; the accumulated cores and stalks of vegetables appeared on the table again as mock salsify *(Schwarzwurzel)*. Goose gizzards, if they had been marinated long enough, boiled, and finally roasted, made a good side dish at supper; the peelings of lemons and oranges were finely chopped, extracted with vinegar, and finally were made into lemonade by adding sugar water.

Even the garbage from groceries, which was no longer fit to eat, found other applications in housekeeping. Sodium silicate served every purpose from preserving eggs to cleaning dirty tiles; damp used tea leaves cleaned the carpet, sauerkraut juice was a marvelous cleaner for brass items, and fresh coffee grounds cleaned cloudy glasses. The cooked-out pork skins and bones were kept cool in the waiting soap crock until the crock was full of leftover fat, back rinds, sausage skins, etc. Then the contents were sold to a soapmaker or, even up to the turn of the century, women made the soap themselves.

Nothing could be wasted, nothing thrown away. Empty cocoa boxes became the holders for cleanser, candle stubs, and matches. Small cardboard boxes later held herbs or powder. Old paper could be used to line cupboards, to clean knives and forks, and, above all, to polish lamps and stove tops.

> Of the many kinds of household leftovers, tins from bouillon make the best spice holders; one simply removes the labels, bronzes them, sews a broad colored ribbon—little ribbon scraps are appropriate here—around the neck of the tin, and writes the contents of the tin on this with ineradicable ink . . .

The most complete possible use of all leftovers demanded of the women ingenuity and experience, but, above all, it required extensive work.

The financial basis of the domestic work of the wife was the housekeeping money provided by the husband, and she was accountable to him for its use. All expenditures had to be proven; not even a penny could be missing from her bookkeeping. The housekeeping money was usually the only source of money under the control of the wife; the main part of the income and, if the occasion should arise, of the fortune, even her dowry, was controlled by the husband. The bookkeeping required of her assured the husband's control and characterized the internal familial power relationships making clear the complete financial dependence of the wife.

The husband was not required to give the wife access to information about his income or his wealth, a fact bitterly deplored by wives in many of their contributions to family magazines. Often the man could not accurately gauge the cost of the household and apportioned too little housekeeping money. Since contractual agreements on the amount of the housekeeping money were unthinkable, the housewife remained dependent on his estimate and often had to beg for every additional penny.

A widely recognized possibility for extending the limited housekeeping money was the cottage labor of the women even in the middle class. Only in this way, in many cases, could they come up with the everyday costs and the extra money for keeping up appearances. Bourgeois women prepared artistic embroidery, crocheted lace and insets, or sewed ready-made clothes at home. Numerous women sought purchasers for their textile handwork and handmade arts and crafts in the women's sections of the newspapers. The money they earned flowed into the household coffers to defray running costs or special expenditures. The homework of bourgeois women had to remain meticulously hidden from the public and frequently also from their husbands. If every form of housework was unacceptable for their class, then any form of paid work was also unacceptable. "Secretly, very secretly, so that no one will notice they [officials' wives] pick up handwork from the shops; secretly, very secretly, they carry it back again—No one should know or be allowed to find out."

The sharp separation of public and private spheres basically shaped the bourgeois lifestyle. The bourgeois housewife, nevertheless, accomplished the physical and psychological reproduction of the family members and supported additionally the professional career of her husband in two ways. On the one hand, she engineered the economy of everyday family life, which helped to cover the high costs of keeping up appearances, and, on the other hand, she made parts of the decor herself. These behaviors of the housewife followed an imminent rationality, which was determined through the constraints of middle-class life. Without the housework of the bourgeois wife providing the daily proofs of social acceptability and the consequent rise of her husband, the material betterment of the family would not have been possible.

Keeping up bourgeois appearances forced the invisibility of housework. Making this work invisible became in itself work, which had to be accomplished in addition to the normal domestic activities. This veiling of housework became its structuring element, and, along with the requirement of thrift and the needs of the family members, determined the work day of the housewives. What appears at first glance to be idleness is revealed, on closer examination, to be difficult and tiresome work.

SUGGESTIONS FOR FURTHER READING

Branca, Patricia. "Image and Reality: The Myth of the Idle Victorian Woman." In *Clio's Consciousness Raised: New Perspectives on the History of Women*, edited by Mary Hartman and Lois Banner, 179–191. New York: Harper Torchbooks, 1974.

———. *Silent Sisterhood: Middle-Class Women in the Victorian Home*. London: Croom Helm, 1975.

Davidoff, Leonore. *The Best Circles: Women and Society in Victorian England*. Totowa, N.J.: Rowman and Littlefield, 1973.

Fallada, Hans. [Rudolf Ditzen]. *Little Man, What Now?* Translated by Eric Sutton. New York: Simon and Schuster, 1933.

Hellerstein, Erna Olafson. "French Women and the Orderly Household, 1830–1870." *Proceedings of the Western Society for French History* III (1976): 378–389.

Oakley, Ann. *The Sociology of Housework*. New York: Pantheon, 1974.

———. *Women's Work: The Housewife, Past and Present*. New York: Vintage, 1976.

Smith, Bonnie G. *Ladies of the Leisure Class: The Bourgeoises of Northern France in the Nineteenth Century*. Princeton: Princeton University Press, 1981.

Strasser, Susan. *Never Done: A History of American Housework*. New York: Pantheon, 1982.

CHAPTER NINE

In the Shadows of the Periphery: Italian Women in the Nineteenth Century

Donna Gabaccia

Studies of women and work have tended to focus on urban occupations in factory, mill, school, and store. Except in Great Britain, however, most women (and men) resided in rural communities well into the twentieth century. Often bypassed by historians, though never by history, these peasants and villagers also experienced the stresses of political and economic change. In this unusual study of southern Italian "women of the shadows," Donna Gabaccia describes a class for whom being unemployed signified not the fulfillment of a Rousseauean fantasy of ideal domesticity, or the achievement of a "conspicuous leisure" essential to urban middle-class status. For these Italian women, lack of gainful employment meant debt and deprivation. The transition from a traditional subsistence economy to a market, or cash, economy, brought them not new opportunities and enhanced self-esteem, but reduced status and increased dependency.

By examining the effects of capitalist agricultural and industrial development on peasant women in Italy, Gabaccia's work shows a female experience significantly different from more familiar stories of urban settings in contemporary western Europe. Using census materials on female occupations and wage rates, records of landholdings, and accounts of changing agricultural techniques, Gabaccia first analyzes the sexual division and distribution of labor in several regions of Italy. She then demonstrates how political decisions affected economic developments that in turn remodeled women's work patterns. Italian unification, by facilitating the creation of national markets and entry into international trade, ultimately forced women into "domesticity." Like Sibylle Meyer (chapter 8), Gabaccia provides a graphic illustration of the inadequacy of the concept of separate public and private spheres. Clearly, the daily lives and family relationships of these Italian women depended on distant decisions by political leaders. This analysis, too, has relevance for an understanding of the effects of agricultural transformation on women's lives in industrializing nations today.

Women in southern Italian life have been portrayed recently as "women of the shadows." That Italy's women should seem shadowy is not surprising. The women of the shadows are invisible not only as women, but as poor, often illiterate rural dwellers, as agricultural workers and peasants, and as residents of a region that became at most a minor power among Western nations. Thus, while historians have outlined women's new roles in the nineteenth century—as factory operative, as middle-class lady or her servant, as feminist—peasant women remain obscure. The very opposite of new, they seem left over from the Middle Ages, occupants of a traditional world untouched by the major events and transformations of the century.

In fact, as this essay will demonstrate, the women of the shadows (like other people without history) become visible precisely when we recognize that they too experienced political centralization, urbanization, and the rise of the factory system. As cities grew, the countryside fed and populated them, and as urban factories produced new and cheap products, the countryside often became an important marketplace for them. Change in the countryside might mean a new crop grown, an old trade abandoned, the search for a cash income, migration, or the loss of kin and neighbors to "better opportunities" elsewhere. Our task, then, is to outline the rural and, more importantly, the gender-specific consequences of the economic, cultural, and political transformation sometimes called "development" or "modernization." This is a worthwhile task. As late as 1890, most of Europe's population lived in the agricultural countryside, especially in Ireland, eastern Europe, the Balkans, and along the Mediterranean, but also in the hinterlands of England, Germany, and France. The average European woman of the nineteenth century was still a rural woman.

Firmly located in Europe's agricultural periphery, Italy has been viewed by scholars as a kind of "school for awakening countries" in today's Third World. To northern European visitors in the nineteenth century, the land seemed astonishingly backward: "almost oriental" was a favored (and telling) comparison. "Backward" is a value-laden expression of a simple reality: the Italian peninsula before 1890 little resembled the European nations which at the time proudly proclaimed themselves models for and pinnacles of human evolution. Although Italians formed a nation-state in the years after 1860, they did not yet share a strong national identity. Even more strikingly, Italy's economy showed few signs of following the example of industrializing northern neighbors. After the commercial and industrial successes of the Renaissance, central Italian industries actually declined through the seventeenth and eighteenth centuries. Modern industrialization began in earnest only around 1900, and only in a few central and northern areas. Until the 1950s, more than half of the Italian labor force worked in agriculture. The very importance of agriculture in Italy was sometimes taken as symbolic of the country's "backwardness." But however different from north European agricultural practice, Italy's agriculture and its countryside were not static and unchanging. Neither were the women of the shadows.

We know from studies of Britain, France, Germany, and the United States that new roles for women—"the lady" and "the mill girl"—accompanied industrialization. Recently, good studies of African, Latin American, and Asian women have told us more about the meaning of political and economic change in peripheral and agricultural regions of the world. In both cases, scholars discovered new forces that relegated women to domesticity. Clearly the policies of the nation-state or the dictates of colonial development agencies play an important role in domesticating women, often by excluding them from a male-dominated public world. (In nineteenth-century Europe, while increasing numbers of men obtained suffrage, women did not; in Africa, modernizing land tenure often meant limiting land ownership to male heads of nuclear families.) At the same time, the transition from a semi-subsistence (or household) economy to a cash (or wage) economy redefined the meaning of work.

Changing patterns in Italian women's work hint at the complexity of domesticity in an agricultural land. In the twentieth century scholars would be puzzled that so few very poor Italian women worked outside their homes. Cultural traits—a Muslim heritage in southern provinces or a more general male obsession with controlling female sexuality—often provided an explanation for the fact that Italian women, when compared to the French or British, rarely worked for wages. Italian culture, it seemed, demanded domesticity of its women. Some scholars even suggested that Italian men's insistence on female domesticity posed an insurmountable obstacle to agricultural or industrial development.

Actually, of course, the women listed in Italian censuses as "without profession and at home" were relative newcomers to Italy, as were housewives in other countries. Only where much productive work had left the household could the housewife exist. That transformation was incomplete in rural Italy in the nineteenth century. At the time of the first comprehensive Italian census in 1871, clerks found relatively few women "without profession"; they counted 50 percent of Italian women as active workers. The large number of working Italian women in 1871 reflected the continued importance for both Italian men and women of small-scale production for family consumption. Wage-earning in Italy (unlike Britain) was not yet central to defining male or female peasants as workers. Both Italian men and women, in a sense, worked in a domestic world.

What distinguished Italy from industrializing nations was that her women became more domestic in subsequent years. While rates of female labor participation in France increased (as women found wage-earning work as textile operatives or domestic servants), rates in Italy declined to less than 30 percent in 1901. This decline was partly an illusion, the result of redefining work as wage-earning; it tells us that Italian men largely claimed wage-earning for themselves. But it is also partially attributable to real changes in women's behavior. Women were less likely to be doing productive work with or without wages in 1901 than in 1871.

A major theme in Italian economic history is the slow decline of Italy's subsistence economy, and the equally slow but persistent growth of capitalist agriculture and industry. In fact, this is the trend of economic development in all western European nations in the nineteenth century: the transition from household production to wage-earning, from production for family use to production for the market, and from small-scale peasant and artisan production to large-scale capitalist production. Focusing on the women of the shadows, however, we might emphasize other themes.

The term subsistence production conjures up images of self-contained and patriarchal peasant and artisan families, working to provide themselves food, clothing and housing, little affected by money and markets. To a degree, such families did shape reality for most Italian women in the early nineteenth century. It is unwise to exaggerate the self-sufficiency of such peasant and artisan households. And it is necessary to outline several important broad variations in how Italian men and women provided for family subsistence in the early years of the nineteenth century.

In much of Italy, peasants enjoyed secure tenure to their land, either through ownership or traditional land rights; they worked small plots of land and grew their own food. If they lived close to a town, they might market any surplus there. By contrast, in parts of southern Italy, semi-feudal social relations persisted. Peasants enjoyed no secure tenure to the land; they cultivated different plots each year on large estates utilizing a three-field system. On their small plots they produced not only staple crops for their own food and garments (oil, grain, linen, sheep), but also a surplus that the estate manager marketed and used to pay land rents to the feudal lord. In areas like these, peasant family subsistence also rested on common rights to the use of land for gathering food and fuel and for grazing small animals. In addition, all over Italy peasant families combined production of food with production of cloth. Here, too, a distinction can be noted between regions with a cottage textile industry and regions where families produced cloth strictly for their own needs.

The division of labor between Italian men and women varied from region to region in the early years of the nineteenth century. In general, married men controlled access to land; few women inherited land or enjoyed rights to its usage. Where land tenure was relatively secure and where small villages were scattered through the countryside, women became an important part of the family work force in the fields, producing food for family consumption. Both men and women marketed small surpluses of eggs, milk, corn, cheese, and so on. Where large estates, herding, and extensive production for the market and concentrated settlement were common, women's agricultural labors were more clearly demarcated from men's. Women gathered, grazed small animals, and generally exploited common usage rights, while men raised grain and herded larger animals. Only at harvest time did women join men on the large distant wheat estates of Sicily, for example, and then mainly as gleaners. The fact that fewer women worked in the fields in such regions cannot be seen simply as a consequence of patriarchal concerns about women working outside the family group, although certainly that played a role. Employers' choices, as well as the very long distances (up to ten or fifteen miles) separating wheat fields from the large compact "agrotowns" of the Italian South, must also be considered.

Almost everywhere in Italy it was women's work at spindle and loom that clothed the family. Girls and mothers worked to produce the cloth and clothing that would become the dowry of daughters at the time of their marriages. (Sons inherited house and/or land.) Where cloth was produced mainly for family needs, men did little. But where cottage industry linked rural workers to city merchants, men might turn their hands in winter to spinning or (more frequently) weaving. In general, where women did little field work, men did little textile work. Local records in such areas might call men "peasants" but women "industrial workers."

The division of labor between men and women in all rural regions changed and became more differentiated in the course of the nineteenth century. The formation of the Italian nation-state can be cited as one important spur to changes in the rural world inhabited by the women of the shadows. Of course, Italy had no formulated plan for development as did colonial agencies or newly independent nations in the twentieth century. Still, the creation of a centralized state stimulated new markets, capitalist agriculture, and greater regional specialization. All in turn encouraged a new division of labor by sex. For women, the economic consequences of unification proved mixed. The legal ending of semi-feudal practices (in the southern provinces) and new inheritance laws after unification allowed small but growing numbers of women access to land. By 1881 more than a third of Italian landowners were female. At the same time, however, the end of feudalism rendered illegal women's gathering and grazing in precisely those areas where women did little field work.

The formation of the Italian nation-state allowed the growth of a unified national market for agricultural and industrial commodities. Through its changing tariff policy (free trade before the 1880s; protection for grain and industrial products thereafter), the state also regulated commercial ties between Italy and other nations. No other events more greatly affected rural Italian women than the import of cheap manufactured cloth and the growth of capitalist agriculture, producing new crops in new ways for markets far from the local piazza.

Historians have shown how the development of the textile industry in France and Britain meant wage-earning options for women. For women in the countryside, however, factory-produced cloth meant unemployment. Although there is much we do not yet know about the decline of Italian rural industries, it seems likely that some Italian women experienced unemployment earlier than others. By the 1880s, 80 percent of Italy's tiny population of female textile operatives lived in only three provinces (Piedmont, Lombardy, and Venice); their numbers and concentration grew substantially by the early twentieth century. In much of northern and central Italy in 1881, women had begun to abandon loom and spindle to purchase cloth. Furthermore, northern Italy's mill girls made up only one-tenth of the women who told census takers in 1881 that they worked as spinners or weavers. Large numbers of southern Italian women still produced cloth for their families, for local sale and for struggling cottage industries. But their numbers, too, were declining. And twenty years later, most women in Italy's South even purchased sheeting for their trousseaux.

The exact timing of Italy's declining rural industries is not yet entirely clear. It seems likely, however, that as cottage industry declined, so too did weaving at home for family use. Folklorists, like Giuseppe Pitré, a Sicilian, commented on the changing occupation of young girls, who no longer sat hours at spindle or loom producing cloth for their own trousseaux. The desire to purchase manufactured cloth probably itself became an incentive for some family members to switch their labors from subsistence agriculture to seek a cash income as either agricultural or industrial laborers. Since Italy's economy offered few rapidly expanding industrial opportunities for either men or women during these years, cash earned in agriculture became increasingly important to many families.

Although individual women may have welcomed liberation from arduous work at the loom, the purchase of cloth also posed a problem. Where would the cash come from? We may never understand precisely how men and women struggled or cooperated to answer this question. But it is possible to describe the context in which differing answers emerged. The development of capitalist agriculture, the growth or decline of local male industries, and regional customs in defining men's and women's tasks all formed parts of that context.

Table 2 describes some representative Italian regions in 1881, and summarizes the work that women did in each (see map, Figure 2). It contrasts two areas where peasant agriculture remained important to three areas where large-scale capitalist agriculture developed fairly early. "Capitalist agriculture" assumed many forms in nineteenth-century Italy. Essential to all forms was the rural entrepreneur who contracted with individuals or families to produce crops which he sold at a profit. The three types of capitalist agriculture summarized in Table 2 represent a rough continuum from less to more capitalist. In the *mezzadria* ("classic sharecropping") system, the Tuscan entrepreneur owned land, houses, vines, trees, and animals; he contracted long-term with peasant families for labor. Peasants still owned some of their own tools, and they divided crops with the landlord, rather than receiving a money payment. The *latifondo* of western Sicily (and Apulia and much of Calabria) evolved from the semi-feudal estates described above. Here, the rural entrepreneur rented a large estate and found short-term sharecroppers (paid in grain) and day laborers (earning a cash wage). In the Po Valley, entrepreneurs owned large tracts of land and paid money wages and provided temporary housing for families of laborers.

Several patterns characterized Italian women's work by 1881. Where women had long worked in the fields (Turin, Abruzzi-Molise, Tuscany, and the Po Valley), they increasingly turned their attentions there as they abandoned their looms. This pattern became most obvious in areas with little capitalist agriculture, like Turin's hinterland. In both Turin and Abruzzi-Molise, women typically concentrated in subsistence production, raising food, while men took whatever wage-earning became available. Men's cash earnings bought property and cloth; women fed the family. In some areas like this, women constituted as much as 70 percent of the agricultural work force in 1881. Usually women also outnumbered men as Table 2 reveals. Men's quest for wages encouraged them to migrate elsewhere while wives, mothers, sisters, and dependent children of both sexes supported themselves on the land. Women in such regions had not in fact moved "beyond subsistence"—even though their work had changed. By 1901 many of the women agriculturalists in regions like these would be listed as housewives, for they worked without wages.

Capitalist agriculture meant different choices for Italian men and women. Women who abandoned their looms sometimes had a harder time finding work in the fields once rural entrepreneurs organized the conditions of employment. Previous habits also worked their influence: women in 1881 were far more likely to work among the Tuscan *mezzadri* than in *latifondo* Sicily. Still, the trend in all areas was similar and clear: growing numbers of men earned wages, providing the cash income that cloth (and other purchases) required, while large numbers of women already in 1881 found themselves listed in the census not as spinners, weavers, or peasants, but as housewives.

Sicily provides an extreme example of this second pattern of adaptation. By 1871, most men working in Sicilian agriculture already worked part-time as wage-earners on the large wheat estates. Their labors purchased food and (where necessary) paid rents or taxes, while women's spinning and weaving still clothed most

Figure 2. Italy in 1881 (Showing Regions Represented in Table 2)

Sicilian families. As cloth production at home declined, Sicilian women sought new work in the fields. (Within a ten-year period, Sicily's women "industrial workers" disappeared from local records to be replaced first by female "peasants" and then, rather swiftly, by "housewives.") Surprisingly, at first Sicilian women actually found work in the fields. In *latifondist* Corleone, for example, women made up almost 40 percent of the agricultural work force in 1881. Thus, not all Sicilian men adamantly forbade wives or daughters to work in the fields or to earn wages. Real agricultural changes, concurrent with the collapse of home textile production, may have helped undermine any male reluctance with hopes of new prosperity, for in the years following Italian unification new crops—especially grapes and oranges, but also nuts, fruits, and olives—began to replace wheat cultivation in western Sicily. These inten-

TABLE 2. Economic Development and Women's Work Patterns, 1881

	Peasant Agriculture		Semi-Capitalist Agriculture		
	Turin Hinterland	Abruzzi-Molise	Mezzadria Tuscany	Latifondo W. Sicily	Po Valley
Percentage of male peasants owning land	50%	59%	20%	18%	15%
Women as percentage of all agricultural workers	50%	40%	32%	16%	34%
Sex ratio	109	114	84	100	96
Women's work: Percentage of women aged nine and over working in					
Agriculture	50%	40%	32%	10%	19%
Textile/clothing production	6%	20%	8%	29%	10%
Housework	22%	23%	44%	44%	39%

Source: Direzione Generale della Statistica, *Censimento della Popolazione del Regno d'Italia al 31 Dicembre 1881* (Rome, 1884).

sively cultivated crops grew conveniently close to town; furthermore, grape and olive harvests overlapped with the wheat ploughing that occupied Sicilian men. Thus, many Sicilian women in the late 1870s and early 1880s earned wages as grape, orange, and olive harvesters, providing the additional cash revenue that cloth purchase required.

During the 1880s, however, all of Sicily's major export crops suffered severe reverses on world markets, and the Sicilian adaptation collapsed in failure. Neither Sicilian men nor Sicilian women could return to subsistence agriculture as could landowning peasants in Turin's hinterland. Not surprisingly, men monopolized wage-earning opportunities in the ensuing crisis; former female agriculturalists as well as women newly liberated from the loom found themselves "domesticated." The unemployed woman became a "housewife."

In claiming wage-earning for themselves, Sicilian men continued to provide food and rents; and in families where sons outnumbered daughters, men's cash earnings might also be diverted to cloth purchase. But in many families the wages of men would not stretch so far; the problem of cloth purchase in particular remained unresolved. Male migration was not a clear answer to this problem as it was elsewhere. Excluded both from the land and from wage-earning, Sicilian women could not easily support themselves and dependent children while men risked migration and the search for cash. A major challenge for Sicilians was the search for female employment. For this reason, Sicilian women were far more likely than other women to migrate. A number of studies of Sicilian women living in the United States point to the very large numbers of such women, even when married, who earned wages in one fashion or another.

Italy's sizeable population of housewives by 1900 included three groups of women: those who produced food without wages for their families, those whose labors in capitalist agriculture were subsumed under a family wage paid to husbands and fathers, and those who might best be considered unemployed textile workers or agricultural laborers. Although housewives, few became ladies. Most Italian men and women confronted domesticity in terms quite different from their counterparts in the middle- and working-classes of France, Britain, and Germany.

In many regions of Italy, housework continued the subsistence production practiced by peasant agriculturalists in previous centuries. While peasant men during the nineteenth century claimed wage-earning for themselves, wage-earning in no way carried with it social status, as did land ownership or secure tenure to land. Thus, the usual hope of male wage-earners was to return when possible to peasant agriculture, in part because of status considerations, in part because they could still achieve on the land a more comfortable standard of living than their wages alone provided. Obviously, the labors of wives and children on the land allowed many peasant men to pursue this hope. Furthermore, throughout much of the twentieth century the political and organizational efforts of Italian wage earners aimed at land reform. Eventually, land distribution enabled many formerly landless men to become peasant agriculturalists, involved simultaneously in production for family consumption and for the market. This means that in large parts of Italy the patriarchal authority of the father over a household economy persisted relatively unchanged. Indeed, capitalist agriculture incorporated patriarchal family traditions, for rural entrepreneurs adopted from peasant agriculture the employment of family work groups.

In other areas of Italy, however, like Sicily, housework evolved instead from women's unemployment. Domesticity and the relations between the sexes had a unique meaning in these regions. Sicilian proverbs, for example, praised housewives as efficient organizers of household consumption but also implied that most women were spendthrifts. Daughters were said to "rob the father"; brothers complained about burdensome sisters; proverbs simply wished unmarried girls dead. That domesticity might elicit male hostility is not difficult to understand. Unlike the food-producing women of the Abruzzi, the unemployed Sicilian women represented an immense cost to male wage earners. Rather than furthering men's hopes of mobility, a Sicilian woman represented a debt to be paid at the time of her marriage in the form of a dowry. Once Sicilian girls had produced their own dowries by weaving cloth and by earning with their spindles to provide for other necessities. Marriages united a girl's property (cloth, clothing, jewelry) to the house, furnishings, or bit of land owned by her bridegroom. As fewer girls labored at the loom or found agricultural wages, their fathers' and brothers' wages provided the dowry; in addition, families shifted formerly male-controlled properties, especially houses, to daughters. In doing so, they sought to compensate the bridegroom for acquiring an unemployable dependent. Men, meanwhile, married "with only their pants," but feared taunts that a wife's dowry stripped them of authority as head of the family. However blinded by their own assumptions, men like these could easily see domesticity as an important component of family poverty.

Scholars and feminists have long debated the complex and contradictory legacy of domesticity in industrializing nations. While imposing severe limits on women, domesticity also offered them an autonomous world of female solidarity and an exalted, morally superior sphere of their own. Modern feminism drew upon and reacted against both aspects of domesticity. Italian domesticity provided Italy's women of the shadows with different constraints and opportunities. Where housework continued to include subsistence production in agriculture, domesticity would never appear as an exclusively female realm as it did in England, France, Germany, or the United States—too many fathers and husbands returned to work and to rule in the domestic world. Furthermore, the status of domesticity, when it overlapped with subsistence production, was a superior one shared by the entire family, not a prerogative of women alone, but a class privilege. By contrast, in areas where peasants lived in large agrotowns far from their fields—as was true in Sicily—an urban woman's world (revolving around textile production) had preceded domesticity. Women's employment brought to this separate world none of the sentimentality associated with a lady's domestic "pedestal" in industrial nations. The most likely to be called housewives were the poorest women. Domesticity did not allow for family peace along traditional lines. Instead, it subjected women to increased male hostility even while it ironically placed in their hands more real property than in the past. Daughters bore the brunt of these changes; wives enjoyed the few benefits. Domesticity added new fuels to sexual tensions long burning in this part of the Mediterranean.

Note: I wish to thank Thomas Kozak, Tessie Liu, Jane Schneider, and Louise Tilly, as well as my editors, for their careful readings of an earlier version of this essay. The term "women of the shadows" is from Ann Cornelisen's book of the same name.

SUGGESTIONS FOR FURTHER READING

Chapman, Charlotte Gower. *Milocca: A Sicilian Village.* Cambridge, Mass.: Schenkman, 1971.

Cohen, Miriam J. *Workshop to Office: Two Generations of Italian Women in New York City, 1900–1950.* Ithaca, N.Y.: Cornell University Press, 1992.

Cornelisen, Ann. *Women of the Shadows.* New York: Vintage, 1976.

Ets, Maria Hall. *Rosa: The Life of an Italian Immigrant.* Minneapolis: University of Minnesota Press, 1970.

Gabaccia, Donna. *Italy's Many Diasporas: Exiles, Elites, and the Workers of the World.* World Diasporas Series. London: University College of London Press; Seattle: University of Washington Press, forthcoming.

Gabaccia, Donna, and Franca Iacovetta. "Women, Work, and Protest in the Italian Diaspora: Gendering Global Migration, Rethinking Family Economies, Nationalisms, and Labour Activism," *Labour/Le Travail,* forthcoming.

CHAPTER TEN

Feminism, Antifeminism, and National Family Politics in Early Third Republic France

Karen Offen

By the end of the nineteenth century two discernible responses to the woman question were apparent: the movement for women's rights that today we term *feminism* and the reaction to it that we label *antifeminism*. In the following study, Karen Offen shows how the development of both forces was shaped by the specific political context of fin-de-siècle France. Demonstrating a synthetic approach that includes the history of ideas, the study of mentalités, analysis of political discourses and institutional structures, as well as demographic data and economic factors, she throws out a challenge to those who continue to limit their studies to the supposedly "separate sphere" of men in politics. They ignore the woman question, Offen contends, "at their peril." The message is instructive in reverse as well: the history of women cannot be divorced from the play of politics and the forces of social and economic change.

To illustrate her method, Offen turns to the history of French feminism. Inspired by the same philosophical heritage that motivated the British and American feminist movements, leaders of the French women's movement were particularly sensitive to the dangers of political radicalism. Though largely republican, they divided on questions of religion and class. But whether Catholic or Protestant or Jew, bourgeois or working-class, they shared the peculiarly French loyalty to family, which embraced financial as well as personal affairs. Therefore arguments for women's rights as autonomous individuals attracted few; responsibility to family and society weighed more heavily than self-fulfillment. To use a term Offen coined elsewhere, they were *relational feminists*. Despite their moderation, however, they provoked a strong antifeminist backlash.

The terms *féminisme* and *féministe* were of French invention. They came into use in France during the last quarter of the nineteenth century, but only gained currency during the 1890s. By 1900 the words were in common usage in English, German, and other Western languages. But at that time they meant something different from what most people think they mean today.

French feminist demands, like those expressed in other Western nations during the nineteenth century, were rooted in the language of Enlightenment political and social criticism. The debate on the woman question had been going on in France for many centuries, but during the eighteenth century its participants focused on problems of women's inferior status in marriage and family law, and on their lack of access to formal education. Indeed, one cannot overestimate the importance throughout Europe of French Enlightenment debate on women, the family, and education, exemplified by Rousseau's controversial antifeminist arguments for democracy among men coupled with the subordination of women. During the nineteenth century the debate grew even more intense, due in no small part to the way women could themselves appeal to the ideological principles of the French Revolution—liberty, equality, fraternity—and to the concept of "rights" that French republicans claimed to represent.

What was new to nineteenth-century debate on the woman question in France was controversy over women's economic activity. At stake was a seemingly insoluble conflict between the emergence of paid employment for women *outside* the household and a vision of the family, shared by French Catholics and anticlerical republicans alike, that precluded it. Echoing the counsel of the historian Jules Michelet, some otherwise staunch republican men reacted adversely to the concept of woman as "worker" and insisted that a "progressive" social structure required male authority within the household itself. Others, more progressive, argued for a thoroughgoing legal restructuring of the family that could emancipate women and incorporate the notion of women as full-fledged economic beings.

French feminist demands during the later nineteenth century were thus shaped within what was still a male-dominated political discourse with a fully-developed range of political identities. Moreover, they were characterized by a distinctive and quite conscious familial orientation, by an overt concern about maternity and womanliness, and by an expressed acknowledgement of the national interest and of women's particular contributions to the nation. This generalization holds particularly true for secular republican feminists, but it also applies, with few exceptions, to a broad spectrum of pro-woman advocates whose affiliations ranged from social Catholicism on the right, to revolutionary socialists and syndicalists on the left. Only the anarchists tended to be rigorously individualistic, but even most French anarchists accepted the social implications of sexual difference and the requirements of reproduction as sufficient rationale for role structuring, even when they attacked the existing property-based institution of marriage.

Fin-de-siècle French feminism can best be understood by Anglo-Americans as a non- or even anti-individualistic form of feminism, which I have elsewhere labeled "relational" feminism. It was based on a theoretical understanding of the relations between the sexes that insisted on their complementarity and interdependence and on a familial base. It posited distinct "manly" and "womanly" sexual natures, and argued for an equitable sexual division of labor in society and in the family. In its secular republican guise, advocates of "relational feminism" argued for a commitment by both sexes to sociopolitical solidarity in the interest of French national welfare. In contrast to today's feminism, French relational feminism was predicated on a combination of biological and cultural differences between the sexes. French feminists, female and male—Catholic, secular republican, and socialist alike—accepted the premises of this gendered system, but rejected the conclusions that had heretofore been drawn from them by such notorious patriarchs as Napoleon I, whose Civil Code had firmly consolidated French marriage and family law around male authority. Since the 1830s French feminists had called for a radical restructuring of these authoritarian laws governing marriage, for the reestablishment of civil divorce, and the revision of many other legal provisions that disadvantaged women. They also argued that women, precisely because they were different from men, must be enabled to make an equitable, yet distinctive contribution to the socioeconomic life of the nation.

During the early Third Republic (1871–1914), French feminist—and antifeminist—discourse was still tightly embedded in the prevailing national socioeconomic and political debates of the period. Not only was France immersed in the dramatic transformation that we now call urbanization and industrialization, but it was simultaneously experiencing a political transition from a highly centralized, authoritarian, and Catholic monarchy, based on an aristocracy of birth, to a more democratic, somewhat fragile, but still highly centralized anticlerical republic, based (as women's rights activist Maria Deraismes put it) on an aristocracy of sex. This double metamorphosis posed a fundamental challenge to the old hierarchical agrarian Catholic French family system and to long-established definitions of what it meant to be a man or a woman in that culture. Although other European nations were experiencing similar problems—and, indeed, Great Britain was providing all continental observers with the most conspicuous examples of urban and industrial problems to avoid—the French case reveals perhaps more than any other that much of the debate over what France had been and was to become was predicated on a politics of gender. Thus France offers an excellent case study of the way in which the social relationship of the sexes itself became a political issue. Moreover, the French case is one of international importance. The impact of French discussion on the woman question was not restricted to Francophone territory; many educated Europeans outside France, from Russia to Spain, and indigenous elites from the Middle East to North Africa and Latin America, attentively followed French public discussion on the woman question and adapted French arguments and solutions to fit their own needs.

French political history during the nineteenth century was marked by continual battles for control of the government. No regime founded in the wake of the French Revolution seemed able to survive more than twenty years. With the establishment of the Third Republic in the 1870s, the battles did not stop. The republicans, who wished to secularize French society, were ever on guard against the monarchists on their right who threatened to overthrow the republic and to reestablish the prerogatives of the king and the Catholic church. On the left, the republicans were under attack by anticapitalist socialists, who insisted that the republican revolution must deliver economic as well as civil and political equality (among men) before its work would be complete. The battle between the secularizing republicans and the monarchist Catholics was only laid to rest in 1904, when the republican regime effected the final separation of church and state by abolishing the government's century-old treaty with Rome. The confrontation with collectivist socialism continued well into the twentieth century.

The conflict between monarchy and republic immediately provoked questioning of male/female relationships and family structure, with the result that women's subordination to men within or outside the family became a very sensitive issue. Throughout the political struggles of the century, the men of both factions fought for a remarkable prize—control of the minds and hearts of women. In keeping with certain civic humanist notions about the importance of education for the training of citizens, a Rousseauean concern with the regeneration of national morality, and a firm conviction that the family (not the individual) was necessarily the cornerstone of the state, one of the first republican actions was to establish a full-blown state-run educational system. Central to their goals was control of the education of girls, not only at the primary level but also at the secondary level. The republicans believed firmly that the sexes should be separately educated, particularly after the age of ten, and that girls should not be taught by men but by well-educated women, themselves trained in republican teacher-training programs. By breaking the Catholic church monopoly on women's education, the republicans hoped to inculcate in future mother-educators, and in their children by extension, a thoroughly secular morality and a loyalty to the republic. By reestablishing civil divorce in 1884 (a longtime feminist demand), they also intended to demonstrate the state's full authority over the institution of civil marriage. These were reforms that enhanced the position of women in French society; they also served the cause of the secular republic.

As the republicans consolidated their hold on power, controversy over the further emancipation of women grew within French republican circles. In the 1890s this controversy became inextricably intertwined with two other factors, both of which could directly affect the political fate of any demands made on the republican government by the women's movement. These two factors were, first, the diminishing importance of the French nation as a world power, due in part (it was believed) to the declining birthrate, and, second, the combined threat of the growing antirepublican, monarchist-identified nationalist movement on the right, and the revolutionary socialist movement on the left. Partisans of the Third Republic correctly viewed both issues as potential threats not only to the continuation of the republican regime, but to the future of the French nation.

The population issue was closely connected to France's sense of its own diminishing international position. France was not the only European nation to experience a falling birthrate in the late nineteenth century, but it was the first to undergo such a decline, the beginning of which can be dated from the last quarter of the eighteenth century. In 1871, France's defeat at the hands of Germany underscored the relationship between population and national might, to France's great disadvantage. It was in the wake of defeat that socially conscious French physicians such as André-Théodore Brochard began to blame France's population problems on the women's maternal indifference, which resulted in high infant mortality, and his Parisian colleague Charles Richet began to blame them on "voluntary sterility." In the 1890s the birthrate figures became even more unfavorable. To demographers this was clear evidence of purposefully controlled fertility. Comparative studies subsequently revealed that, indeed, France had the highest percentage of persons married in western Europe, but these couples did not seem to be reproducing at a rate satisfactory to the republican nation-builders. Worse news came from the 1895 census, which revealed that there had been about eighteen thousand more deaths than births in France that year.

At this point, the second issue emerged. The leadership of the Third Republic came under attack from antirepublican nationalists. These enemies of the republican regime opposed the republic's parliamentary form of government; their ideal was based in an older, unreconstructed authoritarian notion of government that they equated with true French virility. They upheld old aristocratic institutions of the army and the magistracy against all criticism in the controversial Dreyfus case, and argued for the reinforcement of manly prerogatives throughout French society. Central to their vision was the formal subordination of women to men. The prolific nationalist writer Théodore Joran made the point clearly. He castigated feminism because "it allows women to envisage happiness as independent of love and external to love." "Good households," he wrote, "are those where the man considers the woman as an object made for his own personal pleasure and well-being and where the woman believes she ought to please her husband, to serve him, and applies herself exclusively to that end." The nationalist writers insisted, moreover, that feminism itself was "un-French," a "cosmopolitan," "international" import from England and America. It was well known that many members of the republican elite—including leaders of the women's rights movement—were Protestant, Jewish, and active in Freemasonry.

On the left, socialists also criticized the Third Republic. They offered a wide range of solutions to the woman question. The French Workers' Party was on record in favor of women's equality, but other groups took different approaches. These ranged from Aline Valette's advocacy of "sexualisme," based on explicit acknowledgement of women's reproductive function as "production," with the child as "product," to Madeleine Pelletier's insistence on abolishing the family altogether. Meanwhile, in 1892, French socialist deputies to the national legislature, led by Paul Lafargue (Karl Marx's son-in-law), proposed state subsidies for mothers.

In the face of these population concerns, coupled with overt hostility to female emancipation on the authoritarian right and the cluster of controversial ideas on the socialist left, French republican feminists understood that they would have to pursue their own agenda for change in a cautious and politically sensitive manner. Among the feminists' own favored political allies, the male Solidarist republicans, most men insisted—and the women agreed—that the claims of the nation must subordinate all individual claims. The deputies in this group did support a number of reforms that would ameliorate women's position in society by enhancing their assigned roles in the family—through liberalizing divorce laws, giving married women the right to control their own earnings, allowing all adult women to witness civil acts, or even to study in universities and professional schools—but always on the condition that the sexual division of labor in the family be respected. Their touchstone, one that had (and would continue to have) a long history in republican thought on the woman question, was "equality in difference." They were willing to consider women as moral equals but could not accept members of either sex acting as individuals in disregard of their functional context in the nation, which in this case was defined in terms of organic biology and the family. These men would never dream of supporting rights for women independently of—or in conflict with—their assigned maternal roles.

The family ideal envisioned by the Solidarist republicans was composed of two mutually complementary (and ostensibly equivalent) spheres of enterprise, the domestic and the public. The political analogy they liked to invoke was that of minister of foreign affairs and minister of the interior. The domestic sphere became identified with the female, and the public with the male, who even in this restructured version remained legally the head-of-household. This family ideal should not be confused either with the ancien régime patriarchal family insisted on by neo-traditionalist Catholic ideologues, nor with that inscribed by the Civil Code. It is still true, however, that distinctive socially imposed sex roles remained central to the Solidarist approach to sociopolitical organization at the end of the nineteenth century, a view reinforced by their own version of Social Darwinism. Republican Solidarists believed that universal marriage and a sexual division of labor in the family were key features in the social evolution of modern complex societies. Indeed, it was this system, and women's vital role in it, that enlightened republicans hoped to establish throughout France as a norm in order to accomplish the "regeneration" of France. Just as the citizen-conscript would replace the professional soldier as the basis for the new republican "nation in arms," so republican motherhood was to provide the cornerstone of a new secular national morality. "Maternity," as the dramatist Alexandre Dumas *fils* put it, "is women's brand of patriotism."

The arguments of republican feminists were shaped within, and in turn helped to shape, this discourse. They built on it to argue the women's case as one for justice. Their main argument dwelt on the point that the republican principles of liberty and equality should not apply only to men—that the republic must not be a *de facto* aristocracy of sex. This was certainly an appeal to which some republican men were sensitive. It is exemplified by Hubertine Auclert's exposition of the meaning of equality to the delegates at the 1879 Socialist Workers' Congress: "A Republic that keeps women in an inferior situation cannot make men equal. Before you men can earn the right to raise yourselves to the level of your masters, you are obliged to raise your slaves, the women, up to your own level." The appeal for justice still rang true in 1900, when Harlor, a journalist for the all-women's newspaper *La Fronde,* insisted at the International Women's Rights Congress that, "A society that declares *all* human beings born free and equal in rights contradicts its own principle if *all* are not offered the same conditions for development."

In a climate of political discussion sensitive to the population problem and to antirepublican nationalist activity, reformers gave strategic priority to the elimination of social penalties imposed on women by their reproductive role. They argued for generous protective legislation for women workers, for married women's right to control their own earnings, and for the restoration of paternity suits. In short, they reappropriated motherhood in order to argue for its restructuring. They argued for women's rights based squarely on women's claims on the nation as mothers of its citizens. This was not an argument that men in power could overlook.

Women's increasing economic activity outside the household proved to be the most prickly of issues for republican feminists and their allies. In addition to documenting the dropping birthrate, census reports since mid-century revealed that France had led all other Western nations with the highest percentage of women active in the labor force. The percentage of the female population employed in both agricultural and nonagricultural labor rose from 24 percent in 1866 to 38 percent in 1911. Of the several million women in the labor force, the number employed in the nonagricultural sector doubled between 1856 and 1906. Most of the women added to this sector worked in new types of unskilled or semiskilled jobs. The greater proportion of them were young and single, or older and widowed. Still, a sizeable proportion— some 40 percent by 1901—were married women with children.

What most appalled French social critics was that many of these married female workers, the bulk of whom lived in towns and cities, were farming out their newborn infants to other caretakers. Since mid-century this practice had contributed both to the spectacular growth of the wet-nursing industry and to the alarming rates of child abandonment and infant mortality among newborns in urban industrial centers. These tragic developments only increased public opposition to the employment of all women. Both doctors and economists insisted that French society's interests would be best served by enforcing the sexual division of labor and promoting the woman's dedication to her household and children, supported by the male breadwinner. From the 1860s to the 1890s Frenchmen ranging from the liberal Jules Simon to artisans active in the First International Workingmen's Association and Pope Leo XIII all argued that the "solution" to the "problem" of women's labor lay in paying men a "family wage." Men should *become* sole breadwinners. This was an argument that had long been made in England, but it was still relatively new on the Continent.

Feminists as early as the 1830s had objected to such an approach. Working-class women active in the Saint-Simonian movement and in the revolution of 1848 insisted repeatedly that women had a right to work as a guarantee of their independence. In her 1866 study, *The Poor Woman in the Nineteenth Century,* Julie Daubié argued that economic liberalism had deprived women, in the name of equality and liberty, of employments that formerly had been theirs during the old regime. Capitalism and the centralization that accompanied it were the culprits; this new economic system had no respect for what we now call "the rights of gender." In 1868 the socialist Paule Mink, countering the men of the First International, insisted that even though working conditions were often horrible, women required independent work to remain "free and intelligent creature[s]."

By the 1890s French debate on the question of women and work centered on the issue of protective (or restrictive) legislation for women workers. Following an international congress held in Berlin in 1890, most European governments embarked on a program of regulating industrial work. One of the first targets was the employment of women. Even the staunch liberal, Jules Simon, who headed the French delegation to the Berlin Congress, returned to France a convert to government regulation of women's work. After extensive controversy, legislation was finally passed in late 1892 that limited the working hours of women and children in all industrial establishments, and in particular prohibited night work for women. Feminist critics condemned the law in its entirety. Maria Pognon was unequivocal: "The 1892 law was made by antifeminists, who were concerned with reserving all the well-paying work for their constituents; this is the real truth!"

From the 1890s on, republican bourgeois feminists adamantly defended women's right to work against all critics. They denied charges that paid work for women was simply a means for individual aggrandizement, a manifestation of antisocial "egotism." Women went to work not for amusement, one feminist argued, but for survival. Republican feminists called for equitable pay and for married women's right to control their own earnings. But they listened carefully to the findings of doctors such as Adolphe Pinard, who ardently advocated enforced maternity leaves as a means to countering infant mortality among working-class women, and from 1900 on, some called for paid maternity leave and guarantees that working women could return to their jobs without penalty. They sought to ensure that measures designed to "protect infants" or to "preserve the family" were in fact beneficial to women themselves. Even as they demanded, as Nelly Roussel did, women's right to control their own fertility, they pressed for more maternity homes, and for day-care centers and nursery schools where working mothers could leave their children in safety. They advocated improved housing and a variety of social measures that would facilitate family life. At the same time they worked to overturn the law that forbade paternity suits by unwed women and for a law that guaranteed married working women control over their own income. They also continued to press for equal educational opportunity, with an eye to opening more professions to women; to this end, they called for establishment of the *baccalauréat* curriculum in the girls' lycées. They argued that all trades and vocations should be open to women, including the well-paid ones.

Many feminists advocated unionization as one solution for the problems of working women, and a few, such as Marguerite Durand, organized women workers in several trades. By 1911, over one hundred thousand women workers belonged to *syndicats* (unions). These numbers had tripled since 1900, yet women still represented less than 10 percent of the total union membership. Twenty-five thousand of these women belonged to the 162 all-female unions, many of which had been organized under social Catholic auspices. Male trade unions continued to resist admitting women as members. Some still feared that women's low wages would drag down their own, while others were concerned that if women were paid the same higher wages as men, they would be preferred to men by employers because they were more docile. Between 1890 and 1910 some fifty-six strikes by male workers to keep women out of their shops took place. Although the General Confederation of Labor (CGT) supported the case for economic equality and the full inclusion of women workers in men's unions, as partners in proletarianization, working-class sentiment lagged behind.

The problems that plagued a married working woman in early twentieth-century France were epitomized by the Couriau affair. Emma Couriau, a printer like her husband Louis, applied to join the local printers' union in Lyons. The printers had long been among the most militant opponents of women's employment. Their skilled trade was threatened by a combination of technological and organizational changes that allowed employers to recruit women at lower wages, and women had been brought in as strikebreakers during earlier printers' strikes. Not only did the Lyons local deny Emma Couriau's application, despite the fact she was already earning union wages, but its members expelled her husband because he allowed his wife to work. French feminists rallied behind the Couriaus as they appealed the decision at the national level. The leadership of the CGT ultimately supported Emma Couriau's right to work and to join the union, but many workingmen still grumbled about the employment of women and their inclusion in male unions.

Such incidents as this ultimately convinced French feminists that women's nterests could not be advanced, even under a republican form of government, unless hey could break men's hold on political power. It was then that French feminists ιegan to organize for woman suffrage. Between 1909 and 1914 the suffrage movenent became a force to be reckoned with. Unfortunately, the outbreak of war in .914 precluded the long-awaited debate on suffrage in the Chamber of Deputies. Νt war's end France was among the few Western countries that did not enfranchise ts women.

The war exacerbated the situation with regard to women's rights. More women han ever before, especially from the lower and middle bourgeoisie, were employed. Ηeavy war losses (1.4 million dead; over 3 million wounded) intensified French ιational anxiety over the birthrate. The war encouraged both the demand for women workers and for more babies. At the end of the war, nationalist profamily and pronatalist associations (both Catholic and secular) joined forces to lobby against birth control and for tax initiatives and other measures to encourage family growth. In 1920 the republican government stiffened the laws against abortion, outlawed the spreading of contraceptive information, and established medals for motherhood. A symbolic gesture, the nationalistic rhetoric surrounding the medals was nevertheless revealing: the birthrate must be raised so that France could "retain the rank in which victory has placed us" and "permit us to harvest all its fruits." "The Republic ought to testify in a striking manner to her gratitude and respect toward those who contributed the most to maintaining, through their descendants, the genius and civilization, the influence and radiance of France." But neither the women workers nor the problems of motherhood went away. Nor did the birthrate go up. French women's demands and nationalist family politics would remain on a collision course well into the twentieth century.

SUGGESTIONS FOR FURTHER READING

Bell, Susan Groag, and Karen M. Offen, eds. *Women, the Family, and Freedom: The Debate in Documents* II: 1880–1950. Stanford: Stanford University Press, 1983.

Boxer, Marilyn J. "Foyer or Factory: Working Class Women in Nineteenth-Century France." *Proceedings of the Western Society for French History* II (1975): 192–203.

———. "Protective Legislation and Home Industry: The Marginalization of Women Workers in Late Nineteenth-Early Twentieth Century France." *Journal of Social History* 20, no. 1 (Fall 1986): 45–65.

Harsin, Jill. *The Policing of Prostitution in Nineteenth-Century Paris.* Princeton: Princeton University Press, 1985.

Hause, Steven C., and Anne R. Kenney. "The Limits of Suffragist Behavior: Legalism and Militancy in France, 1876–1922." *American Historical Review* 86 (1981): 781–806.

———. *Women's Suffrage and Social Politics in the French Third Republic.* Princeton: Princeton University Press, 1984.

Hellerstein, Erna O., Leslie Parker Hume, and Karen Offen, eds. *Victorian Women: A Documentary Account of Women's Lives in Nineteenth-Century England, France, and the United States.* Stanford: Stanford University Press, 1981.

Hilden, Patricia. *Working Women and Socialist Politics in France, 1880–1914: A Regional Study*. Oxford: Clarendon Press, 1986.

Maruani, Margaret. "France." In *Women and Trade Unions in Eleven Industrialized Countries*, edited by Alice H. Cook, Val R. Lorwin, and Arlene Kaplan Daniels. Philadelphia: Temple University Press, 1984.

McLaren, Angus. *Sexuality and Social Order: The Debate over the Fertility of Women and Workers in France, 1770–1920*. New York: Holmes and Meier, 1983.

McMillan, James F. *Housewife or Harlot: The Place of Women in French Society, 1870–1940*. New York: St. Martin's Press, 1981.

Offen, Karen. "Depopulation, Nationalism, and Feminism in Fin-de-Siècle France." *American Historical Review* 89 (1984): 648–676.

Segalen, Martine. *Love and Power in the Peasant Family: Rural France in the Nineteenth Century*. Chicago: University of Chicago Press, 1983.

Sowerwine, Charles. *Sisters or Citizens: Women and Socialism in France since 1876*. Cambridge: Cambridge University Press, 1982.

European Colonial Holdings, 1914

Figure 3. European Colonial Holdings, 1914

I I I

WOMEN IN THE ERA OF THE INTERVENTIONIST STATE

Overview, 1890 to the Present

By the late nineteenth century Europe had reached a pinnacle of power and influence over much of the rest of the world. There was no question about European technological and military superiority. Historians might still debate the reasons why the Industrial Revolution began in England and not elsewhere—perhaps in the technologically innovative empire of East Asia (China) or the Indian subcontinent with its vibrant textile industry, or even in the Ottoman Empire. But that it occurred in England, because of the trade and exchange advantages generated by English colonial power, and then spread to the European Continent had enormous consequences for intensified global connections. The industrial development of Europe meant a power dominance that Europeans were quick to exploit. Throughout the nineteenth century, for example, the threat of British gunboats sailing through the Dardanelles and pointing their modern weapons at the Topkapi (the Sultan's residence) repeatedly won economic and political concessions for the British Empire and its merchants in Ottoman territory. Not a shot ever was fired. In the last third of the nineteenth century, the Europeans gobbled up Africa, much of Asia, and many islands of the Pacific at a dizzying rate. Britain alone acquired 4.7 million square miles of territory between 1870 and 1900; France amassed 3.5 million and the new German Empire one million. By the turn of the century, nearly one-half billion non-Western people were under the control of Western colonial administrations, although not without protracted and often bloody resistance by native populations. For many ordinary Europeans, and certainly in the eyes of the ruling classes, such successes pointed to unmistakable moral superiority. While the Germans might challenge the British claim that "God was an Englishman," nonetheless there was broad consensus that "man was good, but Western man was better." Where did this leave women—the ones living in Europe but also those under colonial rule with whom ultimately their fate is joined? The twentieth century linked the peoples of the world together more closely than ever before, made all parts of it truly interdependent, and inaugurated a new era in global history.

   In retrospect, this century that opened with European countries enjoying unprecedented and undisputed power and prosperity, ended with a radically new configuration of leading players in world politics. In the wake of two world wars of previously unimaginable violence, and anticolonial revolutions around the globe, peoples of many former colonies in the Americas, Africa, and Asia now achieved political independence and self-determination. Along with those in lands distant from Europe, formerly suppressed populations at home—women, workers, peoples of color—gained new access to political, economic, and social power. Adapting the language of an earlier era, we could say that "revolutions" took place in communications and technology, in law, and in sexual relationships. As we shall see below, all served to give some women of many diverse conditions opportunities beyond their mothers' purview.

The Europe of imperialism and industrial might had its own elites, not only of gender, birth, and status but increasingly of property and wealth. Victors in the struggle for success, they had overseen the unparalleled social and economic changes accompanying the emergence of the new industrial world that we have described in Part II. Furthermore, these leaders had come to share a set of beliefs and commitments to institutional structures that provided a similar framework within which change took place in the various countries of Europe and that they sought to extend to their colonial empires. Historians have called these beliefs "classical liberalism" or "the bourgeois synthesis," implying the existence of a totalizing nineteenth-century world view that shaped attitudes toward political life and economic growth as well as family living and gender roles. Above all, the synthesis meant a commitment to laissez-faire economics. Left to its own devices, an unfettered market economy was believed to offer the best mechanism for economic growth and development as well as for the material welfare of the masses. Thus, the proper role of the state was as night watchman, safeguarding property, maintaining the rule of law, and defending the cause of its citizens abroad—essentially noninterventionist, except for the acquisition of colonies and the "protection" of women and children. The proper form of the state in western and central Europe included parliamentary institutions, acknowledging the claims of peoples to a more direct role in government. Parliamentary government did not necessarily mean democratic rule; the liberal notion of natural rights had not been transformed into democracy. France established effective universal male suffrage from 1871 onward. The new German Empire of Bismarck's creation (1871–1918) also instituted universal manhood suffrage but divided popular authority between the representatives of the states and the people (Parliament) and left in place the Prussian three-class electoral law, which tied male votes to wealth. In 1884, the England of Gladstone passed a suffrage act extending the electorate to about five million male citizens, but this represented only one-sixth of the total population, and in Italy as late as 1913 only seven percent of men could vote. Further east, institutions of representative government developed even more slowly; the Russian czar made concessions to parliamentary rule only in the face of popular unrest during the Revolution of 1905.

Liberal commitments to the bourgeois synthesis, to parliamentary government, market forces, and private property, were matched by a truly optimistic outlook, a strong belief in human rationality, scientific progress, and the superiority of European culture. It included as well, however, an equally strong but potentially disruptive nationalist spirit. Furthermore, none of the ruling groups questioned the significance of the patriarchal family for social stability. Its critical social function was facilitated, most agreed, by a proper and necessary sexual division of labor: men were breadwinners outside the home and women were homemakers. Those who adhered to the synthesis included not only the liberals per se, representing the middle classes of Europe—the captains of industry and commerce, many bureaucrats, and other well-educated professionals—but also many conservatives, large and middling landowners, who were rooted in the older world of agriculture and state service. Overall, they were the beneficiaries of the processes of industrial advance. According to the tenets of Social Darwinism, they were furthering the evolutionary progress of civilization.

Classical liberalism, however, faced serious challenges. One central theme of twentieth-century history is the erosion of faith in the premises of this once influential world view. Socialist and feminist dissent, anticolonial uprisings, new scientific theories, and ultimately two world wars all served to destroy the confidence of and break up the power structures supporting Victorian bourgeois society. Pressure for broadening the suffrage and democratic rule was launched most dramatically by those left outside political power and influence in liberal Europe—by women, workers, and, increasingly, colonial subjects, who turned the liberal theories against the colonists.

For advocates of women's rights, obtaining the vote became the key goal by the early twentieth century, and suffragists could use liberal arguments of natural rights and equality to their own advantage. This strand of feminism was what we now term individualistic, predicated on equality of opportunity irrespective of sex, rather than grounded in women's differences from men. In the years between 1913 and 1922, after protracted struggle, women in twenty European countries and North America received the suffrage and won expanded rights of citizenship (Table 3). In the 1920s and after, it was said that women were "emancipated" by the vote. Is this true? If so, how did women use their new entry into full citizenship to influence political affairs? Did the leaders who claimed to speak for all women recognize different interests based on, say, class or race?

From the early nineteenth century, feminists in many countries not only worked for their sex but forged alliances with workers—another outsider group—for greater social and economic equality. The Russian Revolution of 1917 and Bolshevik political successes provide a most telling example of the rejection of classical liberal premises and institutions. In 1917, Russian Marxists were in a position to make good the century-old commitment of socialism to women's equality. What role did women play in the revolutionary upheavals? Did ideological considerations or more pragmatic requirements of economic development shape Soviet policy toward its female citizens? Did these priorities change over time?

There were also more subtle ways in which classical liberal premises were being transformed in the early twentieth century. The appalling abuses of industrial development under laissez-faire principles—urban slums, child labor, long work hours in factories and workshops under unhealthy conditions, and poor sanitation—provided a rationale for growing government intervention into daily life. Based in part on an optimistic belief in the benefits of governmental manipulation to effect social change, the nations of Europe took unprecedented steps in expanding the range and nature of public power. They moved beyond protective labor laws to

TABLE 3. Timing of States Granting Women Suffrage in National Elections (limited in some instances by special qualifications)

State	Year	State	Year
New Zealand	1893	Luxemburg	1918
Australia	1902	Czechoslovakia	1918
Finland	1906	United States	1920
Norway	1913	Belgium	1920
Denmark	1915	Ireland	1922
Iceland	1915	Mongolia	1924
Netherlands	1917	Spain	1931
Soviet Union	1917	Brazil	1932
Canada	1917	Cuba	1934
Estonia	1917	France	1945
Latvia	1917	Italy	1945
Lithuania	1917	Yugoslavia	1946
Sweden	1918	Romania	1946
Great Britain	1918	Bulgaria	1947
Germany	1918	Belgium	1948
Poland	1918	Albania	1958
Hungary	1918	Switzerland	1970
Austria	1918	Portugal	1976

offer health and disability insurance and old-age pensions, to enlarge municipal services and eventually to introduce unemployment compensation. These policies and other new public commitments inaugurated the era of the welfare state. In the West, from Scandinavia through western Europe to North America, it became a commonplace assumption that governments should be committed to the "general welfare" by providing a wide range of social services. Under communist rule as well, with public ownership of the means of production, the state took an activist role in overseeing social and economic life.

Only in the late twentieth century did the extent of public responsibility, and concurrent intrusion into private affairs, become a subject of popular debate and contestation. By the 1980s, shrinking economic resources in many countries, and by the early 1990s, the collapse of communism in central and eastern Europe, spurred a process of retreat from the welfare state. These shifts in public priorities have had immense and disproportionate impact on some groups of women, as we will see below.

Historians of women have examined the complex ways in which the expansion of public authority altered the relationship between women, their families, and the state. As educational and employment opportunities widened for women and legal changes improved their status and power, growing numbers began to appropriate for themselves the Western ideal of individual self-determination. However, these same changes dramatically increased societal preoccupation with women's roles as childbearers and child-rearers. One result was the development of new professional and governmental agencies that substituted public for traditional family authority and control. Indeed, some historians even speak of the "patriarchal" state in effect replacing the "patriarchal" family.

The evolution of government intervention provided a new framework for women's lives in the twentieth century. The shift is so important that we have called Part III of this book "Women in the Era of the Interventionist State." The new reforms constituted not simply a neutral set of welfare policies, but a powerful force for influencing family life, gender, class, and social relationships; in their implementation in the colonies they worked to establish racial borders through gender patterns. To what extent have public services benefited women? In what ways has the welfare state limited women's autonomy? What are the effects of declining commitments to public services in the 1990s? In the new global age, how do race and gender affect the controversies over social welfare benefits? Can "women," identified as a group, attain "equality" with men? Or is "equality" no longer an appropriate goal?

When seen from the complex perspective of women's rights, state intervention took on some aspects menacing to the goal of greater autonomy. By the early twentieth century, more women were having fewer and fewer children, a fact that did not escape notice by worried male politicians who equated population size with national power. The decline in fertility was a result of complex forces related to the pattern of women's gainful employment and the evolution of the "modern" family. In the pre–World War I era, it led to a population debate and a move by some politicians, organized pressure groups, and even feminists to encourage women to have more children for the sake of the nation—at times even to force the issue by seeking to outlaw abortions and prevent the sale and spread of birth control devices and information. How did European rivalries and imperialism reinforce race consciousness and societal preoccupation with women's sexuality and motherhood? What accounted for an explicit and growing antagonism between the sexes in the prewar period that was exacerbated by the First World War?

World War I can be viewed as a "watershed" in European and world history. It was a shattering event that did a great deal to erode belief in Europe's ruling classes and their values. People asked what kind of society would sacrifice millions of its young men during four long years for such questionable gains. They inquired less intently about the effects of war on women. Yet women's lives were altered by both the world wars of the twentieth century. By disrupting the normal lines of power and social activity, war opened up unparalleled opportunities for women in work and family decision making and made their war experiences very different from men's. Postwar reconstruction, however, sought to reinscribe conservative gender roles and channeled the work of commemoration toward "fallen soldiers" and men's sacrifices. Indeed, the interwar years heightened anxiety about women's political gains and especially about their right to work. Freudian psychology provided a new sexual rationale for older views of "natural" limitations to women's roles. The decades of the 1920s and 1930s also saw renewed efforts to remove married women from the workforce as "double earners" inappropriately competing with men for scarce jobs.

At the same time, in many parts of Europe, but most perniciously in Germany and Italy, fascist movements fed on postwar disillusionment and drew sustenance from their antifeminist "kinder, küche, kirche" (children, kitchen, church) ideal for women. Even some women responded positively to this restrictive vision. Why did fascism appeal to numbers of ordinary European women? How did German fascism (National Socialism) successfully combine sexism and racism in its program for women? Why did similar conditions yield radically different results in Scandinavia?

From the global perspective, the two world wars were but one great civil war from which Europe never recovered its former position of power and influence. In the post-1945 period, indeed, Europe became divided into two hostile ideological camps. Forced to give up most of its colonial territory, it was dwarfed by the superpowers of the USSR and the United States and the rising economic might of Asia. Did the reconstruction of Europe open up new opportunities for women? Did socialist experiments alter women's consciousness? Why did a women's movement re-emerge in western Europe in the 1960s and 1970s? What happened to feminism in central and eastern Europe during the same time frame? Finally, how does the presence of "guest workers," immigrants, and new citizens from former colonies continue to alter the gendered bases of European identity?

Women's Growing Participation in the Labor Force

By the late nineteenth century, a second cycle of economic growth was creating a new industrial and social landscape that altered women's position in the labor market. Although the earlier industrial economy had been subjected to periods of booms and busts, the Great Depression of 1873 to 1896 eroded the classical liberal commitment to free trade. Those depression years were times of declining prices and profits, and the response to the insecurities of uncontrolled markets was the antithesis of economic liberalism: an economic nationalism. The various countries of continental Europe passed restrictive tariffs and treaties that were designed to improve their competitive advantage at the expense of their neighbors. The climate became one of struggle and rivalry, and England, once the unquestioned economic leader, saw its position challenged by the economic successes of the new German Empire and also by those of its former colony across the sea, the United States of America.

State intervention in economic life through protective tariffs not only expressed growing national tensions, it also had important domestic consequences. Along with limiting foreign competition in the national market, government tariff policies reinforced a trend away from the family firm to large-scale enterprises. Cartels and monopolies—agreements among businesses to fix prices, share profits, and control markets—flourished in the protected environment. This was particularly true in heavy industry, which was growing much more rapidly than the older consumer trades such as textiles. New jobs were opening up in metallurgy and engineering, as well as in the electrical and chemical industries; in the main these jobs were taken over by men. There were fewer jobs proportionally for women in the manufacturing sector of the industrial economy.

Nonetheless, one of the most significant socioeconomic trends in the twentieth century has been the steady increase of women working outside the home—aptly dubbed "a subtle revolution." Figure 4 shows the growth in women's gainful employment in select countries between the mid-nineteenth century and the 1990s.

While reflecting the dramatic rise in women's employment over the course of the twentieth century, this trend masks an important shift across economic sectors. Agriculture employed large numbers of women in France, Italy, Russia, and Spain much longer than in nations such as England, Germany, and the United States, which industrialized earlier. In 1911, for example, 41 percent of French and 56 percent of Italian working women, and in Russia an overwhelming 92 percent, were reported in agriculture. Thereafter, wage-earning women in the agricultural sector declined steadily and were replaced by equal numbers going into the service, or tertiary, sector of the economy. Foreshadowing a later trend around the globe, technological advances stimulated an ever-expanding demand for women in clerical and other service jobs. Figure 4 also shows clearly the greater utilization of female labor under the socialist regime in postwar East Germany than in capitalist West Germany.

The shift to service jobs has been the most important long-term change in women's employment patterns. In the first half of the twentieth century, commercial and industrial enterprises increasingly required more typists, secretaries, and file and data entry clerks. As more and more goods were produced, manufacturers required enlarged systems of distribution. Increasing numbers of retail shops opened up in urban centers and they utilized young, single women for sales. As government expanded its services, it too employed new personnel as clerks, telephone operators, and low-level administrators. In time, clerical work became routinized, and the positions that opened up, unlike those of earlier decades when they offered many of the men who held them eventual promotion into management, now provided little chance for advancement. Reduced in status and rewards, these jobs increasingly took on the characteristics of "women's work." Nevertheless, they were coveted by daughters of the middle classes and of aspiring workers, for they were "cleaner" than manufacturing work, offered greater job security, and often carried with them some of the rewards of higher status such as health benefits and paid vacations. They also provided opportunities for women of modest social backgrounds to meet and marry higher-status, white-collar men. Employers, in turn, found in young single women a cheaper, more compliant workforce, whose youthful sex appeal might also enhance the business environment. The clerical labor force became feminized.[1]

The need for a literate clerical workforce was a powerful stimulus driving the expansion of female opportunities also in education. Teaching became an important force for changing women's lives. With their certificates, daughters of the working and lower-middle classes earned admission to the world of white-collar employment and, often, to a culture more sophisticated than that of their origins. While it was generally the mid-twentieth century before female teachers won the right to equal treatment with male teachers, they were among the first professional groups to organize and to claim equal rights. Through the educational reform movement women learned organizational skills they could transfer to other causes, and teachers disproportionately filled the ranks of feminist movements. In France, organized lay teachers were among the most active of female union members.

Since World War II, we are accustomed to consider university training as prerequisite to careers in teaching. Earlier, certification as elementary school teachers

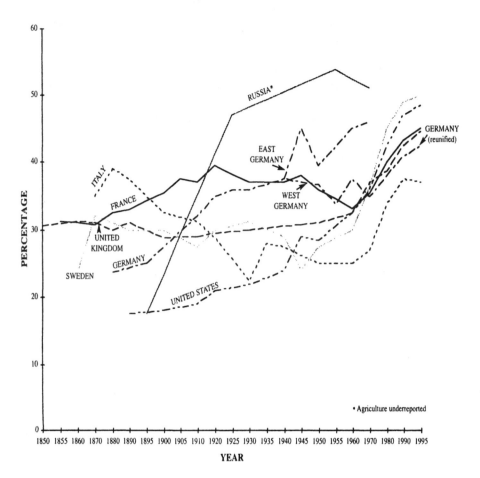

Figure 4. Women's Labor Force Participation as a Percentage of the Total Labor Force in Selected Countries, 1850–1995.

Sources: T. Deldyke, H. Gelders, and J.M. Limbor, *The Working Population and Its Structure* (Brussels: Université Libre de Bruxelles, 1968). OECD, *Labour Force Statistics: Demographic Trends 1950–1990* (Paris: 1979). U.S. Dept. of Commerce, *Historical Statistics of the United States, Colonial Times to 1970,* I (Washington, D.C.: U.S. Government Printing Office, 1975) and *Historical Abstracts of the United States* (Washington, D.C.: U.S. Government Printing Office, 1985). U.S. Dept. of Labor, *Handbook of Labor Statistics* (Washington, D.C.: U.S. Government Printing Office, 1983). Eurostat, *Review/Revue: 1977–1986* (Luxembourg: Office des publications officielles des Communautés européennes, 1988). Eurostat, *Facts Through Figures: A Statistical Portrait of the European Union* (Brussels: European Communities Publishing, 1996). U.S. Dept. of Commerce, Bureau of the Census, *Statistical Abstract of the United States,* (Washington, D.C.: U.S. Government Printing Office, 1997).

required little more than secondary education. In the early twentieth century, teaching closely resembled clerical service, in qualifications, pay, and working conditions. Later, as the requirements for teaching (first in secondary and later in all public schools) were increased to include postsecondary training, teaching began to offer daughters of the middle and upper-middle classes a new profession. In France, where a special normal school for training women to teach secondary school was established at Sèvres in 1881, women teachers helped to challenge the limited principles upon which female education had been based. A shift in emphasis in the education of girls, from moral training alone toward more broad-based and scientific knowledge, contributed as well to a gradual redefinition of women's roles in society.[2]

As a source of employment, however, the schools did not offer women the same ease of admission as the office. Unlike teaching, which required increasing levels of postsecondary education, the expansion of office employment opportunities was facilitated by the public schools, which offered courses in typing, bookkeeping, and stenography, and sometimes even required that girls take them. Due to the vast expansion of demand during the Second World War, women with a secondary school "business education" entered the office in record numbers. In the decades following the war, opportunities for postsecondary education expanded vastly in many countries, offering women as well as men of modest means options previously available only to an elite. However, sex segregation continued to mark the labor force, and the numbers of women in previously male-dominated professions such as medicine and engineering increased most notably in communist countries that faced labor shortages in vital industries, and in the West only after the rebirth of feminism in the late 1960s.[3]

Mass Consumption and the Smaller Family

Growth in the numbers of women in paid labor helped to generate an expanding market for labor-saving devices in the home. Made possible by the advances of earlier decades in cheap steel, electricity, and precision manufacture, by the early part of the twentieth century a whole new range of reasonably priced, consumer-durable goods was being produced, including sewing machines, clocks, bicycles, furnaces, cast-iron stoves, improved cooking utensils, and, later on, electrical appliances like toasters and vacuum cleaners. A series of "universal expositions" held in "Palaces of Industry" in capital cities of Europe between 1851 and 1900 had introduced urban society to the "marvels" that scientific and technological progress made possible. The aim of these events was to teach a "lesson of things." We owe the Eiffel Tower, for example, to the Paris Exposition of 1889. Material improvements were the capstone of a century of progress; mass consumption would fulfill dreams, "merchandise . . . fill needs of the imagination." By connecting "imaginative desires and material ones," the expositions created a new "dream world of mass consumption" that industry and commerce stood ready to serve. So successful was this strategy that by the early twentieth century, Europeans had become their own best customers.[4]

The growing availability of material goods had begun to affect even lower-class families. Aggregate purchasing power was on the rise and real per capita income was increasing. This advance in living standards changed patterns of consumption in highly significant ways. Where once food, clothing, and housing had absorbed working people's total income, improved earnings and changing values were reflected in monies allocated for entertainment and other discretionary spending. Furthermore, with wages rising, particularly in heavy industry, increasing numbers of working-class families could rely on the income of husbands and the wages of their grown children to meet the family's changing material aspirations. More than ever before, daughters—rather than mothers—were out in the workforce. By the early twentieth century a household division of labor that allowed married women to stay at home (but, quite probably, still engage in some wage work) was becoming as characteristic of working-class couples as of those of the middle classes. The onset of consumer mass society changed the nature of the family in the industrialized West, and promoted, as Louise Tilly and Joan Scott call it, the "family consumer economy." As the nineteenth century faded, products once associated primarily with the aristocracy had become available at prices affordable to the middle classes, and consistent with the emphasis on domesticity as a symbol of class status, conspicuous consumption by women played a major role in expanding the consumer society. Now even parts of the working classes became integrated into the world of consumer dreams and desires.

As Part II has already shown, the Western family was becoming smaller, and this was true among all the classes of Europe, not only those living in urban centers but those in many rural areas as well. In part, the advantages of rising living standards prompted lower-class families to limit the numbers of their offspring as it had earlier encouraged the middle classes. Child labor laws and compulsory education helped to change their view of children. Young children no longer were seen as potential earners but rather as dependents, living for longer periods of time on the family income. Better diet and hygiene and public health measures such as municipal water and sewage disposal led to reduced infant mortality and improved the chances of each child for survival to adulthood. Shorter working hours allowed more time for family affairs and parents could begin to devote more attention to their children. Investment in the support and education of children now represented parents' hopes for a better future for the family.

New attitudes coupled with new material conditions produced a notable reduction in fertility levels, as Figure 5 reveals. Crude birthrates (births per thousand population) declined sharply over the period. For example, in Germany overall fertility declined by 60 percent between the date of unification in 1871 and the early 1930s; the trend was temporarily reversed during the Nazi prewar years (1933–39). In France, where the birthrate had declined to 24.6 per thousand by 1880, the population was growing at the slowest rate in all of Europe. In half a century (from 1851 to 1911) the French population rose by only 3.4 million, from a total of 35.7 to 39.1 million people. Across the Channel in England the picture was similar. Marriages of the late 1860s, when they lasted more than twenty years, produced on average 6.2 births; those of 1915, only 2.4 children. This chart shows graphically the convergence among European nations of changing family planning behavior in the second quarter of the twentieth century. Despite the "baby boom" that followed World War II, after 1960 access to new forms of birth control, especially the pill, brought further sharp decreases in birthrates. Looked at in the perspective of a century, the change is so striking as to constitute a "contraceptive revolution." By the 1980s, in several countries of Europe women were no longer having enough babies

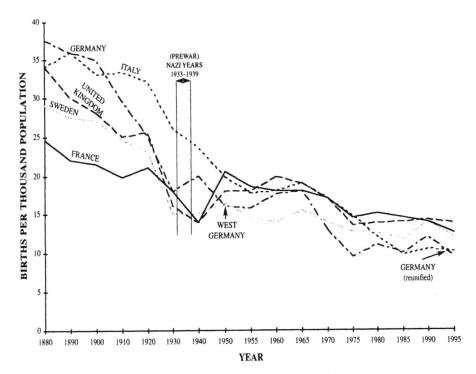

Figure 5. Crude Birthrates (per 1,000 population) for Selected European Countries, 1880–1995.

Sources: B. R. Mitchell, *European Historical Statistics, 1750–1975* (New York: Columbia University Press, 1975); Eurostat, *Women and Men in the European Union: A Statistical Portrait, 1987–1993, 1995* (Brussels: European Communities Publishing, 1996).

to maintain population levels (without in-migration). In 1980 in the twelve countries of the European Community, the total fertility rate (for women aged twenty-five to forty) exceeded 2.0 for only three countries (Greece, Spain, and Ireland). By 1989, it remained higher than 2 only in one country (Ireland). Meanwhile, it had declined to 1.29 in Italy and 1.39 in Spain—both Catholic countries.[5]

The reduction in the amount of time women spend in childbearing and child-rearing has been one of the most significant changes in the female life cycle, especially in light of pronounced increases in longevity in the twentieth century. Most women in the West are no longer caught up in a long series of pregnancies followed by early death. The acceptance of new attitudes and practices that conscious contraception represents marks a major departure in human history. Along with women's increasing labor force participation, it makes possible revolutionary change in the history of women.

Suffrage, Feminism, and Socialism

The emerging consumer society directed its appeal toward housewives and found in the single-family dwelling an expanding market for its goods. Each home would be equipped with its own washing machine, electrical appliances, and other new products. With reduced childbearing, housewives had greater time that could be spent in home management and consumption. For middle-class women in prewar Europe, this meant supervising servants and entertaining for business purposes. For lower-class women, it meant more time for careful marketing, canning, and home sewing. Consumption, however, might not be confined solely to the needs of each individual family, but might involve group purchasing in the interest of economizing. In England and Germany consumer cooperatives that bought in bulk and shared profits emerged in working-class precincts. Discussion in such groups inevitably moved beyond domestic and cooperative matters to questions of politics and class issues, and participation was often the first step in a woman's greater involvement in the outside world.

Whatever the reasons for political awakening, women seeking to change conditions still worked in a public arena that was unfavorable to their efforts. And this difficulty they shared with some of Europe's working classes, who also had no meaningful political voice. We have seen in Part II that feminist organizing began in the nineteenth century and sometimes grew out of religious, moral, and family concerns. Women in groups campaigned for temperance, against prostitution, and, in England and America, for the abolition of slavery. Single women, especially of the middle classes, sought better opportunities for education and employment. The feminist call had also, somewhat tentatively, included the vote, but by the early twentieth century suffrage had been transformed into the key demand—seen by many as the vehicle to carry all the other reforms needed to improve women's position. The intensity of the campaign for the vote varied by country, and reflected the overall political climate; it was strongest in Britain and the United States, two nations fully committed to natural rights philosophy. It was weaker in Germany, where that country's authoritarian structure and ambivalence toward natural rights dampened enthusiasm for suffrage. In France, woman suffrage was caught up in conflicts between church and state, arguments about individual rights and family obligations, and party politics. (See Table 3.)[6]

Suffragists were fighting for a basic principle: the right of women to citizenship in the nation-state. Most rejected the gendered restriction according to which only men attained full citizenship because they bore arms for their country. Indeed, some feminists pressed for women's formal entry into the state by arguing, as the Germans did, that men's military duty (*Wehrpflicht*) was matched by the duty of women's labor pains (*Wehpflicht*). In this push for democracy, furthermore, women could become the allies of workingmen who, in countries with property qualifications for voting, were also disenfranchised. The alliance of woman suffrage and women's movements generally with working-class or socialist parties was more characteristic of European nations than of the United States where socialism was weaker and women drew energy for suffrage essentially from women's clubs and reform societies. While some American suffrage leaders linked the franchise to reforms in women's and children's labor, others, like the English antislavery activists discussed in Part II, also saw in votes for women a key to preserve Anglo-Saxon supremacy against the hordes of immigrants who had moved to American soil, and as an antidote also against the vote by black men.

England had the most well-known and brash suffragists of the twentieth century, Mrs. Emmeline Pankhurst (1858–1928) and her daughters Christabel and Sylvia who, in 1903, founded the Women's Social and Political Union (WSPU). Despite an initial link with the Independent Labour Party (ILP), the WSPU appealed mostly to middle-and upper-class women. It was among the first of the pressure groups in Europe or North America to recognize the importance of the media, and its members undertook outrageous acts to publicize their demands. With the mass demonstration it staged in London in 1910, the WSPU pioneered a tactic adopted by generations of political activists. The "suffragettes," as they were disdainfully labeled but soon called themselves with pride, also attacked government ministers, slapping them or showering them with eggs and tomatoes. They chained themselves to lampposts, attacked property, and went on hunger strikes in jail. In one notable case, Emily Davison threw herself before the king's horse at the Derby, and died for the cause. Across the Channel, the "French suffragette" Hubertine Auclert (1848–1914) and later, the radical individualist doctor Madeleine Pelletier (1874–1939) tried but failed to forge an analogously audacious party.

These militant suffragists were outnumbered by the thousands of women who joined the many other suffrage associations that constituted the National Union of Women's Suffrage Societies, formed in Britain in 1897. One notable leader, Millicent Garrett Fawcett (1847–1929), became active in international feminist councils such as the International Council of Women, the International Woman Suffrage Alliance, and the Women's International League for Peace and Freedom, groups dedicated to advancing the cause of world peace as well as improving the condition of women. Encouraging delegates from such disparate countries as China, Japan, India, Mexico, Egypt, and Syria, in the 1930s they held meetings in Czechoslovakia, Yugoslavia, and Turkey; but most were white Christian women from North America and western Europe, who used the language of sisterhood but never transcended the belief that their role was to lead their "oppressed sisters." At their peak in the interwar period when the councils could count the members of their constituent organizations in the tens of millions, the internationalists were divided by nationality as well as by class. According to historian Leila Rupp, the collective identity the leaders sought to develop as "feminist internationalists" came more easily to those whose countries were no longer struggling for national liberation and who had the individual means to travel to far-flung regions for council meetings.

Millicent Fawcett was among the leaders who brought women's issues to the halls of Versailles during the creation of the League of Nations in 1919–20 and kept humanitarian concerns alive throughout the 1920s. The influence of the pre-war internationalist women continued through the 1930s, and into the formation of the United Nations after World War II. While they of course failed in the larger goal of achieving world peace, the internationalists' work did result in a decision of the League of Nations in 1935 to undertake a worldwide study of the condition of women, which in turn led to the creation of the Status of Women Section of the Economic and Social Council of the United Nations. Rupp sees the work of women's international organizations that began before the first World War as the "prehistory" of the United Nations conferences on women in Mexico City (1975), Copenhagen (1980), Nairobi (1985), and Beijing (1995). One important result of women's continuing international connections has been forcing acceptance of women's rights as basic human rights.[7]

At the national level, suffrage leaders of the prewar era also emerged from the working classes. British suffragists included radical trade union women from the textile districts of Manchester and women in the Cooperative Guilds who drew on their industrial experience to stress suffrage as a means to obtain legislation favorable to women wage-earners. Union women, including Mrs. Dickenson and Mrs. Cooper, Miss Reddish and Miss Silcock, worked hard for Labour candidates in the first two decades of the twentieth century in anticipation of labor support for woman suffrage. But in England, this potentially beneficial alliance of suffragists and labor foundered over differences between those who favored adult suffrage (a call to enfranchise all adults and abolish property qualifications) and woman suffrage (enfranchising women on the same limited basis as men). Suffragists favored a "woman's bill" as a first pragmatic step toward full adult suffrage; most male Labourites favored adult suffrage on principle, although chances of its success were dimmed by Liberal and Tory opposition. Amid the conflict, women suffragists helped conduct a survey inquiring what proportion of the women enfranchised by the limited (women's) suffrage bill would be working-class. When they found the answer to be at least 80 percent, limited suffrage could not be dismissed derisively by Labour as a "Ladies' Bill." This fact, however, failed to cement the alliance in the prewar era.

Continental women like Clara Zetkin in Germany, Dr. Pelletier in France, and Alexandra Kollontai in Russia had similar difficulties in forging effective alliances with socialists and unionists, as we have already learned in Part II. In the first two decades of the twentieth century, these socialist feminists were urging reforms to ease wage-earning women's double burdens as workers and mothers. Unlike the fiery Polish-German radical Rosa Luxemburg (1871–1919), who "regarded her sex as irrelevant," and sought to channel all energies toward promoting revolution, socialist feminists were unwilling to delay change until "after the revolution." Their platform included a call for reform in women's present circumstances. They supported maternity insurance and day-care centers, broadened apprenticeship training to lift women from low-skilled, poorly paid jobs, and equal pay for equal work. In North America, Charlotte Perkins Gilman (who considered herself a socialist) drew architectural plans for kitchenless houses in restructured neighborhoods to overcome patterns of urban space that isolated women and made their domestic work invisible.[8]

But increasingly, socialist women also felt a need to support the bourgeois feminist call for the vote. To demonstrate their position on this issue they pressed for a special day to be set aside to publicize the need for women to vote, which had been monopolized effectively by middle-class feminists. Responding positively, the Socialist Party of the United States set up a national committee to plan demonstrations for the suffrage. The first assembly was held in New York City on March 8, 1908, although subsequently American socialists designated the last Sunday in February as National Women's Day. In Europe similar efforts were underway, spearheaded by socialist feminists of the Second International, an official grouping of socialist parties, trade unions, and political associations. At the women's conference of the International that met in Copenhagen in 1910, Clara Zetkin and Luise Zietz pushed the idea of an International Women's Day, although they did not specify a date. The first was held in Europe on March 18, 1911, and the celebration became a tradition in socialist circles. In 1922, Lenin officially declared March 8 as International Women's Day, because Russian women five years earlier, following the American lead of celebrating the last Sunday in February, had precipitated the first Russian Revolution of 1917 on February 23 (by Gregorian calendar), March 8 in the West.[9]

Despite ceremonial recognition, most male and many female socialists remained skeptical about what they termed "bourgeois feminist" activities and still saw them as diversionary and potentially harmful to working-class unity. Indeed, the success of socialists in portraying feminism as "alien" to working-class women's interests had a long-lasting, divisive effect on women's movements of the twentieth century. Nonetheless, in the late 1960s, International Women's Day was resurrected in the nonsocialist West, and became an occasion for common affirmation of feminist causes, increasingly recognized around the globe.

Restructuring the State: Welfare and Motherhood

By clamoring for political and economic change (and even occasionally questioning the existing sexual hierarchy), working-class organizations posed a real and recognized threat to Europe's ruling classes. Despite a shared rhetoric of revolution, however, not all were revolutionary; many merely wanted a greater slice of the public pie. It was just this combined pressure "from below," however, that convinced many former laissez-faire politicians to institute reforms and redistribute some of the benefits of economic development more equitably. In this fashion, liberalism was transformed into its twentieth-century variant, the welfare state. Germany was the first industrializing country to adopt national welfare programs for wage-earners. Under Otto von Bismarck's guidance, factory workers obtained health insurance in 1883 and accident insurance in 1884; five years later, an old-age pension scheme was passed. The timing of these reforms, which directly influenced passage of similar prewar legislation under Solidarist influence in France during the 1890s and under the liberal governments of Herbert Asquith and David Lloyd George in England between 1906 and 1916, says much about the motives. Bismarck was quite explicit in his hope to wean workers from socialism through welfare capitalism. He sought to suppress the political party of the working class, the German Social Democratic Party (SPD), by securing anti-Socialist laws that were on the books from 1878 to 1890; at the same time, the welfare reforms were a carrot designed to win workers' loyalty and promote socially integrative and conservative sentiments. Increasingly, the nations of Europe and the United States followed Bismarck's lead, instituting progressive income and inheritance taxes to defray the costs of the wide-ranging social services. Germany expanded its commitments during the 1920s, providing unemployment insurance for the first time. The United States followed during the dislocations of the Depression, with Roosevelt's New Deal legislation in the 1930s. So, too, did the Scandinavian countries, where social democratic parties assumed power and cooperated with conservatives to enact broad-ranging welfare legislation.

Welfare provisions and other forms of state regulation are powerful instruments that can shape modern societies along certain lines. Their effects reach far beyond people's "welfare" and "the public good," for they express assumptions about work, proper family life, and gender behavior as well as class ties; therefore, they structure class and gender relationships. For example, social services such as day care, which allow some educated married women to hold well-paying jobs, at the same time exacerbate class differences by offering child-care employees notoriously low wages. However, welfare legislation has helped to avoid class conflict, as Bismarck explicitly intended it should, and this has been done partly by reinforcing traditional gender relationships. In the observation by a Danish author that "what the workers needed was not a revolution but a neat Danish home," lies an unspoken premise that the home be kept neat through woman's work. Benefit plans that offer extensive maternity insurance but deny money for abortion reinforce pronatalist values and limit women's alternatives; the same is true of rules that deprive a single mother of public child support if she cohabitates with a man. She is denied her position as head of household and the man is forced to support the (fictitious) family. While this policy reduces expenditures of public funds, it reinforces women's dependency on men.[10]

Other historic examples of assumptions embedded in the laws are found in the early protective legislation for wage-earning women that was promulgated in Germany, France, and elsewhere. The dominant belief behind this legislation was that a woman, above all, was a mother responsible for her family, and that the state had a duty to help the wage-earning woman fulfill this critical role. In 1891, German legislators passed a law that gave the married working woman a one-and-one-half-hour noon break—so she could rush home and cook the noon meal for her family; and they gradually reduced her workday, including closing by 2 P.M. on Saturdays, so she could have time to clean her home and do the wash on the weekends. These laws remained on the books in Germany until the late 1990s and only then were relaxed slightly to accommodate growing numbers of working women who need to shop after work or on the weekends. Similarly, in 1917, France adopted a five-and-a-half-day work week (the so-called English week) in clothing manufacture (where most women in industry worked), advancing as the primary justification the need of women for time off Saturday afternoon to shop, clean house, and prepare their families for church on Sunday. Whatever the stated intent of these special laws, the actual impact was to reinforce women's double burdens in wage and housework. Unpaid housework, however, was not recognized as socially useful labor and housewives have received no independent claim to pensions or health insurance in the welfare states of the West.

The social definition of women as mothers and homemakers, then, profoundly shaped the laws providing services in the emerging welfare states. It helps account for the remarkable similarity of welfare provisions throughout the West, despite different national traditions and levels of economic growth and development. The political uses made of "motherhood," however, are highly complex. As we will show below, the woman-as-mother model provided a rationale for prewar efforts to intervene into people's lives and force some women, but not others, to bear children. In the interwar years, that same image was at the root of fascist antifeminism in Germany. But the importance of women's maternal role also motivated socialists in Scandinavia in the 1930s to expand welfare services and to provide greater opportunities for women as mothers and workers. When welfare states expanded following the Second World War, they tended to perpetuate long-established gender roles; but simultaneously they added new elements, often modeled on Scandinavian precedents. In Sweden, for example, aid to mothers took on different guises that reflected changing social norms. The "maternity policy" adopted in the early century in the context of high infant mortality rates was transmuted by a socialist government into a general "population policy" during the 1930s. In the 1960s it became a "family policy" that recognized the roles of both parents.[11] Perhaps its most radical aspect was the support provided for unmarried mothers. But social policies providing benefits for women as mothers proliferated even in more conservative societies such as Austria, which developed what Gerda Ruth Neyer terms a "fraternal" welfare state (chapter 15).

In most European countries, at the century's end as well as in its beginning, the birthrate was an important factor in determining national policies. The linkages demonstrated between the changing roles of women and the emergence of welfare states, between private acts, personal responsibilities, and public policies are further evidence of the complex connections between what was once imagined to be "separate spheres."

Motherhood, Empire and Racism

"Motherhood" is not the simple, noncontroversial concept it may appear to be in the common usage "motherhood and apple pie." On the contrary, for early twentieth-century feminists, the population debate that involved women's reproductive capacities took place in a distinctive historic arena. It helped constitute a "domestic" or "familial" feminism, based on a nineteenth-century principle sometimes called "equality in difference," which accepted the sexual division of labor but sought to elevate and highlight the special contributions that women made to the family and society by their uniquely feminine intervention. Feminists could best gain the support of male politicians and public figures when they argued their cause in terms of women's social contributions as mothers and wives, as Karen Offen's case study of the debates in France in the early Third Republic shows (chapter 10). Leaders of women's international organizations aspired to achieve the "motherhood of the world."

But maternalism, as motherhood in its ideological form is sometimes called, could be used in many ways. Noting the many political uses of motherhood and its relationship to such issues as citizenship, race, class, and national identity as well as gender roles, historians Seth Koven and Sonya Michel have called attention to the "protean character of maternalism."[12] In some instances, women themselves sought to appropriate motherhood and make it the basis of a more radical feminist philosophy. This was the case of the German Society for the Protection of Motherhood and Sexual Reform, an influential organization admired by many feminists outside of the Second Empire. The Society had been founded by Ruth Bré in 1904 and later was taken over by Helene Stöcker, a Berlin advocate of changes in sexual and marriage practices. Its program was inspired by the writings of the Swedish social and educational reformer and essayist Ellen Key (1849–1926). Key had sought to restructure society in ways that would put motherhood at the center stage of public life. While

Key was active in the prewar period, her ideas on motherhood directly influenced the characteristics of the emerging welfare state in Scandinavia in the interwar era. Like Key, German Society members were dedicated to elevating motherhood regardless of marital status and sought to extend municipal services to young, unmarried mothers and their children. They set up counseling centers to deal with sexual problems and advocated legal equality for "illegitimate" children. At the same time, they adopted a Neo-Malthusian argument (one favorable to birth control and medical self-help) and fought for the right of women to reject having children under adverse circumstances. The members agitated for the availability and diffusion of birth control information and devices as well as for the decriminalization of abortion laws.[13]

Such goals were controversial; battle lines were drawn. For some groups, the requirements of national growth and strength overrode a woman's right to control her own body. Anti-Malthusian leagues, adopting pronatalist positions, proliferated in prewar Europe and sought official ban on the sale of contraceptives and sex information literature. Nationalist politicians who blamed women's wage work outside the home for the steady fertility decline sought to remove married women from gainful employment in the expectation that then they would have more children. This proposal was debated on numerous occasions (although never enacted) in the parliamentary chambers of France and Germany. It was an antifeminist position that strongly resonated among some workingmen who felt particularly threatened by women's presence in the workforce. The German-National Commercial Employees Union, for example, a union of male white-collar workers that had been organized in the early 1890s to oppose the "degenerative" forces of the modern age, set out to stem the "invasion" of female elements into their profession. Its members openly advocated limiting women's work in service occupations.

Other organizations echoed the turn-of-the-century concern with "race" and "race betterment" as an alternative to the alleged "degeneration" of the nation. For them, absolute population decline was less significant than the question of which groups in society were having the most children. Taking their cue from the prominent Social Darwinist notion of life as a deadly "struggle for existence," their answer was unequivocal—the "unfit." The concept of race as a cultural category became confounded with notions about its alleged biological underpinnings. The prewar population debate shaded inexorably into open discussion of forced sterilization and other eugenic programs under the guise of devising a "science of producing the finest offspring." The "fit," it was feared, were failing to reproduce and only government intervention could reverse the alarming trend.[14]

Because it is seen to culminate in the mass murders and genocide perpetrated by Hitler and Nazi Germany, the eugenics movement of the early twentieth century has elicited considerable—if ambivalent—historical interest. Yet preoccupation with the growth of population in the nineteenth century initially grew out of class questions, as Malthus and his followers drew from birth and death rates inferences about poverty and the quality of life. Workplace insurance and sanitation measures, and to some extent protective legislation affecting women and children, aimed to reduce infant mortality, curtail the spread of infectious disease, and safeguard public health—measures designed to strengthen the nation. Neo-Malthusian prescriptions for contraception also were intended to improve people's chances for a good life. In the late decades of the century, however, as the drive toward expanding overseas empires intensified competition among the leading European countries, discussions over population issues took on more ominous tones.

Imperialist rivalries contributed to a new kind of preoccupation with motherhood. Proponents of "eugenics," a so-called scientific movement to improve inherited human characteristics, focused on women as breeders of "the race." The European powers, which had forced open the doors to China and Japan, now feared what the German Kaiser, William II, termed a "yellow peril," an imaginary horde of Asians inundating Europe. Imperial crises turned into debates over the nation's human stock and revealed considerable class fear and racist sentiment. Britain's Boer War (1899–1902) offers a prime example of these connections. Recruitment of English soldiers from working-class neighborhoods and subsequent investigations of workers' living standards had revealed appalling conditions and poor health and raised fears of lower-class "degenerates" swamping civilized peoples by simply outbreeding them. This outcry came at a time when Labour was beginning to organize working-class people, and class antagonisms, compounded by hatred of the Irish, were running high. Turn-of-the-century England was deluged by books and articles with such revealing titles as *The Problem of the Army, Fertility of the Unfit*, and *Physical Deterioration*. Their aim was twofold: to encourage passage of public legislation designed to curb what was seen as the indiscriminate breeding of lower-class peoples, and to turn middle- and upper-class women into bearers of higher quality citizens. (Intellectual women were thought by some leading eugenicists to produce weak children.) Motherhood of the "fit" was seen by a vocal group as the nation's salvation. As one doctor put it,

> The history of nations is determined not on the battlefield but in the nursery, and the battalions which give lasting victory are the battalions of babies. The politics of the future will be domestics.[15]

With this kind of thinking, it was a small step to use the desire for empire to justify welfare measures at home. More ominously, it was used to advance programs for selective breeding.

Eugenics was also posed as a solution to the fears of prewar anti-Semites in Europe of "rule by foreign Jews." At their murderous extreme, ideas of "race hygiene" led to forced sterilization of persons judged to be racially and morally unfit to reproduce, including entire peoples—Jews and Gypsies. On January 1, 1934, Nazi Germany passed a law identifying nine specific conditions that would permit a "genetic health court" to mandate sterilization that would in its view "prevent lives unworthy of life." The minister of interior suggested the law be applied to some 20 percent of the population. Before the outbreak of war, about 320,000, or almost 0.5 percent of the population, had been forcibly sterilized, and mass sterilization of Jews and Gypsies took place in the concentration camps. German historian Gisela Bock has shown how racist views made it possible for these policies to coexist with an ideology that idealized women's maternal role. "Racist-sexist discourses . . . have portrayed socially, sexually, or ethnically alien women as non-women, and thus as threatening to the norms for all other women."[16]

By portraying people who differed from assumed norms as "alien," racists and imperialists established imaginary borders between themselves and others, between "home" and "empire." Historians have until recently also tended to view the European countries and their empires as separate spheres. In the British case, "one [sphere was] the source of Britishness/progress/civilization, the other precisely that: the other side of the world, the 'dark' continent, the as-of-yet undomesticated space of cultural backwardness."[17] As seen, historians now are better prepared to assess the impact of geopolitical concerns on imperial societies as well as on subject populations. Domestic gender ideologies, carried abroad by missionaries and functionaries of both sexes, determined many of the effects of imperial power on colonial subjects. Experiences with non-European cultures brought reciprocal effects to "home" societies. In Antoinette Burton's words, "Even if most British women did not go to the colonies in their lifetimes, the colonies came to them."[18] In particular, attitudes about women and appropriate gender behavior helped to shape the course of imperialism. When the question arose, for example, of how "Frenchness" was to be defined in determining the eligibility for French citizenship of people of French West Africa in the 1920s, the traditional criteria that had once emphasized only language, service, and allegiance to French law were stretched to include color and culture, including sexual demeanor. Africans were found to be "too ethnically different ever to become culturally French."[19]

If imperialism fueled the population debate and racist politics in Europe, it had, of course, a very direct and disruptive impact on the lives of native peoples of areas that fell under European colonial role. While this book has not focused in detail on women's experiences in the European empires, throughout we have raised significant questions about women's participation in the development of colonial empires. Women were vitally affected by the complex linkages among European politics, economies, and societies and the lives of people in every land they touched. At mid-century, when the British Female Emigration Society was founded, it was intended as a partial solution to the problem of "redundant" (i.e., unmarried) women. By the late nineteenth century, when "the right sort of woman" was encouraged to emigrate in hopes she would bring European values to households in Africa or Asia, many European women accepted "imperious maternity" as their duty. Between 1884 and 1914, some twenty thousand British women took on this charge. While a number of these emigrants saw their ventures as a new form of "female philanthropy," others, such as women bound for South Africa, accepted their charge as a "racial duty."[20]

For some women, service in the colonies served a role similar to that of men who sought employment in distant lands; it provided them a place and opportunity to develop capacities unused at home, especially in projects generally reserved to men. Still other women were motivated by their impulse to improve the lives of colonial women subjects through better education and health care. In a majority of cases, a type of "cultural racism," or assumption of ethnic and religious superiority, undergirded their advocacy for change. As Antoinette Burton points out in chapter 7, women missionaries often began their reform work by denigrating local beliefs and customs. Others, such as Annie Besant (1847–1933), were more appreciative of cultural differences. Besant, who supported home rule in India, believed that Western nations should avoid imposing their values on colonial lands. Suffragist leader Hubertine Auclert (1848–1914), who used her Parisian journal, *La Citoyenne*, to advocate for changing the conditions of life for Arab girls and women in Algeria, recognized the "nefarious influence that French colonialism had wrought upon indigenous society and culture." While she lamented the use of women as a "political pawn," she campaigned unceasingly against child marriage and polygamy, and repeatedly petitioned the government to establish schools for Algerian girls.[21]

The effects of such interventions are not simple to evaluate. Kumari Jayawardena, for example, shows how Besant adopted a double standard, supporting the very traditional caste and gender hierarchies in India that South Asian reformers were struggling to change, while opposing oppressive gender practices in England.[22] In recent years, postcolonialist scholars have emphasized the reciprocity of effects in colonial interactions previously viewed as unidirectional. For example, Inderpal Grewal has shown how the imperial discourse about the "woman 'caged' in the harem, in purdah, becomes the necessary Other for the construction of the Englishwoman presumably free and happy in the home, [while] the discourse of the Englishwoman's association with men and women becomes, for Indian nationalism, a sign of depravity." Grewal finds that depictions of Englishwomen in India as "shameless, immodest and sexually promiscuous" were used as a tool for controlling Indian women. She also points to another negative result of colonial intervention, the replacement of laws supporting female rights to joint property ownership with laws giving sole ownership to men.[23]

The development of new world markets also brought unintended but no less serious consequences for colonial women subjects. In chapter 11, Luise White shows how Kenyan women coped with changes in their rural areas as a result of the incorporation of much of black Africa into the European-dominated world economy. She develops a fascinating connection between the world economy and forms of prostitution, by showing what draught, famine, cattle diseases, and a shift to cash cropping meant for wealthy agriculturists and their daughters, who were expected to help their families out economically.

The African case is not an isolated one. With the spread of white settlements across the Australian continent, for example, a traditional and delicate power balance between aboriginal men and women of the Northern Territory was upset. Colonial administrators and pioneering settlers brought with them their own class and cultural biases, which included restrictive notions about the proper roles of women in society. In the case of Australia, a road was located through the very center of a spectacular area of rocks in the desert. Known as the Marbles, in precolonial times it had been a taboo area for men and the site of women's rituals and celebrations. With construction of the road, however, the area was considered contaminated and no longer accessible for ritual purposes. "Sorrowfully, the women claim they can still hear the old people crying from the caves." Also, consultations to work out settlement patterns took place between aboriginal and white *males,* and women were bypassed in the process of political negotiations.[24]

World War I and the Russian Revolution

In retrospect, that Europeans plunged headlong into war in 1914 seems inevitable. Before 1900 nationalist rivalries were played out in imperial conflicts and wars in far-off lands. But when there was no more territory left to conquer, the focus easily returned to the Continent and settled on disputed claims in eastern Europe. There was a noticeable absence of will to avoid war. Indeed, there was a discernible cultural strain among many educated men that positively welcomed war as the ultimate test of the fittest of nations and the fittest of men—a virulent expression of Social Darwinism that worked simultaneously to construct manhood. The heroes of Italian poet Gabriele d'Annunzio exemplified Nietzsche's "Superman," seeking fulfillment through striving for power and dominance. The Frenchman Georges Sorel idealized violence as a catharsis that might arouse mankind to its highest levels. Expressed in art and philosophy, Sorelian sentiments constituted a revolt against reason, science, and modernity. They were echoed in Germany in the "exaltation" of August 4, 1914, when the overwhelming majority of German parliamentarians voted for war credits and "war [seemed to] signify a release from an intolerable past, a final escape from the emptiness of bourgeois life."[25]

This is not to say that all Europeans acquiesced in war. International peace movements were gathering strength in the early decades of the twentieth century: the Hague Convention of 1899 created an international court of arbitration, and the Second International desperately fought nationalist sentiments and passed resolutions exhorting the world's working classes to reject a call to arms. Furthermore, many feminists and socialists alike thought that as women became more publicly aware, the force of maternal love would be a natural barrier to armed struggle. The International Council of Women and the International Suffrage Alliance held a meeting at the Hague in late April 1915, bringing together internationalist women from countries already at war with each other "to try to stop this scandalous bloodshed," in the words of the Dutch suffragist doctor Aletta Jacobs.[26] When these expectations failed to materialize, some socialist leaders joined wartime cabinets, and most internationalist women and feminists deferred suffrage and other feminist campaigns in order to mobilize women in patriotic causes. However, some notable prewar suffrage leaders maintained their pacifist principles. A well-known Frenchwoman, Hélène Brion, defending herself in court against a charge of treason, declared, "I am an enemy of war because I am a feminist. War represents the triumph of brute strength, while feminism can only triumph through moral strength and intellectual values. Between the two there is total contradiction."[27] Brion went to jail. Despite this lofty individual action, Western feminism has never developed a consistent position on war. Particularly as more women joined the armed forces in Europe and North America in the post-1960s decades, many feminists hailed the step as necessary for women's full incorporation into the nation as equals to men.

World War I was a catalyst accelerating technological, political, and cultural change. It was the first three-dimensional war, fought on land, in the air, and under the sea. It reshaped the map of Europe and ruptured people's lives, yet it had a very different meaning for diverse groups of men and women of Europe. Young men were called on to give their lives for their country; back home, women assumed unprecedented responsibility for the continuity of economic and social life as well as for medical and philanthropic services. As men went off to the front, women took over many social functions that previously had not been open to them and, after the wartime emergency, would once again be closed. In England, women undertook "men's work" as chimney sweeps, truck drivers, farm laborers, cement-makers, and steelworkers. As ticket collectors on English buses, they were labeled "Superwomen." As "Molly the Munitions Maker," they further disproved the "fiction of women's incapacity." By tens of hundreds of thousands, the "munitionettes" earned higher wages than before; and they won new attention from men's trade unions. During the war, the number of Englishwomen employed increased by 1,345,000, of whom nearly all either entered new occupations or replaced male workers. At war's end, however, the prospect of five million returning soldiers in need of employment brought rapid displacement of women workers. Many women were happy to resume traditional roles; others protested. Eight days after the Armistice, on November 19, 1918, six thousand union women marched to Westminster bearing signs, "Shall Peace Bring Us Starvation?" By 1919, 650,000 women were unemployed, of whom 150,000 received no compensation, many for having refused alternative work as domestic servants. Wartime gains disappeared in the postwar depression.

A similar story may be told of France. In March 1915, the Chamber of Deputies resolved "to utilize the feminine labour force to replace the military labour force wherever possible." Factories of all types turned to female employees: manufacturers of soap, drugs, explosives; producers of gas, electricity, and armaments; those producing paperworks as well as metalworks. Transport companies hired their first female drivers, guards, and ticket-takers. Though fewer than their English sisters— perhaps because of the greater demand for women in French agriculture—Frenchwomen left their traditional employment for war work, some 684,000 in armaments factories alone. While some employers reorganized work processes especially to accommodate women, others required performance identical to men's but paid them less. Men's concern that the employment of substitute female labor might permanently depress their own wages led to pressure for equal pay legislation. In July 1915, the first law in France establishing a minimum wage was enacted—quickly climaxing six years of debate—for women homeworkers in garment-making, many newly employed in the military uniform business. Nevertheless, although women's wages rose dramatically, up 400 percent, 500 percent, even 600 percent, rarely did women earn as much as their male counterparts. And most of the financial gains that women made were swallowed up by wartime inflation. After the war's end, as in England, Frenchwomen were encouraged to leave their war jobs. In an effort to prevent widespread unemployment among the returning soldiers, the government offered severance pay to women workers who voluntarily conceded their jobs—but only if they acted by December 5, 1918.

The situation was also very similar in wartime Germany. While Red Cross organizations relying on trained nurses aides supervised the medical needs of injured soldiers and the growing numbers of permanently disabled men, a National Women's Service coordinated much of the philanthropic work on behalf of families left in the home front. With government support, these middle-class women also aided working women to enter munitions factories and take on extensive war work. But mounting political crises in Germany over the inequities of wartime sacrifice eroded dynastic legitimacy. Growing numbers of working women made up consumer protests and joined increasingly hostile strike movements that eventually overthrew the monarchy in November 1918. In Russia, similar political and economic upheaval during World War I introduced the most far-reaching changes in the status of women than experienced anywhere in the Western world. The Russian Revolution of 1917 brought into the daily lives of millions of people questions previously dealt with largely in theory and discussion. Whether or not Russia would have succumbed to revolutionary onslaught without the dislocations of the war is a matter of considerable disagreement among historians. What is clear is that the tsarist government's commitment to industrial growth, dating from the 1890s, strained the traditional political and social systems nearly to the breaking point. The Revolution of 1905 was one clear indication that the autocratic system could not accommodate industrial advance without changing its political and economic structure. War stretched it even further.

The first Revolution of 1917, as we have seen, began on International Women's Day. Women textile workers were the first to go on strike, protesting deepening economic crises—lack of foodstuffs and other necessities, stagnating wages, rampant inflation—and the strike spread spontaneously, particularly after troops garrisoned in the capital of St. Petersburg mutinied. The story of the Provisional Government and Lenin's return from exile in a sealed train provided by the Germans has been told many times and need not be repeated here. Our interest concerns a number of related and less well-known areas. After Lenin successfully led the second, or Bolshevik, revolution in October 1917, a regime pledged to women's rights, reconstruction of the family, communal support of children, and other radical revisions of the social and gender hierarchy took over a backward land of about 128 million "souls." What was the Bolshevik attitude toward "the woman question"? What reforms in women's position did the new Soviet regime seek? How did different women respond to the proposed changes in sexual relationships? How profound was the transformation in women's roles?

Within weeks of wresting power, Lenin appointed the first female cabinet-level officer in the West, Alexandra Kollontai, to serve as commissar of social welfare. Kollontai, who wanted to liberate women by abolishing the family that made them dependent on men, represented the radical wing of socialist feminism. But the force of tradition prevailed over the promise of sexual and social equality. Many women clung to familiar patriarchal forms of family life for purposes of subsistence. Rural women, for example, were hurt by the new government's failure to protect the rights of single women to land. During the period of the civil war that followed the revolution, many women alone (soldiers' wives and widows) were attempting to farm their family's allotment, while at the same time peasant men were demanding large allotments of village holdings and those of former landlords. By 1924, most peasant women who were heads of households had no land whatsoever and had been subjected to considerable humiliation and abuse when they protested the loss of property. This village conflict between men and single women reinforced women's conservatism; survival seemed to require reliance on traditional male-dominated institutions. And most Russian men agreed.

Those women who profited from the Revolution were those who were willing to reject tradition, join the Bolshevik party, and enter politics. This took both "daring and opportunity to move into the new elite. Most Russian women had little of either."[28] Richard Stites (chapter 14) writes that all revolutions cheat their followers in some ways; although the Soviet regime proclaimed full equality of the sexes, in practice, power, authority, and opportunity remained tilted in favor of men (over women) as they were toward industrial workers (over peasants). This is not, however, to deny the very real gains made by women during the Soviet era in education, employment, and personal development.

The New Woman

In the early twentieth century, some radical men and women experimented with new living patterns and sexual relations that went beyond the wife and mother ideal. Older certainties were breaking down at a bewildering rate. The Newtonian universe that had been the model of the physical world for two centuries was coming apart. It had rested on two erroneous assumptions: that both time and space were absolute no matter where one stood in the universe. A young German patent officer, Albert Einstein (1879–1955), destroyed those certainties by his theory of relativity put forth first in the paper *The Electrodynamics of Moving Bodies* (1905). He showed how time and space were relative to the observer and proved that relativity could not be removed. This finding was soon translated by segments of public opinion into a philosophy of relativism of values, mores, and behavior.

Equally significant was the refutation of the optimistic Enlightenment notion of human nature by the work of Sigmund Freud (1856–1939), the Austrian founder of psychoanalysis. For about two hundred years, liberal educated opinion had struggled with the Christian notion of original sin, emphasizing the human capacity for rational self-determination. But Freud, uncovering unconscious aggressive and sexual drives, showed that human beings, while endowed with the potential for reason, also possess strong instinctual drives that conflict with the demands of social existence. He was deeply concerned with the tension between the individual and civilization and believed that civilization had been able to emerge only by repressing basic human instincts, particularly the sexual drives. In Freud's more complex view, human beings might achieve a reasoned existence, but only by bringing instinctual drives to consciousness, and guiding them through rational choice. This integration of rational and irrational was difficult to achieve because of psychological mechanisms such as "repression" and "resistance"; and in any case, human beings were fated to suffer from the struggle to sublimate instinctual drives that was required to live in society. More recent analysts have stressed the extent to which human sexuality itself is shaped by efforts to control it.[29]

Like many other thinkers whose work is seen to define an age, Freud was not alone, nor even the first social analyst to develop a theory about the dominant role of instinctual drives in human experience. The "recovery of the unconscious," as it has been called, drew also on the philosophical works of Friedrich Nietzsche and Henri Bergson, and other intellectual leaders who rejected positivism and emphasized instinct, introspection, and intuition. Indeed, Nietzsche, for example, marked a genealogical line of thinkers who critiqued the authority of reason and the optimism inherent in assumptions about a knowable world. His corpus of work contributed to a powerful "postmodernist" critique of Enlightenment modernity that emerged in the last third of the twentieth century. Studies of sexual science—or sexology—formed a part of this broader analysis and Freud's work on sexuality was preceded by that of Havelock Ellis and Richard Krafft-Ebing. However, Freud's influence on attitudes, behavior, and culture, as well as on science, has been so far-reaching that the founder of psychoanalysis has been compared to Copernicus and Darwin, and the twentieth century labeled "The Freudian Century," signifying a new, truly revolutionary concern with the inner self and its impact on human behavior and social change.

Along with demonstrating the importance of sexual drives in personality development, in dreams, in both conscious and unconscious expression, Freud pointed out the harmful effects of repressed sexuality. Women as well as men suffered numerous physical and emotional illnesses because of unexpressed sexual needs. To the extent that Freud sought change, he wanted to free people from the repressive morality and constraints of Victorian society that caused suffering among his patients. Countering Victorian notions that women were "passionless," he recognized female sexuality as a powerful force, and supported those who defended women's rights to sexual satisfaction. Female frigidity was not innate but socially constructed. The popularizing of his ideas inaugurated a so-called sexual revolution and initiated a debate about the sexually emancipated woman. But Freud, whose views of women reflected his own cultural milieu, was a poor guide, for, like Aristotle and Aquinas, he accepted a male model of human being and depicted women as lesser men. His potentially revolutionary views were used by his followers to reinforce older stereotypes of female passivity.

The Freudian analysis of the development of female psychology defined woman as born deficient, that is, like a castrated man, she was a "mutilated creature," a being without a penis. Jealousy based on "penis envy" underlay female psychic development, which followed one of three possible avenues toward adulthood. Some girls repressed their sexuality and became frigid; others refused to accept the fact of being "castrated" and developed a so-called masculinity complex, characterized by a persistent preference for a childish clitoral masturbation over mature vaginal intercourse and sometimes by lesbianism; and a third, or "normal" group, accepted their "femininity." In this case, through the process of sexual maturation, a girl rejected her mother, longed for her father, and achieved true femininity only after marriage and the birth of a male child, who served as her substitute for the long-desired penis. Such sexual differentiation was reflected in personality types from infancy onward. That these ideas could not sustain a movement for equal sexual freedom is clear, for optimal female development required motherhood. And they were never uncontested. Just one year after Freud published his influential analysis of female psychosexual development, Karen Horney responded with a challenge which countered Freud's notion of "penis envy" by pointing to the presence in "the unconscious of the male psyche [of] the boy's intense envy of motherhood." What women suffered was a "sense of being at a disadvantage socially," a disadvantage that clearly reflected reality. In reconstruing Freud's construction of the "problems of feminine psychology," she wanted to "indicate a possible source of error arising out of the sex of the observer."[30]

Radicals of both sexes nonetheless embraced Freud's ideas in their efforts to experiment with new sexual and marital possibilities, and in the long run, Freud's discovery of powerful, aggressive, sexual instincts in both sexes contributed to movements for sexual liberation. The work of late twentieth-century scholars who deny the biological determination of sex differences offers an even more radical challenge to traditional concepts of women's—and men's—sexuality and to the social roles associated with them. In this view, both biological sex and gender identity are the effects of a repeated series of "performances" that are often assumed merely to reflect, but also serve to construct, notions of femininity and masculinity.[31]

The debate over female sexuality took place in a climate in which some activist men of letters and some "new women" were demanding female emancipation in marriage, culture, and society. The most famous literary proponent of female individualism in that period was the Norwegian playwright Henrik Ibsen (1828–1906). While rejecting the label "feminist," Ibsen believed in the right and the duty of women as well as men to individual development, and recognized that "a woman cannot be herself in the society of the present day, which is an exclusively masculine society, with laws framed by men and with a judicial system that judges feminine conduct from a masculine point of view." In 1879, Ibsen shocked society by producing his now-famous, then infamous, play *A Doll's House*. Nora, wife of Helmer and mother of three, commits two acts that violate male standards. First, in the interest of her husband, she forges a document; then, stunned by his lack of understanding of her motives into recognizing that he treats her as a "silly child," as his "little lark," she walks away from home, husband, and children to fulfill a duty to herself that she sees as "sacred." Before slamming the door, Nora tells Helmer, "I believe that before all else I am a human being."

In the early twentieth century, bohemians in Greenwich Village and Montparnasse and avant-garde playwrights associated with Germany's naturalist theater wrote, argued, and lived in an atmosphere charged with excitement—and ambivalence—centered on the characteristics of the new, sexually emancipated woman. In France, Victor Margueritte's novel *La Garçonne (The Bachelor Girl,* 1922) sold twenty thousand copies in four days, three hundred thousand in its first year, over a million by 1929, although—and no doubt because—it showed a young woman adopting male standards of sexual behavior. Men of solid bourgeois standing, ranging from Léon Blum, later prime minister of France, to Judge Ben Lindsey of Denver, Colorado, published books advocating forms of "trial marriage." It was an exciting era for those involved, even if its immediate impact on the masses of women was minimal. Many ideas were proposed; almost all could agree that some measure of freedom in love was essential to self-development and some even advocated birth control because it permitted the separation of sexuality from reproduction. Emma Goldman (1869–1940), the Russian-born American anarchist, said it probably better than most. The modern woman would achieve emancipation

First by asserting herself as a personality, and not as a sex commodity. Second, by refusing the right to anyone over her body; by refusing to bear children, unless she wants them; by refusing to be a servant of God, the State, society, the husband, the family, etc., by making her life simpler, but deeper and richer. That is, by trying to learn the meaning and substance of life in all its complexities, by freeing herself from the fear of public opinion and public condemnation. Only that and not the ballot, will set woman free, will make her a force hitherto unknown in the world, a force for real love, for peace, for harmony; a force of divine fire, of life-giving; a creator of free men and women.[32]

The fundamental goal of individual self-determination that was part of Goldman's philosophy remained unrealized. The Freudian revolution helped to bring about a change in sexual mores, but it did not include the socioeconomic transformations needed to underpin female sexual independence. Indeed, most of Freud's followers of both sexes rejected the revolutionary implications of his work and, at worst, used it to reinforce demands for social adjustment to conservative values. Henceforth, however, people in the West were more willing to talk about sex and many came to regard sexual pleasure as a legitimate pursuit.

The sexual experimentation and "free love" that began shortly before World War I constituted a "sexual revolution" only for the few, largely limited to the urban middle and upper classes. Most observers surely were horrified by new sexual roles and relationships, including most women. Actresses refused to play Nora and even self-proclaimed radical men expressed considerable ambivalence about the prospect of women's emancipation from traditional roles. Both before and after World War I, the blurring of boundaries between the sexes generated fears of deteriorating values and contributed to a pervasive sense of cultural despair.

The Interwar Years

Until the feminist reinterpretation of history that began in the 1960s, the decade of the 1920s was often described as the time in which women were "emancipated." The woman question was said to be solved. As Table 3 shows, in many countries women now had the vote, and a few sat and deliberated in parliament. Once life settled down after the period of demobilization, they again entered the workforce at a rapid rate, even at the "expense" of male workers (as Germans contended). Reform legislation was codifying these advances, such as the British Sex Disqualification Removal Act of 1919, which opened the higher levels of the civil service, the legal profession, and jury duty to women. Furthermore, the stuffy and quite "proper" prewar world had given way to a new climate of restless vitality and renewed sexual and cultural experimentation.

According to the popular view of the 1920s, it was a crazy age of rising hemlines, bobbed hair, and new leisure activities that, in the United States, included marathon dancing and hand-holding or gum-chewing contests and forays into nightclubs and cabarets where ladies had once not dared to tread. While each specific element in the picture can be backed up by facts, the optimistic conclusions drawn about women's improved status require reassessment. Sandra Gilbert, who describes very vividly the wartime world of men, and of the women left behind in England, probes the underlying "battle of the sexes," a long unacknowledged component of the war and of the postwar decade, whose famous novels, like Hemingway's *The Sun Also Rises,* revealed fears of unbridled female sexuality (chapter 12). Historian Mary Louise Roberts also provides an excellent balance to the conventional view, showing how the postwar perception that women were deserting traditional gender roles came to symbolize the end of Western civilization. Ruins on the battlefield were matched by a ruined culture, a topsy-turvy "civilization without sexes." By obscuring the boundary between what had been constructed as a "natural" division between femininity and masculinity, the "new women" threatened the stability of everything else in a world already shaken by the violence of war.[33]

Some women certainly looked different. The maternal image, exemplified in the United States by the Gibson girl, with her upswept, constrained long hair, her full bosom, narrow waist, wide hips, and concealed legs gave way to La Garçonne, the flapper who boyishly flattened her chest with binders, discarded corsets, lowered her waistline, and displayed her legs in silk stockings. But the flapper dress was seen as a "sexual assault" on men accustomed to women as passive recipients of their sexual advances. Postwar literature, as Gilbert shows, featured woman as bitch. The Parisian designer Coco Chanel, the first woman to achieve fame as a high-fashion couturier, dressed women in tailored suits, white shirts, and men's ties. This style, pioneered in the mid-nineteenth century, now, thanks to new mass marketing and advertising industries, proliferated. "When George Sand dressed as a man in the 1840s, she was likely to remain an isolated phenomenon; when Coco Chanel did the same in the 1920s, she was imitated throughout France and the world."[34]

As women everywhere "bobbed" their hair, the new style was condemned as "indecent and un-Christian," and elicited strong negative reactions on the part of some men, even, according to one report, murder. The "bob" was taken, of course, as a symbol of women's emancipation, the new style seen as a rejection of traditional womanliness and motherhood. Ultimately it would lead to the end of civilization. "Women are cutting their hair as a sign of sterility," wrote Drieu la Rochelle, a French veteran who later became a fascist leader. "A 'being' without a waist, without hips and without breasts, [the new woman] symbolized a civilization without churches, without palaces, and without sexes," concludes Roberts.[35] In her view, such attitudes built upon feelings developed during the war by soldiers resentful of the gap between battlefront and home front, between men's and women's wartime experiences (illustrated strikingly in the photographs on pages 279 and 280). New roles for women now came to suggest anarchy, exemplified by the elaborate fantasies developed about the lives of lesbians described by Carolyn Dean in chapter 13. Lesbians seemed to offer proof of a "volatile female sexuality" that led to "social contamination and moral ruin."

The massive losses sustained by France in the war (which were the greatest among the warring nations) exacerbated fears of "depopulation" prevalent for decades, and contributed to the passage in 1920 of a famous law that instituted severe penalties for advocacy of contraception and abortion. To emphasize the seriousness of its intent to raise the birthrate, the government decreed mere advocacy of abortion a crime punishable by up to three years in prison and three thousand francs penalty. Somewhat lesser penalties—six months maximum—awaited anyone who "for the purpose of contraceptive propaganda, describes, divulges, or offers to reveal . . . the procedures for preventing pregnancy." For historian Roberts, this rapid and "aggressive state intervention in matters of natality and the family," which was followed in 1923 by legislation to prosecute the women seeking abortions, was the result of the "apocalyptic tone" of much natalist propaganda. Clearly the sexual behavior of women was its target, for it did not proscribe the sale of condoms. If maternity was women's counterpart to military service, then the veterans of unprecedented violence and carnage on the battlefield could be assured fewer women would desert their stations. More broadly, by trying to prevent women from escaping their traditional duties, they would squelch, or at least hinder, perceived upheavals in gender roles. "*Not* to assert woman's difference or her maternal, domestic role as primary," Roberts asserts, "would lead to a profound transformation in the meaning of work, marriage, property, and politics in French society and culture."[36] Also in 1920 the French government began to forge medals for mothers: for five living children, bronze; for eight, silver; for ten, gold. On the losing side in this long struggle, French Neo-Malthusians observed, "The rights of women increase. But what is their great duty: to give birth, to give birth again, always to give birth. . . . Should a woman refuse to give birth she no longer deserves her rights."[37] In 1922 the French government rejected votes for women.

As if further inducement to maternity were needed, in 1930 Pope Pius XI presented an encyclical on Christian marriage, declaring contraception a "horrible crime" in the sight of God, who "at times has punished it with death." The physiological, social, and economic emancipation of women, as commonly understood, was characterized by the pope as a "*debasing of the womanly character and the dignity of motherhood and indeed of the whole family* [italics in original]." Through "false liberty and unnatural equality," women became "as among the pagans the mere instrument of man." Women's rights, according to Pius XI, must be adapted to the welfare of the family as authorized by God. The patriarchal family was "not changeable by public laws or at the pleasure of private individuals."[38]

Fascist Antifeminism, Anti-Semitism, and Alternatives to Facism

Adolf Hitler and his followers also proclaimed their dedication to venerating women as mothers. "In my state, the mother is the most important citizen," he declared.[39] But there were mothers and mothers. Nowhere was the contradiction between pledges in support of women and their violation greater than in the Germany that developed in the wake of World War I. While historians hold deeply divided opinions about the impact of Nazi policies on reproduction—and on women's support for the Nazi regime—they recognize both gender and race as relevant categories in matters of birth and death in the Third Reich.[40]

Fascist parties appeared in every country of Europe in the interwar years, although they held power longest in Italy under Mussolini (1919–44) and in the Germany of the Third Reich (1933–45). Fascism fed on a deep sense of malaise and discontent spawned by the war experience and growing rejection of parliamentary liberal government as weak, ineffectual, and pandering to the mediocrity of the masses. Furthermore, fascism everywhere was particularly attuned to stereotypically masculine values: its call was for struggle, strength, and courage. In many cases, early fascist converts had been disoriented soldiers trying to recreate the camaraderie and mutual dependency that they had experienced in the trenches. Equally harsh on men and women who rejected conventional gender roles, the fascists were very much opposed to homosexuality as well as feminism, and they were virulently anti-Semitic.

Women's emancipation, declared Hitler, was a Jewish invention. Women's industrial and professional work and women's rights were part and parcel of the "degeneracy" of the modern world, and fascists were bent on returning women to the home. Antifeminism was a central part of the Nazi ideology. Germany in the 1920s, therefore, offered a stark contrast between the claims of the Weimar Republic (1918–33), which by constitutional law guaranteed women "fundamentally" equal citizenship rights, and the call of the fascists to send women back to the home.

The uneven and incomplete nature of change in the direction of women's liberation accounted for the political responses of many women to these contradictions in the republic. In the first place, a majority of adult women lived off the earnings of their husbands or their children and did not work for wages outside their homes; the trend toward small families with their emphasis on domesticity was continuing. Of the approximately 11.5 million adult women who were working for their living in 1925, fully one-third were in a category of "helping dependents," women who acknowledged to the census taker their secondary economic role in a family business or farm. Their numbers had doubled since 1907. These small establishments, which had difficulty meeting the competition of larger businesses, increasingly were being forced to let the hired help go and rely on the labor of wives. The republic's new labor laws establishing the forty-hour workweek and regulating wages made hired agricultural labor unprofitable, thus increasing the burdens on peasant wives. These developments do not suggest economic advancement or "emancipation" for rural women.

However, during the Weimar Republic, the most bitter contest for jobs occurred in industry and service. It was erroneously believed at the time that women were achieving economic success—indeed their very emancipation—by displacing men. Research by Renate Bridenthal and Tim Mason has proven otherwise,[41] but the political significance of the contemporary view and the backlash that it created remain. What fascism has taught is that myths are important and real if they influence how people act. Even during demobilization at the war's end, there had been public outcry against women's work. It gathered momentum in the unsettled economic conditions of the early postwar period and resurfaced when massive unemployment, caused by the Great Depression of 1929 in the United States, appeared in Germany. In reality, it was the process of economic rationalization that made women's work seem threatening to men. In a burst of effort beginning in the mid-1920s, Germany attempted to discard old plants and equipment and to modernize both industry and agriculture in order to remain competitive in world markets. Rationalization entailed the introduction of labor-saving machines, standardization of parts, and a flow production design that moved goods more swiftly along an assembly line. The new machinery and techniques invaded not only the factories but even the offices. It meant that work became divided into smaller and simpler, more repetitive stages and permitted the hiring of unskilled, cheap labor—and the cheapest laborers were women.

Yet most newly hired women did not replace men; instead, they took jobs in expanding industries that had previously employed women and, now, as women's share of total jobs shifted from agriculture and domestic service to factories and offices, women's work was more easily observed. Furthermore, women as well as men suffered the adverse effects of rationalization. As the new processes led to "speedups" and work became more intense, the conditions of women's labor in many ways deteriorated. Since nothing was done to ease the lot of workers who were both wage-earners and homemakers, many women found it hard to combine paid labor in factories, offices, and shops with running a home. Is it any wonder, then, that the fascist call to "return women to their homes" was favorably received by some working women?

The Nazi party offered alternatives to women's emancipation by glorifying domestic life and its daily routine. There is every indication that this "drive for domesticity" after the Nazis came to power met with tacit approval of many German women. The regime offered tangible benefits to women who stayed at home. As early as the summer of 1933, it provided interest-free marriage loans to young couples as long as the woman withdrew from gainful labor. The money was designed to be spent on furniture and household appliances and to stimulate the depressed economy. The government improved welfare and maternity services and offered family allowances, which increased with the birth of each child. At the same time, it suppressed the sale and spread of birth control devices and information and applied the older antiabortion laws much more strictly. Birth rates were reversed and rose slightly in the period (Figure 5). The controlled public media kept up a constant barrage of propaganda designed to praise and glorify mothers and wives and to enhance their self-respect. The policy was both sexist and racist, however, and reveals the same complex connection between sexism and racism that we saw develop in the prewar period over the population debate.

The glorification of motherhood, which received public support, found its necessary counterpart, from the Nazi perspective, in compulsory sterilization for the sake of racial purity.[42] A new statute in late spring 1933 legalized eugenic sterilization and, in July, the Law for the Prevention of Hereditarily Diseased Offspring ordered sterilization for certain categories of people. All women were affected by the regime's dual policy: so-called Aryan women were hailed as "mothers of the race" and turned into breeders, and non-Aryans vilified as perpetrators of racial degeneration. The Nazis acted on their racist and sexist program with their usual efficiency. They reorganized the medical profession, imposing "hygienic education" and training on the practice of medicine. The sterilization campaign included euthanasia programs aimed at systematically killing the "unfit," as well as perverse experiments on concentration camp victims. The numbers of sterilized "Aryan" Germans noted earlier do not include Jews, who also were victims of mass sterilization for supposed medical purposes. The victims of sterilization were evenly divided between women and men, and came typically from the lower classes. Of the women sterilized, it was servants, unskilled factory or farm workers, jobless housewives married to poor and unskilled workers, prostitutes, and unmarried women who were overrepresented. These women deviated from the norm of acceptable gender behavior. Proper and orderly non-Jewish German workers of either sex were less likely to fall victim to sterilization; "race hygiene" contributed to the maintenance of the class structure as well as the affirmation of the Nazis' standards of proper gender behavior. Tragically, anti-Semitic racism culminated in total war against Europe's Jewish population.

Italian fascism, while less focused on anti-Semitism, shared with German fascism an ideological commitment to limit women to what its leaders defined as traditionally feminine activities. While seeking to adopt the technological advances and enjoy the economic benefits of modern industrial states, and to join the imperialist powers in exploiting colonial empires, Italian fascists tried to hold back concomitant changes of modernity, including new opportunities for women. An oversupply of labor in the 1920s and the militarization of society in the 1930s both provided contexts conducive to propaganda attacking women who deviated from maternal roles. Feminists, condemned as "demodé, spinsterish, and foreign-born," were charged with "obscuring . . . the limits set by nature and consecrated by tradition." They were said to represent "the fruit of the economization of life and moral Jewishification." However, the exigencies of war conflicted with fascist ideology, and by 1940 the Italian regime began to call on women to replace the men it had mobilized by taking work in factories and public offices.[43]

By subordinating the individual and family to nationalistic aims, by breaking down barriers between government and private life, fascist regimes in both Italy and Germany undermined their own ideologically inspired intentions regarding women. In both countries, women's responses to fascism varied by class, religion, urban or rural location, education, generation, and a host of individual characteristics. Historian Victoria de Grazia, suggests, however, that Italian women generally resented and resisted state intervention in private affairs. While some women supported their country's military ventures in Ethiopia in the mid-1930s, women also participated in the armed resistance that developed after September 1943. Drawing on their knowledge of neighborhood and family networks, they were particularly important in the role of courier. Interviewed after the war, these mostly working-class women grounded their determination to resist in their desire to fight injustice done to fathers, brothers, and fiancés, not in abstract political ideologies.[44]

In Germany, a group of students around Sophie and Hans Scholl in Munich called for active sabotage against the regime in the early 1940s. They were brutally suppressed, as was the failed plot of July 20, 1944, on Hitler's life. In both the German and Italian cases, however, most of the population complied with life under the terror of fascism and "resistance" became an individual protest, a work slowdown, membership in a youth gang like the "Edelweiss Pirates" in Essen or Düsseldorf, attendance at a jazz club, or listening to foreign radio broadcasts.[45]

During the interwar period, a combination of factors that affected many nations—reaction against the disruptions and losses due to the "Great War," especially population decline, and economic pressure resulting from the "Great Depression"—had tended to reinforce traditional domestic ideology. Retrenchment against gender role revision took place even in Soviet Russia, where during the 1930s Joseph Stalin (1879–1953) presided over a temporary dismantling of the codes of law that had liberalized marriage and divorce regulations, legalized abortion, and strengthened women's roles in family and society.

Similar demographic and economic problems, however, led to a radically different resolution in Scandinavia. Sweden's neutral position on the northern frontier of Europe had left it less traumatized by World War I. Under the leadership of a remarkable couple, the sociologist Alva Myrdal and her husband, the economist Gunnar Myrdal, both socialists, Sweden moved to solve its population crisis by expanding economic opportunities for women so that, married or unmarried, they could successfully combine work and motherhood. It developed new policies that would set a model for many countries in the years following the war.

Putting into practice ideas advanced decades earlier by their countrywoman Ellen Key as well as by the American Charlotte Perkins Gilman, the Frenchwoman Léonie Rouzade, and the German Helene Lange, the Myrdals used the argument that motherhood is a socially essential function worthy of the highest respect. They convinced Swedish legislators, conservatives along with liberals and social democrats, to enact laws ensuring freedom for mothers by legalizing birth control, abortion, and sex education and protecting the employment rights of pregnant women. To reduce the penalties of pregnancy, Key had demanded that married women be allowed to retain their names, properties, and positions, that parents share equally in duties and rights, and that sexual morality—so loaded against women and especially against single mothers—be centered on "reverence for the child." A measure of the Myrdals' success was Alva Myrdal's statement in the foreword to a 1962 book, *The Changing Roles of Man and Woman:*

> As early as the 1930s, we had succeeded in convincing the Royal Commissions to accept the idea that a career for married women should be viewed as "normal." This was the time when the family role of women first came to be regarded as an ancillary, though highly important part, of her life-plan. The official formulation of the demand was not the "right of married women to work," but rather the "right of working women to marriage and motherhood."[46]

In Myrdal's view, the emerging welfare state should not become, in Sondra Herman's words, a "replacement patriarchy" but "an instrument for women wrestling control of their lives from male-dominated families."[47]

In Denmark, the economic and social crises of the depression years in the 1930s also reinforced the case for expanded welfare services. Led by social democrats, who dominated a coalition with radical-liberals, the welfare state was pushed forward. Reform legislation was passed that broadened social services, including health and unemployment insurance and social security, instituted educational reforms, and curbed the economic might of business monopolies. Through increased social expenditures, the Danish government promoted a higher standard of living and a new degree of equality. Like developments in Sweden, this established a basis in the post–World War II period for the Scandinavian countries to take the lead in reorganizing the workplace to encourage men to assume a greater share in home and family responsibilities, and by amending the maternity leave policy to permit fathers time off for infant care. Few men, however, took advantage of these opportunities to transcend sex role divisions. Gerda Ruth Neyer (chapter 15) explores a similar situation in postwar Austria, where welfare policies continued to rely on and to reinforce definitions of women primarily as mothers and caregivers and men evidently subscribed to these definitions as well.

Mobilizing Women for War

Europe could not avoid another war, because right from the very start the Nazi regime in Germany was bent on aggression. It solved the unemployment crisis by embarking on a massive rearmament program and its response to social tensions was the call for territorial aggrandizement *(Lebensraum),* not internal social and welfare reform. By 1936, however, the regime faced a dilemma, which grew in magnitude as the country embarked on war in September 1939. There was a labor shortage for heavy industrial work and the most obvious source of new recruitment was the married woman who had been encouraged to stay home. Would ideological norms or economic pragmatics prevail? Would the regime channel married women into industrial jobs and later war work? The Nazi government was sensitive to what it thought popular opinion wanted. It believed that its ideological stance on women's proper roles reflected the views of most German families; and, later, it strongly felt that men would fight harder if they knew their wives were not working long hours in munitions and other factories. In stark contrast to Britain, or the United States, the Nazi regime took ineffective measures to mobilize women for the war effort. It made up the shortfall by conscripting laborers from the eastern and western territories it had conquered and transporting them to factories in Germany as forced, slave labor and by working most inmates in designated concentration camps to death.

The governments of England and America sought to solve their labor shortages by ensuring that women did their part for the war effort. The British adopted compulsory registration of women in March 1941, after it was clear that an enormous labor power shortage was developing. From December 1941 onward, women were selectively conscripted into industry, administration, and the armed forces, although British officials favored voluntary compliance and only used compulsion as a last resort. By 1943, it was impossible for a woman under forty years of age to avoid war work; in September of that year, all women under fifty-one years were required to register. Between September 1939 and May 1942, the number of British women in industry alone increased by 1.1 million; by 1943 there were 1.5 million women in the engineering trade, whereas before the war their numbers had been minuscule.

The results were similar in the United States, although the government did not institute civilian conscription but rather embarked on an ambitious propaganda campaign and relied on high wages to sell war work to women. The mass press was particularly important in this effort. The government's main channel of communication with the media was the Office of War Information (OWI), which put out a *Magazine War Guide* informing publishers and writers about the themes that Washington agencies considered useful to the war effort: democracy's struggle, the attitudes of good Americans, the barbarous behavior of the enemy—especially the Japanese whose Asian features were readily caricatured—the importance of meeting production goals. The OWI was also deeply involved in the move to recruit women into the labor force, particularly into prewar male jobs that were short of workers. Magazines were encouraged to publish romances in which women who entered defense industries found fulfillment and the admiration of desirable men in performing such important work for the nation. They changed the typical prewar fiction story that described irreconcilable tensions between marriage and career to show how married women in war work successfully combined both family and labor responsibilities. The recruitment strategy varied by class. For example, magazines like the *Saturday Evening Post,* which had a middle-class readership, often depicted the employed woman in a position of leadership over male subordinates, making courageous and timely decisions. Middle-class women needed to be persuaded to take the step down the social ladder and enter the blue-collar work world, which had less status than their own middle-class lifestyle. Female authority maintained middle-class superiority, despite the loss of status. By contrast, the tales in *True Story,* read by working-class people, rarely showed women in nontraditional positions or those that carried authority. Its readers in real life were unlikely to be found in management roles or professional jobs; also, such portrayal might place working-class women in a position to compete with working-class men. Rather, the themes encouraged working-class women to identify with and be proud of the important contributions of their class. These differences aside, the portrayal of women's war work made it clear that neither middle-class nor working-class women were intended to become a permanent part of the labor force. The American symbol of war work, Rosie the Riveter, proved she could do the job but everyone knew that she was working "only for the duration."[48]

Despite the intended message, however, there is some indication that in the United States, and probably in the other belligerent nations, the war experience was an important one for *married and older* women. After the war, to be sure, women once again were shifted to low-skilled and traditional female jobs. But more and more married women would find a permanent place in the labor force. The changing structure of industry that favored female-typed service occupations soon increased the demand for women workers beyond the supply of the younger and unmarried who had dominated the female labor force in the early part of the century. Simultaneously, demand for greater family income was created by a vast new network of communications media that featured advertisements for all types of attractive goods for personal or household consumption. Demographic shifts in birthrates, marriage and divorce, childbearing, and longevity also served to change women's pattern of paid work. But historians focused on the aftermath of wartime devastation and the emerging Cold War and paid little attention to women and gender issues in the first decades following the war.

European Reconstruction and New Relationships

The European war came to a close with the fall of Berlin in May 1945. The Allied policy of unconditional surrender had meant a land and air battle to the finish. This war, as all wars, took a heavy toll on male life; but it also set a new precedent of deliberately targeting civilian populations, a strategy that has become characteristic of all subsequent civil and international warfare. The loss of life was staggering. Russia sustained by far the highest casualties; indeed, that country absorbed about half of all the war's deaths and casualties, losing 10 percent of its population, an estimated twenty-seven million soldiers and other citizens. Death also claimed about six million Germans, and another twelve million became refugees. France likewise counted deaths in the millions. These losses drastically altered sex ratios. After the war, for example, there were 1,717 women for every 1,000 men in Berlin; in the 1950s the ratio was still 1,353 to 1,000, and more than one-third of all West Berlin households were headed by a woman. It is hardly surprising that before reestablishment of central government in Germany in 1949, much of the work of daily survival lay in women's hands. Berliners tell of female communities and solidarities, of great ingenuity in mastering the arts of barter in the black market, and of endless waiting in lines for food or official papers. Small subsistence gardens sprang up in every nook and cranny, and women grew a variety of foodstuffs for their own family's use as well as for exchange. They took all manner of makeshift jobs. With the return of men came a return to "normalcy." The family of husband, wife, and children reemerged as the norm of private living, and females who headed households (widows with children) were mislabeled "single." Dwellings in new government-subsidized apartment buildings were often reserved for the normative family. When wage labor was reestablished, after being subordinated to exchange through barter in the period of occupation by Allied forces, traditional differentials by sex reappeared.

West German identity was shaped powerfully by understandings of "woman's" place in the trying years of transition to the new democratic state, between the war's end and 1949, when the German Federal Republic that emerged from the three zones of American, British, and French occupation was established. Her day-to-day backbreaking work of survival as the "Woman of the Rubble" (*Trümmerfrau*), however, elided into collective community sacrifice, masking the real labor of women. Indeed, an image of female victimhood stood for general German victimhood. Allegations of female sexual promiscuity, furthermore, seemed to speak of general social disorder and moral decay, turning the period of military occupation—and not the Nazi past—into the nadir of German life. It took the power of feminist consciousness, which reemerged in the 1960s in West Germany, to begin the process of rewriting the tragic but poignant stories of individual women's hardships and survival. In the Cold War, of course, West German identity was also shaped by contrast with the East German state. The German Democratic Republic, resting on socialist principles, and tied to the Soviet bloc, had been proclaimed also in 1949. Significantly, a key ideological mark of East German identity was its broad commitment to women's paid labor, in stark contrast to the Nazi past as well as to the ongoing changes in women's gainful labor in western Europe, which are described below. The German cases demonstrate vividly a point we have stressed in Part III: how central gender images are to the construction of national identity.[49]

With postwar economic recovery and continued expansion and growth came a significant change in the pattern of women's gainful employment in Europe as well as in the United States. In western Europe, where between 1960 and 1973 gross domestic production grew an average of 3.9 percent annually, women's labor force participation increased dramatically. Service jobs continued to multiply for decades, outpacing employment options in industry and opening up the largest area of new positions for women. In 1980, the service sector accounted for two-thirds of female employment in countries of the European Community; by 1987 the figure reached almost three-quarters. By the 1990s, women constituted an average of 41.4 percent of the total civilian labor force in the fifteen countries then comprising the European Union. Figures for individual countries ranged from a low of 35 percent in Greece and Ireland to more than 49 percent in Finland and Sweden—but was high enough everywhere to make women's paid employment a significant factor in the economic lives of individuals, families, and societies. Most strikingly, *married* women's employment rose to levels unparalleled during any previous period of Western capitalist development.

The rapid expansion of the economies of many western European countries in the 1960s helps to explain the steep increases in the employment of married women beginning in that decade, as shown in Table 4. This reversed the trend of the early twentieth century, when even lower-class wives were staying at home if the collective income of their households (from husbands and children) was sufficient to permit them to do so. In the post-1945 period, if the household needed added income or had targeted a special goal such as a better home or a longer vacation, the mother, rather than her children, went out to work. As a result, the increase in married women's employment was steep and steady in most western European countries. Comprising a tiny fraction of the female labor force around the turn of the century, by 1970—a date associated with the "rebirth of feminism"—married workers already accounted for more than 40 percent of all married women in a number of countries.

Others figures, which trace the employment rate of women not by marital status but by the number of their dependent children, also show a considerable increase in working mothers in most countries. As one team of experts on the position of women in the European Community stated in 1993, "Mothers' participation in economic activity is on the increase and its cessation for child-rearing is no longer the dominant model." This observation also reflects a dramatic rise in the numbers of cohabiting or single mothers.[50]

While these changes may be explained by the rising expectations of a consumer society that offered a wealth of new goods and by new demographic patterns, they also express in part the postwar trend toward placing more emphasis on education in family calculations, the education of both mothers and children. Indeed, one may speak of an "educational explosion" in postwar Europe. Parents of all classes now wanted their children of both sexes to spend considerably more time in school, including technical or university training. The greater the degree of education, the larger the likelihood, for both men and women, of gainful employment; but increased schooling plays a more critical role in determining the work patterns of women. The two most decisive factors influencing women's pattern of paid employment across the life cycle are family responsibilities and education. Interestingly, married women who have children later in life are more likely to continue employment with minimal time out, probably due to the mother's opportunity for greater education and higher earning capacity. In some countries, the employment rate for women varies radically with further education. For example, there are sections of Italy where women who graduate from secondary school are four times more likely to be employed than those who drop out.[51]

While once it was thought that the emergence of women's movements in the 1960s in the West "caused" the growth in women's labor participation, the reverse probably is more correct. Both demand and supply factors help to determine the level of women's employment. The growing number of divorces, which accelerated in the 1960s and 1970s, and the rapid rise in never-married mothers, also brought more women with small children back into the workforce. Whether forced by divorce or impelled by desire, far more older women now seek jobs in a market still often geared to the sex appeal of youth or structured to fit male careers. As

TABLE 4. Labor Force Participation Rates of the Female Married Population as a Percentage of All Married Women of Working Age (about 15–65) in Selected Countries.

Year[a]	Britain	Denmark	France	Germany	Netherlands	Sweden	United States
1900	13		(20)[b]	12	5		6
1910	11	24	(21)	26	8	4	11
1920	9	20	29	29		5	9
1930	11	22	26	30	7	10	12
1940		25		35		10	15
1950	23	28	(28)	28	11	15	24
1960	32	31	(31)	36	7	26	32
1970	46	46	38	40	17	56	41
1980	54	66	50	47	32	76	50
1990	59	76	53	54	47	86	58

[a]Actual census years and specific age groups vary.
[b]Figures in parentheses exclude agriculture.
Sources: Hettie A. Pott-Buter, *Facts and Fairy Tales about Female Labor, Family and Fertility: A Seven-Country Comparison, 1850–1990* (Amsterdam: Amsterdam University Press, 1993), p. 201. U.S. Department of Commerce, Bureau of the Census, *Statistical Abstracts,* 1983, 1996.

more women with children went into the labor force, the strains and stresses associated with balancing work and family responsibilities provided the context for the reemergence of concern with the woman question. The conflict between individual and social concerns strikes especially hard at the working mother.

Socialist countries brought even higher proportions of women into gainful employment than western Europe and the United States. According to the national census of 1970, 92.5 percent of all adult women held jobs in the Soviet Union; similar figures apply to East Germany. Comparable data for western European nations in the same year were 48 percent in France and West Germany, nearly 30 percent in Italy, almost 60 percent in Sweden, and 50 percent in the United Kingdom. In addition, nearly 50 percent of all women between fifteen and sixty four years were gainfully employed in the United States. More than western Europe and the United States, the industrial development of the Soviet Union relied heavily on female labor; the leisured housewife was not an accepted social alternative. The Soviet development pattern originated from a mix of necessity and ideology. The country had faced innumerable deaths at the time of the Great Civil War (1918–20) and paid a high price in human life for its collectivization of agriculture and rapid industrialization after 1928. In addition, huge numbers of men had died in the two world wars. Therefore, Soviet Russia had to rely on the labor of women for its push to become an industrialized society. Between 1928 and 1975 the female labor force in the Soviet Union grew from 2.8 million to 53.7, representing an increase from 24 percent to 51.5 percent of all industrial, clerical, and service workers.[52] At the same time, because the socialist leadership acknowledged the importance of integrating women into wage labor outside their private households, they invested heavily (though never adequately) in public services needed to support working mothers. Very high rates of female labor participation were typical also of other central and eastern European countries under communism.

It is now common knowledge that women in socialist nations such as the Soviet Union or East Germany were long burdened by a "double day," which Richard Stites discusses in chapter 14. Ironically, this pattern of women's work has now become typical of most industrial countries. Closer examination of many aggregate employment figures quickly discloses gender differences that reveal a continuing, or even increasing, gap rather than greater equality in the world of work. As sociologist Rose-Marie LaGrave graphically declared, speaking from the perspective of the 1990s,

> The European map of wage labor has its male continent and its female continent, whose contours ignore geographical boundaries and trace instead a hierarchical frontier. The male continent consists of workers and managers, whereas the female one is nothing but a maze of offices. Between these two extremes lies another Europe, a land of gender parity in employment, which is beginning to emerge in retail sales, the skilled trades, technical and related lines of work, teaching, law, and medicine."[53]

The gender gap appears most prominently when figures for part-time work are considered, a pattern that both reflects and reinforces differences in men's and women's employment. Women dominate the ranks of part-time workers. In 1986, 40 percent to 45 percent of working women in Scandinavia and the United Kingdom, 30 percent in West Germany, and 25 percent in Belgium and France were employed part time. In West Germany, a 1984 study showed women comprising 93 percent of all part-time workers. In 1989, more than half of all women in the labor forces of seventeen European countries held part-time jobs; large differences existed across the nations, with the highest percentages appearing in Scandinavia and the countries of northwest Europe. Furthermore, men who work at home tend to be older, women still in their prime earning years. For men, part-time employment serves as a kind of "disguised preretirement," while for women it constitutes a form of "semiemployment." It helps to explain the "feminization of poverty." Offering low wages, lacking such benefits of full-time employment as pensions and advancement opportunities, part-time work "is everywhere the root cause of increased [gender] inequality."[54]

In the late 1980s and the early 1990s, unemployment figures also showed women's greater vulnerability in the work world. Women are more likely to fall into this category in about two-thirds of industrialized countries, often by as much as 50 percent to 100 percent. Figures showed this to be especially true for immigrant women in the Netherlands, Belgium, West Germany, and the United Kingdom, who were far more likely to suffer unemployment than women native to those countries. Immigrants whose country of origin was Turkey, Morocco, Pakistan, and India were most likely to be unemployed, and their labor force participation rates, skill levels, and pay also lagged substantially. Since 1989, women also have born a disproportionate burden of unemployment in eastern Europe, as a result of the transition from "socialism" to capitalist market relations.

Postcommunism: Women "After the Revolution"

As we have seen, accelerating trends of the 1970s, 1980s, and 1990s brought more women into paid employment, and often into higher education and public roles as well. In most national economies, labor needs due to extensive growth in the service sector as well as industry created demand for women's work. Everywhere, but especially in communist countries with command economies and labor shortages, this stimulated efforts to provide an array of public services that facilitated female labor force participation. "Welfare" services such as child care, paid maternity leave, even maternity grants, provided at public expense, aided many working mothers. These efforts to support the "worker-mother" ideal of communist ideology also created employment opportunities for many other women who worked to provide health and child-care support services. These were the programs that Gail Warshofsky Lapidus has termed "affirmative action, Soviet-style." Furthermore, since labor force needs mandated emphasis on scientific and technical training, large numbers of women entered such traditionally male-dominated fields as engineering and medicine. Although women never achieved a proportionate share of managerial positions, nevertheless, Lapidus states that "the sharp line that divided humanistic from scientific orientations in other countries, and therefore the education of women and men, was blurred to a considerable degree in the USSR."

Publicly funded support services, however, while plentiful compared to many Western countries, were never sufficient, and women continued to struggle with the demands of a "double day." It is less commonly recognized that many women in the communist countries carried an additional—a third—burden. This was the duty of public service. The primacy of public obligations for both sexes meant that civic duties played an important role in women's lives under communism. On the one hand, this provided opportunities for far more women to participate in political organizations than in the West, and helps to explain relatively high levels of female participation in political positions. Exhorted by socialist propaganda to participate in the "management of public enterprise," women accepted responsibilities that created for them a "triple burden."[55]

Still, if many allocated time to civic obligations, few attained membership in the ruling elites. Female membership in the Central Committee of the Communist Party of the USSR, for example, between 1918 and 1976 never included more than 4 percent. Women's roles remained largely symbolic and ceremonial: "token women" took their assigned places rather than contend as real political actors for substantive equal power and authority. Quotas, not changed consciousness, were responsible for much of the vaunted equality of the sexes.

Ironically, this emphasis on public participation gave a new and important meaning to private acts. Whatever activities remained outside the control of public authorities took on a special political significance. Personal life, from private relationships to poetry readings, became the locus for a kind of dissent, an "antipolitics." Under these conditions, women and men in the communist countries sometimes developed "an idealized notion of what the private sphere [in the West] stood for." After years of daily struggles with the burdens imposed by the double or triple day, many women came to question the drive of modern Western feminists to attain

greater economic independence and political presence. Their lives contrasted
sharply with the experience of those in Western nations for whom the "private
sphere" historically had represented the exclusion of women from equal employment and equal citizenship. They were keenly aware of the dangers, pointed out by
such Western observers as Jean Bethke Elshtain, in blurring the line between public and private life. In this worldview, it is essential to maintain the family as a
buffer against an authoritarian, interventionist state.[56]

Despite the difficulties faced by the worker-mothers of socialist countries fulfilling responsibilities for women's traditional duties at home, marriage continued
to play a vital role in most women's aspirations. This reflected not only the role of
marriage in obtaining material benefits such as scarce housing. Ekaterina Alexandrova has shown how legal, ideological, and administrative pressures combined to
create the presumption that persons who failed to marry were not "morally stable,"
and hence subject to various penalties. In her view, respectability required conformity with the desire of the government, a kind of "superpatriarchy," to control
the lives of its citizens better by using the family as "labor cell and especially as a
cell of forced social support."[57]

The socialist commitment to sex equality did not protect women from many
types of unequal treatment. While it was the norm for women to be employed full
time, they were also expected to subordinate their own career ambitions to their
husband's and to their children's needs, and many women agreed. For example, a
1988 survey in East Germany reported that only 3 percent of women and 1 percent
of men believed that fathers should delay their career advancement for parenthood,
while 37 percent and 43 percent, respectively, felt that mothers should do so. Women
in the Soviet Union and elsewhere in eastern Europe also suffered from inadequate
access to contraception; there was not a single factory producing contraceptives in
the fifteen Soviet Republics. With legal, or at least decriminalized, abortion often
the only means of reproductive control available, women in large numbers resorted
to abortion, frequently under punitive conditions.[58]

Pretensions to sex neutrality were also undermined by "positive discrimination" in employment, such as the Polish protective legislation that prohibited female
employment in ninety occupations in eighteen fields. On the other hand, working
women were not exempt from heavy labor in industry or agriculture. Women construction workers, even dairy workers and shop assistants, handled loads far exceed-
ing legal limits.

Communism's fall made clear many ambiguities and contradictions in the lives
of women in the newly independent states of eastern and central Europe. While
some gender roles had changed, old-fashioned ideas, officially dismissed as petty
bourgeois and retrograde, had survived amid sharply conflicting images of women.
Studying depictions of women and men in the communist iconography, historian
Eric Weitz found a complex scene.

Oppressed mothers, joyous and living mothers. Slender and active new women
of the 1920s, harassed and exploited workers, cool and elegant patrons of Parisian
shops, partisans wielding machine guns at the side of their proletarian brothers—
the cacophony of female imagery stands in sharp contrast to the stability of male

representations. They do not work together, collage-like, to reveal a movement that understood the complexities of women's lives and developed a comprehensive approach to reaching them in all of their social roles. Instead, they show Communist parties groping unsteadily, lurching from one image to another in the search for some way to appeal to women.[59]

With the fall of communism, state sponsorship of new roles for women disappeared, allowing the resurgence of traditional gender patterns and inequities.

In most former communist states, economic restructuring brought massive unemployment to workers of both sexes. The figures for most countries, however, show that women suffered by far the greatest losses. For example, by 1992 in the former East Germany, 62 percent of women compared to 38 percent of men were reported as unemployed. The number of East German women in upper managerial positions had plummeted from one hundred thousand in 1989 to under one thousand in 1992. According to a study of conditions in postcommunist Russia, 70 percent to 80 percent of the unemployed were women; among those with higher or specialized secondary education, the number rose to 75 percent. Female employees faced discrimination as "expensive labor" for whom support was required in newly privatized sectors of the economy. Not only was it cheaper to send women "back to the home," jobs denied women might become available to unemployed men, who also suffered from economic restructuring. It was now acceptable to discriminate openly, as for example in the ad "Wanted: Engineer (Male)."[60]

The renewed emphasis on women's "purely womanly mission," to use a phrase advanced by Mikhail Gorbachev in his book on "new thinking," coexists with a resurgence of traffic in women for purposes of commercialized sex. Losses of employment for women in professional and service areas were offset partially by growth in previously suppressed types of work. The production of pornography and prostitution flourished anew, and both the demand for and supply of sex workers multiplied. In the Czech Republic, prostitutes reported that they could "earn in one night more than their mothers earn in a whole month in the factory." Along with democratic ideals, a free-market economy brought "degrading, commercialized images of the female that reinforce the widespread devaluation of women," states one historian. The situation was so desperate that growing numbers of eastern European women sold sex on the streets of Istanbul and Ederne.[61]

While asserting that the democratization of Soviet society was "impossible without enhancing the role of women," Gorbachev, his supporters, and his successors have all failed to develop programs geared to women's needs. Beauty contests, a new preoccupation with glamour, and a mushrooming "beauty market" that emphasizes a compliant, sexualized femininity have replaced Soviet-style portrayals of heroic women workers. Sexual liberation, reminiscent of the 1960s and 1970s in western Europe and the United States, is accompanied by images and attitudes that denigrate women and support male domination.[62]

The resurgent "cult of motherhood" has not been accompanied by concern for improving the deteriorating status or living conditions of women. Although women were active in the dissent movements that preceded communism's collapse, for example constituting 50 percent of the membership of Solidarity (which was founded in Poland in 1980 as the first independent trade union in a communist country), they were marginalized when Solidarity gained power. "When we were dissidents, the men needed us and treated us well," states the former Czech activist Jirina Siklova. After the transition, women tended to disappear from political prominence. The decline was most precipitous in Romania, where female parliamentary membership of 34.4 percent in 1985 fell to 5.5 percent in 1990, and in Albania, where their 29.2 percent share in 1986 (down from a peak of 33.3 percent in 1974) diminished to 2.8 percent in 1992. More generally, women's share in representation dropped from about one-third to under 10 percent.[63]

It is important to note that many women welcomed this surcease in their civic obligations. To the extent that "socialist equality" added burdens to people's lives, many women as well as men in the postcommunist period have rejected "equality" as a worthy goal. In the Soviet press of the transition period, "words such as emancipation, egalitarianism and equality were more and more frequently preceded by the adjective 'accursed.'" In Poland, the idea of women's rights is "met with enmity," states Peggy Watson, commenting on a 1994 survey of women in local government that found only 3 percent in favor of special organizations for women. Instead of eliciting new programs for women, the collapse of communism has allowed old patriarchal traditions to reemerge.[64]

Studying the impact of the transition on women in former communist countries, several observers point to a newly prominent discourse that tends to subordinate women's rights as citizens to the goals of nationalist movements. Accompanying state-supported policies to effect change in women's roles had stood the rigorous suppression of traditional religions and ardent nationalisms. At times the gap between socialist ideology and inherited attitudes and customs was so vast it had led to outbreaks of violence against women. In the Moslem lands of the Soviet Union in the 1920s, women had even been murdered by their male relatives for following Soviet urgings to unveil. Seventy years later, long-repressed resistance to gender transformation reemerged in central and eastern Europe, including Russia and the former Soviet Republics. When communist regimes collapsed and women confronted new threats to their economic and political participation as well as social welfare and reproductive rights, these losses in some instances were exacerbated by resurgent nationalisms. Drawing on maternalist images and pronatalist rhetoric, nationalist ideologies served to narrow women's options further. Yet, because of its contrast with the communist deployment of state power to coerce women to work outside the home and to take on new roles, a renascent "woman at home" image could be seen as "new and progressive." Ironically, advocacy of women's rights echoed discredited communist propaganda and seemed retrograde.

The reaction against communism also triggered attacks on women's reproductive freedom. Reversing years of legalized access in most communist countries (excluding the USSR between 1936 and 1966 and Romania after 1966), new laws were passed restricting abortion rights. In Poland, legislation adopted in 1993 limited abortion to instances where a woman's life or health was jeopardized and to pregnancies resulting from rape. In Romania, a revolutionary government that in 1989 took the opposite stance and abrogated the dictator Ceausescu's 1966 abortion proscription in favor of "absolute freedom" of abortion, later modified its position. In the Czech Republic abortion remains legal, but is now deterred by steep fees. In Slovenia and Croatia, abortion is portrayed as a "threat to the nation"; "a fetus is also Croat," declared a political party slogan.[65]

These changes did not go unheeded by advocates of women's rights. Indeed, the campaigns against abortion provoked new efforts to found women's organizations. In Poland, the battle over a proposal to criminalize abortion elicited widespread efforts to establish new women's groups. In 1992–93 the protest movement succeeded in obtaining a million and a half signatures calling for a national referendum on the issue. In Russia about 1993 and 1994, after medical insurance covering abortion was cut back and "right to life" posters appeared in abortion clinics, advocates of abortion rights made collective public health rather than the reproductive freedom of individuals the focus of debate. In Hungary the controversy over abortion became also an "argument in absentia with communism."[66]

Discussing women's roles and women's rights, observers in the west must take care to translate concepts across cultural borders, just as feminisms are difficult to interpret in a globalizing world. The recent history of women in eastern Europe is a case in point. It requires a different feminist sensitivity to varying relationships among public, political, and private aspects of life to understand the choices that women make in specific environments. Along with the restoration of capitalism and political pluralism has come a resurgence of traditional family norms and movements to shift authority that was assumed by the socialist state to individual men. And many women indeed have been eager to replace "socialized reproduction" with "the woman at home" model and a man who shares responsibility for the family.

These new trends must be interpreted in the context of a history of imposed state authority generally unknown in recent Europe outside the communist world. Yugoslavian journalist Slavenka Drakulic captured this conceptual gap in her report on a 1990 trip through Hungary, Czechoslovakia, Poland, East Germany, and Bulgaria. Declaring that "women's lives . . . say as much about politics as no end of theoretical political analysis," she illustrates with tales of daily life endured without the simple necessities taken for granted by women in the West. "After all these years, communism has not been able to produce a simple sanitary napkin, a bare necessity for women. So much for its economy and its so-called emancipation, too." Few Western women can imagine the use and reuse of rags to accommodate their monthly periods. Drakulic highlights the vast gap between Western feminists and the women whose lives she describes by her response to a request she received to write about how feminists choose to contribute to public discourse in eastern Europe from the perspective of critical theory. Shocked at the naiveté of her interrogator, Drakulic wrote, "What does she mean? There is hardly any public discourse."[67]

Public space and civic society, concepts used by liberal feminist political analysts in assessing the status of women, have little explanatory power in a context where men and women both have been deprived of meaningful participation in politics, and private space scarcely exists due to housing shortages. Ironically, some strands of Western feminism share with communism a dubious record of denigrating the realm of private life, the home, and family. State-supported "feminism" like state socialism came to be resisted by many women who lived under communism. Democratization has not been gender-neutral and women have lost disproportionately in employment and political representation, while also suffering especially from cutbacks in public services vital to support their multiple roles. Yet, they should not be viewed as victims, either. They remain potential architects of their world, responding to the challenges of the 1990s and contributing richly different perspectives to the stories of women and social change in Europe.

NOTES

1. Louise A. Tilly and Joan W. Scott, *Women, Work, and Family* (New York: Holt Rinehart Winston, 1978); Ann Douglas, *The Feminization of American Culture* (New York: Avon, 1977).

2. See Jo Burr Mardagant, *Madame le Professeur: Women Educators in the Third Republic* (Princeton: Princeton University Press, 1990).

3. Susan Bachrach, *Dames Employées: The Feminization of Postal Work in Nineteenth-Century France* (New York: Haworth Press, 1984), pp. 61, 119 n. 19; Persis Hunt, "Teachers and Workers: Problems of Feminist Organizing in the Early Third Republic," *Third Republic/Troisième République*, nos. 3–4 (1977): 168–204; James F. McMillan, *Housewife or Harlot: The Place of Women in French Society, 1870–1940* (New York: St. Martin's Press, 1981), p. 55; Linda L. Clark, *Schooling the Daughters of Marianne* (Albany, N.Y.: State University of New York Press, 1984), p. 73; Lee Holcombe, *Victorian Ladies at Work: Middle-Class Working Women in England and Wales, 1850–1914* (Hamden, Conn.: Archon, 1973), p. 46.

4. Susan Strasser, *Never Done: A History of American Housework* (New York: Pantheon, 1982), pp. 67–84; Rosalind H. Williams, *Dream Worlds: Mass Consumption in Late Nineteenth-Century France* (Berkeley: University of California Press, 1982), pp. 58, 65.

5. John E. Knodel, *The Decline of Fertility in Germany, 1871–1939* (Princeton: Princeton University Press, 1974), pp. 246–247; Angus McLaren, *Birth Control in Nineteenth-Century England* (New York: Holmes and Meier, 1978), p. 11; Karen Offen, "Depopulation, Nationalism, and Feminism in Fin-de-Siècle France," *American Historical Review* 89, no. 3 (June 1984):649–652. On "contraceptive revolution," Nadine Lefaucheur, "Maternity, Family, and the State," in Françoise Thébaud, ed., *Toward a Cultural Identity in the Twentieth Century*, vol. V of Georges Duby and Michelle Perrot, eds., *A History of Women in the West* (Cambridge: Belknap Press of the Harvard University Press, 1994), p. 441. On fertility rates, Daniele Meulders, Robert Plasman, and Valerie Vander Stricht, *Position of Women on the Labour Market in the European Community* (Aldershot, Eng. and Brookfield, Vt.: Dartmouth, 1993), p. 22.

6. Jill Liddington and Jill Norris, *One Hand Tied Behind Us: The Rise of the Women's Suffrage Movement* (London: Virago, 1978), pp. 136–137; Amy Hackett, "The German Women's Movement and Suffrage, 1890–1914: A Study of National Feminism," in Robert J. Bezucha, ed., *Modern European Social History* (Lexington, Mass.: D. C. Heath, 1972), pp. 354–379; Steven C. Hause with Anne R. Kenney, *Women's Suffrage and Social Politics in the French Third Republic* (Princeton: Princeton University Press, 1984); Eleanor Flexner, *Century of Struggle: The Woman's Rights Movement in the United States* (Cambridge: Belknap Press of Harvard University Press, 1959); Ellen Carol Dubois, *Feminism and Suffrage: The Emergence of an Independent Women's Movement in America 1848–1869* (Ithaca, N.Y.: Cornell University Press, 1978).

7. Leila J. Rupp, *Worlds of Women: The Making of an International Women's Movement* (Princeton: Princeton University Press, 1997), quotation on p. 75; see also pp. 34, 220, 224–225.

8. Marilyn J. Boxer and Jean H. Quataert, eds., *Socialist Women: European Socialist Feminism in the Nineteenth and Early Twentieth Centuries* (New York: Elsevier, 1978); Jean H. Quataert, *Reluctant Feminists in German Social Democracy 1885–1917* (Princeton: Princeton University Press, 1979); Dolores Hayden, *The Grand Domestic Revolution: A History of Feminist Designs for American Homes, Neighborhoods and Cities* (Cambridge: MIT Press, 1981).

9. Temma Kaplan, "On the Socialist Origins of International Women's Day," *Feminist Studies* 11, no. 1 (Spring 1985): 163–171.

10. Jennifer G. Schirmer, *The Limits of Reform: Women, Capital, and Welfare* (Cambridge, Mass.: Schenkman, 1982); Elizabeth Wilson, *Women and the Welfare State* (London: Tavistock, 1977).

11. Ann-Sofie Ohlander, "The Invisible Child? The Struggle for a Social Democratic Family Policy in Sweden, 1900–1960s," in Gisela Bock and Pat Thane, eds., *Maternity and Gender Policies: Women and the Rise of the European Welfare States, 1850s–1950s* (London and New York: Routledge, 1994), pp. 60–72.

12. Seth Koven and Sonya Michel, "Introduction: Mother Worlds," in id., eds., *Mothers of the New World: Maternalist Politics and the Origins of Welfare States* (New York: Routledge, 1993), pp. 1–42, quotation on p. 5.

13. Cheri Register, "Motherhood at Center: Ellen Key's Social Vision," *Women's Studies International Forum* 5, no. 6 (1982): 599–610.

14. Richard J. Evans, *The Feminist Movement in Germany 1894–1933* (London: Sage, 1976), pp. 120–130, 178–182; McLaren, *Birth Control*, pp. 141–154, 188.

15. C.W. Saleeby, *Parenthood and Race Culture* (1909), quoted in Anna Davin, "Imperialism and Motherhood," *History Workshop: A Journal of Socialist Historians* 5 (spring 1978): 9–65, quotation on p. 29.

16. Gisela Bock, "Racism and Sexism in Nazi Germany: Motherhood, Compulsory Sterilization, and the State," in Renate Bridenthal, Atina Grossmann, and Marion Kaplan, eds., *When Biology Became Destiny: Women in Weimar and Nazi Germany* (New York: Monthly Review Press, 1984), pp. 271–296, quotations on pp. 279, 288. It is not well known that this German law was said to be influenced by a California law, developed in the 1920s. See Stefan Kuhl, *The Nazi Connection: Eugenics, American Racism, and German National Socialism* (New York: Oxford University Press, 1994), p. 39.

17. Antoinette Burton, "Rule of Thumb: British History and 'Imperial Culture' in Nineteenth- and Twentieth-Century Britain," *Women's History Review* 3, no. 4 (1994): 483–500, quotation on p. 484.

18. Inderpal Grewal, *Home and Harem: Nation, Gender, Empire, and the Cultures of Travel* (Durham, N.C.: Duke University Press, 1996), p. 4; Burton, Ch. 7 above.

19. Alice L. Conklin, "Redefining 'Frenchness': Citizenship, Race Regeneration, and Imperial Motherhood in France and West Africa, 1914–40," in Julia Clancy-Smith and Frances Gouda, eds., *Domesticating the Empire: Race, Gender, and Family Life in French and Dutch Colonialism* (Charlottesville, Va.: University Press of Virginia, 1998), pp. 65–83.

20. For an examination of the theoretical and political implications of work dealing with women and colonialism, see Jane Haggis, "White Women and Colonialism: Towards a Non-recuperative History," in Clare Midgley, ed., *Gender and Imperialism* (Manchester and New York: Manchester University Press, 1998), pp. 45–75. On emigration, Julia Bush, "'The Right Sort of Woman': Female Emigrators and Emigration to the British Empire, 1890–1910," *Women's History Review* 3, no. 3 (1994): 385–409, quotations on pp. 384, 397.

21. On Besant, Kumari Jayawardena, *The White Woman's Other Burden: Western Women and South Asia during British Rule* (New York: Routlege, 1995), pp. 123–34; on

Auclert, Julia Clancy-Smith, "Islam, Gender, and Identities in the Making of French Algeria, 1830–1962," in id. and Gouda, *Domesticating Empire*, pp. 154–174, especially pp. 167–172, quotation on p. 170. See also Steven C. Hause, *Hubertine Auclert: The French Suffragette* (New Haven: Yale University Press, 1987), pp. 132–148.

22.   Jayawardena, *White Woman's Other Burden.*

23.   Grewal, *Home and Harem,* pp. 53–55, quotations pp. 53, 54.

24.   Diane Bell, "Women's Business is Hard Work: Central Australian Aboriginal Women's Love Rituals," *Signs* 7, no. 2 (1981): 314–337.

25.   Fritz Stern, *The Politics of Cultural Despair: A Study in the Rise of the Germanic Ideology* (New York: Doubleday, 1965), pp. 256–257.

26.   Rupp, *Worlds of Women,* p. 26.

27.   Susan Groag Bell and Karen M. Offen, eds., *Women, the Family, and Freedom: The Debate in Documents,* II: 1880–1950 (Stanford: Stanford University Press, 1983), pp. 271–272.

28.   Barbara Evans Clements, "Working-Class and Peasant Women in the Russian Revolution, 1917–1923," *Signs* 8, no. 2 (1982): 215–235.

29.   Thomas Laqueur, *The Making of Sex: Body and Gender from the Greeks to Freud* (Cambridge: Harvard University Press, 1990); see also Michel Foucault, *The History of Sexuality,* 2 vols. (New York: Vintage, 1980).

30.   For Freud, see "Some Psychical Consequences of the Anatomical Distinction between the Sexes," excerpted in Bell and Offen, *Women, the Family, and Freedom,* II, pp. 330–334; for Horney, "The Flight from Womanhood: The Masculinity Complex in Women as Viewed by Men and Women," *International Journal of Psycho-Analysis* 7, pts. 3–4 (July–October 1926), in ibid., pp. 334–338.

31.   See e.g., Judith Butler, *Gender Trouble: Feminism and the Subversion of Identity* (New York: Routledge, 1990).

32.   In Leslie Fishbein, "The Failure of Feminism in Greenwich Village before World War I," *Women's Studies* 9, no. 2 (1982): 281

33.   Mary Louise Roberts, *Civilization without Sexes: Reconstructing Gender in Postwar France, 1917–1927* (Chicago: University of Chicago Press, 1994).

34.   Ibid., p. 67.

35.   Ibid., pp. 20, 63.

36.   Ibid., pp. 99, 102, 210–211.

37.   McMillan, *Housewife or Harlot,* pp. 191–192.

38.   Bell and Offen, *Women, Family, Freedom,* II, p. 310.

39.   Quoted by Ute Frevert, *Women in German History: From Bourgeois Emancipation to Sexual Liberation,* trans. Stuart McKinnon-Evans with Terry Bond and Barbara Norden (New York: Berg, 1990), p. 207.

40.   See e.g., Atina Grossmann, "Feminist Debates about Women and National Socialism," *Gender and History* 3, no. 3 (Autumn 1991): 350–358.

41.   Renate Bridenthal, "Beyond 'Kinder, Küche, Kirche': Weimar Women at Work," *Central European History* VI, no. 2 (June 1973): 148–166; Tim Mason, "Women in Germany, 1925–1940: Family, Welfare and Work," Parts I and II, *History Workshop* (Spring 1976 and Autumn 1976), pp. 74–113; pp. 5–32.

42.   Gisela Bock, "Racism and Sexism in Nazi Germany: Motherhood, Compulsory Sterilization, and the State," *Signs* 8, no. 3 (1983): 400–421; Renate Bridenthal, Atina Grossmann and Marion Kaplan, eds., *When Biology Became Destiny: Women in Weimar and Nazi Germany* (New York: Monthly Review Press, 1984).

43.   Victoria de Grazia, *How Fascism Ruled Women: Italy, 1922–1945* (Berkeley: University of California Press, 1992), pp. 281–283.

44. Ibid., pp. 278–288.

45. Detlev J. K. Peukert, *Inside Nazi Germany: Conformity, Opposition and Racism in Everyday Life,* trans. Richard Deveson (New Haven: Yale University Press, 1987).

46. In Shari Steiner, *The Female Factor: A Study of Women in Five Western European Societies* (New York: G. P. Putnam's Sons, 1977), p. 245.

47. Sondra R. Herman, "Alva Myrdal and Swedish Reform, 1929–1956," *Journal of Women's History* 4. no. 2 (Fall 1992): 82–112, quotations on p. 82.

48. Leila J. Rupp, *Mobilizing Women for War: German and American Propaganda, 1939–1945* (Princeton: Princeton University Press, 1978), p. 181; Maureen Honey, "The Working-Class Woman and Recruitment Propaganda during World War II: Class Differences in the Portrayal of War Work," *Signs* 8, no. 4 (1983): 672–687.

49. Elizabeth Heinemann, "The Hour of the Woman: Memories of Germany's 'Crisis Years' and the West German National Identity," *American Historical Review* 101, no. 2 (April 1996): 354–395; Elizabeth H. Tobin and Jennifer Gibson, "The Meanings of Labor: East German Women's Work in the Transition from Nazism to Communism," *Central European History* 28, no. 3 (1995): 301–342; Mary Fulbrook, *The Divided Nation: A History of Germany, 1918–1990* (New York: Oxford University Press, 1992).

50. On "dominant model," Meulders, Plasman, Stricht, *Position of Women,* p. 22.

51. On "educational explosion," Rose-Marie LaGrave, "A Supervised Emancipation," trans. Arthur Goldhammer, in Thébaud, ed., *Toward a Cultural Identity,* p. 470; on correlation between education and employment, Meulders, Plasman, Stricht, *Position of Women,* p. 20.

52. Gail Warshofsky Lapidus, ed., *Women, Work, and Family in the Soviet Union* (Armonk, N.Y.: M. E. Sharpe, 1982); "Comparative International Statistics," No. 1519, *Statistical Abstract of the United States* (Washington, 1984), p. 872.

53. LaGrave, "Supervised Emancipation," p. 468.

54. Ibid., pp. 481–488; Frevert, *Women in German History,* p. 300; Liisa Rantalaiho and Raija Julkunen, "Socioeconomic Restructuring and Crisis in Gender Contracts," *Journal of Women's History* 5, no. 3 (Winter 1994): 11–29, quotation on p. 14; and Anne-Wil K. Harzing, "The Labour-Market Position of Women from Ethnic Minorities: A Comparison of Four European Countries," in Anneke Van Doorne-Huiskes, Jacques Van Hoof, and Ellie Roelofs, eds., *Women and the European Labour Markets* (Heerlen, The Netherlands: Paul Chapman Publishing, 1995), pp. 53–71.

55. Gail Warshofsky Lapidus, *Women in Soviet Society: Equality, Development, and Social Change* (Berkeley: University of California Press, 1978), quotations on pp. 123, 124; on "triple burden," Barbara Einhorn, *Cinderella Goes to Market: Citizenship, Gender and Women's Movements in East Central Europe* (London and New York: Verso, 1993), p. 32.

56. Ibid., pp. 6–7. For Elshtain, see *Public Man, Private Woman: Women in Social and Political Thought* (Princeton: Princeton University Press, 1981).

57. In 1990, the Budapest housing council had a waiting list of 70,000 for 7,000 flats; in Warsaw, the wait was estimated to be 20 to 30 years; Einhorn, *Cinderella,* p. 57. On pressures to marry, Alexandrova, "Why Soviet Women Want to Get Married," p. 39, in Tatyana Mamonova, *Women and Russia: Feminist Writings from the Soviet Union* (Boston: Beacon Press, 1984), pp. 31–50, quotations on pp. 49, 50.

58. For survey, Einhorn, *Cinderella,* p. 29; on abortion, Michele Rivkin-Fish, "Post-Communist Transformations and Abortion Politics: Reflections on Feminist Strategies and 'Choice,'" *Critical Matrix* 8, no. 2 (1994), 103.

59. Eric D. Weitz, "The Heroic Man and the Ever-Changing Woman: Gender and Politics in European Communism, 1917–1950," in Laura L. Frader and Sonya O. Rose, eds.,

Gender and Class in Modern Europe (Ithaca, N.Y.: Cornell University Press, 1996), pp. 311–352, quotation on pp. 314–315.

60. On unemployment in former East Germany, Marilyn Rueschemeyer, "Women in the Politics of Eastern Germany: The Dilemmas of Unification," in id., ed., *Women in the Politics of Post-Communist Eastern Europe* (Armonk, N.Y.: M. E. Sharpe, 1994), pp. 87–116, especially p. 95; and Myra Marx Ferree, "German Unification and Feminist Identity," in Joan W. Scott, Cora Kaplan, and Debra Keates, eds., *Transitions, Environments, Translations: Feminisms in International Politics* (New York: Routledge, 1997), pp. 46–55, especially p. 47. On Russia, Anastasia Posadskaya, "A Feminist Critique of Policy, Legislation and Social Consciousness in Post-socialist Russia," in id. et al., eds., *Women in Russia: A New Era in Russian Feminism*, trans. Kate Clark (London and New York: Verso, 1994), pp. 164–182, especially p. 170. On expensive labor, Bridger, Kay, and Pinnick, *No More Heroines?*, p. 5.

61. Mikhail S. Gorbachev, *Perestroika: New Thinking for Our Country and the World* (London: Collins, 1987), p. 117. After praising the advances made by women and applauding their contributions in nontraditional roles to the development of the Soviet Union and to the defeat of fascism, Gorbachev states, "We failed to pay attention to women's specific rights and needs arising from their role as mother and home-maker." On prostitutes, Hana Havelkova, "Transitory and Persistent Differences: Feminism East and West," in Scott, Kaplan, and Keates, eds., *Transitions, Environments, Translations*, pp. 56–62, quotation on p. 57. On degrading images, Barbara Evans Clements, "Current Developments in the Study of Women in Russia," *Journal of Women's History* 10, no. 1 (Spring 1998): 192–197, quotation on p. 196.

62. Olga Lipovskaya, "The Mythology of Womanhood in Contemporary 'Soviet' Culture," in Posadskaya et al., eds., *Women in Russia*, pp. 123–134, quotation on p. 127.

63. Ruth Rosen, "'Male Democracies, Female Dissidents," *Tikkun* 5, no 6 (1990): 101, quoted by Einhorn, *Cinderella*, p. 148. See Einhorn, "Where Have All the Women Gone? Politics and Participation," Ch. 5 in *Cinderella*. Also Fatos Tarifa, "Disappearing from Politics: Social Change and Women in Albania," in Rueschemeyer, ed., *Women in . . . Postcommunist Eastern Europe*, pp. 133–151, figures on p. 148. See also Susan Gal, "Gender in the Post-Soviet Transition: The Abortion Debate in Hungary," *East European Politics and Societies* 8, no. 2 (Spring 1994): 256–286; Einhorn, *Cinderella*, pp. 151 and 177 n. 11; and Elizabeth Waters and Anastasia Posadskaya, "Democracy without Women Is No Democracy: Women's Struggles in Postcommunist Russia," which includes an interview with Posadskaya in June 1994, in Amrita Basu, ed., *The Challenge of Local Feminisms: Women's Movements in Global Perspective* (Boulder, Colo.: Westview Press, 1995), pp. 351–373. Women's representation in the Russian Duma dropped from 33.3 percent to 5.6 percent between the late 1970s and 1991; ibid., p. 369.

64. On relief from civic burden, see Wolchik, "Women and the Politics of Transition in the Czech and Slovak Republics," in Rueschemeyer, ed., *Women in . . . Postcommunist Eastern Europe*, p. 16; Mary Ellen Fischer and Doina Pasca Harsanyi, "From Tradition and Ideology to Elections and Competition: The Changing Status of Women in Romanian Politics," in ibid., pp. 201–233, especially p. 220; and Einhorn, *Cinderella*, p. 167. On rejection of "equality," see ibid., p. 168 and Bridger, Kay, and Pinnick, *No More Heroines?*, p. 36. For survey, Peggy Watson, "Civil Society and the Politics of Difference in Eastern Europe," in Scott, Kaplan, and Keates, eds., *Transitions*, pp. 21–29, especially p. 22.

65. On Polish legislation, Wanda Nowicka, "Two Steps Back: Poland's New Abortion Law," *Journal of Women's History* 5, no. 3 (Winter 1994): 151–155. On Romania,

Doina Pasca Harsanyi, "Romania's Women," *Journal of Women's History* 5, no. 3 (Winter 1994): 30–54, especially p. 47. On Czech Republic, Elzbieta Matynia, "Finding a Voice: Women in Postcommunist Central Europe," in Amrita Basu, ed., *Challenge of Local Feminisms,* pp. 374–404, especially p. 387. On Croatia, Renata Salech, "The Postsocialist Moral Majority," in Scott, Kaplan, and Keates, eds., *Transitions,* pp. 79–97, quotation on p. 85.

66. On petition, Matynia, "Finding a Voice," pp. 398–399; on Russia, Rivkin-Fish, "Post-Communist Transformations," pp. 102, 119–120; and Waters and Posadskaya, "Democracy without Women," especially p. 370; on Hungary, Gal, "Gender in the Post-Soviet Transition," p. 261.

67. Slavenka Drakulic, *How We Survived Communism and Even Laughed* (New York: W.W. Norton, 1991), pp. 30, 124–125, 127. In 1991 she stated that the title of her book "feels wrong"; p. xvii.

CHAPTER ELEVEN

Prostitution, Differentiation, and the World Economy: Nairobi, 1899–1939

Luise White

With European industrialization, imperialism, and the rush for colonies in the second half of the nineteenth century, the focus of Western history must necessarily broaden to areas outside of Europe. Luise White takes us to Kenya, a British colony in East Africa, in the first third of the twentieth century. The rural population was already differentiated into "rich and poor and everything in between" and was facing continuous pressures as a result of increased white settlements, crop failures, cattle diseases, and the introduction of cash crops into the countryside. Prostitution in Nairobi was one response by daughters to a sudden decline in the economic fortunes of their wealthy families. The form it took was determined by economic needs. One of White's most innovative points is that sexuality is not just a "personal and private matter," but can be shaped by forces other than personal desire. It is best described "by the language of family and kin." Prostitutes worked as daughters, accumulating for their fathers what they had been unable to do through the more traditional method of marriage. Prostitution, therefore, is not marginal or aberrant, but economically rational behavior, as the Frenchman Dr. Louis Villermé recognized in his 1847–48 study, when he labeled it "the fifth quarter" of women's day.

White's pathfinding study rests on oral interviews. Oral history is a rewarding approach for uncovering contemporary women's experiences, a corrective for biases and omissions in written texts. As White has noted elsewhere, "people are excellent chroniclers of their immediate past, however unheroic, illegal, or unpleasant that past might have been." She worked as well with more traditional historical documents in the archive of the colonial office, using fruitfully the records of the Medical Department, heir to records of the Contagious Diseases Act, that dealt with medical regulation of prostitution and housing.

We tend to think that sexual relations are personal and private matters. While we may read dozens of books advising us on how to achieve intimacy, we generally believe that decisions about who sleeps with whom, where, for how long, and under what kinds of encouragement are the results of passions so personal that they cannot be studied systematically. We believe this partly because we see matters such as sexual attraction and choosing a partner as timeless qualities, where choice is personal, so personal as to make any serious inquiry difficult, if not pointless. But how do we know what is personal and what is not? Perhaps if we look at those sexual relations that are the most furtive—conducted in alleys and doorways not because either party likes it better that way, but because those are the only spaces available for such acts—we can see people brought together by forces other than their personal desires. Perhaps we can begin to observe people who occasionally sleep together because of cattle diseases, falling food crop prices, and increased cash crop production.

In this essay I want to look at two forms of prostitution that developed in Nairobi, Kenya between 1899 and 1939. Both forms, or ways for women to conduct the sale of sexual access to themselves, emphasized brief sexual relations with customers rather than night-long fictions of matrimonial bliss, and both forms were known for the aggressiveness with which women sought their customers. All the labor forms, in Nairobi and presumably elsewhere, were determined by specific crises in rural society and the women's relationship to housing in the town. In Kenya there is no evidence, oral or written, of anything that could be even vaguely construed as pimping: when women prostitute themselves, they retain all their earnings. How a woman prostitutes herself—with which form—indicates the urgency with which she requires money. In Kenya the women who walked the streets (*watembezi* in Swahili, widely spoken in Nairobi) were precisely those women who took the pennies from sex conducted in doorways back to the stunted agricultural economies of East Africa, and enabled their families to recoup some of the losses the world economy had forced upon them. It was the women who quietly waited in their rooms for men to come to them (*malaya* in Swahili), the ones who provided the widest range of domestic services, including cooked food and bath water, and had the most discreet and circumspect of relationships, who accumulated capital for themselves, and most definitely not for their families.

Nairobi was founded in 1899 at the foot of the fertile highlands that were to be taken over by white settlers. Built around a swamp where no one had lived before, everyone who came there, black or white, female or male, was a migrant of some sort. Europeans came to settle because Kenya offered more opportunities than they might otherwise inherit in their homes; African men came because their inheritance was substantially delayed (by the untimely combination of natural disaster and European conquest), and because they were forced to do so. From 1902, a tax was levied on married men, payable in coin that could most easily be obtained by working for Europeans. Young African men were observed to work to pay their fathers' taxes (polygamous men had higher tax rates), and then work to enhance their own inheritance. They left the wage labor force once they married, and to secure a still larger supply of male laborers, in 1910 a tax was introduced on all males over sixteen.

Why did women come to Nairobi, and why did they become prostitutes? We know that they became prostitutes because there were simply no jobs for women then or in the next forty years. Some came to set themselves up as independent heads of households. "In those days," said one widow, "I didn't get another husband; there was another way to make a living then." Another woman said, "At home, what could I do? Grow crops for my husband and my father. In Nairobi, I could earn my own money, for myself." But most women came to help their families. By the end of the nineteenth century those families were primarily agriculturalists already differentiated into rich and poor and everything in between. In almost all those families women and livestock were the traditional elements of wealth, exchange, reproduction, and, of course, status. They could be exchanged for each other and they could reproduce more like themselves. They were integral elements in the cycle of family formation and they were at the same time investments. Thus, men with many wives could produce more daughters and grain with which to exchange for livestock, and young men would work for their fathers so that they would eventually be given the livestock with which to wed. The most valuable livestock was cattle, then sheep, then goats.

In the 1890s, a devastating series of cattle epidemics swept through Eastern Africa. By 1897, central Kenya was struck by drought, famine, and smallpox. It had the effect of turning the world (and its values) inside out—with as many as 60 percent of all the local cattle dead, famine devalued the remaining cattle and, indeed, everything but foodstuffs. Agriculturalists dominated, and men with many wives could find no one to marry their daughters and thus replenish their herds. Virtually an entire generation of wealthy men faced an end to their way of life. All the available evidence points to the fact that these men's dwindling status and wealth was restored and restocked by their daughters' prostitution. These women already knew that permanent sexual access to them had an exchange value; they simply transformed the location and control of the work so that they sold repeated sexual access to themselves to many men. Thus, as early as 1899 daughters of the hardest hit pastoralist people, by all accounts the Masai, were observed to be the "loose women" in Kenya's rudimentary townships, and by 1909 some three hundred Masai *watembezi* prostitutes were arrested in Nairobi.

How do we know that these women were the daughters of wealthy fathers? How do we know they were not impoverished young women who sought through prostitution to better their own lives? First of all, we know that in the years before World War I, prostitutes earned roughly between four and eight times what male wage-earners did (partly due to the low value of the currency at that time), so that any rapid gains accruing to the older generation would almost have to have come from prostitutes' earnings. Secondly, we know because these women, the *watembezi*, left prostitution once the requisite number of livestock were acquired. Those women who came from impoverished households also came to Nairobi, and the best evidence I have indicates they and they alone became *malaya* prostitutes.

The pre–World War I interaction of the colonial state, the Masai, and other pastoral peoples provides an excellent example of a sequence of destocking, prostitution, and livestock acquisition. Masai herds were decimated in the epidemics of the 1890s and their economy seriously undermined; Masai women seem to have been active in prostitution even before Nairobi was established, and in the early years of this century they were said to dominate Nairobi prostitution. Meanwhile, pastoral peoples in western Kenya, an area largely unaffected by the cattle epidemics, raided British installations (see Figure 6). The British led Masai soldiers in punitive expeditions against the Kipsigis and Nandi, and by 1905 it was esti-

Figure 6. East Africa in 1905.

mated that 55 percent of Nandi cattle had been taken to Nairobi. The Masai soldiers were paid in goats that they parlayed into cattle (at rates of about fifteen goats
per cow), just as prostitutes' profits were invested in livestock. In 1911, when Masai
herds were said to approach their nineteenth-century levels, there was a noticeable
Masai retreat from prostitution and wage labor. By 1907, however, colonial officials began to observe an increasing number of Kipsigis and Nandi women entering prostitution, replacing the Masai women and accosting men on settlers' farms
and on the streets of Nairobi. These women, too, were said to buy livestock with
their earnings, at rates that were at least double what the Masai had paid, as white
settlement brought about a demand for meat that slowly began to raise the value of
cattle. According to contemporary male authors, by 1909 Nandi women were "notorious" throughout Kenya and by 1913 "the most enlightened" Nandi were those
prostitutes who had returned home after a few years in Nairobi—presumably they
knew the most English and belonged to the wealthiest families.

What were these women doing? They were doing through prostitution what in
better times they would have done through marriage: stock their fathers' herd and

keep livestock values competitive. They had to restore their fathers' property—cattle, not daughters—to its earlier level of prestige. That they were doing this in the streets, in alleys, loudly, aggressively, testifies to the urgency with which monies were required. For despite how disrespectful the *watembezi* form looked, despite its emphasis on brief sexual encounters in less than sensual surroundings, the means of accumulation was anything but disorderly: it was aggressive and swift by design; it matched high risks with high profits. It would then seem that anything more than occasional *watembezi* prostitution was not caused by dire poverty; it was the response of relatively wealthy families to a sudden decrease in their wealth. Young women became streetwalkers not as a survival strategy, but to help their families maintain previous levels of differentiation—and most of these women did not just survive, they prospered.

During World War I prostitution in Nairobi changed. The *watembezi* form still dominated, indeed it took on a revitalized dimension in pursuit of British and South African troops during the war, but its practitioners tended to be long-term residents of Nairobi, not immigrants from newly impoverished societies. "It was extra money, we went to pick beans and had a man in secret; sometimes a woman would go . . . just for the men," said a teenage woman who had been born in Nairobi. World War I *watembezi* were on the whole older than the young women who had sought men on the streets and back alleys of the prewar city. Wartime *watembezi* earned large sums, but they saved their cash or bought urban real estate. They could not have bought cattle with their earnings had they wanted to, so successfully had pastoralist fathers and daughters managed to reconstruct and reestablish the value of their herds.

Unlike pastoralists, many East African cultivators prospered from the events of the 1890s and the coming of colonial rule. Not only were they able to sell grain at exceptionally high rates of exchange to other Africans, they fed the European expansion into East Africa as well. Until World War I, African agriculturalists dominated local and export markets, and many of the Kikuyu farmers in central Kenya became wealthy. Until the ravages of military conscription during World War I and the rapidly increased white settlement after the war, the Kikuyu had sent relatively few sons into wage labor and fewer daughters into prostitution. The combined weight of white farmers' land-grabbing, and legislation introduced to prevent further white farmers' labor shortages, reduced many Kikuyu farmers to resident laborer status on European farms. Nevertheless, many Kikuyu "squatters" and cultivators on their own farms were able to produce and sell surplus crops. By the mid-1920s the increased production of maize and rice in other parts of the country began to erode the profits Kikuyu farmers could get for potatoes and millet in Nairobi. The price of potatoes, for example, had increased by 57 percent between 1924 and 1928 and the prices of other Kikuyu crops had risen as well: fewer people bought them. By 1928, both Kikuyu chiefs and *malaya* prostitutes in Nairobi complained about married Kikuyu women coming to town as if they were selling vegetables, but prostituting themselves with workingmen in the alleys of the African areas, and returning to their homes before dark. It seems very likely that these Kikuyu *watembezi* were not acting out of any immorality or personal insecurities; they were engaging in prostitution so that they could maintain the standard of living that only a few years before they had obtained solely through the sale of their farm produce. This *watembezi* prostitution was not about any preference for sex conducted in doorways and bushes, but about keeping a standard of living buoyant in the face of declining food profits.

Cattle diseases and state-sponsored destocking do not qualify as an incursion of the world economy into peoples' private lives. Rising crop prices are facts of life for farmers all over the world, and are not a unique characteristic of colonized peoples. To see how the world economy influences what we think of as intimate behavior, we have to look at those crops introduced specifically by colonial powers for the specific reason of making their colonies pay off: cash crops. Coffee, tea, cotton, sugar, and tobacco are a few examples. Among critics of imperialism, cash crops have an importance almost unmatched by any other colonial introduction: they are almost never edible crops; they take up arable land that might be better used for food crops; they are often produced on plantations and concentrate local labor in such a way as to remove people from food production. They are often produced at gunpoint. This list could go on for pages, but the most significant thing about cash crops is that they draw producers into a worldwide system of supply and profit and loss that is determined by conditions far outside the country producing the coffee, tea, or sugar. Unlike mining—the wholesale extraction of a country's wealth—cash crop production pits various countries' producers against each other. Coffee growers in Kenya do not compete with each other, they compete with coffee growers in Brazil and Colombia and Sumatra. The amount they pay their workers in each of these countries has nothing to do with how hard these men and women work; it has to do with the competitive value of their coffee crop relative to that of coffees produced thousands of miles away under different conditions. The only real influence local producers have on profit is quantity, but this can backfire when demand drops. In most colonies it was a crime for Africans to uproot their cash crops when prices were low and plant food crops instead. Some scholars have argued that cash crop production enabled Africans to resist the depredations of wage labor, but this argument fails to tell us what happens when the cash crop is not wanted, or is overproduced, or is deemed obsolete by the production of synthetics. The introduction of cash crops made African cultivators as dependent on the health and stability of world markets as they were on the rainfall.

It is this kind of dependence that determines not only who becomes a prostitute, but the duration of the services prostitutes provide. The process does not happen overnight, but it does happen with great clarity. In 1903 the German colonizers of what was to become Tanganyika (when it was handed over to the British at the end of World War I) introduced coffee to the Haya people on the western shore of Lake Victoria, a thousand kilometers (six hundred miles) from the sea. They did not concentrate coffee in plantations, but gave some to every large farm. Before the War, coffee did well in the fertile hills of Bukoba, but it was not until the worldwide boom of the 1920s that Haya producers began to see spectacular profits. By the mid-1920s the wealthier Haya were almost heady with success; they hired laborers from the neighboring Belgian colonies to come pick their coffee and "squat" on their land, and as Christians they ceased exchanging their daughters for livestock and requested and received a cash bride-price, which by about 1927 was the equivalent of $175 or more. Unlike many African peoples, the Haya permitted divorce, and fathers returned the bride-price in full. Thus, in 1930 when the world price of coffee dropped a staggering 90 percent, Haya producers were in trouble; it was not even worth their while to ship their produce to the coast, but they had laborers living on their farms who demanded payment nonetheless. Although the problem lay in cash crop production, the solution was found in women. Young wives were divorced and fathers repaid the bride-price, shifting the problem back on themselves—a generation of fathers now had to come up with cash to repay their own increasing debts and refurbish the foundations of a sagging cash crop economy. How the decision to solve this problem was made within individual households is not known, but within two or three years Haya women in their early twenties appeared in large numbers on the streets of Kampala (Uganda), Dar es Salaam (Tanganyika), and Nairobi.

Haya women did not walk in the streets in these towns; instead they rented rooms in the African areas and sat outside their houses and solicited men from there. This was called the *Wazi-Wazi* form, from a slang term for Haya common in Nairobi. Haya women scandalized the more sedate and circumspect prostitutes of these areas, who saw such open solicitation and aggressive behavior as a threat to their respectability and their profits. Haya women were known for shouting out their prices to men, and they took these men into the four-by-eight foot rooms they shared with other Haya immigrants for brief sexual encounters, for which they received just about 17 percent of the world price of raw coffee beans. Between 1930 and 1935 the world price for a thirty-five-pound bag of coffee beans varied between three and seven shillings. In those same years, *Wazi-Wazi* prostitutes in Nairobi charged fifty cents—one half of one shilling—for sexual intercourse. *Malaya* women were justifiably upset since this had the overall effect of lowering the price for brief sexual relations for all prostitutes, at a time when most *malaya* prostitutes earned perhaps a third more than male laborers did. *Wazi-Wazi* prostitutes were also said to fight with the men who refused to pay them and call on their neighbors for help—practices unheard of by both *malaya* and *watembezi* women in 1930s Nairobi. An old woman born near Nairobi in about 1900 said that the biggest change she observed in her lifetime was that after the mid-1930s "women beat up men." According to a younger *malaya* woman, cash was so important to a Haya woman that she "would risk her blood to get her money." Indeed, it was so important to Haya women that they were reputed to send money home each week or month, and if a Haya woman died in Nairobi her friends would take her body and her money the hundreds of miles back to Bukoba. Why did Haya women do all this? Clearly because the advantages and opportunities of being a daughter of a well-to-do coffee-growing family outweighed the disadvantages of being a prostitute in Nairobi.

How did the colonial state respond to streetwalkers and *Wazi-Wazi* women? While it was not in the interests of public order that women be allowed to call out a price to men as they returned from work, there were few arrests of *watembezi* prostitutes in colonial Nairobi, and none of Haya women. More than any other kind of political entity, colonial states do not act with one voice, let alone motivation; they mediate between different and competing interests—the government at home, the settlers it must protect, the African leaders who make ruling easier, and the Africans who must be made to work in colonial enterprises, but in ways that do not antagonize any of the groups above. Although we might think that no state encourages prostitution, these particular interest groups had nothing against it. In Nairobi and other cities, the presence of prostitutes and the amenities and cooked food they sometimes offered, made the task of getting urban Africans back to work day after day somewhat easier. It also reduced African wages just enough to keep them at work a few months longer than they otherwise would have stayed. Moreover, the colonial police were busy with the Africans the state made into criminals, those Africans who broke the law by spending more than a month looking for work in Nairobi, or leaving an employer before their labor contract had expired. The state knew about Haya and *watembezi* women, but found them more of a service than an offense. The values of accumulation and entrepreneurship subsidized solid, Christian, patriarchal households on the western shore of Lake Victoria and helped extend the laboring time of hundreds of badly needed unskilled African workers in Nairobi.

No new forms of prostitution emerged after 1939. While the *watembezi* form dominated World War II prostitution, it did so under special circumstances, only some of which could be identified as young women's family labor. That no new forms emerged after the mid-1930s is especially significant, and may well mark a point of transition in East African agricultural history. The biggest change in African colonial history has nothing to do with barbarism and civilization, nothing to do with tribe and nation. It has to do with a transition around the issue of Africans' participation in wage labor. In most of Africa in the era before World War II, wage labor was a means by which Africans could supplement their farm production. It was not something they relied on solely for their subsistence. The monies earned working enhanced farming, however unwillingly and hesitantly that labor was originally undertaken. By World War II, in those areas where most men were migrant laborers, wage labor became the means by which most people subsisted, and farming itself was dependent on the cash migrant laborers brought home. So atrophied were the agricultural systems of these parts of Africa that women farmers could not plant maize or cotton or beans unless their husbands, working on tea estates in Kenya or the docks of East Africa, sent them the money to buy seeds—even subsistence required an assist from wage labor. These areas also sent a steady stream of prostitutes to towns, but they went as independent accumulators, not as daughters bailing their families out of trouble. Elsewhere, African agriculture took off in ways that colonialists had not fully expected—and in fact were to complain about—and these families did not have daughters who became prostitutes. That no new forms of prostitution emerged after 1939 testifies to the impoverishment of the poorest peasant households; they continued to have crises, but they no longer attempted to solve them—if they could be solved at all—from within the family.

Note: Virtually all the information in this essay comes from 170 interviews conducted with women who had been prostitutes in Nairobi between about 1909 and 1960, and twenty-six men who had visited prostitutes between 1917 and 1960; these interviews were conducted by myself and my assistants, Paul Kakaire and Margaret Makuna, without whom the research would have been impossible.

SUGGESTIONS FOR FURTHER READING

Bujra, Janet M. "Women 'Entrepreneurs' of Early Nairobi." *Canadian Journal of African Studies* IX, 2 (1975): 213–234.

Cooper, Frederick. *From Slaves to Squatters: Plantation Labor and Agriculture in Zanzibar and Coastal Kenya, 1890–1925.* New Haven: Yale University Press, 1980.

Geiger, Susan. *TANU Women: Gender and Culture in the Making of Tanganyikan Nationalism, 1955–1965.* Portsmouth, N.H.: Heinemann, 1997.

Hay, Margaret Jean, and Sharon Stichter, eds. *African Women South of the Sahara.* London: Longman, 1984.

Hershatter, Gail. *Dangerous Pleasures: Prostitution and Modernity in Twentieth Century Shanghai.* Berkeley: University of California Press, 1997.

Mwangi, Meja. *Going Down River Road.* London: Longman, 1977.

Petrik, Paula. "Capitalists with Rooms: Prostitution in Helena, Montana, 1865–1900." *Montana: The Magazine of Western History* 31 (1981): 28–41.

Schmidt, Elizabeth. *Peasants, Traders and Wives: Shona Women in Zimbabwe.* Portsmouth, N. H.: Heinemann, 1992.

Vail, Leroy, and Landeg White. "'Tiwani, Machambero!' Forced Cotton and Rice Growing on the Zambezi." *Journal of African History* 19 (1978): 239–263.

van Onselen, Charles. "Prostitutes and Proletarians." *Studies in the Social and Economic History of the Witwatersrand.* New York: Longman, 1982.

Walkowitz, Judith R. *Prostitution and Victorian Society.* Cambridge: Cambridge University Press, 1980.

White, Luise. "A Colonial State and an African Petty Bourgeoisie." In *Struggle for the City: Migrant Labor, Capital, and the State in Urban Africa,* edited by Frederick Cooper, 165–191. Beverly Hills: Sage, 1983.

———. *The Comforts of Home: Prostitution in Colonial Nairobi.* Chicago: University of Chicago Press, 1990.

———. "Prostitution, Identity, and Consciousness in Nairobi during World War II." *Signs* 11, no. 2 (1986).

CHAPTER TWELVE

Soldier's Heart: Literary Men, Literary Women, and the Great War

*Sandra M. Gilbert**

From the ancient Greeks on, the theme of war has figured prominently in Western historiography, but as is true of the historical tradition generally, the literature saw war mainly from the male perspective. This is changing now, as women's historians and literary critics take up the topic. Sandra Gilbert's chapter on the Great War—World War I—is an excellent case in point. As Gilbert shows, the war functioned in many ways to liberate women, but "ended up emasculating [men], depriving them of autonomy, confining them as closely as any Victorian women had been confined." This unusually sensitive study of "war images" is based on literary fiction, the poems and novels of male modernist writers like D. H. Lawrence and Ernest Hemingway, and the works of female authors like Radclyffe Hall, Alice Meynell, Madeline Ida Bedford, and Virginia Woolf. Literary fiction and poetry can be used as sources for reconstructing an historic era because they reflect the prevailing spirit of the times refracted through the artistic imagination. Gilbert examines literary works that deal with themes like eroticism between men and men and women and women, which polite society handled only with great restraint. She uncovers a true "battle of the sexes" that accompanied the battles of the Great War. Gender tensions directly fed into the mood of anxiety, self-doubt, and intensified misogynist resentment which, "in the words of Rebecca West, was 'strikingly the correct fashion . . . among . . . the intellectuals'" in the postwar period.

As we have all been told over and over again, World War I was not just the war to end wars; it was also the war of wars, a paradigm of technological combat which, with its trenches and zeppelins, its gases and mines, has become a diabolical summary of the idea of modern warfare—Western science bent to the service of West-

*This chapter is an abbreviated version of an article by the same title that appeared in *Signs: Journal of Women in Culture and Society* 8, no. 3 (1983): 422–450. We thank Sandra M. Gilbert for her willingness to help revise and shorten it. Full citations are in the *Signs* article. We thank the University of Chicago Press. Copyright © 1983 by the University of Chicago. All rights reserved.

ern imperialism. That this apocalyptic Great War involved strikingly large numbers
of men as well as shockingly powerful technological forces, moreover, has always
been understood to intensify its historical significance. The first modern war to
employ now familiar techniques of conscription and classification in order to create gigantic armies on both sides, World War I, as we have all been taught, virtually completed the Industrial Revolution's construction of anonymous dehumanized man, that impotent cipher who is frequently thought to be the twentieth
century's most characteristic citizen. Helplessly entrenched on the edge of No Man's
Land, this faceless being saw that the desert between him and his so-called enemy
was not just a metaphor for the technology of death and the death dealt by technology, it was also a symbol for the state, whose nihilistic machinery he was powerless to control or protest. Fearfully assaulted by a deadly bureaucracy on the one
side, and a deadly technocracy on the other, he was No Man, an inhabitant of the
inhumane new era and a citizen of the unpromising new land into which this war
of wars had led him.

Of course, as we have also been taught, these many dark implications of World
War I had further implications for twentieth-century literature. From D. H.
Lawrence's paralyzed Clifford Chatterley to Ernest Hemingway's sadly emascu-
lated Jake Barnes to T. S. Eliot's mysteriously sterile Fisher King, the gloomily
bruised modernist antiheroes churned out by the war suffer specifically from sexual wounds, as if, having traveled literally or figuratively through No Man's Land,
all have become not just No Men, nobodies, but *not* men, *un*men. That twentieth-
century Everyman, the faceless cipher, their authors seem to suggest, is not just
publicly powerless, he is privately impotent.

Obviously, however, such effects of the Great War were in every case gender-
specific problems, problems only men could have. Never having had public power,
women could hardly become more powerless than they already were. As for private impotence, most late Victorian young girls were trained to see such "passionlessness" as a virtue rather than a failure. Yet women, too, lived through these years,
and many modernistic writers seem to suggest that, oddly enough, women played
an unusually crucial part in the era. In D. H. Lawrence's 1915 "Eloi, Eloi, Lama
Sabacthani," for instance—a representative, if somewhat feverish, wartime poem—
the unmanning terrors of combat lead not just to a generalized sexual anxiety but
also to a sexual anger directed specifically against the female, as if the Great War
itself were primarily a climactic episode in some battle of the sexes that had already
been raging for years. Drawing upon the words Christ cried out as he died on the
cross, the creator of Clifford Chatterley here presents the war metaphorically as a
perverse sexual relationship that becomes a blasphemous (homo)sexual crucifixion.
As battle rages and death attacks, the speaker assumes, in turn, the terrifying roles
of rapist and victim, deadly groom and dying bride. Lawrence's perversely revisionary primal scene is made even more terrible, however, by the voyeuristic eyes
of a woman who peers "through the rents / In the purple veil" and peeps "in the
empty house like a pilferer." Like the gaze of the Medusa, her look seems somehow responsible for male sufferings.

Can this be because the war, with its deathly parody of sexuality, somehow
suggests female conquest? Because wives, mothers, and sweethearts were safe on

the home front, did the war appear in some peculiar sense their fault, a ritual of sacrifice to their victorious femininity? Through a paradox that is at first almost incomprehensible, the war that has traditionally been defined as an apocalypse of masculinism seems here to have led to an apotheosis of femaleness. If we reflect upon this point, however, we must inevitably ask a set of questions about the relations between the sexes during this war of wars. What part, after all, *did* women play in the Great War? How did men perceive that role? More specifically, what connections might there be between the wartime activities of women and the sense of sexual wounding that haunts so many male modernist texts? Most importantly, did women themselves experience the wound of the war in the same way that their sons and lovers did?

If we meditate for a while on the sexual implications of the Great War, we must certainly decide, to begin with, that it is a classic case of dissonance between official, male-centered history and unofficial female history. For not only did the apocalyptic events of this war have a very different meaning for men and women, such events were in fact very different for men and women, a point understood almost at once by an involved contemporary like Vera Brittain, who noted about her relationship with her soldier fiancé that the war put "a barrier of indescribable experience between men and the women whom they loved." The nature of the barrier thrust between Brittain and her fiancé, however, may have been even more complex than she herself realized, for the impediment preventing a marriage of their true minds was constituted, as we shall see, not only by his altered experience but by hers. Specifically, I will argue here that as young men became increasingly alienated from their prewar selves, increasingly immured in the muck and blood of No Man's Land, women seemed to become, as if by some uncanny swing of history's pendulum, ever more powerful. As nurses, as mistresses, as munitions workers, bus drivers, or soldiers in the "land army," even as wives and mothers, these formerly subservient creatures began to loom malevolently larger, until it was possible for a visitor to London to observe in 1918 that "England was a world of women—women in uniforms," or, in the words of a verse by Nina Macdonald, "Girls are doing things / They've never done before . . . All the world is topsy-turvy / Since the War began."

"*All the World is topsy-turvy / Since the War Began*"; that phrase is a crucial one, for the reverses and reversals of No Man's Land fostered in a number of significant ways the formation of a metaphorical country not unlike the queendom Charlotte Perkins Gilman called Herland, and the exhilaration (along with anxiety) of that state is as dramatically rendered in wartime poems, stories, and memoirs by women, as are the very different responses to the war in usually better-known works by men. Sometimes subtly and subversively, sometimes quite explicitly, writers from Alice Meynell to Radclyffe Hall explored the political and economic revolution by which the Great War at least temporarily dispossessed male citizens of the patriarchal primacy that had always been their birthright while granting women access to both the votes and the professions that they had never possessed. Similarly, a number of these artists covertly or overtly celebrated the release of female desires. In addition, many women writers recorded drastic (re)visions of society that were also, directly or indirectly, inspired by the revolutionary state in which they were living. For, as Virginia Woolf put it in a crucial passage from *Three*

Guineas, "So profound was [the] unconscious loathing" of the daughters of educated (and uneducated) men for "the education" in oppression which all women had received, that while most "consciously desired [the advancement of] 'our splendid Empire,'" many "unconsciously desired" the apocalypse of "our splendid war."

Not surprisingly, however, the words as well as the deeds of these women reinforced their male contemporaries' sense that "All the world is topsy-turvy / Since the war began" and thus intensified the misogynist resentment with which male writers defined this Great War as an apocalyptic turning point in the battle of the sexes. Not surprisingly either, therefore, the sexual gloom expressed by so many men as well as the sexual glee experienced by so many women ultimately triggered profound feelings of guilt in a number of women: to the guilt of the female survivor with her fear that "a barrier of indescribable experience" had been thrust between the sexes, there was often added a half-conscious fear that the woman survivor might be in an inexplicable way a perpetrator of some unspeakable crime. Thus, the invigorating sense of revolution, release, reunion, and re-vision with which the war paradoxically imbued so many women eventually darkened into reactions of anxiety and self-doubt as Herland and No Man's Land merged to become the Nobody's Land T. S. Eliot was to call "death's dream kingdom."

From the first, World War I fostered characteristically modernist irony in young men, inducting them into "death's dream kingdom" by revealing exactly how spurious were their visions of heroism, and—by extension—history's images of heroism. Mobilized and marched off to the front, idealistic soldiers soon found themselves *im*mobilized, even buried alive, in trenches of death that seemed to have been dug along the remotest margins of civilization. Here, all the traditional categories of experience through which the rational cultured mind achieves its hegemony over the irrationality of nature were grotesquely mingled, polluting each other as if in some Swiftian fantasy. From now on, their only land was No Man's Land, a land that was *not,* a country of the impossible and the paradoxical. As Robert Graves notes, "The average life expectancy of an infantry subaltern on the Western Front was, at some stages of the War, only about three months," so that a universal sense of doom, often manifesting itself as a *desire* for death, forced the wild man soldier to ask, with the speaker of one of D. H. Lawrence's poems, "Am I lost? / Has death set me apart / Beforehand? / Have I crossed / That border? / Have I nothing in this dark land?" (see Figure 7).

With no sense of inherited history to lose, on the other hand, women in the terrible war years of 1914–18 would seem to have had, if not everything, at least something to gain: a place in public history, a chance even to make history. Wrote one former suffragist, "I knew nothing of European complications and cared less. . . . I asked myself if any horrors could be greater than the horrors of peace—the sweating, the daily lives of women on the streets. . . ." Ultimately, such revolutionary energy and resolute feminism, together with such alienation from officially important events, was to lead to a phenomenon usefully analyzed by Nina Auerbach: "Union among women . . . is one of the unacknowledged fruits of war," and particularly during World War I, there was "a note of exaltation at the 'Amazonian countries' created by the war, whose military elation spread from the suffrage battle to the nation at large." For, of course, when their menfolk went off to the trenches

Figure 7. Hospitalized Veterans in England (Reproduced with permission of the Trustees of the Imperial War Museum, London.)

to be literally and figuratively shattered, the women on the home front literally and figuratively rose to the occasion and replaced them in farms and factories. Picture after picture from the Imperial War Museum's enormous collection of photos portraying "Women at War" illustrates this point. Liberated from parlors and petticoats alike, trousered "war girls" beam as they shovel coal, shoe horses, fight fires, drive buses, chop down trees, make shells, dig graves (see Figure 8).

Though it may be a coincidence, then, there is ironic point to the fact that Charlotte Perkins Gilman's *Herland,* with its vision of a female utopia created by a cataclysm that wiped out all the men, was published in Gilman's feminist journal *Forerunner* in 1915, and at least one feminist noted the accuracy of a cartoon in *Punch* depicting two women who "did not think the war would last long—it was too good to last." When the time came for demobilization, many women wept at the ending of what they now saw as the happiest and most purposeful days of their lives. For despite the massive tragedy that the war represented for an entire generation of young men—and for their grieving wives, mothers, daughters, and sisters—it also represented the first rupture with a socioeconomic history that had heretofore denied most women chances at first-class jobs—and first-class pay.

Inevitably, the enthusiasm and efficiency with which women of all ranks and ages filled in the economic gaps men had left behind reinforced the soldiers' sickened sense that the war had drastically abrogated most of the rules that had always organized Western culture. From the first, after all, it had seemed to the man at the front that his life and limbs were forfeit to the comforts of the *home* front, so that civilians, male and female, were fictive inhabitants of a world that had effectively insulated itself from the trenches' city of dreadful night. Ultimately, this barely veiled

Figure 8. Women's Land Army Workers in England (Reproduced with permission of the Trustees of the Imperial War Museum, London.)

hostility between the front and the home front, along with the exuberance of the women workers who had succeeded to (and in) men's places, suggested that the most crucial rule the war had overturned was the rule of patrilineal succession, the founding law of patriarchal society itself. For as the early glamour of battle dissipated and Victorian fantasies of historical heroism gave way to modernist visions of irony and unreality, it became clear that this war to end all wars necessitated a sacrifice of the sons to the exigencies of the fathers—and the mothers, wives, and sisters.

That such a generational conflict was not just associated with but an integral part of the sexual struggle fostered by the war is made very clear in a poem by Alice Meynell, a long-time suffrage fighter, who accurately foresaw that through one of the grimmer paradoxes of history the Great War might force recalcitrant men to grant women, the stereotypical peacemakers, a viable inheritance in patriarchal society. In fact, her "A Father of Women" seems almost to explain the sexual anxiety of D. H. Lawrence, who actually lived with her family during part of the war, for the speaker of this verse answers some of the questions Lawrence had asked in "Eloi, Eloi, Lama Sabacthani": "Our father works in us, / The daughters of his manhood. Not undone / Is he, not wasted, though transmuted thus, / And though he left no son." She goes on to tell "The million living fathers of the War" that they should finally "Approve, accept, know [us] daughters of men, / Now that your sons are dust." Ostensibly so calm and sympathetic, her last phrase can be read almost as a taunt, though it is certain she did not intend it that way. You have killed your sons, she seems to say, so now your daughters will inherit the world.

Even the most conventionally angelic of women's wartime ministrations must have suggested to many members of both sexes that, while men were now invalid and maybe in-valid, their sisters were triumphant survivors and destined inheritors. Certainly both the rhetoric and the iconography of nursing would seem to imply some such points. To be sure, the nurse presents herself as a servant of her patient. "Every task," writes Vera Brittain of her days as a VAD (Voluntary Aide), "had for us . . . a sacred glamour." Yet in works by both male and female novelists the figure of the nurse ultimately takes on a majesty which hints that she is mistress rather than slave, goddess rather than supplicant. After all, when men are immobilized and dehumanized, it is only these women who possess the old (matriarchal) formulas for survival. Thus, even while memoirists like Brittain express "gratitude" for the "sacred glamour" of nursing, they seem to be pledging allegiance to a *secret* glamour—the glamour of an expertise which they will win from their patients. "Towards the men," recalls Brittain, "I came to feel an almost adoring gratitude . . . for the knowledge of masculine functioning which the care of them gave me."

Not surprisingly, this education in masculine functioning that the nurse experiences as a kind of elevation is often felt by her male patient as exploitation; her evolution into active, autonomous, transcendent subject is associated with his devolution into passive, dependent, immanent medical object. In *A Farewell to Arms,* Hemingway's Frederic Henry clearly responds with a surface delight to being cared for and about by Catherine Barclay. Yet there is, after all, something faintly sinister in her claim that he *needs* her to make "unpleasant" preparations for an operation on his wounded knee and something frighteningly possessive in her assertion that "I get furious if [anyone else] touch[es] you." Similarly, in *The Sun Also Rises,* Hemingway's Jake Barnes, consoled by the nymphomaniac Brett Ashley as he lies limply on his bed, cannot forget that she "was a V.A.D. in a hospital I was in during the war" and fell in love with him because "she only wanted what she couldn't have," a line that ambiguously implies a form of perverse penis envy as well as a species of masochistic desire. More openly, Lawrence writes in "The Ladybird" about a wounded middle European prisoner who tells a visiting English Lady with whom he is falling in love that she must "let me wrap your hair round my hands like a bandage" because "I feel I have lost my manhood for the time being." Hopelessly at the mercy of his aristocratic nurse, this helpless alien adumbrates wounded males who also appear in works by women—for example, the amnesiac hero of Rebecca West's *The Return of the Soldier,* whom a former girlfriend restores by gathering his "soul" into "her soul"; and Lord Peter Wimsey, in Dorothy Sayers's *Busman's Honeymoon,* who is so haunted by memories of the war that he confesses to his bride that "you're my corner and I've come to hide."

Where nurses imagined by men often do seem to have sinister power, however, the nurses imagined by women appear, at least at first, to be purely restorative, positively (rather than negatively) maternal. The "grey nurse" whom Virginia Woolf describes in a notoriously puzzling passage in *Mrs. Dalloway* is thus a paradigm of her more realistically delineated sisters. Knitting steadily while Peter Walsh dozes, she seems "like the champion of the rights of sleepers" who responds to "a desire for solace, for relief." Yet even she is not an altogether positive figure. Like "The Greatest Mother in the World" depicted in Alonzo Earl Foringer's 1918 Red Cross War Relief poster—an enormous nurse cradling a tiny immobilized male on a doll-sized stretcher—Woolf's grey nurse evokes a parodic *pietà* in which the

Virgin Mother threatens simultaneously to anoint and annihilate her long-suffering son, a point Woolf's imaginary male dreamer accurately grasps when he prays "let me walk straight on to this great figure, who will . . . mount me on her streamers and let me blow to nothingness with the rest." Does male death turn women nurses on? Do figures like the pious Red Cross mother experience bacchanalian satisfaction as, in Woolf's curiously ambiguous phrase, they watch their patients, one-time oppressors, "blow [up] to nothingness with the rest?" A number of texts by men and women alike suggest that the revolutionary socioeconomic transformations wrought by the war's "topsy-turvy" role reversals did bring about a release of female libidinal energies, as well as a liberation of female anger, which men usually found anxiety-inducing and women often found exhilarating.

On the subject of erotic release, a severely political writer like Vera Brittain is notably restrained. Yet even she implies, at least subtextually, that she experienced some such phenomenon, for while she expresses her "gratitude" to men from whom she learned about "masculine functioning," she goes on to thank the war that delivered their naked bodies into her hands for her own "early release from . . . sex-inhibitions." Significantly, too, as if to confirm the possibility that Brittain did receive a wartime sex education, Eric Leed records the belief of some observers that "women in particular 'reacted to the war experience with a powerful increase in libido.'" Was the war a festival of female misrule in which the collapse of a traditional social structure "permitted," as Leed also puts it, "a range of personal contacts that had been impossible in [former lives] where hierarchies of status ruled"? In their different ways, notorious heroines like Hemingway's Catherine Barclay and his Brett Ashley are set sexually free by the war, as are Lawrence's famous Connie Chatterley, his Ivy Bolton, and his Bertha Coutts, all of whom contribute to the impotence of his Clifford Chatterley and the anxiety of his Oliver Mellors.

Significantly, however, where men writers primarily recounted the horrors of unleashed female sexuality and only secondarily recorded the more generalized female excitement that energized such sexuality, women remembered, first the excitement of the war and, second (but more diffusely), the sensuality to which such excitement led. Thus, where most male writers—at least after their earliest dreams of heroism had been deflated—associated the front with paralysis and pollution, many female writers imagined it a place of freedom, ruefully comparing what they felt was their own genteel immobilization with the exhilaration of military mobility. In her "Many Sisters to Many Brothers," Rose Macaulay articulated their envy of the soldier's liberation from the dreariness of the home and the home front: "Oh it's you that have the luck, out there in blood and muck." To women who managed to get to the front, moreover, the war did frequently offer the delight of (female) mobilization rather than the despair of (male) immobilization. After all, for nurses and ambulance drivers, women doctors and women messengers, the phenomenon of modern battle was very different from that experienced by entrenched combatants. Finally given a chance to take the wheel, these post-Victorian girls raced motorcars along foreign roads like adventurers exploring new lands, while their brothers dug deeper into the mud of France. Retrieving the wounded and the dead from deadly positions, these once-decorous daughters had at last been allowed to prove their valor, and they swooped over the wastelands of the war with the energetic love of Wagnerian Valkyries, their mobility alone transporting countless immobilized heroes to safe havens.

For many women, moreover, but perhaps in particular for lesbian women like Willa Cather, whose inability to identify with conventional "femininity" had always made their gender a problem to them, the war facilitated not just a liberation from the constricting trivia of parlors and petticoats but an unprecedented transcendence of the profounder constraints imposed by traditional sex roles. Most dramatically, this transcendence is described in Radclyffe Hall's two crucial postwar fictions— her short story entitled "Miss Ogilvy Finds Herself" and her more famous *The Well of Loneliness.* In the first, the aging lesbian Miss Ogilvy remembers, as she is being demobilized, that her ambulance was "the merciful emblem that had set [her] free," and mourns the breaking up of the "glorious" all-female unit she has led. Similarly, Stephen Gordon, the "invert" heroine of *The Well,* feels at the outset of the war like "a freak abandoned on a kind of no-man's-land" (and Hall's metaphor is significant) but soon finds herself paradoxically metamorphosed into a member of a new women's battalion "that would never again be disbanded." For, explains Hall, "war and death" had finally, ironically, given "a right to life" to lesbians like Stephen, women who refused the traditions of femininity and the conventions of heterosexuality alike.

To be sure, specifically erotic release was frequently associated with such a right to life, for Vera Brittain's sex education was complemented by the romantic permission given, in various degrees, to heterosexual characters like Miranda in Katherine Anne Porter's "Pale Horse, Pale Rider" and to lesbian heroines like Miss Ogilvy and Stephen Gordon. In the first work, Porter's protagonist, falling in love with a young soldier, meditates happily on the "miracle of being two persons named Adam and Miranda" who are "always in the mood for dancing." As for Miss Ogilvy, she goes off on a vacation where Hall grants her a dream of unleashed desire in which, transformed into a powerful primitive man, she makes love to a beautiful young woman, enthralled by the "ripe red berry sweet to the taste" of the female body. Similarly, Stephen Gordon meets her lover, Mary Llewelyn, when they are sister drivers in the allegorically named "Breakspeare" ambulance unit, and after the war they too achieve a "new and ardent fulfillment" on a honeymoon in Spain.

Perhaps more important than the female eroticism that the war energized, however, was the more diffusely emotional sense of sisterhood its "Amazonian countries" inspired in nurses and VADs, land girls and tram conductors. As if to show the positive aspect of the bacchanalian bonding that some male writers feared, women like Vera Brittain, May Sinclair, and Violetta Thurstan remembered how their liberation into the public realm from the isolation of the private house allowed them to experience a female (re)union in which they felt "the joys of companionship to the full . . . in a way that would be impossible to conceive in an ordinary world." For Radclyffe Hall, too, the battalion of sisters "formed in those terrible years" consisted of "great-hearted women . . . glad . . . to help one another to shoulder burdens."

It is also, of course, true that the Great War produced for many men a "frontline experience replete with," as Paul Fussell puts it, "what we can call the homoerotic." From Herbert Read, who wishes one of his dead soldiers to be kissed not by worms "but with the warm passionate lips / of his comrade here," to Wilfred Owen, who sends his "identity disc" to a "sweet friend," imploring "may thy heart-beat kiss it, night and day," male combatants frequently feel for each other "a love passing the love of women." Significantly, however, where the liberating sisterhood experienced by women was mostly untainted by hostility to men—where it was, in fact, frequently associated with admiration for male soldiers or identification with male heroism—the combatants' comradeship seems as often to have been energized by a disgust for the feminine as it was by a desire for the masculine. The war between the front and the home front, that is, issued in an inextricable tangle of (male) misogyny and (male) homosexuality, so that Owen, say, reproaches female "Love" while praising beautiful "lads."

The male comradeship fostered by the isolated communities of the trenches, moreover, was continually qualified by rifts between men that were not just acci-dental but essential consequences of the war. Most obviously, the No Man's Land that stretched between allies and enemies symbolized the fragmentation of what Sigmund Freud called the "wider fatherland" in which, as Freud sorrowfully noted, European men no longer dwelt, though they had "moved unhindered" in it before the war. "Strange Meeting," perhaps Owen's most famous poem, stunningly dram-atizes this disintegration of male love, with its vision of brotherly doubles meeting in a "dull tunnel" where one tells the other that, "I am the enemy you killed, my friend."

But if the war forced men like Lawrence, Freud, and Owen to qualify their dreams of brotherhood by confronting the reality of No Man's Land and imagin-ing themselves as nightmare citizens "without a land," it liberated women to imag-ine a revisionary worldwide Herland, a utopia arisen from the ashes of apocalypse and founded on the revelation of a new social order. In a range of genres—poems and polemics, extravagant fantasies and realistic fictions—women writers articu-lated this vision repeatedly throughout the war and postwar years. Gertrude Ather-ton's popular fantasy, *The White Morning,* for instance, told a utopian tale of the takeover of Germany by a female army, while Dorothy Harrison, one of the pro-tagonists of Sinclair's *The Tree of Heaven,* has a mysteriously epiphany when she is confined at Hollowell Prison as part of the prewar suffrage battle, an epiphany that turns out to be a proleptic vision of how women will get the vote in "some big, tremendous way that'll make all this fighting and fussing seem the rottenest game."

For many women such intimations of social change were channeled specifi-cally through the politics of pacifism. From Olive Schreiner, whose meditation on "Women and War" had argued that the mothers of the race have a special respon-sibility as well as a special power to oppose combat, to Charlotte Perkins Gilman, whose Herland was an Edenically peaceable garden because its author believed women to be naturally nonviolent, feminist activists had long claimed that, in the words of Crystal Eastman, "woman suffrage and permanent peace will go together." Indeed, like the trade unionist Mrs. Raymond Robins, whose opinions were other-wise very different, Eastman had confidence that "it is the first hour in history for the women of the world. This is the woman's age!" Precisely because these thinkers were uniformly convinced of woman's unique ability to encourage and enforce peace, however, there is sometimes an edge of contempt for men implicit in their arguments. But it is in Virginia Woolf's *Three Guineas,* the postwar era's great text of pacifist feminism, that such hostility to men comes most dramatically to the surface, in the form of violent antipatriarchal fantasies paradoxically embedded in an ostensibly nonviolent treatise on the subject of "how to prevent war." Perhaps, Woolf even hints in an early draft of this New Womanly book of revelation, the devastation wrought by war is a punishment (for men) exactly fitted not only to the crime of (masculine) war-making, but to other (masculine) crimes. Even in the more subdued final version of *Three Guineas* she seizes upon the imperative to prevent war as an excuse for imagining a conflagration that would burn down the old male-structured colleges of "Oxbridge," representative of all oppressive cultural institutions, and substitute instead an egalitarian and feminist "new college, [a] poor college" where "the arts of ruling, of killing, of acquiring land and capital" would not be taught.

Later in *Three Guineas,* moreover, Woolf rebels even against the rhetoric of writers like Schreiner and Eastman, observing sardonically that "pacifism is enforced upon women" because they are not in any case allowed to offer their services to the army. Thus, most radically, she puts forward her famous proposal that "the daughters of educated men" should refuse to join their brothers in working either for war *or* peace, but should instead found a "Society of Outsiders" based on the principles that "as a woman, I have no country. As a woman, I want no country. As a woman, my country is the whole world." To be sure, Woolf recommends as part of this proposal a passive resistance to patriarchal militarism significantly similar to that advocated by many other feminist pacifists. But at the same time, with its calculated ex-patriotism and its revisionary vows of "indifference" to the uncivilized hierarchies of "our" civilization, her Society of Outsiders constitutes perhaps the most fully elaborated feminist vision of a secret apocalyptic Herland existing simultaneously within and without what she called in that volume England's "splendid Empire," a righteous and rightful woman's state energized by the anti-war passions the war produced in women. In some part of herself, therefore, Woolf may well have shared the apocalyptic delight that Hesione Hushabye bizarrely expresses when bombs begin falling at the end of Bernard Shaw's *Heartbreak House:* "Did you hear the explosions? And the sound in the sky: it's splendid: it's like an orchestra: it's like Beethoven." As patriarchal culture self-destructs, those it has subordinated can't help feeling that the sacrifices implied by "the sound in the sky" might nevertheless hold out the hope of a new heaven and a new earth.

Given the fact that the war functioned in so many different ways to liberate women, it seems clear that more than simple patriotism caused some leaders of the women's movement quite early to recognize a connection between feminist aspirations and military effects. In 1915, for instance, *The Suffragette,* the newspaper of the English Women's Social and Political Union, was renamed *Britannia,* with a new dedication: "For King, for Country, for Freedom." At last, it must have seemed, women could begin to see themselves as coextensive with the state, and with a female state at that, a Britannia, not a Union Jack. And as we know, the female intuition expressed in that renaming was quite accurate; in 1918, when World War I was over, there were eight and a half million European men dead, and there had been thirty-seven and a half million male casualties, while all the women in

England over the age of thirty were finally, after a sixty-two-year struggle, given the vote. Not too much later all the women in America over the age of twenty-one achieved the same privilege. For four years a sizable percentage of the young men in England had been imprisoned in trenches and uniforms, while the young women in England had been at liberty in farm and factory. Paradoxically, the war to which so many men had gone in the hope of becoming heroes ended up emasculating them, depriving them of autonomy, confining them as closely as any Victorian women had been confined. As if in acknowledgement of this, Eric Leed tells us, doctors noted that "the symptoms of shell-shock were precisely the same as those of the most common hysterical disorders of peacetime, though they often acquired new and more dramatic names in war: 'the burial-alive neurosis,' 'gas neurosis,' 'soldier's heart,' 'hysterical sympathy with the enemy' . . . what had been predominantly a disease of women before the war became a disease of men in combat."

Because women developed a very different kind of "soldier's heart" in these years, "wearing the pants" in the family or even "stepping into his shoes" had finally become a real possibility for them. Yet of course that triumph was not without its darker consequences for feminism. Because male artists believed even more strongly than their sisters did that soldiers had been sacrificed so that some gigantic female could sleep surrounded by, in Wilfred Owen's words, a "wall of boys on boys and dooms on dooms"; because they believed, with Hemingway, that a Lady Brett was a sort of monstrous antifertility goddess to whose powers the impotent bodies of men had ceaselessly to be offered up; because, finally, with Lawrence they "feared" the talents of liberated "poetesses" like H.D. at least as much as they admired them, the literature of the postwar years was marked by an "antifeminism" which, in the words of Rebecca West, was "strikingly the correct fashion . . . among . . . the intellectuals."

Inevitably, many women writers themselves internalized the misogyny that actuated such antifeminism. Heroines like Hall's Miss Ogilvy and her Stephen Gordon, for instance, who had been briefly freed by the war, ultimately succumb to the threat of a reconstituted status quo. Miss Ogilvy dies almost directly as a result of the sexual "dying" that climaxes her dream of erotic fulfillment, and Stephen Gordon is assaulted by "rockets of pain" which signal "the hour of our death" as she surrenders Mary Llewelyn to the male lover who she decides is Mary's rightful spouse. At the same time, the guilt of the survivor is specifically articulated by one former nurse who defines her culpable numbness in a dreadful confession: "She [a nurse] is no longer a woman. She is dead already, just as I am . . . a machine inhabited by a ghost of a woman—soulless, past redeeming." Most theatrically, perhaps, Katherine Anne Porter expresses in "Pale Horse, Pale Rider" this nurse's feeling (and what might have been a universal female sense) that if men are sick, they must have fallen ill because women are sickening. After her heroine, Miranda, down with influenza, has had a terrifying dream about her lover, Adam, in which "he lay dead, and she still lived," she learns that her disease has contaminated him, and indeed, he has died and she has lived, kept going by a "fiery motionless particle [which] set itself . . . to survive . . . in its own madness of being."

Eventually, therefore, repressed by what was still, after all, a male-dominated community, and reproached by their own consciences, many women retreated into embittered unemployment or guilt-stricken domesticity after World War I. "Generally speaking, we war women are a failure," confesses a character in Evadne Price's *Women of the Aftermath.* "We had a chance to make ourselves solid in the working market . . . and came a hell of a cropper in most cases." To be sure, as J. Stanley Lemons and others observe, women's "peacetime levels [of employment] were [still] significantly higher than the prewar situation." Nothing would ever be the same again. But no war would ever function, either, the way this Great War had, as a battle of the sexes which initiated "the first hour in history for the women of the world." World War II certainly was to be as much a war against women civilians as it was against male combatants, with a front indistinguishable from the home front. As Virginia Woolf anticipated in *Three Guineas,* in fact, it was to be a war whose jackbooted Nazis, marching for the Fatherland, enacted the ultimate consequences of patriarchal oppression, so that Sylvia Plath, protesting against her imprisonment in "daddy's" black shoe, would fear that "I may be a bit of a Jew." In 1944, moreover, in her war-shadowed "Writing on the Wall," H.D. was to return to Radclyffe Hall's definition of "no-man's-land" as a "waste land" for "inverts" (Hall) and "hysterical women" (H.D.) while more recently, in a revision of the metaphor that Hall's Stephen Gordon temporarily transcended, Linda Pastan was to see her own body as a "no man's land" over which sons and husbands battle, and in 1981 Adrienne Rich was to publish a poem which despairingly declared that "there is no no man's land," by which she clearly means there is still no Herland. With Rich, all of these women would understand themselves to be participants in an ongoing "war of the images" whose possibly apocalyptic dénouement has not yet really been revealed, though the combats of the early twentieth century offered enduring possibilities of vengeance and victory, female anxiety and feminist ecstasy.

Suggestions for Further Reading

Auerbach, Nina. *Communities of Women: An Idea in Fiction.* Cambridge: Harvard University Press, 1978.

Borden, Mary. *The Forbidden Zone.* Garden City, N.Y.: Doubleday, Doran, 1930.

Bradbury, Malcolm. "The Denuded Place: War and Form in *Parade's End* and *U.S.A.*" In *The First World War in Fiction,* edited by Holger Klein. London: Macmillan, 1976.

Braybon, Gail. *Women Workers in the First World War: The British Experience.* London: Croom Helm, 1981.

Brittain, Vera. *Testament of Youth.* New York: Macmillan, 1933.

Cadogan, Mary, and Patricia Craig. *Women and Children First: The Fiction of Two World Wars.* London: Golancz, 1978.

Cook, Blanche, ed. *Crystal Eastman on Women and Revolution.* New York: Oxford University Press, 1978.

Cott, Nancy. "Passionlessness: An Interpretation of Victorian Sexual Ideology, 1790–1850." *Signs* 4, no. 2 (Winter 1978): 219–236.

Fussell, Paul. *The Great War and Modern Memory.* New York: Oxford University Press, 1975.

Greenwald, Maurine Weiner. *Women, War and Work: The Impact of World War I on Women Workers in the United States.* Westport, Conn.: Greenwood, 1985.

Lane, Ann J., ed. *The Charlotte Perkins Gilman Reader.* New York: Pantheon, 1980.

Leed, Eric. *No Man's Land: Combat and Identity in World War I.* Cambridge: Cambridge University Press, 1979.

Lemons, J. Stanley. *The Woman Citizen: Social Feminism in the 1920s.* Urbana, Ill.: University of Illinois Press, 1973.

Matthews, Caroline. *Experiences of a Woman Doctor in Serbia.* London: Mills and Boon, 1916.

Nicolson, Nigel. *Portrait of a Marriage.* London: Weidenfeld and Nicolson, 1973.

Reilly, Catherine, ed. *Scars upon My Heart: Women's Poetry and Verse of the First World War.* London: Virago, 1981.

Schreiner, Olive. "Women in War." Chap. 4 in *Women and Labour.* 3d ed. New York: Frederick Stokes, 1911.

CHAPTER THIRTEEN

Lesbian Sexuality in Interwar France

Carolyn J. Dean

Since the reemergence of women's history in the 1970s, feminist scholars continue to debate the bases of female subjectivity. For some, drawing on Enlightenment epistemological assumptions about social construction, sexual identity became a historical and social product constructed through gender ascriptions. Others turned to "the body" itself in an effort to explain the physiological and psychological aspects of sexual difference. Carolyn Dean, indeed, offers a complicated reading of lesbian sexuality in interwar France demonstrating the fluidity of sex and gender, male and female, masculinity and femininity. She returns to the body as image and sexuality as practice. Drawing on medical texts, literary fiction, journalism, and public discourses, she traces the politics of lesbian sexuality, which reemerged as a problematic simultaneously reinforcing and undermining the conservative gender order after the disruptions of the Great War. Fantasies of female same-sex desire, hidden yet omnipresent, worked to construct "all" women, seemingly standing for a volatile female sexuality. As Dean notes, "the line between the degenerate homosexual body and the normal heterosexual body . . . could not be clearly drawn." These same fantasies, however, were appropriated and rearranged by lesbians in their struggles to give voice to their own identity.

Novels, newspapers, and political discourse after the Great War (1914–18) manifested changing attitudes toward female homosexuality. In the late nineteenth century, political and cultural commentary demonized lesbianism in the context of the low birth rate and feminist challenges to normative heterosexuality: literary and medical narratives predictably emphasized the sterility of same-sex desire and its consequent threat to the size and health of the population. But by the end of the war, the lesbian became one of the symbolic centers of moral and political anarchy. The war necessitated that women take over men's jobs, earn higher salaries, and thus gain political and social autonomy. The main consequence, as an alarmed critic put it, was that men could no longer tell the difference between honest and deviant women, since now all women "smoke, drink . . . drive cars. . . ."

Many scholars argue that lesbians were perceived (and often perceived themselves) as visible gender deviants at the end of the century. But after the war, the clearly demarcated line between lesbians and other women was no longer so obvious, and a wide range of commentary began to focus instead on lesbians' invisibility. As Jean de Mézerette put it in 1939, "Pederasts flaunt themselves, flagellants hide no longer, drugs can be easily found; but young women who love women have an irritating tendency to dissimulate their tastes. Nevertheless, [lesbianism] is, I believe, a pervasive practice in France."

I will argue that Mézerette was interested in exposing the dangers of female sexuality for which the lesbian, often unidentified and unidentifiable, was the privileged emblem. Thus lesbian invisibility was not just the function of cultural negligence but the product of a cultural obsession with female sexuality expressed dramatically in interwar French cultural commentary. The reality that lesbians were present in every walk of life but difficult to identify as such became part of an elaborate fantasy about the secretive, elusive nature of the lesbian. Moreover, that fantasy also formed the parameters within which self-described lesbians forged an alternative language for their own sexuality.

French cultural commentary targeted the increasing visibility of urban male homosexual subcultures in order to argue that gay men should be more discrete and not "flaunt" their preferences. Journalists decried men's putative snobbery, their sense of superiority, their cliquishness and ostentatious tendencies. Discussion about male homosexuality proliferated in part because of André Gide's open defense and celebration of male same-sex love in *Corydon* (1924), but the literature concerned with female homosexuality was just as voluminous—and perhaps more so, because it was included in an increasingly vast pornographic repertoire. But while gay men sexualized the male body by putting it on display, by transforming themselves into objects rather than subjects of desire, in the French postwar cultural imagination lesbian sexuality refused to show itself. Although many commentators bemoaned "mannish" women and accused them of lesbianism, most popular texts seemed to be far more invested in unmasking lesbians who eluded identification.

Drawing on nineteenth-century themes in which lesbians were located predictably in aristocratic circles and among working-class women (specifically prostitutes), one medical book obsessively discussed methods for detecting women who desired women. The author claimed that wealthy lesbians, always accompanied by poodles, walk discretely on the Champs-Elysées in quest of other women. When their eyes met, "each performs a rapid motion of the tongue and lips; this is the conventional sign, adopted by tribades to signify, 'I am on the lookout for a woman.'" Another doctor Caufeynon insisted that since "sapphic" practices were masturbatory, lesbians might be found rubbing themselves against the table where they smoothed linen or profiting from the movement of the sewing machine. When he inquired about the practices of women in textile factories, the foreman claimed that such behavior was so common he no longer paid attention. Finally, in nearly every book about lesbians, prostitutes, weary of men and of "common" pleasures, were notorious tribades.

According to the discourse, when lesbians were not moving surreptitiously through public space, they were almost always (unlike gay men) behind closed doors; either lesbianism was the irresistible vice even "normal" women succumbed to when protected by the anonymity of sex clubs, or it was practiced like a religion whose temples looked like any other house on the block. Many of the discussions about lesbians or the semipornographic texts offering a glimpse behind those doors drew on a famous fantasy first articulated by Pidansat de Mairobert in 1784 about the "Secte des Anandrynes"—a secret lesbian sect reserved for aristocrats, including Marie-Antoinette. In keeping both with late eighteenth- and nineteenth-century references to that fantasy, the highbrow literary critic Octave Uzanne identified the Secte in 1921 as the origin of underground lesbian communities. And in an anonymous 1933 pornographic work, the heroine meets a "Maréchale B" who promises to introduce her into the sect, and a critical text published the same year invoked its rituals.

Most books did not invoke the sect directly, but used images of secret chambers and clubs to describe the world lesbians putatively inhabited. Although these spaces retain their aristocratic trappings, interwar narratives effectively democratize them. Aristocrats and prostitutes ceased to be the privileged repositories of lesbian desire; bourgeois women were now as likely to enjoy lesbian affairs. In Willy's *Le Troisième Sexe,* in Charles-Louis Royer's *Le Club des damnés,* in Georges Anquetil's *Satan Conduit le bal* and in Charles-Etienne's novelistic series about the homosexual underworld—and these works hardly exhaust the list—these secret places, metaphorically behind or underneath the visually accessible urban landscape, become oddly coextensive with that landscape. Anquetil notes that both pederasts and lesbians have penetrated public life and even "austere bourgeois dwellings." In 1927, Willy signaled a "pandemic of androgyny" and claimed that "this noble vice [homosexuality]" was now "dangerously democratized."

Royer's club dwellers and Charles-Etienne's characters represent the bourgeoisie, and lesbians are its privileged symbols. In *Le Club des damnés,* female same-sex desire symbolizes all the "damned" who frequent the underworld; the hero's companion, lured away from him by other women, acted like a "femme damnée, who behaves in spite of herself, as if in the grip of an insatiable, tormenting fever." In the beginning of Charles-Etienne's 1919 novel *Notre Dame de Lesbos,* the hero Julien attends a costume ball. Upset by the number of homosexuals in attendance, he writes a nasty article about the "third sex." After it is published, he learns to his surprise that he has alienated many friends whose homosexuality he had not suspected. Moreover, he eventually learns that the woman he loves is a lesbian, and the rest of the novel is devoted to her life. In this and many other of Charles-Etienne's novels, the author characterizes interwar French society in terms of the contagion, debauchery, and duplicity he associates with female homosexuality: not only are bourgeois women unable to resist the advances of other women; the boundaries between the lesbian and other women prove to be porous and the difference between perverted women and other women cannot be clearly articulated. In most interwar writing with (homo)sexual themes, the French social body had not simply been contaminated by ever more numerous lesbians; the line between the degenerate homosexual body and the normal heterosexual body could not be clearly drawn.

Commentators thus presumed that female homosexuality was both pervasive and unmarked; in so doing, they raised the suspicion that any woman might be a lesbian. Although the pseudonymous Dr. Alibert approvingly quoted another expert on the art of recognizing lesbians—"generally they wear dresses exactly similar, they have the same jewels, and they say they are sisters"—he also insisted that "taking into account the ease with which they [women] trample upon all conventions, it must be admitted that the majority have a predisposition to vice." This description of lesbians is remarkably imprecise. More significant, however, Alibert insisted that all women are potentially lesbians and warns husbands that sapphism is so contagious they ought not to expose their wives to "known" lesbians for fear of producing "committed sapphists." Dr. Caufeynon used the same language to argue that most women may become lesbians because the moral laws implicit in social organization made by men are wholly incompatible with women's nature. The lesbian, then, is no longer a clearly defined creature: instead, she cannot be easily distinguished from any other woman.

Medical men used a model of gender deviance to make the very distinctions between normal and perverted women they also claimed were not feasible. Since the late nineteenth century and into the postwar period, French medical men drew distinctions between congenital ("innate") and acquired lesbianism (between "tribades" and "sapphics," respectively) made elsewhere in the United States and Europe. In so doing, they linked congenital homosexuality to gender deviance—the "masculine" behavior and dress of "tribades"—and acquired homosexuality to "vice"— the momentary impulses of otherwise normal "feminine" women. The "real" lesbian was masculine, and most doctors did not believe the "feminine" woman's lesbianism was a choice; instead, they conceived it as a predictable if unfortunate reaction to male betrayal and egotism. At the same time, doctors and writers did not sustain this model of gender deviance, a theoretical impasse that became more pronounced after the war. Increasingly in the interwar years, they did not draw clear distinctions they claimed existed between the devouring, congenital, masculine tribade and the devoured, acquired, feminine sapphist.

Although tribades are cold and calculating—this is especially true in interwar flagellation pornography, in which lesbian flagellants are a predominant feature— their desire for pleasure is so uncontrollable they find it only in extremes of pain. Indeed, their desire is so insatiable only self-annihilation can relieve their torment. Hence, according to the writer Sylvain Bonmariage, the lesbian is a "cold-hearted," "self-involved egotist" whose pleasure nevertheless "devours her soul, her senses, and her flesh. . . ." The Professor Malherman—likely a pseudonym—argued that lesbians find a particular joy in hurting others, but that they find the greatest pleasure in their own sexual degradation. According to the popular writer Maryse Choisy, lesbians are known for their "tyranny" and "crimes of jealousy," but this masculine imperiousness is inseparable from the "constant sexual irritation" characteristic of female insatiability. The Italian doctor Cesare Lombroso's tribade who threatens to tear her lover's entrails out is no different from Marcello Fabri's sapphist who eviscerates her partner.

The doctors and writers who insisted on the lesbian's gender deviance also suggested that she confounds gender, that she represents the intrinsic volatility of a female sexuality that is always both active and passive, agent and victim, contaminated and contaminating. She is visibly perverted womanhood and yet her body is the hidden, fantasmic repository of the dangerous, annihilating, and undomesticated sexuality within all women—the normal woman's uncanny double. In this way they depicted lesbians as the secret agents of the social contamination explicitly associated with the moral ruin of postwar France. The containment of the fantasized dangers of female sexuality depended on the fantasy of lesbian invisibility that made all women suspect and yet sustained the illusion of a specific group of women against whom society might mobilize and from whom society required protection. Thus, the boundaries between normal and perverted women were sustained even as all women were subject to more intense regulation.

This construction of lesbian invisibility also offers a context within which to understand interwar lesbians' own narratives about sexuality. The French writer Colette's famous, breathtakingly condescending portrait of lesbianism as a surrogate for maternal love—her book *Le Pur et l'impur* (first published in 1932 under another title)—remains the standard account of lesbianism during this period. Moreover, most literary histories of lesbianism in Paris focus primarily on Anglo-American expatriates. But less well known French lesbians transformed the dominant and negative construction of lesbians' elusiveness into an affirmative valuation of lesbian sexuality. They scorned both maternity and masculinity—at least as tropes Colette and others used to characterize lesbian desire—and replicated in positive terms the cultural fantasy of an intrinsically volatile, elusive, annihilating sexuality.

These would-be poets paid homage to the memory of the lesbian expatriate poet Renée Vivien, who starved herself to death in 1909. Vivien was English but adopted a French pen name, wrote in French, and enjoyed enormous success during her lifetime. She was the lover of the wealthy American Natalie Barney, whose Parisian salon was a famous gathering place for elite lesbians and gay men, among others. An entire portion of Colette's book is devoted to an affectionately negative characterization of Vivien (Vivien's poetry is overrated, she lisps, she nails her windows shut, and is absurdly secretive). Unlike Colette, many French male writers repudiated Vivien's lesbianism—either by denying it outright or claiming her homosexual reveries constituted nothing more than a *poetic* identification with her heroine Sappho. But many lesbian writers insisted that Vivien's sexuality was paradoxically so refined it could not be satiated in this world. Moreover, as Henriette Willete wrote, "Shadow was her friend," as if Vivien's desire for closed, stifling spaces and her discretion were continuous with purity rather than with impurity. Vivien is the agent of her destruction not because lesbian sexuality is intrinsically impure but because it is pure, too "chaste" in its passion, too passionately chaste.

Their reading of Vivien is a long way from Colette's characterization, and from other portraits. Whether Colette was right or not about the "real" Vivien is irrelevant; most important, the women who cherished Vivien fashioned visions of their own sexuality after prevalent constructions of female same-sex desire as intrinsically elusive. The relationship between these figurations of lesbian desire and the dominant rhetoric of lesbian invisibility is homologous: both discourses employ the fluidity of the lesbian who cannot be pinned down or identified either to regulate female desire, or in the case of Viven's acolytes, to escape regulation. I have focused primarily on dominant rhetoric. But Vivien's lesbian admirers used dominant discourses about lesbian elusiveness to figure a presence so immaterial it was never in danger of being erased. They fetishized Vivien's death, it would seem, as a means of staying alive—hence the love of concealment in their work, their invocation of an ethereal and highly eroticized body whose sensuality is omnipresent and yet intangible. This is certainly not the only form of self-representation lesbians employed during the interwar period. But the celebration of Vivien demonstrates clearly how those representations are shaped not only by gender deviance—lesbians consciously or unconsciously appropriate and transform discourses about their "manliness." They are also shaped by discourses about the dissolution of gender boundaries: here, lesbians refashioned cultural fantasies about their inability to be bound to a stable gender identity. Those women conceived an eroticism that could not be effaced because, like the difference between honest and deviant women, it could not be definitively located.

SUGGESTIONS FOR FURTHER READING

Albert, Nicole. "Sappho Mythified, Sappho Mystified, or the Metamorphoses of Sappho in Fin-de-Siècle France." In *Gay Studies from the French Cultures: Voices from France, Belgium, Brazil, Canada, and the Netherlands,* edited by Romme Menes-Leite and Pierre Olivier de Busscher, 87–104. New York: Haworth Press, 1993.

Benstock, Shari. *Women of the Left Bank: Paris 1900–1940.* Austin: University of Texas Press, 1986.

De Jean, Joan. *Fictions of Sappho, 1546–1937.* Chicago: University of Chicago Press, 1989.

Merrick, Jefferey, and Bryant T. Ragan, eds. *Homosexuality in Modern France.* Oxford: Oxford University Press, 1996.

Roberts, Mary Louise. *Civilization without Sexes: Reconstructing Gender in Postwar France. 1917–1927.* Chicago: University of Chicago Press, 1994.

Stambolian, George, and Elaine Marks. *Homosexualities and French Literature: Critical Contexts, Critical Texts.* Ithaca, N.Y.: Cornell University Press, 1979.

CHAPTER FOURTEEN

The Russian Revolution and Women

Richard Stites

Based on his wide experience researching and writing Russian history, Richard Stites offers a broad synthesis of women's place in the Russian revolutionary tradition and postrevolutionary society. His story begins with the reforming sentiments of the 1850s and 1860s, at a time of debate over the nature and course of the emancipation of serfs. He points to midcentury as the first phase of women's participation in the reforming movements and identifies three influential, if distinct, approaches: the feminist, which was essentially a movement by women for women; the nihilist, which was a countercultural current stressing the personal values of equality; and the radical, which sought total emancipation of all through socialism. The second phase was inaugurated by the tsarist government's commitment to industrialization and shift to parliamentary politics. It saw the growth of political parties, and many on the left, including the Marxists, feared the feminist revival as diversionary. In 1917, however, the significance of the half-century debate over the woman question became clear. Women's equality was among the many promises made by the new Bolshevik leadership, as were workers' control over factory production, educational advances, and ethnic self-determination. Despite the regime's public commitment to women's rights, however, the persistence of older notions of women's subordinate role hampered greater strides toward gender equality, as did continuous priority dilemmas that placed women's issues secondary to other societal and developmental goals. Besides, the regime was poor and could not afford extensive social support. It was only in work—as wage earners in social production—that the possibility of individual independence was extended to Russian women. There was less success in transforming family relationships and role divisions within the family.

Women's participation in the Russian Revolution of 1917 was conditioned—both in its successes and in its failures—by a long and interesting prehistory. The explosive events of 1917 can be explained only partially by the physical, military, and social environment of the moment. To this analysis must be added a legacy of images, beliefs, feelings, and attitudes shaped in the two generations preceding the revolution: the Populist Revolt (1860–81), an almost purely upper-class affair; and the revolution of 1905 (1890–1914), a nationwide, all-class uprising. Recent scholarship on peasants, workers, nationalities, soldiers, sailors, and other groups has demonstrated clearly that long-standing attitudes and circumstances of life are important factors in the molding of revolutionary (and counterrevolutionary) behavior. The same applies to the history of women: although deep study of working-class women's lives has just begun, research on the development of women's consciousness and on women's movements in the major revolutionary episodes of the nineteenth and early twentieth centuries indicates the main peculiarities of women's political activity in the great Russian Revolution of 1917.

Although the growth of "women's consciousness"—a refusal to accept traditional social roles—began in early nineteenth-century Russia, the woman question as a social issue burst onto the public scene only in the late 1850s and early 1860s. Why? Part of the reason was the general atmosphere of a political "thaw" under a new, reforming tsar, Alexander II (r. 1855–81), the deep shame over the Russian defeat in the Crimean War (1854–56), and a sense of euphoria connected with the imminent emancipation of the serfs (1861). Social and economic factors were also at work: the specter of serf emancipation and the prospect that females of the serf-owning class could be thrown onto the economy awakened an impulse among some young, gentry women to prepare for economic and personal independence. No less crucial was the emergence of a new generation of intelligentsia males whose social outlook—known as "nihilism" or a sweeping negation of accepted values—included egalitarianism, an attack upon elitist manners and conventions, and a determination to practice their beliefs in everyday life. From this milieu, which also spawned a wave of revolutionaries, emerged the first important writings on women's equality. Russian radicalism was almost unique in its demands for women's equality and the demands coincided with a new stage of women's perception and self-perception.

Motivations, impulses, and responses of Russian women themselves were complex and diverse, with the simultaneous appearance of three distinct approaches to the woman question: feminism, nihilism, and radicalism. Though there was much overlapping, shifting, and interlocking of these three currents at first, they eventually sorted themselves into separate ways. Russian feminists were in many ways similar to Western ones. They sought not revolution or even personal sexual emancipation, but launched rather a legal and moderate movement led by women on behalf of women. By social origin, the leaders and founders were mostly noblewomen. One should not be tempted to derive a deterministic sociology from this fact: the first nihilist and radical women came essentially from the same background. The feminist leader Anna Filosofova was the wife of a tsarist general, but Sofya Perovskaya, assassin of the tsar in 1881, and Alexandra Kollontai, a Bolshevik commissar in 1917, were daughters of generals. But the feminists chose very consciously to define the needs of women as something separate from general social struggle and the liberation of all the people. Their aims were modest and their achievements impressive: charity for poor girls, mutual assistance, self-directed activity in a land where this was in short supply, and educational and professional opportunities. Largely through their efforts, universities and medical courses became available to Russian women in the 1870s, a notable feat for any European country at that time.

Nihilism was not a political movement in the 1860s; it was rather a mentality and a style of personal liberation. Like their male colleagues, nihilist women stressed their independence, their modernity, and their contempt for the established order by means of physical appearance and symbolic gestures: short hair, plain (sometimes dirty) clothes, a defeminized manner, cigarette smoking, and brusqueness in speech. Nihilism was part of a countercultural revolt like those of nineteenth-century European bohemians, fin-de-siècle decadents, or American hippies of the 1960s. Their values were equality, science worship, progress, and disdain for old Russian ways and customs—including religion, the family, and the highly stratified class system. Wives and daughters broke with their families, migrated to St. Petersburg and Moscow, enrolled in courses, joined circles and communes, and in general scandalized polite society. Many women who went through this counterculture moved on to political radicalism and even terrorism. Others did not. Nihilism was not coterminous with revolution for people of either sex. Even among women who admired Nicholas Chernyshevsky's *What Is To Be Done?* (1862)—a utopian novel about women's emancipation—were those that remained deaf to its radical message and contented themselves with borrowing its devices of fictitious marriages, women's cooperatives, and communes for personal, social, and sexual emancipation.

Nihilist and radical women are often linked in the study of the revolutionary movement of the 1860s. But as far as women are concerned, radicals had more in common with active feminists than with those—called "egoist" nihilists—who defined emancipation as a personal affair. The feminists and the radical women had larger goals. For the latter, this meant emancipation of all the people, especially the toiling peasants, through socialism. They also shared an almost religious sense of service and self-sacrifice. In a brilliant book on the subject, Barbara Engel has shown how their strategy of sacrifice and martyrdom—while endowing the revolution with a symbolic halo—diminished their feminist sensibilities and led them to downplay or ignore special problems of the female population. This does not mean that the feminist impulse was absent among radical women. Many of the most active women in the populist movement of the 1870s went through a crucial phase of womanly self-definition before turning the personal into the political. Female revolutionaries also maintained networks of moral and psychological sustenance, a phenomenon that has survived strongly into the present.

Who were the radical women and what did they do? Most of the several thousand females who participated in the revolutionary movement between the 1860s and 1880s were from privileged Russian families—gentry, professionals, government officials, and military officers—with an increasing admixture of merchants' and priests' daughters, women of the lower classes, Jews, Poles, and other nationalities. In the tiny circles of the 1860s, women acted as adjuncts, recruiters, messengers, and were sometimes manipulated by radical men such as the notorious Sergei Nechaev. In the 1870s, with the "Movement to the People," hundreds of women migrated into the factories and villages in search of the "socialist" peasant, propagandizing, and falling into police dragnets. Hundreds were arrested and incarcerated or sent into Siberian exile. An era of assassination was inaugurated when Vera Zasulich fired a shot at a high police official in the capital in 1877. When disillusionment with peasant revolutionary potential and fear of open exposure led a branch of the movement—the People's Will—to a campaign of terror in the years 1879–81, women were even more prominent numerically, constituting about one-third of that body's all-powerful executive committee. One leader, Sofya Perovskaya, directed the final assault on the tsar that took his life in March 1881, after which she and her coconspirators were hanged in a public square in St. Petersburg. Both the murder and the executions induced social shock.

But failure attended the symbolic victory of the revolutionary Populists: no revolution occurred, peasant socialism did not emerge, and the People's Will gradually disintegrated. The Populist episode left a dual legacy for radical women: it encircled them with the aureole of martyrdom and revolutionary honor and it endowed them with a myth of moral courage and indomitable power. But it often led their followers to continue the "pure radical" notion of the Great Cause, to the detriment of feminist concerns; and it also failed to win women a place of equal power and creativity in the revolutionary movements.

The second phase of the revolutionary movement in Russia occurred in an altered social context. Russia's rapid industrialization added dramatically to the number of urban factory women, prostitutes, and domestic servants. Peasant women followed their menfolk—and sometimes went independently—into the wage workforce in the cities, the slums, and the proletarian working-class quarters. Female domestics were the most ignored by social critics (and the least studied to this day), though they were very prominent in the urban housing revolution that erupted in Russia after the Bolshevik Revolution. In the eyes of the cultural and religious elite, prostitutes became a symbol of a moral decadence that was allegedly engulfing Russian society. Factory women, as Rose Glickman's superb study has shown, had to face hostility and abuse on two fronts: in the exploitativeness of the factory system itself; and in the home where male "proletarian virtue" often excluded decent treatment of wives and daughters.

The partially successful revolution of 1905, which produced civil rights, a free press, a parliament, and dozens of new public institutions, also thickened the social and political texture of Russia. Into the maelstrom of revolutionary politics rushed peasants, workers, the middle classes, and national minorities of many levels of cultural development. To represent their interests and those of the forces of order and stability, a whole spectrum of political parties appeared, most of which deliberated openly in the Duma, or parliament, created in 1906. The right-wing parties that inscribed fatherland, faith, and tsar on their banners avidly opposed feminism and women's suffrage. Conservatives sometimes fudged the issue but were generally hostile. The Liberal Party (Kadets) divided at first—thinking other matters more important than votes for women—but grudgingly came round to support them. All the leftist parties—the Marxist Social Democrats (both Bolsheviks and Mensheviks), the Socialist Revolutionaries, and the anarchist groups—supported equal rights for women in principle, though only the Marxists proclaimed it publicly and unambiguously. But in practice many leftists viewed the woman question as a minor cause that should be subsumed under a grander perspective of all-Russian liberation and the destruction of the tsarist system. The radicals of 1905 were less interested in fighting for sexual equality in part because they rested comfortably on the radical myth that these things had already been decided in the 1860s.

While women were accepted as equals in the parties of the left, as individuals they were much less prominent in the leadership than they had been a generation earlier. The steady influx into the socialist parties of workers whose attitude toward women was not as advanced as those of the intelligentsia may also have been responsible for a certain downgrading of the role of women. It must be kept in mind, however, that for many women who sought a role in political life, the socialist parties seemed the only genuinely hospitable home. One development that made some Marxists suspicious of what they called "feminist" concerns was the emergence of the Russian women's suffrage movement around 1905. The feminist movement of 1905 was complex. In one sense it was a continuation of "classical" feminism of the 1860s, a movement of women for women and emphatically not a class struggle, nor ready to bury its cause under some larger one defined by men. This focus on women as a constituency that cut across class lines and the willingness of some feminist groups to accept a limited property suffrage was quite enough to besmirch it in the eyes of most Marxists as "bourgeois." The charge was not wholly accurate or fair, quite aside from the complex meaning of the word bourgeois in the Russian context.

In the first place, almost all feminists—conservative, liberal, or "social"—saw women's emancipation as part of the liberation of all oppressed peoples, though not via "proletarian" revolution or neopopulism. They had upheld the revolution of 1905, and supported a whole range of reforms that benefited everyone. Secondly, an important component of the feminist movement was specifically interested in the labor movement, working-class women, factory conditions, the right to strike, and so on. Some of these feminists were even Socialist Party members. But they usually found themselves rebuffed by party leaders who frowned upon "separatist" tendencies. By 1906, the feminists—reshuffled several times—had parted company with the revolutionary movement and continued their fight for the vote. They did not get it until 1917, but in the course of their campaigning they continued what their mothers had started—building self-confidence and organizational experience and effecting changes in women's lives in education, law, and social protection.

The populist tradition devoid of organized feminism continued strong among those women who shared with radical men the belief that everything about the emancipation of women had already been said and that there was no need for a special women's movement. For Maria Spiridonova, a fiery schoolteacher from Tambov province, the hallmark of a political woman was personal valor and action. During the 1905 revolution she avenged the scourged peasants of her province by shooting dead the general who had led the punitive expedition against them. After ten years in exile she returned to European Russia in 1917 and became a leader of the ultraradical left Socialist Revolutionaries. Spiridonova evinced no interest whatsoever in feminism, seeing herself as already the equal of men and seeing the revolution as the focal point of her life. Vera Zasulich, ex-terrorist and Menshevik Marxist, considered special meetings and organizations for women within Social Democracy unnecessary. Such women harbored the shortsightedness of successful women of the past (monarchs and writers, for example) who, seeing their own record as "proof" of women's ability, ignored feminist concerns. The multitude of professional revolutionary women of all parties in the revolutions of 1905 and 1917 who shied away from the suffrage movement distinguished the Russian experience from that of England where violence found a place inside the feminist movement itself. It also reinforced male notions that attention to women's problems was provincial and harmful.

The "proletarian women's movement," in contrast, was an attempt to synthesize one brand of radicalism—Marxism—with feminism. Formulated by the German Clara Zetkin, and adapted to Russian conditions by Kollontai and Nadezhda Krupskaya (Lenin's wife), it rejected "bourgeois" feminist movements of women for women, reaffirmed the alliance of men and women in the class struggle for a proletarian revolution, but insisted on the special needs and concerns of women within the proletarian movement. Working-class women in particular were beset by problems of illiteracy, low political consciousness, unequal pay, absence of maternity benefits, sexual harassment on the job, and even abuse from their proletarian husbands. The Marxist feminists believed that these concerns were real, that organized feminism—with its suspected class bias—could not alleviate them, and that male socialist leaders poorly understood them and gave them insufficient attention. In 1905, Kollontai, still a Menshevik, helped to launch a special campaign to enlist women workers in the Social Democratic labor movement and to fight the feminist organizations in Russia. This struggle culminated at the first Women's Conference in 1908 when the two currents confronted each other in a mood of hostility. Thereafter, feminism went into decline. The Marxist women's movement revived on a very modest scale in 1912–14 when the Bolsheviks launched a newspaper called *The Woman Worker* and began celebrating the European socialist holiday, International Women's Day.

Tsarist Russia collapsed in the middle of World War I. By then the lives of women had changed significantly since the onset of the revolutionary movement in the 1860s. In spite of its many backward features, that collapsing state was not some sort of feudal "old regime." For women of many classes, new public spaces and sites of interaction had opened up gradually in the three decades after 1861, and very rapidly thereafter. Among them were certain courts where women could litigate, revolutionary circles admitting women (of any ethnic group), families of inter-marriage, university courses, factory workshops and yards, and places of culture and entertainment. Theater audiences in the capitals became very diverse at mid-century and the national scene grew in numbers. The net of provincial showplaces provided points of convergence for genders and classes. Actresses and singers traveled far and wide in search of success and personal expression. New identities were formed around these sites that differed from those of the early nineteenth century: imperial court, gentry salon, ballroom, market place, church, cabin, or brothel. The swelling of geographical and social mobility created integrating forces for both sexes and pointed toward what in the West was called civil society. Dense and continuous connection through friendship, travel, correspondence between, for example, feminists and performing artists of Russia with those of Europe was an index of this endless remaking of identities and sensibilities.

Russia's sufferings in World War I (1914–17) threw earlier feminist-versus-revolutionary controversies into the shadows, reduced old organizations to shambles, and kept many revolutionary leaders out of touch with Russian reality. Thus, on the eve of the 1917 revolution, the woman question, having won attention in the last years of the monarchy, was practically dormant. The revolutionary year 1917 began with the overthrow of the monarchy, and was followed by an uneasy and undefined alliance of the "bourgeois" parties in the Provisional Government and the moderate socialist leaders in the Soviets (workers' councils). It ended in October with the Bolshevik seizure of power and the creation of a new revolutionary regime under Lenin. At no time did the women's struggle dominate the proceedings, but a struggle there was nonetheless. All the old factions went to war again. The urban uprising in the capital that caused the collapse of the monarchy was begun by a demonstration in support of International Women's Day; and both Mensheviks and Bolsheviks attempted to organize and recruit women workers throughout the year. The feminist organizations came out of the doldrums, united, and petitioned the Provisional Government for the vote—which they received along with sharpened barbs from the Bolshevik women's organizers for presuming to speak for lower-class women. All the rhetoric and the insults of 1905 revolution were trumpeted again by both sides.

But the feminists found a fresh cause with an ironic twist: the Women's Batallions of Death. If women of the revolutionary tradition could shunt feminism aside in favor of the Great Cause of social revolution, other women could do the same for another Great Cause: defending the fatherland. In the summer of 1917, while regular troops were melting away during the Provisional Government's last and ill-fated offensive against the Central Powers, Russian women volunteers, organized into batallions, were trying to stiffen the lines against the invaders. In the last act of 1917, the dramatic but anticlimactic storming of the Winter Palace (headquarters of the Provisional Government), a unit from the Women's Batallions defended while Bolshevik Red Guards, some women among them, took the palace.

For the Bolsheviks "the day after the revolution" had at last come when, after generations of postponement of "smaller" questions for the sake of the larger, the former had to be faced and solved. But the day after the revolution never came. As in the past, there were always good reasons why certain things had to wait—equality, harmony, cooperation, abundance, social justice, all the furnishings of the utopian dream world. The first inkling that the revolution was not over but only beginning was the Civil War (1918–21), where perhaps as many as eighty thousand women served in combat, medical, support, espionage, partisan, and administrative roles. For these women the Great Cause—and not the rights of women—arose once again as the all-embracing mission in life. They fought, they suffered, and they died, sometimes horribly, as they had done in the struggle against autocracy, once again projecting an unparalleled image of nobility and sacrifice, an image reflected in the posters and stories of the Civil War. It was in fact one of the greatest sagas of women at war in modern times, a saga to be repeated in excruciating and terrible detail when Nazi Germany invaded Russia in 1941. It must be remembered that the women on the anti-Bolshevik side of the Civil War also suffered, died, or went into tragic exile forever. As in all the previous episodes of the revolutionary tradition, the Bolshevik women were more often deputies, auxiliaries, assistants, nurturers, and teachers, than the possessors of raw power and monumental stature.

The Marxist-feminist synthesis of the prerevolutionary years was not wholly forgotten or abandoned. Lenin proclaimed again and again the complete equality

of the sexes in all realms of life—and he was the first political leader in power ever
to do so. His regime, with the assistance of women advisors, legislated equal pay
for equal work; proclaimed full political, juridical, and educational equality; legalized abortion; and liberalized the divorce system, making woman a full partner in
the family. More importantly, recognizing that laws do not make a social revolution and that the best arbiters of women's affairs were women themselves, the Bolsheviks launched a movement for women's self-activity; the Zhenotdel, or women's
section of the Communist Party (1919–30). Under the leadership of Kollontai and
others, the Zhenotdel, a national network of women organizers, spread the news of
the revolution, enforced its laws (especially against errant and brutal husbands), set
up political education and literacy classes for working-class and peasant women,
fought prostitution (now outlawed), lifted the veil physically and metaphorically
from the faces of women in the Muslim republics, an area barely touched by the
currents of women's liberation thought before 1917.

A seldom noted effect of the Russian Revolution on women was to hurl them
across the vast expanses of the new Soviet state. Upper-class women of nineteenth
century Russia had been at home in the spas of the Caucasus and among the dress-
makers of Paris and other European cities. Officers' wives, and those of the exiled
Decembrists, had known life on the frontier. Radical and nonradical women had
haunted the university halls of Zurich. And a few hundred had seen battle on the
shores of the Crimea, in Serbia, and in Poland during the tsarist wars. But the Soviet
regime ushered in a new era of travel and, for some, adventure. The tens of thousands
of Bolshevik women who fought in the Civil War saw action from Estonia to Baku
and Vladivostok. The sparse prerevolutionary foreign settlements in central Asia now
swarmed with activist women—Zhenotdel, Godless League members, Komsomol,
workers, officials, and teachers. Contact between Russian and non-Russian women
and men has been barely touched in the scholarship, except for the dramatic campaigns to emancipate the Muslim "women of the East." In the 1930s and during the
war, this diasporic movement widened enormously as women traveled out to industrial sites, flew to the Arctic Circle and, in 1945, marched to Berlin.

The energy of Zhenotdel leaders was prodigious and their social ambitions
vaulting; but their organization always remained weak, its efforts underfinanced,
and their aims held in dubious repute by many male Bolshevik leaders. Why? Bolshevik leaders endorsed the principle of equality of the sexes, but most had no interest in the rapid emancipation of women. Those who did often thought in terms of
what one scholar has called "mobilization for modernization"—the deployment of
women's energies in modern productive labor for the sake of the regime or of society—another version of the Great Cause. It is tempting to attribute this to the "treachery" or "hypocrisy" of Bolshevik males, but name-calling does not add much to
historical understanding. All revolutions, in a sense, cheat their supporters and mass
participants, just as almost all societies exploit their poorest and weakest members.
The communist revolutions of our time in Yugoslavia, China, Cuba, Vietnam, and
other places that have gone back on their promises to women are no different, except
that they promised more and thus found it harder to keep their word. Like many
revolutionaries in Russia before them, the Bolsheviks interpreted "equality" as complementarity, specialization, or division of labor. Since there were no titles or rules

of entry that mentioned gender, Bolsheviks came to assume that theirs was a community of equals even though some had more power, did more writing, or, after coming to power, had bigger rations. Bolshevism could not break with the deep conviction that women, though "equal" in valor and revolutionary consciousness, were by nature better at support, sustenance, and nurturing.

In their public statements and symbols, Bolsheviks neither demeaned women nor put them on a pedestal. There is no equivalent to Marianne, symbol of the French Republic, in Soviet heraldry—though it had been used by tsarism in World War I. The posters, medallions, and symbols of the revolution show man and woman, side by side, apparent equals in struggle and in labor. But a closer look at those symbols of the earliest months and years often shows women (sickle in hand) depicted as representing rural life, agriculture, the peasantry, and fertility; while men (hammer in hand) represented the city, industry, workers, production. In a subliminal way, early Bolshevik symbolism reflected a view of women as passive, pliant, and reproductive. Although the Bolsheviks proclaimed from the very outset a moral and social alliance between peasants and proletarians and between town and country, the alliance was always an unequal one in favor of the urban over the rural.

In the 1920s Bolshevik men and women tried through public statements and institutions to reduce this dichotomy. With the emergence of Stalinism in the 1930s, things changed drastically. The Zhenotdel was abolished with the explanation that women were now actually equal to men and that its work was no longer needed—a palpable misstatement. Wives of engineers and managers were publicly exalted for their work in beautifying the home and their husbands' offices. In art, the ascetic and determined women revolutionaries were replaced by gushing images of supermothers and heroines of domesticity in order to match new pronatalist policies. If the early Bolshevik male leaders were conditioned by a cultural block to renege on the promises of women's equality, some of them at least had made an effort to recall these promises. Stalinists of the 1930s quietly, and sometimes rudely, repudiated the old intelligentsia norms of political respect for women, and reverted to many of the patriarchal attitudes and life patterns of the old regime. The authoritarian style of Stalinism, the brutal warlike atmosphere of strife, and the economic imperatives of the five-year plans were partly responsible for this reversion. The industrial revolution of the early 1930s pushed peasants into the cities and workers and lower-class urban elements up into positions of power and responsibility, and with them came still unreconstructed attitudes toward women, the family, and sexuality.

Can this be called a counterrevolution in women's emancipation? It is true that laws of 1936 criminalized abortion and made divorce extremely difficult—another reversion to the tsarist era. But the divorce law seems to have been widely supported by the masses of Soviet women who were tired of the "sexual freedom" of the 1920s that led to abandonment and serial polygamy for males. The industrialization drive brought harsh living conditions to many—to say nothing of the terrors wrought by collectivization and famine policies. But against this must be set an extremely progressive system of female education, professionalism, and affirmative action designed to pull everyone into productive labor.

The successors of Stalin rendered their verdict by liberalizing the divorce and abortion laws and keeping intact the educational opportunities for women—though in practice thay never delivered equality in school or the workplace. Post-Stalinist reform in the status of women was, like much else after 1953, partial and selective. Attitudes and structures remained as in Stalin's time: women were to work in the economy and were expected to work a second shift in the home; they were segregated into lower-paying professions and into lower-paying ranks in all professions. There was ferment, quiet newspaper campaigns and lobbying for amenities that are central to women's lives. But nothing except pallid and formulaic statements about male responsibilities and the ritual claims of equality was done by the state to diminish the deep patriarchal attitudes toward women. Only after the onset of *perestroika* and *glasnost* and then the collapse of the Soviet Union could women organize themselves into truly independent political entities.

In retrospect, the revolution—and the revolutionary movement that preceded it—seems a failure in respect to women's position in Russian society. This is not wholly true. Soviet women enjoyed wide opportunities in science, technology, medicine, and other professions that were rarely found in the West until a few decades ago. That gap has closed and women's activism in Europe and the United States—to use a favorite Soviet expression—"caught up and overtook" that of Soviet women. For the new feminist movements that are now in place in post-Soviet Russia, the lessons of the Russian Revolution should be clear: "larger" issues and causes—however noble—should not be permitted to swallow women's issues or independent feminism. Russian males would be well advised to look hard at the reality of women's lives, a reality that is clearly visible behind the tatter of old slogans and symbols.

SUGGESTIONS FOR FURTHER READING

Atkinson, Dorothy, Alexander Dallin, and Gail Warshofsky Lapidus, eds. *Women in Russia.* Stanford: Stanford University Press, 1977.

Bergman, Jay. *Vera Zasulich: A Biography.* Stanford: Stanford University Press, 1983.

Bernstein, Laurie. *Sonia's Daughters: Prostitutes and Their Regulation in Imperial Russia.* Berkeley: University of California Press, 1995.

Clements, Barbara Evans. *Bolshevik Feminism: The Life of Aleksandra Kollontai.* Bloomington, Ind.: Indiana University Press, 1979.

Clements, Barbara Evans, Barbara Alpern Engel, and Christine D. Worobec, eds. *Russia's Women: Accommodation, Resistance, Transformation.* Berkeley: University of California Press, 1991.

Clyman, Toby W., and Judith Vowles, eds. *Russia through Women's Eyes: Autobiographies from Tsarist Russia.* New Haven: Yale University Press, 1996.

Edmonson, Linda. *Feminism in Russia, 1900–1917.* London: Heinemann Educational, 1984.

Engel, Barbara Alpern. *Between the Fields and the City: Women, Work, and Family in Russia, 1861–1914.* Cambridge and New York: Cambridge University Press, 1994.

Engel, Barbara Alpern, and Anastasia Posadskaya-Vanderbeck, eds. *A Revolution of Their Own: Voices of Women in Soviet History.* Translated by Sona Hoisington. Boulder, Colo.: Westview Press, 1998.

Farnsworth, Beatrice. *Aleksandra Kollontai: Socialism, Feminism, and the Bolshevik Revolution.* Stanford: Stanford University Press, 1980.

Glickman, Rose L. *Russian Factory Women: Workplace and Society 1880–1914.* Berkeley: University of California Press, 1984.

Goscilo, Helena, and Beth Holmgren, eds. *Russia—Women—Culture.* Bloomington, Ind.: Indiana University Press, 1996.

Kelly, Catriona. *A History of Russian Women's Writing, 1820–1992.* Oxford: Clarendon Press; New York: Oxford University Press, 1994.

————, ed. *An Anthology of Russian Women's Writing, 1777–1992.* Translated by Catriona Kelly. Oxford and New York: Oxford University Press, 1994.

Lapidus, Gail Warshofsky. *Women in Soviet Society.* Berkeley: University of California Press, 1978.

Mamonova, Tatyana, ed. *Women and Russia: Feminist Writings from the Soviet Union.* Translated by Rebecca Park and Catherine A. Fitzpatrick. Boston: Beacon Press, 1984.

Pushkareva, N[atalia] L[vovna]. *Women in Russian History: From the Tenth to the Twentieth Century.* Translated by Eve Levin. Armonk, N.Y.: M. E. Sharpe, 1997.

Stites, Richard. *The Women's Liberation Movement in Russia: Feminism, Nihilism, and Bolshevism 1860–1930.* Princeton: Princeton University Press, 1978.

Worobec, Christine. *Peasant Russia: Family and Community in the Post-Emancipation Period.* Princeton: Princeton University Press, 1991.

CHAPTER FIFTEEN

Gender and the Austrian Fraternal Welfare State After 1945

Gerda Ruth Neyer

The welfare state has been a subject of active and impressive scholarship since the reemergence of the women's movement and women's history starting in the late 1960s. The research shows not only its crucial importance for understanding women's work and family lives as well as changing definitions of citizenship in the twentieth century, but also for powerfully shaping class, race and gender relations in society. Social welfare policies—from protective labor laws to measures to improve infant health to new space and ventilation in factories and workshops— profoundly impact daily life, differentially affecting, however, life's chances for women based on their class, race, familial position, or sexual orientation. Scholars disagree, however, over the fundamental characterization of the welfare state. For many feminists, early welfare interventions merely substituted the state for the father's authority, which perpetuated women's dependency; here, the welfare state is seen as "patriarchal." More recently, others have stressed its "maternalist" character, drawing attention to organized women's agency in effecting welfare policies oriented toward the needs of women and children. These policies, however, often extend middle-class norms into working-class lives. In a radical break with both formulations, Gerda Ruth Neyer offers a new way to think about the welfare state. Based on a careful examination of parental leave policies after 1945, she labels the state "fraternal," implying an orientation "which tries to secure men's independence as individuals by treating all men as equal vis-à-vis women and by denying women equality with men by treating them either as women (i.e., non-men), as mothers, or as wives." Neyer offers a feminist analysis and critique of this complicated gendering process. What has been its impact on married and single mothers in different occupations? Significantly, in the move toward legislative uniformity under the European Union since 1995, many of the concrete gains which supported women's rights to work and to children in Austria have been abridged.

Theorists of the welfare state classify Austria as a conservative-corporatist and/or familistic welfare state indicating that its policies are directed towards the "family" and towards sustaining status differences among various occupational groups. Compared to "liberal" welfare states (Australia, Canada, Great Britain, the United States), which offer only modest social insurance and social assistance, and to "social democratic" welfare states (especially the Nordic countries), which grant universalized access to highly developed systems of social security and social services, Austria's insurance programs cover separately groups such as blue-collar workers, civil servants, farmers, and the self-employed. Benefits also exist to support the family, but social infrastructure services, such as child care, to substitute for unpaid work within families are not widely available.

Feminist scholars have criticized these welfare state classifications on various grounds. The most important objections pertain to the failure of these categories first, to evaluate women's unpaid work (as mothers and/or as wives) in its relation to the welfare state benefits; second, to incorporate non-employed women's welfare status into these models; third, to analyze the welfare state's function in creating and sustaining power differences within the "family" (i.e., among couples); and, fourth, to illuminate the extent to which welfare state provisions support or hamper women's and men's autonomy and independence, either as individuals or as mothers or fathers. To view welfare states from a perspective which includes these gender considerations requires a reconceptualization of the welfare state itself. Feminist scholarship, indeed, suggests its redefinition as a state which uses social policies as interventions into civil society in order to structure and regulate it. Welfare state policies are thus designed to shape social institutions and/or social relations. If we apply this definition to an investigation of the Austrian welfare state, we arrive at a different classification of its type. The Austrian welfare state may be described as a "fraternal" welfare state, a welfare state which tries to secure men's independence as individuals by treating all men as equal vis-à-vis women and by denying women equality with men by treating them either as women (i.e., non-men), as mothers, or as wives.

This essay attempts to exemplify the fraternal features of the Austrian welfare state by depicting the development and key assumptions of the Austrian Parental Leave Policies after 1945. In essence this policy-cluster comprises two types of welfare state legislation: the Maternity Protection Law and the Parental Leave Law. The Maternity Protection Law, which was introduced in Austria in 1885, aims at protecting mothers' and children's health through employment protection provisions for women during pregnancy and after childbirth. These regulations include a prohibition of employment for non-self-employed and unemployed women for a minimum of 16 weeks before and after childbirth with full income replacement, and benefit payments for self-employed women to hire assistance during that time. The Parental Leave Legislation, which was enacted in 1957, enables mothers (and since 1990 fathers, too) to take a paid leave of absence in order to care for their child. Currently more than three-quarters of all women giving birth are entitled to parental leave benefits and almost all of these mothers (98 percent) take advantage of the option; but hardly any of the fathers do. While the first measure is widely accepted, the second one has been highly contested ever since its introduction. The structure of the Austrian welfare state has been one of the central measures to legitimize the persistence of gender-differences in Austria. The parental leave benefits favor men's independence through welfare state support for women.

In 1957, women in Austria were for the first time given the opportunity to take an (initially unpaid) six-months parental leave at the end of their maternity protection leave. At the same time, the Christian-conservative and the socialist coalition government annulled provisions dating from the time of the Nazis whereby firms had to set up their own nursery schools or to contribute to the financing of public or private day nurseries in their vicinity. Thus, social policy set the stage for the private care of (young) children by their mothers.

In 1960, maternity leave was increased to a year and income-related parental leave benefits were introduced. They varied according to family form, income, and size. Single mothers (and those responsible for the upkeep of their families) received parental leave benefits equivalent to their unemployment benefit entitlements. Married mothers received maximally half of the latter. In the case of married women, the husband's income was counted towards the parental leave benefit so that the latter could be further reduced or completely eliminated. Entitlement to parental leave benefits demanded that the mother abstain from gainful employment and devote her time primarily to the care of her child.

The parental leave policy of the 1950s and 1960s did not view women as individuals, but exclusively as "mothers," as caretakers of their children and their families. Since only mothers were entitled to parental leave, fathers were such "freed" from any caretaking obligations. Despite this gendering of parenthood, the Austrian welfare state policy of the 1950s and 1960s did not adhere solely to a "male breadwinner"–"dependent wife" model. The parental leave laws indirectly conceived of women as "breadwinners," too, since the parental benefit did not replace women's individual income but became part of the family income. In line with other family policy measures, especially family and child allowances (both usually paid to the father or husband), the parental leave policy thus intended to reduce the financial obligations of fathers/husbands towards their dependents. The parental leave policy, therefore, may be viewed as a welfare state policy which tried to ease the economic costs of maintaining a family for fathers/men. At the same time, given the fact that women had to interrupt their gainful employment while on parental leave, the laws increased the economic costs of mothering for women.

With the onset of the one-party Socialist government (1970–83), the policies of the Austrian welfare state underwent profound changes. It was the intention of the government to universalize welfare state benefits. In 1974 parental leave regulations were revised in a way which incorporated the aims of the government to "modernize" society as well as preserve the traditions of a mother-centered policy. The new regulations made it easier for young women, unemployed women, and women who had more than one child to meet the requirements for drawing parental leave benefits. Parental leave benefits were separated from family income, raised substantially, and transformed into an income-unrelated benefit. The income-unrelated benefit comprised two rates: a standard rate for married mothers and a 50-percent higher rate both for single mothers and for married mothers whose husbands had insufficient or no income. For single mothers unable to work after their parental leave for want of child-care facilities, special benefits were introduced which could be granted until the child's third birthday.

The government saw the amendment to parental leave legislation as part of its efforts to increase women's labor force participation and to ensure women's independent existence either through employment or through social benefits. However, since entitlements to parental leave benefits remained restricted to mothers, the parental leave policy adhered to its feminization of parenthood. Moreover, with the exception of parental benefits, all other family benefits continued to be paid usually to the husband or to the father of the child. Welfare state policies of the 1970s thus "individualized" women as far as their personal income was concerned, but continued to subsidize men/fathers with respect to their monetary and nurturing responsibilities toward their wives and children.

Since the emergence of the second feminist movement in the early 1970s, parental leave policies and their gender-segregating effects have come under repeated criticism. Feminists proposed changes of the parental leave policy along two major lines: first, that labor market policies and parental leave policies be altered to allow women to combine gainful employment and motherhood according to their needs, and, second, that fathers be entitled to obtain parental leaves. Only the latter proposal was partially put into law, though embedded in a "package of measures for the family" which still gave priority to mothers' caring duties. The parental leave laws introduced by the Social-Democratic and Christian-conservative coalition government in 1990, furthermore, combined a number of important provisions. These included the extension of parental leave and parental leave benefits until the child's second birthday; the option for fathers to draw parental leave benefits, yet only if the mother pursued gainful employment; the option of a sharing of parental leave benefits between the parents; the option of part-time work with a reduced rate of parental leave benefits for both parents in the child's second year of life or for one parent in the child's second and third year of life; the granting of half-rate parental leave benefits until the child's second birthday to non-self-employed working women who have no claim to parental leave benefits; the granting of half-rate parental benefits to self-employed women in farming and business until the child's second birthday; and, finally, the introduction of a reemployment allowance for firms in which a woman or a man has availed her(him)self of her (his) right to a two-year parental leave.

Significantly, these provisions presented a whole range of family-oriented measures that were far more than a mere amendment to the provisions in force between 1974 and 1989. On the normative level they recognized the fact that children require care over a longer period of time and that this care should not only be the sole responsibility of mothers. The granting of allowances to groups that had previously not been eligible for parental leave represented a partial allocation of responsibility to society. The work of caring, however, remained privatized and widely feminized. The needs of parents for greater flexibility in their arrangements for the care of small children were not respected sufficiently. Priority was given to employers' claims concerning their organizational needs. Parental leave could only be shared by the parents once; parents had to decide within four weeks of the child's birth how they wished to structure the whole period of parental leave until the child's second birthday. There was no legal right to part-time work. In essence these new provisions did not create the social, economic, occupational, and caring conditions for women—and especially for single women—to be able to live with children on equal terms with men.

Nevertheless, the government and the parliament considered the amendments as promoting gender equality and "equal treatment of both genders in the world of work." This marks a shift in the legitimation of gender-specific social policies from one based on notions of motherhood to the principles of equality and equal rights, with equality, however, varying according to which gender it is applied to. While fathers were given the opportunity to go on parental leave, women's opportunities—especially those of single mothers—to arrange parental leave, caring, and gainful employment according to their needs were hardly enhanced.

With Austria's entrance into the European Union and in compliance with the Maastricht criteria to tighten the budget, two "Structural Adjustment Laws" were passed in 1995 and 1996 which led to massive cuts in parental leave benefits. Drawing parental leave benefits was made more difficult by extending the employment period necessary to qualify for them. The 50 percent higher parental leave benefit for single mothers was replaced by a loan which must be repaid by the parent not drawing benefits—usually the father. The paid parental leave benefit period was reduced by half a year, unless the child's father takes half a year of parental leave. (This rule also applies if the father is not eligible for parental leave benefits or if the mother has no contact with the child's father.) The periods of possible part-time employment and of eligibility for special benefits for single mothers (after the parental leave period) were reduced accordingly. In addition, women claiming special benefits as single mothers must present a confirmation from the local council that child care facilities are not available and the local council must pay the federal authorities a third of the cost of the special benefits for single mothers.

These provisions not only imply significant benefit reductions for women but also a shift towards a "post-patriarchal" social policy. In apparent accord with feminist demands that welfare state policies should focus more on men's responsibilities as fathers, the "family" was re-institutionalized as the basis of the parental leave policy. The draft for the legislation foresaw making parental leave benefits dependent on the family income and financing the (higher) benefits for single mothers by introducing a right for the mother to claim maintenance from the father for herself. The laws enacted assume that all women live or have lived in a relationship with a man who has the potential to support them financially. In a return to the values that shaped welfare legislation in the 1950s and 1960s, women are, thus, no longer viewed as independent individuals who have a right to their own income, either through employment or through welfare state benefits. Rather they are placed in a relationship dependent on the child's father, and this relationship, then, is made a basis for welfare state claims. By re-introducing female dependency as the norm of parental leave policies and by making parental leave benefits for women dependent on men's willingness to resume their fatherly duties and thus contribute to gender equality, the Austrian welfare state establishes itself as a "post-patriarchal" welfare state. The 1995 and 1996 provisions also disclose the main features of parental leave legislations, which have contributed to generating the gender-specificities of the Austrian welfare state.

With the Structural Adjustment Laws, the paid period of parental leave benefits was reduced by half a year, unless both parents go on parental leave. In addition to losing the financial benefits for the months reserved for fathers, women also lose the social security entitlements that go with them. Due to the lack of child-care facilities for children under the age of three, most women do not have a chance to resume employment after the parental leave and find it difficult to secure their own income and acquire social security coverage. Welfare state policies in Austria ignore the gender and social differences that exist with regard to labor market opportunities, income, caring obligations, and private family arrangements. They subject all women and men to the same conditions with regard to participating in the labor force and being included independently in the welfare state benefit systems, despite the fact that pregnant women, single mothers, and mothers with small children are hardly able to meet the requirements. Ironically, the grounding of welfare state regulations in fictitious assumptions about gender equality contributes to a gender unequal distribution of the risks of parenthood as well as perpetuates a differential access to the labor market and the welfare state systems.

Furthermore, the legislative change replaces the 50 percent additional leave benefit for single mothers and for married/cohabiting mothers whose husband/partner had little or no income by a loan. In the case of single mothers, the loan is granted only if the mother names the child's father to the local authorities. In a similar way, single mothers drawing special benefits (after parental leave) have to prove that they are living alone and this may imply increased surveillance by local authorities into women's home situations. The state, thus, restricts women's rights to self-determination and autonomy by making welfare state benefits dependent on the woman's willingness to disclose her sexual relationships to the authorities. In the case of married/cohabiting women, the mother must agree to repay the loan herself if the father is unable to do so. The state forces the mother, who needs additional benefits, to assume the father's responsibilities if he fails to comply with his legal obligations. Welfare state regulations, therefore, curtail women's independence with regard to private life, yet at the same time enlarge their economic responsibilities with regard to familial dependents.

The measures taken in 1995 and 1996 represent a partial return to social policy legislation which works to structure the economic relations between women and men. Parental leave legislation, as well as welfare state legislation in general, has always assumed that married and cohabiting women would be supported financially by their husbands and partners. With the introduction of the parental leave loan for single mothers, this principle of maintenance has been extended to partnerships that do not necessarily exist. The law's justification for this extension was that married and unmarried fathers should be treated equally with regard to their financial obligations towards their children's mothers. This made putative equality between men the norm for social policy decisions. However, this norm of equality revives a fraternal view of gender relations in which men are regarded as equal and women are regarded as dependent on men. Moreover, men's equality is measured with respect to their economic obligations towards their dependents, while women's needs and dependency are viewed largely in non-economic terms. For example, a father's contribution for maintaining his child's mother during parental leave was set at a rate which amounts to only 32 percent of the standard rate that is officially acknowledged as the poverty level for a single person in Austria.

Since 1995, single mothers also face greater pressure to provide their own child care. If claiming special benefits after their parental leave, they must provide a local council's certificate confirming that no suitable child care facilities are available; by law, however, the local council must refund the federal authorities a third of the cost of these special hardship benefits. With this provision, an open conflict which has been raging for years between the federal authorities and local councils about the building of child care facilities apparently has been settled at the expense of the local councils. The latter are required to set up care facilities for young children. But the local councils have passed the problem on to women, confirming the availability of adequate childcare facilities even when this was not the case or when the conditions were intolerable for the woman and child concerned. In this way many women lost their benefits after parental leave. The conflict between two institutions—the federal authorities and the local councils—has been transformed into a conflict between the local councils and the individual woman. By converting the problem of child care into a conflict between institutions and women, the problem is individualized and privatized. Women's efforts to make the privatized forms of child caring a matter of public policy are, thus, turned into the very opposite, a new form of privatization.

Outlook

The history of parental leave policy in Austria reveals the gap that separates a policy supportive of women from a social policy which includes women. A policy in women's interests must strive to reduce the power gap between men and women in the social, economic, and family spheres and bring about autonomy for both genders. A policy with such aims involves a fundamental revision of the principles and concepts of the welfare state which until now has contributed not to the breakdown of gender-specific inequalities but to their production and maintenance. This change would require welfare state policies which make it possible for women and men with children to live and work while assuring women's independence and autonomy with respect to their private, public, and economic situation. Austria's entrance into the European Union has at the same time narrowed and enlarged women's chances to bring about these changes. It is important to note, as seen in the Austrian case, that the existing European Union social policy directives lag behind the scope of national regulations. The European Union policy of situating working women similarly to men has, however, opened up opportunities for improving women's employment status, though the range of possibilities remains constrained due to the limitations of the European Union gender policy as a policy of "equality of employability"—with men as the norm. The future development of the welfare state and its gendering effects will thus largely depend on women and their abilities to use national and international policies to change welfare state structures in a feminist way.

Suggestions for Further Reading

Bock, Gisela, and Pat Thane, eds. *Maternity and Gender Policies: Women and the Rise of European Welfare States, 1880s–1950s*. London: Routledge, 1991.

Campbell, Beatrix. *Wigan Pier Revisited: Poverty and Politics in the 80s*. London: Virago, 1984.

Gordon, Linda, ed. *Women, the State, and Welfare*. Madison, Wis.: University of Wisconsin Press, 1990.

Hernes, Helga Marie. *Welfare State and Woman Power: Essays in State Feminism*. Oslo: Norwegian University Press, 1987.

Koven, Seth, and Sonya Michel. *Mothers of a New World: Maternalistic Politics and the Origins of Welfare States*. New York and London: Routledge, 1993.

Lewis, Jane. *The Politics of Motherhood: Child and Maternal Welfare in England, 1900–1939*. London: Croom Helm, 1980.

———, ed. *Women and Social Policies in Europe: Work, Family and the State*. Aldershot, Eng.: Edward Elgar, 1993.

Pateman, Carole. *The Disorder of Women: Democracy, Feminism and Political Theory*. Stanford: Stanford University Press, 1990.

———. *The Sexual Contract*. Stanford: Stanford University Press, 1988.

Sainsbury, Diane, ed. *Gendering Welfare States: Combining Insights of Feminist and Mainstream Research*. 2d ed. London: Sage, 1996.

Schirmer, Jennifer G. *The Limits of Reform: Women, Capital and Welfare*. Cambridge, Mass.: Schenkman Publishing Company, 1982.

Wikander, Ulla, Alice Kessler-Harris, and Jane Lewis, eds. *Protecting Women: Labor Legislation in Europe, the United States, and Australia, 1880–1920*. Urbana, Ill.: University of Illinois Press, 1995.

Wilson, Elizabeth. *Women and the Welfare State*. London: Tavistock Publications, 1977.

CONCLUSION

The Rebirth of Feminism
and Its Challenges

Historians tend to consider anything that has happened within the past half-century—or even the last century—as "contemporary history." Many argue that such events are too recent to provide the long perspective necessary to understand historical change. Yet we conclude our book with comments on European women's movements in the period since World War II. And we look to the changing global context of European feminisms, as more and more immigrants and former colonialists have settled in Europe's heartland, raising profoundly unsettling questions about the basis of European identity and challenging its gendered definitions and limits.

In the decade of the 1960s, despite widespread prosperity, public concern in Europe and the United States about the Vietnam War, student protest movements on both sides of the Atlantic, civil rights riots in American cities, a general strike in France, among others, had combined to produce a heightened sense of alienation among the younger generations. Many young Germans, for example, were disturbed deeply by the materialism of their parents and their complicity in, and silence about, the Nazi past. Youth in France and the United States attacked bureaucracies that seemed too rigid to respond to their needs. These protest movements in western Europe and America provided the context for the founding of new women's movements. They drew as well on the ongoing efforts of older women in government, media, and elsewhere who were working to change existing discriminatory laws and practices that limited women's opportunities in employment and public life. New demographic and family patterns that increased significantly the years of life many women might spend as single individuals also underscored the perceived need for a reconstruction of gender roles.

On August 26, 1970, in New York City, tens of thousands of women marched in celebration of the fiftieth anniversary of the suffrage amendment. In France, in the same year, women achieved public notice at a demonstration at the Tomb of the Unknown Soldier by laying down a wreath dedicated to the one who was more unknown than the soldier—his wife. Communications now spread quickly across international boundaries, reawakening in many countries of the Western world dormant feminist movements and stimulating political actions of many types, including a drive for new research and teaching about women's lives that ultimately helped produce books like *Connecting Spheres*. Since 1989 feminist voices have been heard again in the countries of central and eastern Europe. Furthermore, there have been parallel feminist awakenings in many of the new nations created out of Europe's former colonies, where independent research centers also pursue studies about women, and encourage action against such practices as female genital mutilation.

Feminist progress, however, reflects multiple contexts. Postwar ideals of democracy and egalitarian principles led European governments, even in some cases when not pressed by mass feminist advocacy, to adopt policies favoring equal education and employment rights. In the Netherlands and France, for example, as one recent author states, governments "instigated change from above with surprising speed [even] when relatively little pressure was exerted on them." Changing cultural values help to explain such action. Arguably the single most important factor facilitating the rebirth of feminist movements, however, came by way of technology; namely, the development and diffusion of the contraceptive pill. The ability of masses of women, for the first time in history, to control their own fertility, through contraception as well as generally increased access to abortion, has proved to be the most critical factor in awakening women's consciousness to new possibilities. In a survey conducted in Belgium in 1987, women were asked to identify the three most important changes that had occurred to improve women's lives in the twentieth century. Far and away the most popular choice was "the pill," chosen by 70 percent. Another 29 percent mentioned the vote, followed by 28 percent who picked the washing machine.[1]

Crystallizing experiences of the early 1970s included the publication in France and West Germany as well as the United States of manifestos proclaiming "I had an abortion," by hundreds of prominent women. Lucia Chiavola Birnbaum reports that Italian feminists "gathered testimony from thirty thousand women on maternity, sexuality, and abortion and published the accounts." Gisela Kaplan reports that in West Germany, France, and Italy half a million women (per country) marched in favor of abortion rights, and millions more expressed their support. By the 1980s a majority of women in all the countries of western Europe reported using contraceptives (save Spain, where the figure was 47 percent). In 1981 the voters of Italy passed a referendum supporting a new law permitting legal abortion; by the end of the 1990s, Catholic Italy manifested the lowest birthrate in the world. The desire to control fertility, and to assert autonomy in other aspects of life, coexists today with recognition of the importance to society of motherliness and the traditional maternal values of care, support, and nurturance, which exist independent of gender.[2]

However well motivated or supported by women or by government leaders, feminist movements face many challenges in the evolving global society. The socialist government of François Mitterand, for example, after his election as president of France in 1981 with strong support from women voters, created a Ministry of Women's Rights and increased funding for this office tenfold over its counterpart in the previous administration. The economic constraints of global interaction prompted the socialist government, however, to renege on its promises. Since the 1980s, in the United States feminist gains have provoked considerable backlash, astutely orchestrated by groups whose financial considerations or social conservatism turn them against new gender and sexual relationships and family arrangements that may entail new priorities, including enhanced and costly quality child care available for all children or benefits for domestic partners. In eastern Europe, the status of many women has declined absolutely, due to restrictions on social welfare programs that once encouraged women's labor force participation; in the western parts of Europe, "downsizing" threatens the whole welfare apparatus, with its unemployment, health, and pension guarantees. Immigrant and refugee women face formidable obstacles to their well-being; they are often convenient targets for racist policies designed to safeguard "national" cultures. Ethnic warfare has revived rape and other violence explicitly directed against civilian women.

The pending transformation of European nation-states into a European Union, with its international codes of law, seems to spell reduction of social welfare benefits targeted to women and their families. In many instances, the levels of support promised by the Union are less than existing benefits in individual member countries, as Gerda Neyer shows for Austria. At the same time, within the industrialized world there are growing gaps between rich and poor. Standards of living, measured by prenatal care infant birth weight and nutrition, among other indices, are deteriorating for a permanent underclass, which seriously threatens ideals of equality and challenges feminist goals, strategies, and alliances. Nonetheless, there have been many positive and probably irreversible changes in women's condition and status. "Choice" in its broadest meaning is now more widely available to more classes of women, including the option whether or not to marry or to have children, and to take advantage of higher education that increases economic opportunities.

As this book has shown, efforts to transform public and private lives along lines of greater sex equality have not followed a simple, linear progression, nor will they in the future. It has taken the work of many activists and scholars to create the feminist consciousness that today recognizes the diversity of cultures and multiple individual needs inherent in the now worldwide effort to change gender relations. The tripartite scheme once used to classify feminist approaches—liberal, socialist, radical—has given way to new understandings more inclusive of women of color and nonnormative sexualities as well as of persons of varying classes, ethnicities, and nationalities. The need to avoid generalizing about "women" in feminist analyses while also building coalitions for feminist practice poses a difficult challenge but also offers hope for future effectiveness.

At the end of the twentieth century, which witnessed the demise of the heady optimism of the nineteenth, we have learned to avoid grand narratives and universal pronouncements in favor of diverse, specific statements and particular objectives. Feminisms take on many meanings reflecting specific political, cultural, and historical environments. Probably the leading task now facing feminist activists and theorists is the difficult effort to integrate the desire for "equality" into the practices of daily life and simultaneously to insist on changing society to accommodate gender and other differences. Along with Kumari Jayawardena, we see the problem as achieving "universality with diversity," a vision that places feminisms in constant dialogue, through struggle and accommodation, to accomplish the tangible goals of specific women and the ideals of many women's movements.[3]

We can assert with confidence, however, that the path to a more egalitarian world requires knowledge of the past—indeed, multiple knowledges that have been lacking for too long. In our view, hope lies in the still new and developing scholarly field we call women's studies. Today, the fastest growing frontier for studies by, for, and about women lies distant from its origins in the geographic territory of the United States, England, and continental Europe. Research, teaching, and special projects in women's history and other disciplines have now appeared in more than one hundred countries around the globe. Since women's studies serves to keep alive feminist ideas, this multiplicity of voices bodes well for the future. We hope that our collective work, too, advances these efforts toward equality and justice.

NOTES

1. Gisela Kaplan, *Contemporary Western European Feminism* (New York: New York University Press, 1992), pp. 13, 174.
2. Because of the long eclipse of women's history, few knew of a precedent set forty years earlier by women in Germany; ibid., pp. 14, 17, 107; on France, p. 197, on Germany, p. 168. Lucia Chiavola Birnbaum, *Liberazione della donna: Feminism in Italy* (Middletown, Conn.: Wesleyan University Press, 1986), p. 104.
3. Kumari Jayawardena, *The White Woman's Other Burden: Western Women and South Asia during British Colonial Rule* (New York: Routledge, 1995), p. 18.

CONTRIBUTORS

Barbara Franzoi Bari is professor of history at the College of Saint Elizabeth in New Jersey, where she was awarded the CASE-Carnegie professorship for excellence in teaching. Author of *At the Very Least She Pays the Rent: Women and German Industrialization, 1871–1914* (1985), she is currently working on a book about Catholic congregations in nineteenth-century Prussia.

Marilyn J. Boxer is an Affiliated Scholar with the Institute for Research on Women and Gender at Stanford University and Professor of History at San Francisco State University, where she served as vice-president for academic affairs (1989–96). She is author of *When Women Ask the Questions: Creating Women's Studies in America* (1998) and contributing coeditor with Jean Quataert of *Socialist Women: European Socialist Feminism in the Nineteenth and Early Twentieth Centuries* (1978).

Antoinette Burton is Associate Professor of History at the University of Illinois, Urbana. She is the author of *Burdens of History: British Feminists, Indian Women, and Imperial Culture, 1865–1915* (1994) and *At the Heart of the Empire: Indians and the Colonial Encounter in Late-Victorian Britain* (1998), as well as numerous articles on race, nation, empire, feminism, and colonialism. She is currently at work on a book-length project about Indian women writers and the architectural idioms of memory and home.

Lyndel Butler has previously assisted with translations of *Reigen* by Arthur Schnitzler and the correspondence of Einstein with Queen Elizabeth of Belgium. She taught German in high school and college and currently works in the home health care industry as a trainer and systems developer.

Carolyn J. Dean teaches history at Brown University. She is the author of *The Self and Its Pleasures: Bataille, Lacan, and the History of the Decentered Self* (1992), *Sexuality and Modern Western Culture* (1996), and *The Frail Social Body and Other Fantasies in Interwar France* (forthcoming).

Donna Gabaccia is the Charles H. Stone Professor of American History at the University of North Carolina at Charlotte. She is the author of many books and articles on immigrant life in the United States, and on Italian migration worldwide. Her most recent books are *From the Other Side: Women, Gender and Immigrant Life in the United States* (1994); *We Are What We Eat: Ethnic Food and the Making of Americans* (1998) and *Italy's Many Diasporas: Elites, Exiles, and Workers of the World* (forthcoming).

Sandra M. Gilbert, Professor of English at the University of California, Davis, is co-author with Susan Gubar of *The Madwoman in the Attic* (1979), followed by the three-volume *No Man's Land: The Place of the Woman Writer in the Twentieth Century* (1988, 1989, 1994); coeditor with Gubar of *The Norton Anthology of Literature by Women* (1985, 1996); and author of five books of poems, most recently *Ghost Volcano* (1995), as well as *Wrongful Death: A Memoir* (1995). She is currently at work on a study of the poetry of grief entitled, "The Fate of the Elegy."

Sarah Hanley is Professor of History and Law at the University of Iowa, and a recent Guggenheim Fellow. She is the author of *The Lit de Justice of the Kings of France: Constitutional Ideology in Legend, Ritual, and Discourse* (1983, French edition 1991) and *Les Droits des femmes et la loi salique* (1994). Recipient of the Koren Prize for best article in an American, Canadian, or European journal in 1989 and the American Political Science Association prize for the best article in Politics and History in 1997, her forthcoming book is *State Building in Early Modern France: Law, Litigation, and Local Knowledge.*

Maryanne Cline Horowitz is Professor of History and Title IX Officer, Occidental College, and Associate, University of California, Los Angeles. She is the author of *Seeds of Virtue and Knowledge* (1998); editor of *Race, Gender, and Rank: Early Modern Ideas of Humanity* (1992) and *Race, Class, and Gender in Nineteenth-Century Culture* (1991); and coeditor of *Playing with Gender: A Renaissance Pursuit* (1991), *Politics of Gender in Early Modern Europe* (Sixteenth Century Journal, 1989), and *Renaissance Rereadings: Intertext and Context* (1988). Her Web site is http://www.oxy.edu/~horowitz/home.

Olwen Hufton is Leverhulme Research Professor of History at Merton College, Oxford University. She is the author of *The Poor of Eighteenth Century France* (1975), *Europe: Privilege and Protest, 1730–1789* (1980, rev. ed. 2000), *Women and the Limits of Citizenship in the French Revolution* (1992), *The Prospect Before Her: A History of Women in Western Europe, 1500–1800* (1995) and other works.

Sibylle Meyer studied sociology in Berlin and has worked as a research fellow in the Institut für Zukunfsstudien und Technologiebewertung and the Technical University of Berlin. Since 1993, together with Dr. Eva Schulze, she has served as Director of the BIS—Berliner Institut für Sozialforschung, GmbH. Dr. Meyer has written numerous books and articles on housework, family, the technologies of gerontology as well as on new technology and services for the private household.

Gerda Ruth Neyer is a political scientist at the Institute for Demography at the Austrian Academy of Science, Vienna. She teaches in the field of women's history and the theory of the welfare state at the University of Vienna. She is Visiting Professor at Stanford University (1997–99) where she is affiliated with the Institute of International Studies and the Institute for Research on Women and Gender. She is author of numerous articles on parental leave, and social and labor market policies from a feminist perspective.

Karen Offen is senior scholar at the Institute for Research on Women and Gender, Stanford University. She is the author of *European Feminism(s), 1700–1950: A Political History* (2000). Her research interests encompass the comparative history of women and feminisms, and her current work focuses on gender issues in European political and intellectual history, with a particular emphasis on Francophone cultures.

Mary Elizabeth Perry has published four books and many articles on marginal groups in early modern Spain. Her books *Crime and Society in Early Modern Seville* (1980) and *Gender and Disorder in Early Modern Seville* (1990) each won the Sierra Book Award. She has received a Fulbright Fellowship and grants from the American Council of Learned Societies, the Comite Conjunto Hispano-Norteamericano, the Del Amo Foundation, and the National Endowment for the Humanities. Adjunct Professor of History at Occidental College, she is also Research Associate at the UCLA Center for Medieval and Renaissance Studies.

Jean H. Quataert is Professor of History at Binghamton University, State University of New York, where she has transformed her teaching of German and European history to include global perspectives. She is author of *Reluctant Feminists in German Social Democracy* (1979) and, most recently, *Staging Philanthropy: Patriotic Women and the National Imagination in Dynastic Germany, 1813–1916* (2000).

Joan W. Scott is Professor in the School of Social Science at the Institute for Advanced Study (Princeton, New Jersey). Her publications include *Gender and the Politics of History* (1988), *Only Paradoxes to Offer: French Feminists and the Rights of Man* (1996), and many other works. She is coeditor *of Transitions, Environments, Translations: Feminisms in International Politics* (1997).

Richard Stites is Professor of History at Georgetown University. He is the author of *The Women's Liberation Movement in Russia* (1978), *Revolutionary Dreams* (1989), and *Russian Popular Culture* (1992).

Frank Tallett is Senior Lecturer in the Department of History at the University of Reading. He is author of *War and Society in Early Modern Europe, 1495–1715* (1992) and, along with Nicholas Atkin, is the editor of *Religion, Society and Politics in France since 1789* (1991), *Catholicism in Britain and France since 1789* (1996), and *The Right in France, 1789–1997* (1998).

Luise White is associate professor of history at the University of Florida. Her first book, *The Comforts of Home: Prostitution in Colonial Nairobi,* won the Herskovits Prize for the best book of the African Studies Association in 1991. Her second book, *Blood and Fire: Rumor and History in East and Central Africa,* is forthcoming.

Merry Wiesner-Hanks is Professor of History and former Director of the Center for Women's Studies at the University of Wisconsin-Milwaukee. She is one of the editors of the *Sixteenth Century Journal,* and the author of *Working Women in Renaissance Germany* (1986), *Women and Gender in Early Modern Europe* (1993), *Gender, Church and State in Early Modern Germany* (1997), and numerous articles on various aspects of women's lives and gender structures in early modern Europe, especially Germany.

INDEX

Breinigsville, PA USA
31 July 2010
242740BV00005B/6/A